FROM FRINGE
TO FLYING CIRCUS

'*From Fringe to Flying Circus*, is precisely that, a lovingly written and produced history of the 20 years of stage, radio and TV comedy that began with the four shorthaired satirists of *Beyond the Fringe* in 1960 and which now zooms off into the stratospheric ruderies of *Monty Python*.' Robert Hewison *The Evening Standard*

'Clever Mr Roger Wilmut has managed to dissect and describe a certain stream of recent humour – the satire of the 1960s and the surreal zaniness of the 1970s – without losing any of the fun of it.' *The Economist*

'A very welcome, often very funny book . . .' *The Paperback and Hardback Buyer*

FROM FRINGE TO FLYING CIRCUS

Celebrating a unique generation of comedy 1960 – 1980

Roger Wilmut

Preface by Bamber Gascoigne

Designed by Kate Hepburn
METHUEN LONDON LTD

A Methuen Paperback
FROM FRINGE TO FLYING CIRCUS
ISBN 413 50770 X
First published in Great Britain 1980
by Eyre Methuen Ltd
Copyright © 1980 by Roger Wilmut
This edition published 1982
by Methuen London Ltd,
11 New Fetter Lane,
London EC4P 4EE
Made and Printed in Great Britain by
Fakenham Press Limited,
Fakenham, Norfolk

Prologue
'Miner' by Peter Cook; 'Edna' by Barry Humphries; 'Telegram' by Alan Bennett; 'So That's the Way You Like It' by Peter Cook, Alan Bennett, Jonathan Miller and Dudley Moore

Chapter 1
'Sermon' by Alan Bennett; 'So That's the Way You Like It' by Peter Cook, Alan Bennett, Jonathan Miller and Dudley Moore; 'Aftermyth of War' by Peter Cook, Alan Bennett, Jonathan Miller and Dudley Moore; Kenneth Tynan review by *The Observer*; Bernard Levin review by *The Daily Express*; 'T.V.P.M.' by Peter Cook; 'Black Equals White' by Peter Cook; 'The Suspense is Killing Me' by Peter Cook, Alan Bennett, Jonathan Miller and Dudley Moore; Alistair Cooke review by *The Guardian*; 'The Great Train Robbery' by Peter Cook

Chapter 2
'First Things First' by David Frost; 'The Mine Disaster' by John Cleese and Alan Hutchison; 'It Can't End Like This' by John Cleese and Bill Oddie; Seddon review by *The Observer*; 'Judge Not' by John Cleese; review of *Cambridge Circus* by Walter Kerr

Chapter 3
Jonathan Miller article by *The Observer*; 'Sex investigations' by David Frost and Christopher Booker; 'Henry Brooke' by David Frost and Christopher Booker; 'He and She' by Eleanor Bron and John Fortune; 'Disraeli' by Christopher Booker

Chapter 4
'Lady Pamela' by Eleanor Bron; 'Kenyatta' by John Bird; 'Wilson' by John Bird; 'Virginia Woolf' by Alan Bennett; 'Appeal' by John Bird and Eleanor Bron; 'Lucid Intervals' by John Bird and John Fortune; 'Before the Wedding' by Eleanor Bron and John Fortune

Chapter 5
'On Going to the Excuse-me', 'Antiques', 'Children's Party', 'Heidi' and 'Forty Years On' by Alan Bennett

Chapter 6
'World Domination League' and 'One Leg Too Few' by Peter Cook; 'On the Bus', 'Frog and Peach', *Bedazzled*, 'Black Magic' and 'Mini Drama' by Peter Cook and Dudley Moore

Chapter 7
'Alone in the Country' by John Cleese; 'Goodnight Darling' by John Cleese and Bill Oddie; 'Three Babies' by David Hatch; 'Othello', 'Spot', 'Fish Jokes' and 'Teapot' by Bill Oddie; 'Star Trek' by Graeme Garden

Chapter 8
'Crete' by John Cleese and Graham Chapman; 'Three Men on Class' by Marty Feldman and the estate of John Law; 'Hendon' by Michael Palin and Terry Jones; 'The Story So Far' and 'The Wonderful World of the Ant' by Marty Feldman, John Cleese, Graham Chapman and Tim Brooke-Taylor; 'Psychiatrist' and 'Sheepdog Trials' by John Cleese and Graham Chapman; 'Magna Carta', 'Buffies' and 'Dr Findish' by Graeme Garden and Tim Brooke-Taylor

Chapter 9
The Goodies – all extracts by Graeme Garden and Bill Oddie, with Tim Brooke-Taylor

Chapter 10
'James Watt' and 'Come Out to Play' by Michael Palin, Terry Jones and Eric Idle; 'Stonehenge', 'Latin', 'Battle of Hastings' and 'F. R. Launcelot' by Michael Palin and Terry Jones

Chapter 11
All extracts copyright Python (Monty) Pictures Ltd

Chapter 12
'Gibberish' by Eric Idle; *Fawlty Towers* by John Cleese and Connie Booth

Contents

11.

12.

Performance Photographs

Performance Photographs

Acknowledgements

It would have been quite impossible for me to write this book without the help I received from many people. Special thanks are due to Roger Hancock for the original idea, and for constant help and encouragement; and to those who gave me interviews: Humphrey Barclay, John Bird, Christopher Booker, Eleanor Bron, Tim Brooke-Taylor, Graham Chapman, John Cleese, Peter Cook, William Donaldson, Jim Franklin, Graeme Garden, Terry Gilliam, Sir Hugh Greene, David Hatch, Richard Ingrams, Neil Innes, Terry Jones, Jonathan Miller, Bill Oddie, Michael Palin, Tony Palmer and William Rushton; and Alan Bennett, who wrote me a long letter in lieu of an interview.

The book would have been dull indeed without the script extracts to illustrate it; for permission to quote from their work I am grateful to Alan Bennett, John Bird, Christopher Booker, Connie Booth, Eleanor Bron, Tim Brooke-Taylor, Graham Chapman, John Cleese, Peter Cook, Marty Feldman, John Fortune, David Frost, Graeme Garden, David Hatch, Barry Humphries, Alan Hutchison, Eric Idle, Terry Jones, the estate of John Law, Jonathan Miller, Dudley Moore, Bill Oddie and Michael Palin. Thanks also to *The Observer*, *The Daily Express*, *The Guardian*, *The Sunday Times*, and Walter Kerr; and to Faber and Faber for permission to quote from *Forty Years On*.

Thanks for General Help and Useful Information are due to Steve Body, Patrick Gowers, Anne Henshaw, Hugh Macdonald, Christine Miller and Tony Rushton; for the loan of scripts, to Humphrey Barclay, John Cleese and Michael Palin; and for lending photographs, scrapbooks, posters, programmes, books and record covers (for use as marginal illustrations), to: Humphrey Barclay, Tim Brooke-Taylor, Jonathan Cape Ltd, Alexander H. Cohen, William Donaldson, Eyre Methuen Ltd, Faber & Faber Ltd, Christopher Falkus, Futura Publications Ltd, Terry Gilliam, Kate Hepburn, Eric Idle, Terry Jones, Michael Joseph Ltd, Martin Lewis, Bill Oddie, Orion Films Ltd, Michael Palin, Tony Rushton, Geoffrey Strachan, Weidenfeld & Nicolson Ltd.

For permission to reproduce book covers and record sleeves, thanks to: Jonathan Cape (for *The Body in Question*), Eyre Methuen Ltd (for *Dud and Pete: The Dagenham Dialogues*, *Ripping Yarns*, *Bert Fegg's Nasty Book for Boys and Girls*, *The Brand New Monty Python Bok* and *Papperbok*, *Monty Python and the Holy Grail (Book)*, *Monty Python's Life of Brian*, *Animations of Mortality*, *Monty Python's Big Red Book*, *Is Your Marriage Really Necessary*, *The Balloons in the Black Bag* and *The Rutland Dirty Weekend Book*), Faber & Faber Ltd (for *Forty Years On*, *Habeas Corpus* and *The Old Country*), Futura Publications Ltd (for *Hello Sailor*), Michael Joseph Ltd (for *Timothy*), *Private Eye* (for a front

Acknowledgements

cover and a 'Mrs Wilson's Diary' cartoon), *The TV Times* (for a front cover and a *Doctor in the House* listing), Magnum Books Ltd (for *Life and Other Punctures*), Weidenfeld & Nicolson Ltd (for *Chaucer's Knight*, *The Goodies File*, *The Goodies Book of Criminal Records*, *The Making of the Goodies Disaster Movie*, *Fawlty Towers* and *Fawlty Towers Book 2*); Kay Gee Bee Songs Inc. (for AB 4073 *Monty Python Live at City Center*), BBC Records (for REB 233 *The Rutland Weekend Songbook*, REB 73M *Monty Python's Flying Circus* and REB 377 *Fawlty Towers*), Charisma Records (for CAS 1103 *The Album of the Sound Track of the Trailer of the Film of Monty Python and the Holy Grail*, CAS 1063 *Monty Python's Previous Record*, *Monty Python Live at Drury Lane*, CAS 1049 *Another Monty Python Record*, CAS 1140 *The Sound of Edna*, CAS 1080 *The Monty Python Matching Tie and Handkerchief*, CAS 1123 *Housewife-Superstar* and DC 19783 *The Monty Python Instant Record Collection*), Cube Records (for TOOFA 14 *The Music of Dudley Moore* and HIFLY 26 *The Clean Tapes: The Very Best of Peter Cook and Dudley Moore*), Decca Record Co. (for SPA 416 *The World of the Goodies* and PA 311 *The World of Dud and Pete*), EMI (for PMC 1145 *Beyond the Fringe* and PMC 7024 *I'm Sorry, I'll Read That Again*), Island Records Ltd (for ILPS 9601 *The Secret Policeman's Ball* and ILPS 9434 *Derek and Clive (Live)*), Polydor Ltd (for 2382 556 *The Innes Book of Records*), United Artists Records Ltd (for UAS 29492 *How Sweet to be an Idiot*), Virgin Records (for V 2094 *Derek and Clive Come Again*), Gerald Scarfe (for VR 4 *Here Comes the Judge*) and Warner Brothers Records (for K 56751 *Monty Python's Life of Brian* and K 56459 *The Rutles: All You Need is Cash*).

The publishers have made every effort to trace all copyright holders; apologies are due for any errors or omissions in the credits, which, if they come to light, will be corrected in future editions.

Rare tape recordings, gramophone records and video tapes were kindly lent by Peter Copeland, Terry Jones, Vaughan Lipscombe, D. Jeremy Stevenson, Geoffrey Strachan, Peter Tatchell and Victor Van Amerongen.

Documentary research was done with the aid of BBC Radio and Television Script Libraries and Registries, Sound Archives, Gramophone Library, Written Archives Centre at Caversham and News Information; the British Film Institute and the British Institute of Recorded Sound.

Special thanks to BBC Film Library for access to their material, and to Terry Jones for access to rare Python films.

Finally, thanks to Martin Noble for compiling the index; to Tim Smith for checking through the typescript; and to Peter Copeland for invaluable research assistance and criticism of the typescript as it progressed.

Roger Wilmut, March 1980

Introduction to the Paperback Edition

The original, hardback, edition of this book went to press in March 1980 – a date which can be seen, with hindsight, to mark the end of an era as far as the protagonists are concerned. Since then, most of them have been striking out on their own more and more; and indeed many of them are moving well into the Big Time.

The most notable of these is of course Dudley Moore, with his resounding success in the films *10* and *Arthur*; Terry Gilliam has established himself as a successful film director with *Time Bandits*, which he scripted with Michael Palin; Eric Idle has invaded the West End theatre with his play *Pass the Butler*; John Cleese has co-directed a further Amnesty special, *The Secret Policeman's Other Ball*; while literary endeavours include Graham Chapman's *A Liar's Autobiography*, Graeme Garden's *The Seventh Man*, Bill Oddie's *Little Black Bird Book*, and Terry Jones's *Fairy Tales*.

All this indicates that the twenty-year period covered by the present book has indeed come to a close, and that we are now well into a new and different period; so I have not attempted to bring the narrative up to date. Nor have I altered the final speculative chapter, which was written from the viewpoint of the end of this first era.

The subsequent and current happenings belong to another book – *From Flying Circus to . . .?* – which perhaps I will write some day. Watch this space – around the year 2000.

Roger Wilmut, March 1982

Preface

It is a shock to discover that one's most vivid memories are a part of history. Indeed, in this book's terms, of prehistory. I have been wheeled on to tell what it was like in those distant days, the fifties, before Mr Wilmut's story begins and when Jonathan Miller and Alan Bennett, his Adam and Methusaleh, were fresh-faced youngsters. Well, it was splendid. Like each new wave, we thought we were spearheading a revolution. In our own way we were, in the sense of helping to get rid of what had gone before. But it wasn't a revolution that would lead anywhere. Kerensky's rather than Lenin's.

I arrived in Cambridge in the autumn of 1955. My ambitions were theatrical, and we were all aware that Cambridge provided an unusually effective springboard into the professional theatre. Peter Hall had gone down a couple of years before and was already Director of the Arts Theatre in London. I had the impression that the summer show of the Footlights transferred every year for a season in the West End, and was intrigued to discover from this book that it was only the two previous shows, in 1954 and 1955, which had done so. Perhaps it is in the nature of undergraduate experience, with an entirely new generation every three years, to regard a two-year pattern as a permanency.

Revue seemed to me the quickest way to lasting fame, so I wrote some sketches, submitted them to the Footlights, and soon found myself in the strange dinner-jacketed all-male world of 'smoking concerts' that Roger Wilmut describes. As he says, the mood was less intimidating than might have been expected. Criticism of someone else's effort was much inhibited by imminent scrutiny of one's own. All actors are darlings backstage.

This was a time when revue was a staple diet of the West End, with two or three such shows on at any moment. A few performers were individual enough to stand outside the main stream – I remember chiefly the upper-class eccentricities of Joyce Grenfell (who spent a considerable part of one evening skipping round and round the stage in ever-decreasing circles, singing of how she was going to pick a flower at the top of a hill, then in the centre of the stage stooped to pluck it, and gradually skipped her way round and down again), and the endearing performances of delightfully trivial material by Michael Flanders from his wheel-chair and Donald Swann at the piano. But the main stream itself was a lugubrious affair, the tired tail-end of a tradition that went back to glorious beginnings with Noël Coward in the twenties. The topicality of the run-of-the-mill revues was that of The Tatler, and their lyrics, with thumping rhythms and elaborate rhymes, had more than a touch of the W. S. Gilberts. A large proportion of the routines were songs shared out in snippets between three characters in line abreast on the stage. I remember that the only number I managed to get into the Footlights summer show at the end of my first year was on precisely this theme. It was performed by one man from such a trio. The sketch consisted of the truncated snatches which had been his part in several routines of this type, with the refrain:

> I'm the man on the left,
> Left out on the left,
> The last in the line out of three,
> The man who's sung bits
> Of various hits,
> That's me.

There was one revue of the early fifties which had broken the usual mould and which – to me at any rate – was a great inspiration. This was *Cranks*, both written and directed by the brilliant choreographer John Cranko, who died when only in his forties. As well as introducing the charms of the young Annie Ross, *Cranks* had a freshness of vision, even a poetic quality, which came I think from two things. Instead of the tired topicalities of ordinary revue, it offered a surreal but very relaxed mixture of word patterns, non-joky songs and languid dance. And whereas other revues were made up of sketches submitted by many different writers, and were put on stage by a director assisted by someone else in charge of movement, *Cranks* – in all respects except the final performance – was the work of one man.

In my second year at Cambridge I discovered for myself the practical basis of Cambridge's theatrical advantage. The A.D.C., or Amateur Dramatic Club, had something which Oxford lacked – a splendid small theatre, properly equipped, and exclusively in the hands of undergraduates. The club only used the stage a week or two each term for its own productions. For the rest of the time the theatre could be hired by any other group, taking over the working of the entire building, with one's own set designer, scene painters, props people, wardrobe mistress, ticket and programme sellers, poster painters, lighting buffs, stage manager, actors, director and even impresario, who did really stand to lose his investment. In my case, the impresario was a member of my own college, Peter Durlacher, who inherited some money and decided to gamble £200, the cost of putting on a show for a week, in presenting a college revue. On the strength of that one number in the prestigious Footlights revue (one more than anyone else in my college had provided) I was invited to write the show. The man on the left, left out on the left, the last in the line out of three had given me my big break. With John Cranko in mind, I blandly insisted on directing the whole thing as well and so found myself launched on one of the more unexpected adventures of my life. An intoxicating sell-out during our week at Cambridge was followed by the excitement – which recurs again and again during the pages of this book – of not quite believable discussions with professional managers, in my case Michael Codron, and eventually a production in the West End. I had come up with the foolish title *Share My Lettuce* (I was intrigued to read Mr Wilmut's account of everyone else's equally painful search for titles) and the motif of edible greenery frequently caused us to be confused with Julian Slade's much better known *Salad Days*. The confusion had a certain relevance since the two shows shared a flavour (fresh and silly) which was effective at the time but embarrassing in retrospect.

During the whole of my last year as an undergraduate *Share My Lettuce* was on in the West End, which left me with the brief and mistaken impression that I was an up-and-coming man of the theatre. I had a weekly royalty cheque coming in (on average about £80) but indulged in only one major extravagance. This was a magnificent new overcoat in green Harris tweed costing eight guineas, a display of unashamed opulence and vanity which caused as many disapproving remarks as if I had turned up in a Rolls Royce. I considered myself now too grand to write unpaid for the Footlights, but patronized smoking concerts to cast an elderly and benevolent eye on the new talent. It was during the next year, 1958–9, when I was away in America, that things would hot up with the arrival on the Cambridge revue scene of the first superstar since Jonathan Miller. I first saw the newcomer in action when he was presiding over a Footlights dinner. It was in October 1959, some four months – as it turned out – before the birth of Prince Andrew. When we rose to our feet for the loyal toast, the company was already in a mellow mood. Gentlemen, said the president, the Queen. The Queen, we all intoned, the Queen, the Queen. But the president was not done. He mumbled on, with the dreadful deadpan intensity which would later be known as the trade mark of E. L. Wisty. 'And all who sail in her,' raising his glass again in an excess of loyalty. It was Peter Cook. In characteristic form, as we were soon to discover.

From that time on, before the story of this book even begins, I was just an interested bystander, a has-been in the comedy business, and exactly the sort of person you get to write prefaces. *Cranks* and *Share My Lettuce* were the avant-garde of revue in the fifties, but the whimsicality of both shows – for even *Cranks* would seem whimsical now – was replaced by something much tougher and more fruitful in *Beyond the Fringe,* and our zaniness was far outpaced by what the so-called 'Oxbridge Mafia' have achieved on television during the seventies. Of those television triumphs, by a generation younger than mine, I have been only an intermittent and admiring viewer, and part of the reason why this book fascinated me was that it pulled together so many separate and half-perceived strands. I was also amazed to discover quite how many of the familiar funny faces of modern television came from Cambridge, and to a lesser extent Oxford. Clearly this is an area for the Equal Opportunities Commission. In the field of light entertainment fifteen years of socialism have got us nowhere.

The successes of my own age group (roughly Jonathan Miller to Eleanor Bron) were naturally more exciting to me than those of the youngsters hard on our heels. I suppose each generation must have an intoxicating moment of realizing that its own members can get things going on their own account in the wide world. For me that moment was The Establishment. This was something quite different from our lot merely being presented on stage or between hard covers by older people (though I now realize that Michael Codron, the dreadfully wise old person who put on *Share My Lettuce* in the West End, was 27 at the time). This was a case of one of the gang, Peter Cook, finding premises in Soho, having them done up and furnished, finding a cast (not to mention cooks, waiters and chuckers out), preparing a launch and inviting in the world. For a year or so it was a very special pleasure, of a type that I haven't known since, to drop in at The Establishment in the certainty of seeing friends, among the audience as well as on stage. There was an immediacy, a sense of danger and the unexpected, particularly in the impromptu question-and-answer sessions which were part of the bill of fare.

I shall always remember with pleasure one of John Bird's more brilliant sallies. He was on stage in the persona of President Kennedy, and we were invited to fire questions at him. Kennedy had recently returned from a visit to Moscow. 'Mr President,' came a question from the floor, 'what was your impression of Mr Kruschev?' Rehearsing the President's very particular New England twang had been a necessary preparation for the role. So had a mastery of the relentlessly balanced phrases which were his style of oratory. But no one in the audience was quite prepared for the perfection of the reply. After a due moment's pause for reflection, President Bird delivered his verdict:

His arms were not so short that they did not reach his waist. Nor were they so long that when he walked they brushed the ground. I recognised in him a man, like other men.

I firmly believe that the question was not planted. But if you insist that it was, well then that – like everything else in this admirable book – is show business.

Bamber Gascoigne

Prologue

English comedy has a history as long as it is varied. In the Middle Ages no
baronial dining hall was complete without its jester; and the comedies of
Shakespeare, the savage and scurrilous political satire of the eighteenth century, the circus clowns and the early music-hall all form part of the English
tradition – a continuing and changing tapestry of laughter.

Categorization of comedy is a chancy business; but, conveniently ignoring
those performers who fall outside the main fashion, it is possible to see the
history of twentieth-century comedy as dividing itself into three principal
styles. The first, which dominated the years up to the Second World War, was
music-hall. The many halls up and down the country were the main form of
entertainment for the working classes before broadcasting and the cinema
established themselves, and a successful artist could 'work the halls' for a
lifetime on a handful of good sketches or songs. Seen today, on archive film,
performers such as George Robey, Lily Morris or Gus Elen can still rock an
audience with laughter at comic routines which had been polished over thirty
years.

This opportunity to perfect their work by constant repetition in front of
different audiences was denied the next generation of performers, who made
their reputations on radio and television. The 'NAAFI comedians', as they
have been called, were those who gained their first experience during the
Second World War in ENSA and other organizations formed to entertain the
troops. When the war ended, they spilt over into civilian life, and people such
as Tony Hancock, Harry Secombe, Peter Sellers, Spike Milligan, Graham
Stark and Robert Moreton came to dominate radio and, later, television. In
particular Milligan wrote and performed in *The Goon Show*, together with
performers Secombe and Sellers, producing a radio comedy series which
remains unsurpassed for inventiveness, sheer craziness and an explosive use of
the medium which did not so much break conventions as trample them
underfoot. The BBC is rather proud of *The Goon Show* nowadays, but at the
time the subversive, irreverent and often delightfully dirty jokes were rather
too much for them, and the programme was almost executed on many
occasions.

The Goon Show was a major influence on many of the people who formed
the 'third wave' of comedy – the university comedians. There had been a
handful of university-trained performers during the 1950s; Michael Flanders
and Donald Swann cornered the market in elegantly witty songs, while cartoonist and musician Gerard Hoffnung organized two hilarious comic concerts
and made a speech to the Oxford Union in 1958 which remains one of the

funniest solo performances ever recorded. The real watershed, however, came in 1960 when four young men opened in a revue called *Beyond the Fringe* at the Edinburgh Festival. They took Edinburgh, and later London, by storm and paved the way for the so-called 'satire-boom' of the early 1960s. More importantly, they also broke the ground for a group of marvellously inventive and talented comedians, most of whom had two things in common – education at Oxford or Cambridge Universities, and no original intention of going into show business. Of course, as Bill Oddie points out, 'you can't read show business at university'; but the fact remains that, had they not been sidetracked, the world might have gained three doctors, two solicitors, an advertising executive, a literary critic and a number of other solid citizens – and lost an immeasurable amount of laughter.

It may seem strange that people whose sights were fixed on a degree and a career should allow themselves to be deflected in this way. After all, those who go to any university – whether at the taxpayer's expense or their parents' – are ostensibly there to gain the degree which is proof of three years intensive education. However, it is fortunately not as simple (or as dreary) as that. All universities – and in particular the old-established ones of Oxford and Cambridge – act as greenhouses where, protected from the harsh winds of the outside world, the students can take the opportunity to develop any talents they may find in themselves; in fact, not only to put down roots, but to flower. The fact that some of them wilt when they are taken out of the greenhouse is a necessary risk of the operation. The sun must have been particularly warm in the late fifties and early sixties, for a number of rare and colour-

ful blooms who managed to take root in the difficult soil of broadcast comedy had all been cultivated at Oxford or Cambridge during this period.

Anyone who managed to avoid exposure to television, films and stage from 1960 onwards – a Martian, say, or a BBC Programme Planner – could have taken advantage of a unique opportunity to see what they had been missing when, on 1, 2 and 3 April 1976, almost all the people in this group came together for a special show in aid of Amnesty International, called *A Poke in the Eye With a Sharp Stick* and given at Her Majesty's Theatre, London.[1]

The items were many and varied, and the audience greeted most of them as old friends. The team from the imaginative and highly successful television series *Monty Python's Flying Circus* – John Cleese, Michael Palin, Terry Jones, Graham Chapman and Terry Gilliam, but without Eric Idle – were present and not at all correct; they performed a noisy and complicated trial scene, with Peter Cook substituting for Eric Idle. The sketch (cannibalized from four separate sketches in the original television series) involved a witness in a coffin and a long argument about whether Basingstoke is in Hampshire or West-phalia; and ended with a song, 'Anything Goes', written not by *the* Cole Porter but by *a* Cole Porter.

Apart from assisting the *Monty Python* team, Peter Cook also resurrected the monologue in which he had first introduced the strange character he later named E. L. Wisty. Staring fixedly at a point some twelve feet above the heads

1976 Amnesty Show: Peter Cook as E. L. Wisty

of the stalls, he explained in a near monotone why he would rather have been a judge than a miner:

Terry Jones

> 'The only trouble with the mining community is that conversation tends to be a bit on the boring side. If you want to hear a boring conversation, just pop down my mine. Stuff like: "Hello – I've just found a lump of coal" – "Have you really?" – "Oh yes, no doubt about it, this black substance is coal all right" – "Jolly good, the very thing we're looking for." I've tried to inject a little intellectual substance to the conversation down the mine – I said to a fellow miner the other day, I said: "Have you heard of Marcel Proust?" He said, "No, he must work down another mine."'

Graham Chapman narrated a demonstration, written by Terry Jones and performed by other members of the *Monty Python* team, in which various basic comedy gags – pratfalls and custard-pie-throwing included – were subjected to a detailed analysis. Neil Innes, one of the few non-university performers, sang an all-purpose Bob Dylan-type protest song; Eleanor Bron performed a superb parody, written by Michael Frayn, of the sort of public speech which is all too liable to wind up any amateur charity concert; and Barry Humphries, a welcome Australian interloper, appeared in the guise of the housewife-superstar Dame Edna Everage:

> 'A lot of my countrymen say rude things about you – they do! – just because you have the lowest standard of living in the world, and I don't think that's *fair*! I think that's mean and horrid, and I think they're awful. Because I know that England will rise again – it will! It will! Say to the level of Sicily or Ethiopia . . .'

Alan Bennett

The senior member of the cast, Alan Bennett – who displayed, as always, a disconcerting ability to look twenty years younger and sound twenty years older than his actual age – performed a monologue in which he attempted to dictate a telegram to an over-helpful telephone operator ('We seem to be drifting into a kind of redundant intimacy'):

> '. . . and then I want to end it, if I may: "NORWICH". Norwich, yes . . . well, it's an idiomatic way of saying "Knickers off ready when I come home". You see, it's the initial letters of each word. Yes, I *know* "knickers" is spelled with a 'K'. I *was* at Oxford, it was one of the first things they taught us. And in an ideal world it would be "KORWICH", but I don't think it carries the same idiomatic force. "BURMA"? – no, I hadn't come across that – what's that? "Be upstairs ready, my angel" – well, yes, I like that – I don't think it would do in this case, for strictly topographical reasons – because Miss Prosser lives in a basement flat; and if she *was* upstairs ready, she would in fact be in the flat of the window dresser from Bourne and Hollingsworth, and I don't think she would want that – and I certainly don't think *he* would.'

The three lively performers known individually as Tim Brooke-Taylor, Graeme Garden and Bill Oddie, but collectively as 'The Goodies', could hardly perform the complicated stunts which characterized their television series; instead they sang several of Bill Oddie's songs, including the hit number 'The Funky Gibbon'.

John Cleese and Michael Palin performed the *Monty Python* sketch about the dead parrot – perhaps the most famous consumer complaint in history; Eleanor Bron, John Fortune and John Bird appeared in a couple of brief and witty sketches; and Jonathan Miller (who also directed the show) appeared with Peter Cook and Alan Bennett (with Terry Jones standing in for Dudley Moore) in one of the sketches from *Beyond the Fringe* – the devastating spoof of Shakespeare at his most tragical-pastoral-historical-unintelligible:

Jonathan Miller

> 'Oh good my Lord, unstop your ear and yet
> Prepare to yield the optic tear to my experience,
> Such news I bring as only can crack ope
> The casket of thy soul.
> Not six miles hence
> There grows an oak whose knotty thews
> Engendered in the bosky wood doth raise itself
> Most impudent towards the solstice sun –
> So saying there did die and dying so did say.'

The show ended with the entire cast assisting Michael Palin in a jolly song about a transvestite lumberjack, bringing to a close an occasion which was plainly enjoyed by the cast as much as the audience.

A Poke in the Eye With a Sharp Stick was something of a family reunion. The story of these performers between the sudden public acclaim of university humour in 1960 and this Amnesty special, and from there on to the end of their first twenty years, is the subject of this book. Because the careers of the people involved crossed and re-crossed, as partnerships formed and different shows with changing casts came and went, producing a kind of Lobster Quadrille, it

1976 Amnesty Show: Monty Python's 'Lumberjack Song' – Carol Cleveland, Michael Palin, and (kneeling) Graham Chapman, Terry Gilliam, Terry Jones, John Cleese; (standing) John Fortune, John Bird, Barry Humphries and Jonathan Lynn

is not possible to tell the story strictly chronologically. The narrative, which might fairly be compared to a railway main line from which various branch lines radiate at different places, will follow each branch to its end before returning to the mainline at the point at which it left, and moving along the narrative to the next branch. . . . Where a group of performers are left for a time there will generally be a reference ahead to their reappearance; and the 'family tree' at the end of the book may be of some help in keeping track of individual performers, even if it does look like a particularly neurotic game of snakes and ladders. Because many of the people concerned have been active in other fields – theatre directing, writing, or straight acting – it has also been necessary to draw boundary lines which inevitably will sometimes seem (and sometimes are) a trifle arbitrary; but the narrative aims to cover the careers as comic writer/performers of the people involved with the minimum number of flash-backs (or 'flash-forwards').

This, then, is the story of the 'Oxbridge Mafia', as they have been called – the generation who created the sharp eye of *Beyond the Fringe*, the uninhibited exuberance of *The Goodies*, the brilliant inventiveness of *Monty Python's Flying Circus*, and much more . . . the story of the people who, quite without intending to, came to dominate British humour in the sixties and seventies.

1.
The University Revues; 'The Last Laugh'; 'Beyond the Fringe' in London and New York

Cambridge University has always attracted more notice to its revues than Oxford, and indeed the whole tradition is stronger at Cambridge. If the blame is to be apportioned for the near take-over in the last 20 years of British humour by the 'Oxbridge Mafia', most of it must go to the unsung heroes who founded the Cambridge University Footlights Club in 1883.[2] The club's title was given to it by a Mr M. H. Cotton; and the mainstay of the club during the early years of this century was a don of King's College called Rottenburg, who wrote several of the early shows. He was a devotee of athletics, and the atmosphere of the club at this time has been described as 'decidedly hearty'.

The early shows were in the form of musical comedies. They were sharply satirical in tone, but only on a very parochial level – for this was an age of much slower communications, and the happenings of an entire university year would still be 'topical' at the time of the show. One such was the 1913 show, *Cheer-oh Cambridge*, which starred Jack Hulbert, later a famous entertainer. In 1919 came the first revue, *Reconstruction*; it was a success but it was not until 1924 that there was another revue, called *Bumps*. Later revues starred people such as Jimmy Edwards and Richard Murdoch, who went on to become successful professional comedians.

Since membership of the club was limited to men, female impersonation was a necessary performing art until 1932 when 'real women' were included in the cast for the first time. The result was felt to be such an unmitigated disaster that the following year's show was called *No More Women* and it was not until the early 1960s that female membership of the actual club was allowed, although a few women appeared in the revues from the late fifties onwards.

The club was, at any rate by the 1950s, rather élitist. New members had to be proposed for election by existing members, and would be invited to perform at an audition; if they were thought suitable they were then invited to join. The presidency of the club, on the other hand, was passed on – feudally – from each president to the next. The Footlights was a university club but some individual colleges staged their own revues and informal 'smoking concerts', where anyone was welcome to try out material on an audience who, since they would probably be trying out their own material shortly, were disposed to be encouraging. 'Smoking concert' is a delightfully old-fashioned term. It dates from the end of the last century, when Masonic Clubs and other organizations, as well as university colleges, would hold concerts to which ladies (who did not smoke) were not invited; this meant that the gentlemen might not only smoke, but also be entertained by items of a rather broader nature than would otherwise be thought polite. By the 1950s, however, the college smoking concerts were simply informal gatherings where relatively impromptu performances could be given.

At the end of the university year, in June, the Footlights revue proper would be mounted for a two-week run, in the Arts Theatre at Cambridge, using the best material and performers to emerge from the smokers. It was not unusual for each revue to tour briefly, usually to Oxford and occasionally as one of the unofficial entertainments mounted on the 'fringe' of the Edinburgh Arts Festival in August, before disappearing as the participants took up their intended careers.

There had been a couple of visits to the West End of London in the 1930s by the Footlights Club, when Jack Hulbert brought revues down; but apart from this no public attention was drawn to the Footlights Revues until 1954, when *Out of the Blue* played briefly in the West End. Among the cast was Jonathan Miller.

If 'Oxbridge Mafia' is an accurate description of the performers this book is about, then Jonathan Miller must surely be the Godfather. Though born on 21 July 1934, he is not the oldest – Alan Bennett beats him to that by a couple of months – but he was the first in the public eye. He first showed signs of performing talent at school, doing what he describes as 'mocking take-offs of the radio and television, and slightly surrealist monologues'; and, while still at school, made three appearances with schoolfriend Michael Bacharach in a BBC Radio programme called *Under Twenty Parade* on 10 March, 18 March and 7 April 1953. He was billed as 'John Miller', and he and Bacharach performed fairly basic lampoons on radio presentation – the weather forecast, police messages and so on – which are about what one would expect from lively sixth-formers.

He went to Cambridge later that year, to study medicine. As a result of performing one of his monologues in a 'Poppy Day' revue run by his college, he was noticed by the secretary of the Footlights Club. He never actually joined the club, as he was not really interested in the whole atmosphere of smoking concerts and so on. 'I acted in one play, and in two Footlights revues – occasionally taking part in some of the other sketches, but mostly just doing my own monologues – and I did those in 1954 in the show which came to London called *Out of the Blue*, which was produced by Leslie Bricusse, and included Frederic Raphael and people like that.'

Miller did two monologues in this show – 'Down Under' and 'Radio Page', as well as appearing as the Village Idiot in Gordon Pask's sketch 'Truly Rural', as Brutus in Geoffrey Brown's 'Rome on the Range', and in a couple of other minor rôles. Leslie Bricusse went on to be co-author of the book, music and lyrics of musicals such as *Stop the World I Want to Get Off* and *Pickwick*, while Frederic Raphael's work included the series of television plays *The Glittering Prizes*, based on his days at Cambridge, and many novels.

Out of the Blue opened at the Phoenix Theatre, London, on 6 July 1954; it attracted a few favourable reviews, and led the way for the next year's revue, *Between the Lines*. When *Between the Lines* opened in Cambridge, the *Daily Telegraph* reviewer headlined his brief item on it 'Danny Kaye of Cambridge'. He went on to describe Miller as being more like Danny Kaye than Kaye himself – a label Miller spent some time trying to live down. This, and later labels such as 'The Doctor of Mirth', applied once he had gained his medical degree, have left him with a jaundiced view of the press. The Danny Kaye label arose 'because I had an antic element to my performance, because I capered around and looked peculiar, and had red hair and a long nose – there was that sort of glib jumping to conclusions which happened. In fact as a boy of thirteen or fourteen I was very interested in Danny Kaye, and rather carried away by him.'

When *Between the Lines* opened in London at the Scala Theatre, on 28 June 1955, Miller again drew most attention from the critics, with honourable mentions for other members of the cast, including Brian Marber (the president of the Footlights Club that year), Peter Woodthorpe (who went on to be a successful actor), Trevor Williams and John Pardoe (later a leading Liberal politician); but neither of these revues was seen as likely to have any influence in the long term. Miller: 'They were still on the rump of the old tradition – there was still an awful lot of stuff with people walking on in blazers and flannels and boaters, and singing songs about Proctors and "Going down for the last time" and punts, and things of that sort. But there were elements of things which later appeared in shows like *Beyond the Fringe*; there were satirical, rather biting little sketches, which were written by people like Freddy Raphael – but still cast in an old fashioned, rhyming verse form.'

Out of the Blue: Jonathan Miller explains how Australians transport cattle

These were the first glimmerings of the harder edge of humour which was to come. The outside world was beginning to impinge on the Cambridge greenhouse for the first time – although the initial reaction to the austere post-war world of rationing was an attempt to recapture some of the feeling of elegance and style of which the war had deprived people. Miller remembers: 'The smart thing in Cambridge in the early fifties was to be queer – rather wittily queer; and therefore people feigned queerness as a way of escaping, or seeming to escape, from the austerity.' Of course, at this time actual homosexuality was not the socially acceptable condition it is today, and what Miller's

3

contemporaries were presumably aiming for was the affected elegant wittiness of an Oscar Wilde. Within this rather artificial atmosphere were the beginnings of a more cynical social awareness; Miller himself did not do National Service because he was training to be a doctor, but many of his contemporaries at Cambridge did – and in a few cases had actually fought in the war – and Miller thinks that this may have been partially responsible for the hard edge which was beginning to appear. There was also a general public feeling, especially among the young, of disenchantment with the established order during the mid-fifties, brought about by such events as the Suez crisis and growing alarm over the testing and proliferation of nuclear weapons. The spirit of the times was well caught by John Osborne's 1956 play *Look Back in Anger*, which led the press to coin the phrase 'Angry Young Men' as a description of Osborne and similar writers. Miller, however, was not an Angry Young Man: 'I was a privileged young man with a decent Public School education and nothing to complain about, and therefore I wasn't angry or annoyed. I was slightly *nettled* by things, but that was because I was amused by them rather than really outraged.'

There was also a growing link between the people who were interested in drama and those who were active in university journalism. Miller stresses the importance of the Cambridge magazine *Granta*, which had been founded in the 1880s. 'In the years that I was at Cambridge it was taken over by Mark Boxer – later, he did the "Life and Times in NW1" cartoons in *The Times* with Alan Bennett, and he started the *Sunday Times* colour magazine – he started the whole business of really sharp, satirical, graphically aware layouts and designs in *Granta* – he got sent down for publishing a blasphemous poem. A lot of the

Springs to Mind – Footlights' 1958 May Week Review. Cast: Timothy Birdsall, Michael Collings, Fred Emery, David Johnson, Joe Melia, David Monico, Geoff Pattie, Adrian Slade, Bill Wallis.

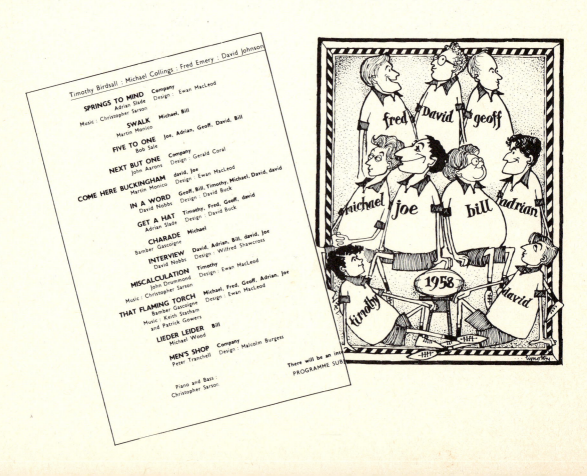

people who wrote for, and edited, *Granta* knew the theatre, Amateur Dramatic Club, Footlights people, so you have to take account of what people wrote in journals in Cambridge in the fifties, as well as what they actually performed on stage.'

Miller left Cambridge in 1956, and then·spent three years as a medical student at University College, London. He appeared in two hospital revues, directing one of them; again, there were signs of a turning outward from the parochial concerns of the hospital. Like the Footlights revues, and indeed the professional West End revues, they began to look at the world and, as Miller says, 'If you look at the world at all, you're bound to become satirical about it.'

While still at Cambridge, Miller appeared in a radio programme, *The Man From Paranoia*, broadcast on 9 September 1955; written by Allan Grant and Ted Taylor, and described as 'A Thing for Radio', it told the story of a Cambridge don who owns a singing goldfish. Then, while at medical school, he made nine appearances in *Saturday Night on the Light*, a lively magazine programme, performing his own monologues. One of them, a speculation occasioned by the sale of four hundred pairs of trousers by the London Passenger Transport Lost Property Department, later found its way into *Beyond the Fringe*. These broadcasts were in 1957 and 1958, and were followed in 1959–60 by a further twelve appearances in the successor to *SNOL*, *Monday Night at Home*. 'And that's my career in showbiz.'

While Jonathan Miller was at medical school, Peter Cook was becoming the leading light in the Cambridge Footlights Club. Cook was born on 17 November 1937. While still at school he had had several short items published in the 'Charivaria' section of the comic magazine *Punch*, as well as writing a few things for school consumption: 'I wrote a terrible play about Martians landing in a suburban part of England. I can't remember what happened, except that the Martians behaved more normally than the people in suburbia. Then I wrote the words for a musical comedy for the Marionette Society – it was called *The Black and White Blues*, and had the hideously naïve premise of a sort of rock-and-roll vicar who went to Africa to convert the natives with a mixture of Christianity and Hot Rhythm. It really was quite appalling, what I remember of it.'

One of his comic creations reverberated into his professional career, in the form of the character who became known as E. L. Wisty. Wisty first came to the public eye (though not by name) in the monologue about the miner who wanted to be a judge, but the basis of the character was laid while Cook was at school: 'I developed a character there which was based on a guy who used to work at the High Table, called Mr Boylett. He used to say very strange things like: "I saw a stone, and I thought it might be valuable because I thought I saw it move, so I hoped to sell it." There was absolutely no meaning to this – he thought he saw things move – and this became a sort of catchphrase within the school.'

Cook was, like many of the subsequent university humorists, a great fan of *The Goon Show*. 'I used to go sick every Friday to listen to *The Goon Show* in the sanatorium – there was a sort of understanding between me and the matron. I remember my parents and my aunts and so on – it wasn't that they couldn't stand *The Goon Show*, but they always thought it was very *loud* – however much the sound was turned down they still thought it was *loud*. They were completely unaware of the hidden vulgarity in it.'

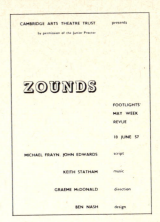

CAMBRIDGE ARTS THEATRE TRUST presents
by permission of the Junior Proctor

ZOUNDS

FOOTLIGHTS' MAY WEEK REVUE

10 JUNE 57

MICHAEL FRAYN, JOHN EDWARDS script

KEITH STATHAM music

GRAEME McDONALD direction

BEN NASH design

CAMBRIDGE ARTS THEATRE

FOOTLIGHTS PRESENT

ANYTHING MAY . . .

SOUVENIR PROGRAMME ONE SHILLING

5

While still at school, Cook submitted a script to the BBC which was just a *Goon Show* pastiche, using the ready-made characters, and got a kind letter back from Peter Titheradge saying that it was a good Goon script, and suggesting that he write something of his own. In fact he wrote nothing else while at school, apart from 'a completely Nazi treatise on how the "unintelligent working class" should be sterilized! People say I've got more reactionary in my old age, when in fact I've moved to the left from my very solid Nazi position at the age of sixteen!'

Although he should have done National Service when he left school in 1956, he contrived to fail the entrance. 'I was allergic to feathers – I mean I *had* been allergic to feathers and I had grown out of it, but it was still on my medical record. They asked me if I would sneeze if I was in a barrack room full of feather pillows – an unlikely situation, I thought – but I said, truthfully, "Yes" (because everybody sneezes at some time or another), and so I was unsuitable.' This left him with a year to fill in before he could be admitted to Cambridge. 'I spent that time in France and Germany – where I went to these awful satirical nightclubs. I thought they were terribly bad – I spoke reasonably good French and German, and I thought the humour was very juvenile – says he at the age of eighteen! But that was when I formed at the back of my mind the idea of forming the Establishment Club – I didn't know it was going to be called that at the time. I thought, very early on, "Why isn't there the equivalent of this in London?" For a long time my major fear was that somebody would do the obvious and start it before me – it seemed such an obvious idea.'

Cook went on to Cambridge in 1957, where he read French and German literature at Pembroke College. 'I didn't do much writing in my first year because I felt the Footlights was a tremendously élite club – I was too bashful to even consider applying for it.'

In his second year at Cambridge he summoned up enough courage to do an audition for the Footlights Club. He performed an 'I thought I saw it move' monologue which was very well received. From then on writing and performing became his main interest – he did just enough work to get his degree.

Cook took part in the 1959 Footlights revue, *The Last Laugh*, which also starred Timothy Birdsall and Eleanor Bron. The director was John Bird. Bird, who was born on 22 November 1936, had come to Cambridge in 1955 to read English. He went on to research the history of naturalistic drama, a subject in which his interest waned when he discovered that he would have to learn Russian in order to quote Chekhov, and Norwegian in order to quote Ibsen. He was at Cambridge for four years, and was originally mainly associated with the Amateur Dramatic Society for whom he directed several plays, including *The Bald Prima Donna* by Ionesco. He also distinguished himself by staging N. F. Simpson's surrealist play *A Resounding Tinkle* in its complete version, which was supposed to be unstageable; the cast included Peter Cook, in his first straight rôle. On the strength of this, Bird was offered a job as assistant director at the Royal Court Theatre in London, which had originally staged *A Resounding Tinkle*, but in the one-act version.

Bird's final contribution to Cambridge life, before leaving in 1959 to take up this post, was to direct the Footlights revue. He was invited to do this by the Footlights Club but, as he was not much interested in revue, agreed to do so only on condition that he could have a completely free hand.

The Last Laugh was certainly quite unlike any Footlights revue before or since. It was very ambitious, and very politically-orientated. Bird: 'It was a complete disaster, really, in a way . . . the first night ran about four-and-a-half hours. I was told it was the first Footlights revue to be booed on the first night. It settled down after that, but there were a lot of very difficult technical things – back projections – and they didn't get a proper rehearsal.' The show also broke new ground on the musical side by having a ten-piece modern jazz band, under the direction of Patrick Gowers.

Bird had insisted on Eleanor Bron being in the cast – he followed the 1957 revue in refusing to have any drag acts, which had been normal since the episode in the 1930s. Bron was then in the second of her three years at Cambridge, where she was reading modern languages. She had really wanted to go into acting, but had been persuaded out of it and saw herself as heading for a career in publishing.

Being such a sharp contrast with the usual light-hearted Footlights revues, *The Last Laugh* was not very well received, and got a bad review in the local paper. Approval for it came from one unexpected source. Bird: 'Alistair Cooke was in Cambridge; he came to the first night. He had some American friends with him, and he wanted to show them what a Footlights revue was like. He wrote a wonderful review of it in *The Guardian*.'

Cooke's long review, published in *The Manchester Guardian* on 10 June 1959, was certainly enthusiastic. He described briefly the rather vapid pre-war Footlights revues, and expressed his surprise at the completely different vein of *The Last Laugh*. He enthused at considerable length about Patrick Gowers's music, and went on:

> The whole show is acted with never a fumbling line or gesture, and since it is inconceivable that a dozen undergraduates can appear as full-fledged professionals, the only sensible inference is that in Mr John Bird, the club has a broth of a director. In fact, if the West End does not soon hear of John Bird, Patrick Gowers, Geoff Pattie and Peter Cook, the West End is an ass.
>
> In bringing in Miss Eleanor Bron, the club has passed up the easy guffaws available in all public demonstrations of transvestism. Incidentally, they have got themselves a very fetching dish, if I may coin a phrase. She has a wolf-whistle figure, a confident pout, and needs only to practice singing in pitch . . . to be something of a threat to the hoydens of the London Pavilion. She is from Newnham [College]. Newnham is something else that seems to have changed since my day.

The Last Laugh attracted the attention of William Donaldson, who at that time was a theatrical producer in a small way. (He has since become something of a literary scamp, having written two books – *Both the Ladies and the Gentlemen* and *The Balloons in the Black Bag* – embroidering his experiences while living off a call-girl's earnings, and the best-selling *Henry Root Letters*.) Donaldson mounted a revised version of *The Last Laugh*, under the title *Here is the News*, with a professional cast including Sheila Hancock and Cleo Laine.

Donaldson: 'I've always held firmly to the opinion that John Bird was much the cleverest of all these people. In my day, he was the guru, he was the clever one. He changed the idea of revue at Cambridge from being old-style smoker jokey thing – he taught me that revues shouldn't be jolly little songs about Hermione Gingold and Liberace, but that the targets should be political. This

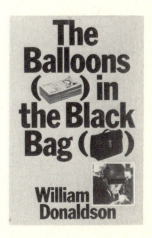

revue was very very hard indeed – I think it was brilliant. I put it on – it didn't actually come to London – Oxford and somewhere, and it collapsed. I think it was sensational, and if it had come to London, *Beyond the Fringe* wouldn't have had any impact at all. *Beyond the Fringe* was funnier – it worked, and this one didn't.'

Patrick Gowers, the musical director of *The Last Laugh*, thinks that Donaldson is being over-enthusiastic. He remembers nearly every sketch as ending with a stated or implied death – John Bird says this was because he often couldn't think of any other way of ending the sketches. *Here is the News* rehearsed in London for four weeks in the hope of a theatre becoming available, but in the end it was abandoned. It was to some extent ahead of its time, with its political content and a strong anti-nuclear-armament standpoint, for audiences who were still expecting revues to be light-hearted rather than disturbing.

The Last Laugh stands out as the only Cambridge Footlights revue to attempt to be directly politically satirical. In the following year, 1960, Peter Cook was the president of the Footlights Club and wrote most of the material for that year's revue, *Pop Goes Mrs Jessup*, which he describes as 'entirely frivolous'. It was seen by theatrical producer Michael Codron, who asked Cook to contribute to a professional revue starring Kenneth Williams and Fenella Fielding. This was *Pieces of Eight*, which played at the Apollo Theatre in London in 1960, receiving favourable if not enthusiastic reviews.

Cook: 'I loved that revue – it was Old Fashioned Revue, which was eventually killed off by *Beyond the Fringe*. I found nothing wrong with it. The other main contributor was Harold Pinter – I was very cross at the time because royalties were awarded on the amount of time your contributions took up. Well, Harold Pinter's contributions took up an immense amount of time because he'd written all these pauses into his sketches . . . which I called the "pay pause". I eventually submitted a sketch to Michael Codron which consisted almost entirely of significant pauses. But he knew perfectly well what I was up to, and it was rejected. It was an odd combination, Pinter and me – I've always been stuck with this thing that most of my ideas are only worth about five minutes. I love the sketch form.' *Pieces of Eight* was followed in 1961 by *One Over the Eight*, again with Cook's contributions based on pieces he had performed at Cambridge. 'By the time I left Cambridge I had acquired an agent, and was a "professional writer".'

Cambridge, and in particular the Footlights revues, has always seemed to be more in the limelight than Oxford; but Oxford also had a tradition of revues and smoking concerts. One of the more self-effacing contributors to this field was also one of the most talented – Alan Bennett, born slightly more than two months before Jonathan Miller, on 9 May 1934, and thus the senior partner in the group which was to be formed. He says: 'My first venture into revue was during National Service. I was studying Russian at the Joint Services School in 1956, and I wrote and performed some sketches with Michael Frayn, who was on the same course. I can't recall what the sketches were about. I imagine they were full of private jokes about the Russian course, and depended for their reception upon the audience being drunk or otherwise well-disposed.

'I then went to Oxford, where I had no theatrical ambitions. I might have acted a bit, but I was overawed by the people who did. I lived a college rather

8

than a university life, and steered clear of the Oxford University Dramatic Society and the Experimental Theatre Club.'[3]

Exeter College, where Bennett studied, had a tradition of smoking concerts. 'I started to do occasional sketches for these, and then put together a concert with Russell Harty, who lived on the same staircase – this would be in 1956.' This concert saw the first appearance of the biting parody of a particularly meaningless kind of sermon, now fortunately out of fashion (partly because of this skit), which was later included in *Beyond the Fringe*:

Beyond the Fringe: Alan Bennett's sermon

'As I was on my way here tonight, I arrived at the station, and by an oversight I happened to go out by the way one is supposed to come in; and as I was going out an employee of the railway company hailed me. "Hey, Jack," he shouted, "where do you think you're going?" That at any rate was the gist of what he said. But, you know, I was grateful to him; because, you see, he put me in mind of the kind of question I felt I ought to be asking you here tonight. Where do you think you're going?

'Very many years ago, when I was about as old as some of you are now, I went mountain climbing in Scotland with a very dear friend of mine. And there was this mountain, you see, and we decided to climb it. And so, very early one morning, we arose and began to climb. All day we climbed. Up and up and up; higher and higher and higher. Until the valley lay very small below us, and the mists of the evening began to come down, and the sun to set. And when we reached the summit we sat down to watch this magnificent sight of the sun going down behind the mountain. And as he watched, my friend very suddenly and violently vomited.

'Some of us think Life's a bit like that, don't we? But it isn't. Life, you know, is rather like opening a tin of sardines. We are all of us looking for the key. And I wonder, how many of you here tonight have wasted years of your lives looking behind the kitchen dressers of this life for that key. I know I have. Others think they've found the key, don't they? They roll back the lid of the sardine tin of Life, they reveal the sardines, the riches of Life, therein, and they get them out, they enjoy them. But, you know, there's always a little bit in the corner you can't get out. I wonder – I wonder, is there a little bit in the corner of your life? I know there is in mine.'

Bennett says: 'It took about half an hour to write, and was, I suppose, the most profitable half hour's work I have ever done. Once I had hit on the form I used to be able to run up sermons for all sorts of occasions, choosing texts almost at random from any book that came to hand.

'I also used to do imitations of the Queen's Christmas broadcast. I imagine various people were doing similar sketches around the same time, and it has always seemed to me that what was subsequently labelled "satire" was simply this kind of private humour going public.'

Another Oxford graduate, John Bassett, was the person responsible for the beginning of *Beyond the Fringe*. Jonathan Miller sees him as 'a much unsung and under-celebrated person – he was a sort of undergraduate entrepreneur. He put on jazz bands and played in them, and fixed up gigs for May Balls, and so forth – and sometimes arranged cabarets. As a double deal to get his jazz band in he would arrange to get Alan Bennett performing, or Dudley Moore, or someone like that.'

Dudley Moore was born on 19 April 1935. In 1979 he told *The Observer*: 'I was a very serious pompous child. I spent the first seven years of my life syphoned off in hospital beds and wheel chairs with a club foot. I had special boots, and – just like Rumpelstiltskin – the only way I could express my rage was by stamping on the floor until it collapsed and gave way. It was my leg onto which I projected all my feelings of inadequacy and self-loathing.'[4]

When he went to secondary school, he turned to clowning to protect himself from the inevitable bullying and jokes about Hopalong Cassidy; of course his work suffered, apart from his natural flair for music, which he went on to study at Magdalen College, Oxford. 'I felt dwarfed by the social ease of the people who'd come from public schools. I couldn't stand the sound of their voices – they seemed so in charge of themselves. So I tried to imitate them. My vowels still got back to Dagenham very easily, though I let them slip and slide anywhere nowadays.' He became involved in stage and cabaret activities, and expanded his musical interests to include jazz, developing an attractive style of jazz piano playing which later became a major part of his career; he also developed a style of impromptu clowning which at times had a subversive undercurrent to it. This undercurrent made itself felt in some of the *Beyond the Fringe* sketches – for example in the sketch with Bennett and Miller discussing philosophy, which was liable to be interrupted by off-stage and unscripted remarks of the 'Nurse – the screens!' variety.

In 1960 John Bassett, having left Oxford, was assisting Robert Ponsonby, who was then running the Edinburgh Festival. From the mid-fifties onwards this annual feast of drama and music also had the added attraction of unofficial performances by various small and often experimental theatre and revue groups (including the Cambridge Footlights) – the 'Fringe' of the Festival. Ponsonby suggested that the Festival itself might have an official late-night revue, instead of letting the Fringe have the monopoly in that field; Bassett suggested Moore and, at Moore's instigation, Bennett – both from Oxford – and suggested that they could be balanced by two Cambridge people.

Jonathan Miller: 'Bassett had been at school with my wife's sister, and therefore vaguely knew of me. I was a doctor by this time – I'd just qualified. I was doing my first house job. People always get this wrong – they always somehow think that I was at Cambridge – I'd been down from Cambridge for three years. I remember Bassett came round to the casualty department while I was doing a job – I was there with a dressing in my hand at the time I was talking to him.' Miller agreed to meet the others, and also suggested Peter Cook; he fully intended, however, to go on with medicine: 'I still fiercely regret the distraction. I think that was a bad thing I did. Much better to have been a very funny comic undergraduate and forget about it – but I got onto this terrible treadmill.'

The four had what Miller describes as 'a rather guarded and hostile encounter' over a meal, at which they 'instantly disliked each other and decided that it might be a profitable enterprise'. Bennett remembers: 'We warily took one another's measure. Peter was very funny and, to my alarm, very fluent. He appeared to be able to ad lib excellent material in monologues of spiralling absurdity. Since my output was rather limited I had the slight feeling I was there under false pretences – a feeling that never really left me.' Cook says: 'We eyed each other vaguely suspiciously – in those days Alan was chronically shy ... Dudley had a terrible piece that was some mime about a violin which behaved like a baby – really shocking – whenever I wish to score a point I say "Let's do the violin and baby mime."'

If Cook had been prone to listening to advice the show might never have happened. 'My agent at the time advised me against getting involved with "a little amateur revue up in Edinburgh". I said I'd like to do it – it would only be two weeks – then he negotiated me £110 as opposed to the others' £100, which after his commission left me with £99 – I didn't pay much heed to his advice after that.'

Bassett suggested that the four should pool the best of their existing solo material, and write additional material together to bring the length up to an hour: he also pushed the four of them into rehearsing. Bennett: 'The title *Beyond the Fringe*, which none of us was keen on, came from Robert Ponsonby – it was intended to imply that what we were doing was beyond the capabilities of the Fringe. The best of the stuff that went into *Beyond the Fringe* was old material, sketches we had tried and tested before. Some of the new sketches had some bite – I am thinking of the sketches about nuclear warfare, the myth of the last war, a sketch about capital punishment. These got the show a name for being topical and satirical in a mode at that time associated with American stand-up comedians – Mort Sahl, Lenny Bruce, and Nichols and May. But really we were having it both ways. Most of the stuff was in the tradition of English revue – light, silly, but very funny. It was well observed and to the point. It wasn't in the terrible school of "How would it be if . . ." revue writing, where people came on dressed as garden gnomes or whatever. It did actually treat the audience as intelligent people who read the papers – and read papers other than *The Stage*.'

One of the aspects of *Beyond the Fringe* that was to attract the most attention was the bareness of the staging. There was no stage set to speak of, and no costumes – the cast wore suits and dark sweaters. Peter Cook: 'Part of the style of the show came from the lack of money. We'd have been delighted to have had a hundred chorus girls dancing about.' Miller sees the staging as a more deliberate decision: 'We resolved not to have scenery – because we didn't have enough money to put it up – and then we suddenly realized there was a virtue in it. What was new about the show was that it moved fast, was undecorated, and therefore it appealed to that sort of late fifties Brechtian appetite on the part of people like Kenneth Tynan for the sort of "new brutalism" of the late fifties theatre. It didn't depend on illusionism; it didn't depend on pretty girls; it didn't depend on musical interludes in a "seriously though" moment – the whole thing depended on trying to make people laugh as much as possible, as hard as possible, about things that were actually the case.'

There were some musical interludes from Dudley Moore, but there was nothing serious about them. One was a devastating impression of 'Little Miss Muffett' as it might have been arranged by Benjamin Britten and sung by a particularly wobbly Peter Pears; another was a witty arrangement of 'Colonel Bogey' which displayed a remarkable reluctance to come to an end. Moore remembers: 'I think that I've always had an ear for styles, and in fact it was written when we were in Edinburgh – I think it was the night before, because I can only work to deadlines. I remember writing it in this peculiar flat somewhere where we were all ensconced. In fact the never-ending cadence wasn't something that I'd written in – I'd written a long cadence, but it went so well that I just improvised and made it longer and longer.'[5]

Classical drama was not exempted from the team's attentions, and their Shakespeare sketch entitled 'So That's The Way You Like It', is probably the best parody ever written of the bard at his most historically obscure.

COOK: Sustain we now description of a time
When petty lust and overweening tyranny
Offend the ruck of state.
Thus fly we now, as oft with Phoebus did
Fair Asterope unto proud Flander's court
Where is the warlike Warwick
Like to the mole that sat on Hector's brow,
Fairset for England, and for War.
(Enter Miller and Bennett)

MILLER: And so we bid you welcome to our court,
Fair cousin Albany, and you, our sweetest Essex,
Take this my hand, and you, fair Essex, this,
And with this bond we'll cry anon
And shout Jack Cock of London to the foe.
Approach your ears and kindly bend your conscience to my piece,
Our ruddy scouts to me this hefty news have brought:
The naughty English, expecting now some pregnance in our plan,
Have with some haughty purpose
Bent Aeolis unto the servis of their sail.
So even now while we to the wanton lute do strut
Is brutish Bolingbroke bent fair upon
Some fickle circumstance.

BENNETT
COOK   }: Some fickle circumstance!

Peter Cook, Jonathan Miller,
Alan Bennett, and Dudley Moore
in *Beyond the Fringe*

Beyond the Fringe: Moore,
Miller, Cook and Bennett in
the Shakespeare parody as
seen by American cartoonist
Al Hirschfeld

MILLER: Get thee to Gloucester, Essex. Do thee to Wessex, Exeter.
    Fair Albany to Somerset must eke his route.
    And Scroop, do you to Westmoreland, where shall bold York
    Enrouted now for Lancaster, with forces of our Uncle Rutland,
    Enjoin his standard with sweet Norfolk's host.
    Fair Sussex, get thee to Warwicksbourne,
    And there, with frowning purpose, tell our plan
    To Bedford's tilted ear, that he shall press
    With most insensate speed
    And join his warlike effort to bold Dorset's side.
    I most royally shall now to bed,
    To sleep off all the nonsense I've just said.
    (They exit. Re-enter all four, as rustics.)
MILLER: Is it all botched up, then, Master Puke?
BENNETT: Aye, and marry is, good Master Snot.
MOORE: 'Tis said our Master, the Duke, hath contrived some naughtiness
    against his son, the King.
COOK: Aye, and it doth confound our merrymaking.
MILLER: What say you, Master Puke? I am for Lancaster, and that's to say
    for good shoe leather.
COOK: Come speak, good Master Puke, or hath the leather blocked up thy
    tongue?

MOORE: Why then go trippingly upon thy laces, good Grit.
COOK: Art leather laces thy undoing?
MOORE: They shall undo many a fair boot this day.
ALL: Come, let's to our rural revel and with our song enchant our King.

Very properly, the 'play' ends with a battle.

(Enter Cook and Miller, with swords)
MILLER: Why then was this encounter nobly entertained
And so by steel shall this our contest now be buckled up.
Come, sir. Let's to it.
COOK: Let's to it.
Good steel, thou shalt thyself in himself thyself embowel.
MILLER: Come, sir. *(They fight)*
Ah ha, a hit!
COOK: No, sir, no hit, a miss! Come, sir, art foppish i' the mouth.
MILLER: Art more fop in the mouth than fop in the steel.
(They fight again. Cook 'hits' Miller)
MILLER: Oh, God, fair cousin, thou hast done me wrong.
(He dies)
Now is steel twixt gut and bladder interposed.
COOK: Oh, saucy Worcester, dost thou lie so still?
(Enter Bennett)
BENNETT: Now hath mortality her tithe collected
And sovereign Albany to the worms his corse committed.
Yet weep we not; this fustian life is short,
Let's on to Pontefract to sanctify our court.

Beyond the Fringe opened at the Lyceum Theatre, Edinburgh, at 10.45 p.m. on Monday 22 August 1960. Critical reaction was excellent, although the major public acclaim did not come until the show opened in London in May the following year. How it got to London is a comic story in itself. William Donaldson, who had just had his disaster with John Bird's *Here is the News*, was probably the only London producer who didn't go to Edinburgh to see *Beyond the Fringe*.

'I think I assumed I wouldn't get it, because its reputation was enormous immediately. I'd just had this terrible flop, so I thought the last person they'd give it to anyway is this fool – and I was only about twenty-three – so I didn't bother to go near the place. A friend of mine was Peter Cook's agent. His contribution to *Beyond the Fringe* was to try to persuade Peter Cook not to do it – and then he didn't even go up to the opening – he'd never met the other three at all – and he came to me with all the notices after it had opened. He said "I think we ought to get this – this looks rather good." I said "You'll be lucky." He said "No, I'll get it – you stay here", and he flew up to Edinburgh . . . and they all hated him – Cook hated him, the other three hated him. . . . Anyway, within twenty-four hours he'd persuaded four intelligent strong-minded men that he should represent all of them, and that his friend Willie Donaldson was the *only* person qualified to do the show in London. How he'd been able to persuade them was that I was so stupid and inexperienced that I wouldn't interfere with what they wanted to do, whereas every other impresario who knew his business, and knew what he was doing, would interfere with it.

'We all went out to dinner, at the White Elephant I recall, and I just sat stunned, and stared at them, and said how clever they were, and how I wished I'd seen the show – and they signed with me! Most extraordinary! The only thing they were a bit doubtful about was whether I'd be able to get a theatre – because apart from anything else I was bankrupt at the time, the Bird revue had bankrupted me. In fact as soon as the word got out that I owned this show all these impresarios who'd been up to Edinburgh were begging and pleading with me to let them in on it. In the end I let Donald Albery in on it because he promised us one of his theatres. He was the only other producer who hadn't seen it, and he didn't know what the hell he'd bought – he came to the final run-through. I said "What do you think?" He said "Who's the one with the spectacles?"; so I said "That's Alan Bennett", and he said "Oh, we've got to get rid of him, he's no good."' (Bennett remembers Albery as saying that 'it would be all right except for the fair-haired one', adding 'I did understand what he meant'.)

Before coming to London the show played Cambridge, where it went down very well, and then did a week at Brighton. The Brighton audiences, however, seemed not to appreciate the new style in revue; the cast performed to the sound of seats banging up and walking sticks taking people out of the theatre. Donaldson: 'It got the most terrible notices – there was the worst review of a show I've ever read in my life, which said "The only thing you can say for this frightful show is at least they wrote it themselves, so they're not messing up anybody else's material." At the end of every show there were only three people left in the theatre – and we had all these notices from the national critics saying it was the funniest thing ever – and we thought we'd imagined the whole thing . . . and Albery panicked so much he wouldn't give us a theatre. In the end we squeezed into the Fortune Theatre because David Jacobs [a lawyer, not the well-known broadcaster] came down to see it at Brighton and he thought the show was so bad it would keep the Fortune warm for a show belonging to another client of his – a revue with Bernard Cribbins – he thought it would run for about six weeks. Then it opened, and the rest is history, as they say.'

Beyond the Fringe opened at the Fortune Theatre on 10 May 1961, and was immediately hailed as a satirical masterpiece – a label which the performers found rather disconcerting. Cook: 'Certain parts of it *were* satirical – the capital punishment sketch, the sketch I did as somebody who'd joined the Beaverbrook press, the "Aftermyth of War" – which upset quite a few people, who thought it was an attack on people who laid down their lives in the war, when in fact it was a parody of the films.'

BENNETT: I'll always remember that weekend war broke out. I was at a house party at Cliveden with the Astors and we sat around listening to the moving broadcast by Mr Churchill, or Mr Chamberlain as he then was. I remember turning to my husband and saying, 'Squiffy, *où sont les neiges d'ans temps?*' But I did not feel then that all was quite lost and immediately afterwards I got on the telephone to Berlin to try to speak to Herr Hitler, who had been so kind to us on our last visit to Germany that summer. Unfortunately the line was engaged. There was nothing I could do to avert the carnage of the next six years.

(Sound of an explosion)

MOORE: Mr Charles Spedding of Hoxton remembers:

COOK: I'll never forget that day that war was declared. I was out in the garden at the time, planting out some chrysanths. It was a grand year for chrysanths, 1939, I had some lovely blooms. My wife came out to me in the garden and told me of the Prime Minister's announcement of the outbreak of war. 'Never mind, my dear,' I said to her, 'you put on the kettle and we'll have a nice cup of tea.' *(Sound of an air-raid siren)*

MOORE: Put out that light! All over Britain, the humble little people showed the same spirit of courage. *(Sound of an air raid. Miller enters with a tea trolley)*

MILLER: You could always tell the difference between theirs and ours. Ours has a steady sort of reliable British hum, rather like a homely old bumblebee. Theirs, on the other hand, has a nasty intermittent whine rather like a ghastly foreign mosquito.

BENNETT *(off, on microphone)*: Meanwhile, as invasion threatened, England was blanketed in security. *(Cook and Moore enter with a signpost)*

COOK: Wait a moment, now. We'll put Ipswich round there.

MOORE: We'll put Lyme Regis where Ipswich was.

COOK: And we'll put Great Yarmouth where Lyme Regis was. There, now, that should fool the Boche. Bye-bye, then. Here – how do we get home?

MILLER: Home. The very word had a sort of comforting sound, didn't it? Homes whose very foundations were built upon the air. Young men, scarcely boys, tossed aside youthful things and grew up overnight in the grimmer game that is war. A game where only one side was playing the game. Young men flocked to join the Few.

MOORE: Please sir, I want to join the Few.

MILLER: I'm sorry, there are far too many.

COOK: From the rugby fields into the air.

MILLER: From the squash courts into the clouds.

BENNETT: From the skiffs into the Spitfires.

MILLER: This was war.

BENNETT: I had a pretty quiet war, really. I was one of the Few. We were stationed down at Biggin Hill. One Sunday we got word that Jerry was coming in – over Hastings, I think it was. We got up there as quickly as we could, and everything was very calm and peaceful. England lay like a green carpet below me, and the war seemed worlds away. I could see Tunbridge Wells, and the sun glistening on the river, and I remembered that last weekend I'd spent there with Celia that summer of '39, and her playing the piano in the cool of the evening. Suddenly, Jerry was coming at me out of a bank of cloud. I let him have it, and I think I must have got him in the wing because he spiralled past me out of control. As he did so – I will always remember this – I got a glimpse of his face, and, you know – he smiled. Funny thing, war. *(There is the sound of hearty singing. Cook enters)*

COOK: Perkins! Sorry to drag you away from the fun, old boy. War's not

	going very well, you know.
MILLER:	Oh my God!
COOK:	We are two down, and the ball's in the enemy court. War is a psychological thing, Perkins, rather like a game of football. You know how in a game of football ten men often play better than eleven –?
MILLER:	Yes, sir.
COOK:	Perkins, we are asking you to be that one man. I want you to lay down your life, Perkins. We need a futile gesture at this stage. It will raise the whole tone of the war. Get up in a crate, Perkins, pop over to Bremen, take a shufti, don't come back. Goodbye, Perkins. God, I wish I was going too.
MILLER:	Goodbye, sir – or is it – au revoir?
COOK:	No, Perkins.

But satire was not a word the group had ever used in connection with their writing. Miller says: 'There were targets we wanted to hit – Alan had certain people he wanted to lampoon – I was interested in lampooning productions of Shakespeare, not because I had a burning indignation against them but because I just wanted to get them right. None of us approached the world with a satirical indignation. We had no reason to – we were all very comfortably off, and doing very nicely. Alan was all set to be an academic at Oxford, Dudley was doing very well as a jazz musician – and Peter and I came from professional middle-class families anyway, and had nothing to complain of. What made the show work was that we resolved not to make these conditional propositions, which were always the basis of old-fashioned revue – "wouldn't it be funny *if* ...". Our idea was "isn't it funny *that* ...". – let's observe what actually goes on, imitate it, and remind people by the shock of recognition how absurd things are. We knew it was funny before we put it on, because it made us laugh a good deal, but we didn't think it was a revolution. It was only when Kenneth Tynan shoved this banner into our hands – it was rather like Charlie Chaplin [in *Modern Times*] finding himself at the head of a communist parade. I think the banner was thrust into our hands by that first Sunday review by Ken Tynan.'

Tynan's review, headlined 'English satire advances into the sixties', appeared in *The Observer* on 14 May 1961. He described the scenery – such as it was – and the performers, and also described the opening sketch in some detail. Assessing the show as 'the funniest revue that London has seen since the Allies dropped the bomb on Hiroshima', he described some more of the sketches, and concluded:

> It can justly be urged against the show that it is too parochial, too much obsessed with BBC voices and BBC attitudes, too exclusively concerned with taunting the accents and values of John Betjeman's suburbia. *Beyond the Fringe* is anti-reactionary without being progressive. It goes less far than one could have hoped, but immeasurably farther than one had any right to expect.

Perhaps more significant was Bernard Levin's review in the *Daily Express* on the morning after the first night, in which, imbued with the euphoria of

> English satire advances into the Sixties

The NEW HELL-RAISERS

A whiff of grapeshot is all you'll get from us

And so it is. Mad? Yes they are. Understand them if you dare. They are young—original—writers— actors. JONATHAN MILLER *(left in the photograph) is a doctor.* PETER COOK *an undergraduate. They talk better than most of us wish we could. You will still be talking about them fifty years hence. Start now.*

what was certainly a very funny show, he went overboard with enthusiasm. Announcing that the Theatre had 'come of age', having been given the key of the door and shown how the lock works by the four young men, he said that his first reaction was one of gratitude:

> Gratitude that there should be four men living among us today who could come together to provide, as long as memory holds, an eighth colour to the rainbow. Satirical revue in this country has been, until now, basically cowardly. First, it has picked on the easy targets. Second, however hard it hit its targets . . . it left its audience alone, to leave the theatre as fat and complacent as it came in.

With mounting enthusiasm he listed the targets of the show, going on to say:

> The satire then is real, barbed, deeply planted and aimed at things and people that need it. But this is still not all. For the final target . . . is the audience. It is they who . . . are thoroughly, healingly, beneficially, beautifully, and properly shaken up in the process. The four good, great men who have done this thing to and for and in the name of all of us have written and performed the whole thing themselves.

Whoever it was thrust the banner into their hands, Miller feels that they found themselves at the head of a procession they didn't belong to: 'And we've been lumbered with it ever since. Having gone off and done something else, they say, "Oh, the old satirical verve has gone, I see – the revolutionaries have certainly found themselves very comfortable houses to live in – the young 'Fringers' have gone soft". We were soft from the very start. We'd always lived in houses like that.'

One of the sketches which attracted the most attention was Cook's lampoon of the Prime Minister, Harold Macmillan. Cook says: 'My impersonation of Macmillan was in fact extremely affectionate – I was a great Macmillan fan. He did have this somewhat ludicrous manner – but merely because it was the first time for some years that a living Prime Minister had been impersonated on the stage, a great deal of weight was attached to it.'

> 'Good evening. I have recently been travelling round the world, on your behalf, and at your expense, visiting some of the chaps with whom I hope to be shaping your future. I went first to Germany, and there I spoke with the German Foreign Minister, Herr . . . Herr and there, and we exchanged many frank words in our respective languages; so precious little came of that in the way of understanding. I would, however, emphasize, that the little that did come on it was indeed truly precious.
>
> 'I then went on to America, and there I had talks with the young, vigorous President of that great country, and danced with his very lovely lady wife. We talked of many things, including Great Britain's position in the world as some kind of honest broker. I agreed with him, when he said that no nation could be more honest; and he agreed with me, when I chaffed him, and said that

no nation could be broker ... This type of genial, statesmanlike banter often went on late into the night.

'Our talks ranged over a wide variety of subjects including that of the Skybolt Missile programme. And after a great deal of good-natured give and take I decided on behalf of Great Britain to accept Polaris in place of the Skybolt. This is a good solution because, as far as I can see, the Polaris starts where the Skybolt left off. In the sea.

'I was privileged to see some actual photographs of this weapon. The President was kind enough to show me actual photographs of this missile, beautiful photographs taken by Karsh of Ottawa. A very handsome weapon, we shall be very proud to have them, the photographs, that is, we don't get the missile till around 1970 – in the meantime we shall just have to keep our fingers crossed, sit very quietly and try not to alienate anyone.

'This is not to say that we do not have our own Nuclear Striking Force – we do, we have the Blue Steel, a very effective missile, as it has a range of one hundred and fifty miles, which means we can just about get Paris – and by God we will.

'While I was abroad, I was very moved to receive letters from people in acute distress all over the country. And one in particular from an old-age pensioner in Fyfe is indelibly printed on my memory. Let me read it to you. It reads, 'Dear Prime Minister, I am an old-age pensioner in Fyfe, living on a fixed income of some two pounds, seven shillings a week. This is not enough. What do you of the Conservative Party propose to do about it?' *(He tears up the letter)* Well, let me say right away, Mrs McFarlane – as one Scottish old-age pensioner to another – be of good cheer. There are many people in this country today who are far worse off than yourself. And it is the policy of the Conservative Party to see that this position is maintained.'

Beyond the Fringe: 'TVPM' – Cook as Harold Macmillan

Michael Frayn was in the audience on the second night, and later, when the script was published, wrote in the introduction: 'The couple in front of me, as sound a pair of Young Tories as I have ever heard cachinnate, were right with us, neighing away like demented horses, until the middle of Peter Cook's lampoon on Macmillan, when the man turned to the girl and said in an appalled whisper, "I say! This is supposed to be the Prime Minister", after which they sat in silence for the rest of the evening. God knows what cherished family prejudices they had betrayed by then.'[6]

Part of the attraction of the show was the quite different characters of the four participants. Alan Bennett: 'We were never likeminded. I was the edgiest person on stage – the one who didn't look as if he ought to be there. I often felt the audience disliked me – "Oh, *he's* come on again." I used to do a sketch with some sort of bite to it, a kind of upper-class figure talking about various topics – capital punishment, South Africa – all worthy liberal stuff. Peter always referred to it, with justification, as the Boring Old Man sketch. When I'm writing nowadays and get into a certain mode of writing I recognize it as the Boring Old Man coming out.'

Bennett seems determined to under-rate himself. Miller says: 'He had a sort of pin-sharp accuracy – an absolutely unflinching accuracy of portraiture. Everything else I have ever seen other people do since has always seemed to be extremely blurred. He was a miniaturist – perfect when he came on. I was a very good clown; and Dudley was a very very funny antic and endearing musical clown – in addition to being rather a good actor. Peter Cook's things are in the world of N. F. Simpson and Harold Pinter. Peter's accuracy is the genuine accuracy of recording a slightly schizophrenic thought process – he's an accurate observer of mad thought. He created a picture of disordered thinking which was just funnier than anyone – much better than Pinter. I infinitely prefer Peter's tramps to any of the tramps that appear in *The Caretaker*. He was wonderful at creating stolid, imperturbable upper-class fools – and this weird E. L. Wisty – a great comic creation.'

Bennett's observation of the others is as pointed as one might expect. 'Jonathan was sometimes inspired on the stage but he gets bored very easily and would often throw the whole performance away because the audience had failed to respond to some remark. As often as not they hadn't heard it, as he talked too fast. His boredom would annoy Dudley, who is a very conscientious performer, plugging away right till the end even on a bad matinée. Peter has a kind of madness on stage. His performance would often be quite dangerous, on the edge of embarrassment. I don't think this stems from any conviction, though I suppose the most fruitful area of comedy does lie in that direction; it's simply that he has the kind of self-confidence which doesn't take into account audience reactions. He had the sketch about Macmillan, and one evening Macmillan came to the show. Peter therefore went several steps further, remarking on the Prime Minister's presence in the audience. Macmillan buried his face in his programme, and the audience, out of embarrassment, gradually froze. This didn't stop Peter. On he plunged. Someone with less self-confidence would have been guided by the atmosphere. I suppose one is braver when one is younger, though.

'The Queen came one night, incognito, in a party with Sir Alec Douglas-Home. I was at the time doing a Boring Old Man sketch about corporal punishment in which I said the word "erection". The management asked me to delete this on the night of the Queen's visit. I priggishly refused. I cringe to think of it today. I suppose I must be one of the few people who have said "erection" in front of the Queen. I wish I hadn't. I don't suppose either of us profited from the experience.'

The great strength of *Beyond the Fringe* was that it quite simply was – and still is – a very funny show. The gramophone record made during one of the performances in the Fortune Theatre stands up excellently; even those sketches whose satirical points are now dated, such as the Civil Defence sketch, are still funny. The performances of all four are remarkably self-assured – their voice production is excellent (whereas the early appearances of many of the other Footlights members betray a lack of experience in projecting for a theatre audience) and the comic timing is perfectly judged.[7]

Beyond the Fringe: 'Bollards' – Miller, Moore and Cook 'camp it up'; Bennett is the 'butch cameraman'

The show's sketches range from the satirically barbed to the plain silly, such as the 'Bollards' sketch, in which three very effeminate male models suddenly assume a strong appearance of masculinity in order to advertise cigarettes. This sketch attracted the attentions of the Lord Chamberlain's office, which then held absolute control over what might or might not be said or done on the British stage. In this case it was the *stage directions* which apparently came in for criticism – the direction 'enter two outrageous old queens' having to be amended to 'enter two aesthetic young men'. (Bennett complains that in this sketch 'I was somehow relegated to the butch cameraman role. I was never allowed to camp it up.')

Another sketch, 'Black Equals White', was one of the first to lampoon black politicians, pre-dating John Bird's Kenyatta and Amin imitations by several years.

MILLER: Everywhere the black man is misrepresented. For example, recently I went in London to see the play 'T'ings ain't what dey used to be'; and in this play, there was a black man who was layin' around all over de place, doin' nothin', implying that all black men are layabouts.

COOK: Surely, Mr Nobitsu, you might say the same play implied that all white people were pimps or prostitutes.

MILLER: Well dat is fair comment. There can be no progress, Mr Edwards, until you English men stop looking down your noses at us Africans.

COOK: *(looking down his nose)* Yes, I think I see what you mean. . . .

MILLER: Black equals white – no taxation without representation – black equals white.

COOK: Mr Nobitsu, one thing rather puzzles me about you, and that is your hair is extremely straight, and your complexion seems to be white in colour.

MILLER: Dat is perfectly true. I have recently undergone an operation to straighten my hair and also to remove de pigmentation from my skin.

COOK: Doesn't this rather fly in the face of your principles?

MILLER: Not at all. I feel I can represent the interests of my people best by speaking to the white man on his own ground. Besides, it is the only way in which I can get lodgings.

The policy the four had set themselves of concentrating on being funny, and letting the satire take care of itself, is the great strength of the show. Indeed the technique of writing to please themselves, adopted by many of the comic writers who started at university in this period, is one of the main reasons for the enduring nature of the best of their work. In the case of *Beyond the Fringe*, it was the sections of the script that contained social comment which attracted the most attention, and this has perhaps tended to alter the balance of the show in people's memories. Quite unconsciously the show met a need, which was just beginning to arise in the public mind, for a satirical edge to humour. Michael Frayn, in his introduction to the published script, suggests: 'Conceivably the demand arose because after ten years of stable Conservative government, with no prospect in 1961 of its ever ending, the middle classes felt some vague guilt accumulating for the discrepancy between their prosperous security and the continuing misery of those who persisted in failing to conform by being black, or queer, or mad, or old. Conceivably they felt the need to disclaim with laughter any responsibility for this situation, and so relieve their consciences without actually voting for anything which might have reduced their privileges.'[8]

The sketches in *Beyond the Fringe* are witty, sharp, and to the point; and never too long. Assuming a reasonable level of intelligence in their audience, the writers shine a mocking light on many of the prejudices and follies of the day, without ever needing to blind their audiences in the glare. Among the subjects which up to then had not been considered normal for the West End theatre was that of capital punishment, exposed as folly in a sketch of admirable brevity. Alan Bennett played the prison governor, Dudley Moore the guard, and Jonathan Miller the condemned man.

MILLER: Is it going to hurt?

MOORE: Look, I wouldn't worry about that if I was you, sir. You take a tip from me. I've seen hundreds come and go. Relax – let yourself go loose. You're in experienced hands – he's a craftsman, sir.

MILLER: Is it going to hurt?

MOORE: Well, I suppose it's rather like a visit to the dentist. It's always worse in anticipation. But you won't see any of the apparatus if that's what you are worried about – you'll have a little white bag over your head.

MILLER: What white bag?

MOORE: It's just a little white bag, sir. They make them in Birmingham. But I can't explain to you what goes on out there, I'm not here for that sort of thing – am I now? You wait till the Prison Governor comes down – he'll set your mind at rest. Really he will.

(*Enter Bennett*)

Beyond the Fringe: Moore, Bennett and Miller in the capital punishment sketch

BENNETT: Morning, and a lovely day it is too. Though there will be rain before the day is out. Fine before eleven, rain before seven. You know what they say.

MOORE: So you'll be missing the rain, sir, won't you?

BENNETT: I don't mind saying, you know, there's been an awful hoo-ha in Parliament about you, and so far as I can see the Home Secretary doesn't like this business any more than you do. But you know what parliamentary procedure is, and the case being sub judice and all that, anyway we'll see if we can't do something about it afterwards. You know, when I was at school I was a bit of a lad, and whenever I used to get into a scrape my headmaster used to say to me, 'Now look here, I'll give you a choice, you can either be gated for a fortnight, or you can take six of the best and we'll forget all about it!' Well, like any self-respecting lad I used to take six of the best – what's the difference between this and capital punishment?

You don't want to be cooped up for the rest of your life.

MILLER: Yes, I do want to be cooped up for the rest of my life.

BENNETT: Come along, now, you're playing with words.

(A bell starts tolling. Miller and Bennett exit up stairs. Bells. Crash, off. Enter Cook in the silence.)

COOK: I think it should be done in public.

Beyond the Fringe ran for over a year with the original cast, until they took it to America, when a substitute cast including Bill Wallis, Robin Ray and Joe Melia took over. It transferred to the Mayfair Theatre in 1964, and ran in a revised version until 24 September 1966. The show had changed the face of British Theatre to the extent that the old-fashioned type of revue disappeared from London; and by widening the scope of acceptable humour it helped to open the way for the 'satire boom' which included BBC Television's *That Was the Week That Was* and Peter Cook's satirical nightclub The Establishment (which he had opened while *Beyond the Fringe* was running in London). The story of these will be told in Chapter 3.

Beyond the Fringe was produced in New York by Alexander H. Cohen. Peter Cook remembers: 'I still had the same agent; the show was being bid for by Alex Cohen and David Merrick – Merrick was one of the most successful producers on Broadway, and Alexander Cohen had done Nichols and May, and Flanders and Swann, so he had a reputation for "Nine o'clock theatre" – and my agent said, "We don't want to turn this into a Dutch Auction", which is precisely what I *did* want to turn it into, I wanted to get as much money as possible. Anyway, we went with Alexander H. Cohen.'

The show opened at the John Golden Theatre on 27 October 1962. Alistair Cooke wrote in *The Guardian*:

The four irascibles of the non-establishment, the cast of *Beyond the Fringe*, came to New York on Saturday night to present their clownish commentary of the world before Cuba. It was the unhappiest date for an opening night in the most paralysed theatre week of the season. The audience, composed of every devil-may-care in New York, was a big one but the critics didn't get around to their reviews till this morning [29 October]. To the delight of the transatlantic *Fringe* fans, who were there in sufficient numbers to cue the natives when the accents grew unintelligible, Messrs Miller, Bennett, Moore and Cook repeated the *coup de théâtre* of their 1961 London opening. And there is hardly a review this morning that is less than delirious ... This tumult of acceptance is a puzzle to many shrewd theatre men here who deplored the quartet's decision not to adapt their material to American themes, or their strangulated tripthongs to the ears of a people to whom a vowel is a vowel is a vowel. But they make no concessions, a British trick Oscar Wilde discovered before them. In a way their success is a reprise of the old, and most popular, visiting lecturers, who pitied their audience, said so, and made a mint.

Peter Cook says: 'We couldn't have geared our approach to America – I don't think any of us had ever been there. Alexander Cohen took the absolutely correct view that it would become an immensely chic show in the States, and the fact that it was English and we hadn't altered a word would be a sort of built-in snob merit.' Miller: 'There were things which the Americans liked because they *were* English, and they were getting a sort of ethnic "buzz" out of little bits of Limey eccentricity. But it was actually international in many ways – it was about "isn't it funny being alive".'

After all this time together it was hardly surprising that these four very different young men were starting to get on each other's nerves. Jonathan Miller says: 'I had a row with Alan in New York. ['Didn't we all' agree Cook and Moore.] There was a round table in a sort of Green Room where we used to sit and eat the most disgusting institutional sandwiches which were brought up from some sort of hideous cemetery underneath the theatre – and in the tension of the interval something sprang up between us, and I remember tipping the table up, and racing out in a high dudgeon – or trying to race out in a high dudgeon, because what happens is you always forget that the door opens the opposite way to the one you think it's going to. Which punctures the dudgeon.'

Cook upset Miller one night by wandering on to the stage during the philosophy sketch with Miller's newly born baby: 'I said "This has just arrived", and he said something like "Put it in the fridge". He was furious because he felt I might have dropped it.'

As the long run wore on, the four also found themselves increasingly tending to break up with laughter on stage. Miller says: 'Strangely enough, this didn't work against us. In most shows, if the actors do start to break up and giggle on the stage, the audience becomes very hostile indeed. But actually, they went along with us more and more – the more we laughed, the more they enjoyed it. I think this was partly because they knew that the show belonged to us entirely. I think they felt we were discovering something which was amusing, and they were in on some sort of secret. Had there been real scenery, and real props, and real costumes, I think it would have been very embarrassing indeed.'[9]

The show ran very successfully for about a year, and returned in a new version in 1964, with Paxton Whitehead acting Jonathan Miller's rôles, and

Beyond the Fringe: 'On the whole I had rather have been a judge than a miner' – Peter Cook

25

with some new material – including an interview between Cook and Bennett arising out of the 'Great Train Robbery' which neatly encapsulates their different approaches.

COOK: Well, I'd like to make one thing quite clear at the outset – when you speak of a train robbery, this in fact involved no loss of train. It's merely what I like to call the *contents* of the train which were pilfered – we haven't lost a train since 1946, I think it was, the year of the great snows – we mislaid a small one. They're very hard to lose, you see, being so bulky – a train is an enormous thing compared for example to a small jewel, a tiny pearl for example might fall off a lady's neck and disappear into the grass, or the gravel, or wherever she was standing – in the sea, even, and disappear underwater – whereas an enormous train, with its huge size is a totally different kettle of fish. . . .

BENNETT: I think you've made that point rather *well*, Sir Arthur . . .

Beyond the Fringe rapidly became, and remains, a legend. Miller says: 'None of us could ever do it again – we're too self-conscious about it – we know what we're up to. It would need all of us in the state of innocence again.' The mood of the time which helped make it such a success had gone – as Bennett says: 'There are cows, but they're not sacred any more.' Miller: 'Sacred cows are not sacred in their own right; cows are blessed, and they become sacred – it's the same cow, all that's happened is that some ceremony has been performed on the cow. That's all there is to sacredness. In the time that has lapsed between our rather lurching attack on the dairy and what's happened now, publicity and television has gone on, and public figures have been seen on television – it's very hard for someone to be sacred when they're seen visually a lot of the time.'[10]

With the ending of the first American run, the partnership split up. Cook and Moore went on into show business, and Chapter 6 will be devoted to their exploits; while Alan Bennett became a successful dramatist by way of television comedy (Chapter 5).

Miller had intended to go back into medicine, having been sidetracked first by the London and then the American run: 'By that time I think I had begun to think that other things might be more interesting. Not actually performing – I had no intention of going on performing at all – I never really liked doing very much of it. I became interested in directing by pure accident when George Devine, at the end of the London run of *Beyond the Fringe,* asked me if I wanted to direct a John Osborne play – because presumably it had a slightly satirical edge to it, so he thought "Let's get one of those satire boys to come into it" – like trying to get a specialist plumber.'

Miller sees directing as the nearest thing in the theatre to medicine: 'There's a diagnostic task involved, in recognizing human behaviour and reconstituting it.' He worked for the BBC-TV programme *Monitor*, and also directed a television film version of *Alice in Wonderland* which looked at the story from quite a different angle. 'I was taught to do that as a scientist – there's no point in reprinting Newton's Laws of Motion – you look at things as if they haven't been looked at before. I was interested, when I did *Alice,* in looking at dreams. I was interested in what dreams were really about – that's what Lewis Carroll was interested in. There were certain things which intrigued me about

26

his writing: his Victorianism, the melancholy of growing old, and the sadness of losing childhood, which is what the whole book's about. It isn't just a charming fairy story which entertains middle-class children.'

Since then he has concentrated largely on theatrical and operatic production – with a return to medicine for the 1979 BBC television series *The Body in Question*. His productions – and also the various TV documentaries which have shown him at work on them – demonstrate a fiercely burning intelligence which illuminates whatever he is working on in quite a new light. It is not always a comfortable light.

Miller is still unhappy about the association with satire which clings to him in the minds of the press. 'I hate the whole idea of that satire movement – I don't even like the idea of being identified as part of that lineage. Satire is just an awful idea, really.'

But the last word on *Beyond the Fringe* should come from Alan Bennett: 'I can't say I look back to *Beyond the Fringe* with any nostalgia, feeling I was more of an onlooker than a participant. Looking back on it now I think of it as the work of another person. A year or two ago I had to go to dinner at Downing Street. It was in Harold Wilson's Camelot period, when actors and sportsmen used to rub shoulders at Number Ten. The Wilsons met the guests as they came in. He asked what I did, and I said I was now a playwright, but that I'd started off in revue. "Oh dear," said Mary Wilson, "not one of those revues where there's nothing on the stage and the actors wear black sweaters?" I had to say that I meant just that. *"Beyond the Fringe,"* said Mr Wilson: "But you weren't one of the original four, surely?" One felt a bit like Trotsky, eliminated from the history of the revolution.'

Cambridge Circus, Lyric

This clever revue written by various authors, and with music by Hugh Macdonald and Bill Oddie, had its first London presentation at the New Arts on July 10th, before transferring to the Lyric on August 14th. Designed by Stephen Mullin, with costumes by Judy Birdwood and lighting by Tim Fell, "Cambridge Circus" is directed by Humphrey Barclay and presented by Michael White by arrangement with the Cambridge Arts Theatre Trust.

THE CAST

BILL ODDIE, TIM BROOKE-TAYLOR, GRAHAM CHAPMAN, JOHN CLEESE, DAVID HATCH, CHRIS STUART-CLARK and JO KENDALL.
Directed by HUMPHREY BARCLAY

Left: Bill Oddie, Graham Chapman, Jo Kendall and John Cleese in "Sing Sing", popular skit on an International song contest.

Above: "Judge Not", an hilarious court scene parody with, L to R., John Cleese, David Hatch, Tim Brooke-Taylor and Chris Stuart-Clark. Right: Tim Brooke-Taylor and Chris Stuart-Clark in an Elizabethan frolic "Swap a Jest" and, far right, a moment from the sketch "Patients for the Use Of" showing Tim Brooke-Taylor and Bill Oddie. This revue, incidently, is the 80th anniversary production of the famous Cambridge Footlights Dramatic Club, and has been welcomed in London as a pleasant change from recent over-sophisticated satirical shows.

36

2.
Footlights Revues 1961, 1962, 1963 – 'Cambridge Circus'; Oxford Revues; 'Cambridge Circus' on tour

Meanwhile, back in the greenhouse – specifically the greenhouse of the Cambridge University Footlights Club – a further generation of comedians was flowering in the sunny atmosphere of the early 1960s. *Beyond the Fringe* had very little effect on them. Any subsequent influence that it and the satire programmes, such as *That Was the Week That Was*, had on the Footlights consisted largely of a feeling that there was quite enough satire to go round and that the Footlights would do better to concentrate on being inventive and funny. 'Back to music-hall' was the cry by 1962 and 1963.

In the year 1960–61, however, one of the leading lights of the Footlights Club was a future leader of the satire movement – David Paradine Frost. Frost was born on 7 April 1939, the son of a minister of the Methodist Church. While other future Footlighters were gaining experience in school plays, Frost benefitted from some training as a lay preacher. He was highly successful, and the experience taught him how to compose and present his ideas, as well as giving him a good grounding in public speaking.

He studied English at Cambridge from 1958 to 1961; he was also a tireless organizer – he found time to edit *Granta* and contribute to *Varsity* as well as being closely involved in the Footlights Club. In the 1961 Footlights Revue he was certainly the star. A tape recording exists of that revue, and it is not just hindsight that causes the two clearest personalities to stand out to be those of Frost himself, and another member of the 'Oxbridge Mafia' – Humphrey Barclay.

Barclay was born on 24 March 1941, and had what he describes as 'a frightfully conventional upbringing, from a very huntin', shootin' and fishin' family'. One of Barclay's less sporting-minded relatives, however, was his cousin Julian Slade – an earlier member of the Footlights Club, and best known as the composer of the hit musical *Salad Days*. Slade encouraged Barclay to try for the Footlights Club, but Barclay doubted his ability to get into it. Instead he entered the Amateur Dramatic Society when he got to Cambridge. 'I think I went along to try and design, and either I misunderstood it, or there was a very strange rule that if I wanted to be a designer I had to do an audition anyway. So I got put into plays, usually playing sanctimonious vicars.'

He read classics, originally with a view to going into, perhaps, the Foreign Office – until he decided that the Foreign Office sounded too much like hard work. 'I thought perhaps there would be something vaguely connected with television, or showbiz, which I could have an administrative capacity doing – and luckily enough, that's the way it ended up.' Indeed, he has ended up as the Head of Comedy for London Weekend Television.

Barclay was asked to join the Footlights Club and appeared in that 1961 revue. Another person of later importance, who did not actually appear that year but wrote a small amount, was John Cleese, then in his first year at Cambridge.

Cleese was born on 27 October 1939, in Weston-Super-Mare. 'My parents were old-ish – my father forty-six and my mother forty – when I was born as an only child, after fourteen years of marriage. I think I was very protected. We were lower-middle-class – Dad's dad had been a solicitor's clerk and Mum's father had been one of Weston-Super-Mare's "leading auctioneers". We were very middle-class, and very correct. The atmosphere on social occasions was very pleasant, but it seems, when I look back on it, more dominated for me by the fear of doing something which was socially incorrect than it was by really enjoying oneself.'

He showed little sign of his future talents at school. 'I do remember one solitary incident – I was stuck in bed with a cold, when I was about ten, and I remember writing a couple of pages of alleged dialogue in an exercise book, based on Jewell and Warris [a popular comedy double-act on radio at the time]. I was in a couple of school plays – I played in *Twelfth Night* – who's the pain in the arse in that? – Malvolio – very badly, completely without any understanding or ability; and I never had any ability as an essayist either. When I went to Clifton College, I remember that from very early on I used to write down jokes – particularly from *The Goon Show,* which was of course our great joy in those days. Because I was a very tall, I suppose really quite shy, and rather solitary only child – I was quite happy to be on my own. I think I used the fact that I could make people laugh to make relationships with people that I otherwise wouldn't have had much of a relationship with. I was one of the clowns in the class, but always one of the least courageous.'

When he left school in 1958 he was unable to go straight to Cambridge, because he was in the first year of people who did not have to do National Service when it was abolished, and there were twice the usual number of people trying to get to university that year. He taught at his old prep. school for two years, and entered Cambridge in 1960. 'I was put up for Pembroke College, which unfortunately I didn't get into, and I got into Downing College, which I've always thought was a very poor college, simply because it did absolutely nothing for me except provide me with two exceptionally good law tutors. But otherwise there was no attempt by the college to involve me, and I soon got out into digs, in my second and third years, which were ideally situated right in the middle of town, a hundred yards from the Footlights Club and three hundred yards from the Law School. I used to spend most of my time in Pembroke College with Tim Brooke-Taylor and Chris Stuart-Clark and Bill Oddie and people like that.'

He tried for the Footlights Club largely because he had been encouraged to do so by his friends at Clifton College. 'I had organized a house entertainment which had some quite good things in it – we pinched things from Flanders and Swann – and I did a sixth form entertainment in which I did a wonderful satirical attack on my housemaster, whom I cordially disliked, which included one joke so vicious that it made another member of the staff actually fall off his chair laughing.

'They'd all said at Clifton "You'd better go into the Footlights" – so when I went to Cambridge I went to this guildhall where each society used to have its little stall to advertise its "wares". I went up to the Footlights stall – I said, "I'm interested in joining," and they said, "Well, what do you do? Do you sing?" Well, my jaw hit the floor – I think I was the only one in the history of my school who was not *allowed* to sing, I was so bad – I had to do extra Greek – and I said, "Well, no"; and they said, "Oh, well, do you dance?" – well, of course, if there's anything I'm worse at than singing, it's dancing. So I said, "No," and they said, "Well, what do you do?", and I said, "I make people laugh" – and I blushed the colour of a beetroot, and ran – literally. And if it hadn't been for a very close friend of mine called Alan Hutchison, who happened to have been at school with the treasurer of the Footlights, I don't know that I'd have ever have got in.'

He did get in, and although he took no part in the revue in 1961, he did contribute a few items to the script. The recording of that revue, which was called *I Thought I Saw It Move* and ran from 6 June to 17 June 1961, shows a lively but fairly amateur standard of performance, with a rather higher standard from Frost, Barclay and Mike Burrell. John Wood – now better known by his stage name, John Fortune – is also to be heard in a couple of really rather odd sketches. The music is of an unusually high standard, mostly in the mainstream jazz style, from a small group directed by Hugh MacDonald, who was also musical director on the two subsequent revues.

Peter Cook had left the year before but, as can be detected from the title, his influence was still strongly felt – particularly by David Frost, who seems to have been suffering from something of a Peter Cook fixation at this stage. Frost made several appearances – one as a harlequin in a sketch with an unusual use of pathos, for him – and another in a monologue, written by him in a sub-Peter-Cook style, called 'First Things First', which stands out as being much sharper in approach than the surrounding material. He starts, in true Cook fashion, by bemoaning his routine life:

> '. . . And me wife's pregnant – or she would be, if I had anything to do with it. But I don't seem to meet very many marriageable bits any more. It's the Americans. Kennedy, and that Chester Boles. They're all young, you can see it in the papers. Or it's the Russians. My landlord's a spy. He *looks* like a spy. Well, he doesn't look like one, actually, that's really what clinches it. I can just see him, sitting there practising his vowel sounds in the Ukraine. And I was supposed to be seeing the Prime Minister at eleven, but I hadn't finished boiling my underpants. First things first, after all. I'm so busy. I've got this part-time job, you see, as a hangman. It's all grist to the mill, isn't it. I mean, you're all over by five past nine. A bit like a paper round. Less variety, but it's more concentrated. Mind you, sometimes it's later than five past, but then you have difficult customers in any trade. Mind you, I'm not saying there's a great future in it. If anything, the bottom's dropping right out of it, what with all these people agitating, and things. Well, I say "people", but in fact they're socialists. No, I mean, if the thing fails three times, the prisoner's released. And shot.'

The show contained several good sketches – particularly 'Ask-It Casket', performed by Mike Burrell and Hugh Walters, and written by Geoffrey Paxton (set in a department store with such departments as the Trouser Browser, the Bra Bar, and so on); a neat quickie with a hell-fire preacher and a heckler ('You're a dead loss' – 'No I'm not, I'm a prophet'); and a BBC-type news parody read by Humphrey Barclay, which included this mildly 'black' item written by John Cleese and Alan Hutchison:

> 'The Mine Disaster. This evening, prospects of a successful rescue are rapidly diminishing. Nevertheless, whilst any hope remains, operations are being continued by floodlight. Betsy, the eight-year-old Collie belonging to the Clark family of Mabshurst in Cornwall, who has been trapped on a ledge a hundred and twenty feet down a disused tin mine, is weakening, despite quantities of brandy and rabbit lowered to her. Earlier, Mr Clark and his son Ronald tragically fell to their deaths during the descent, when within barking distance of the dog. Julia, Mr Clark's teenage daughter, then descended, and actually reached the ledge; but fell to her death when bitten by the dog. Mrs Clark (thirty-nine), the one surviving member of the family, said before attempting the perilous descent this evening: "Inhumane people will say this is madness, but I know it is what my husband would have wished."'

David Frost left at the end of that term; and so in fact did so many people that junior members of the club suddenly found themselves on the committee after only a few weeks membership. Barclay became the secretary; Robert Atkins, who had not appeared in the 1961 revue but had written a couple of items for it, became the president; and another second-year student, Tim Brooke-Taylor, became the treasurer.

Brooke-Taylor was born on 17 July 1940. He did no acting as such at school – Winchester – because they had 'a very old-fashioned attitude towards actors – "it encouraged boys to show off" – it wasn't a school orientated towards doing plays, which was a shame. But at the end of each term the house I was in – it was a boarding-school – put on an impromptu revue. My housemaster, a very shrewd old bachelor, wrote "No doubt if his A-levels fail, Tim could become a film star, or, as he would probably prefer to be, an old-time music-hall comedian" – which was extraordinarily shrewd.

'Then when I went to the Derbyshire Education Committee to beg them for a grant to Cambridge – Father had died and there wasn't any money – they said, "What are you going to do besides work the whole time?" I was thrown by that, slightly, because I wasn't expecting to work *that* hard – and the Footlights flashed into my mind, because my brother had been a member of the Footlights – he'd been there nine years before, about the same time as Jonathan Miller – so I said, "I'll join the Footlights." I wouldn't have *dared* join if I hadn't promised I would. But it was obviously very important to me, because when I did an audition piece for the Footlights I had sleepless nights for ages – I really was worried about not being elected a member. It was something I really liked – I liked the people, and the fact that it wasn't theatrical, people died the death and it didn't matter.'

In his first year – 1960–61 – Brooke-Taylor read economics and politics, to avoid having to read Roman law; and then he read law, swopping notes with John Cleese. He read law because 'my family were all lawyers, so it was the simple thing to do – and I liked law. I still do. A lot of medical people do comedy as a release – a lot of lawyers do it because there is so much scope; the cases we used to have were so hysterically funny in a sick sort of way. I used to start giggling the minute somebody said, for example, there was this runaway coach and horses, and round the corner was a pregnant woman – by that stage I was giggling; and then she gave birth to an idiot child – and it went on and on . . . There was an old woman who was literally locked in the lavatory, and she had to climb out, so she put one foot on the lavatory bowl, and the other foot on the toilet roll – well, by that stage I'd gone . . . *All* the stories were incredibly sick, of course, because somebody's suing somebody else. There's so much scope – I think the best sketch we did by far was the courtroom sketch in *Cambridge Circus*.'

He had started by auditioning for a Pembroke College production of *The Rivals*. 'I think there were thirty-one parts and thirty-two people auditioned, and I failed to get a part . . . I auditioned for a Pembroke Players smoking concert, which had a terrific reputation – Peter Cook had done it for three years – and that show went very well; mostly written by Geoffrey Paxton – Bill Oddie was in it . . . and I did a piece out of that as an audition for the Footlights.'

The revue that year, 1962, included Barclay, Cleese, Brooke-Taylor and another unsuspecting future professional comedian, Graham Chapman.

Chapman was born on 8 January 1941. 'From the age of seven or eight I was a very avid listener to radio comedy; and always at the back of my mind I think I wanted to do that sort of thing; but of course that's not an idea that attracts itself to parents, and security does. Particularly after a war. I was brought up to think that being a doctor represents a pinnacle of that kind of security – should there be another war, for instance – or possibly a solicitor. Or a vet. Security I think was the order of the day for the parents of most of my generation. But I always had a hankering to write – and perform – the two seemed in my mind to be linked. I suppose that's because of Spike Milligan who I knew was writing *The Goon Shows* – I always took particular note of who was *writing* the shows.

'When the time came at school to think about the future – I was thinking of medicine merely because my brother was at medical school – I saw a piece of the Cambridge Footlights Revue televised, so I thought, "I'd like to go to Cambridge!" I hadn't realized that had entered my thinking – it had subconsciously – so I found out about how to get to Cambridge . . . so that's where I went to do my medicine rather than straight to a London hospital.'

He didn't join the Footlights Club until his second year, because any prospective member had to be invited first to do an audition, and then, if that was satisfactory, invited to join. 'I eventually got in by mounting a revue separately, at my college, with a friend. We arranged for ourselves to be quite funny, I think, by serving a great deal of claret before the performance began; and we invited – quite by chance – most of the committee of the Footlights. So we were elected.'

Chapman has contrived to forget most of his early comic work, quite deliberately. 'I do remember a sketch about a drama teacher which was just an excuse for doing a silly mime, out of which came the wrestling sketch which has been with me ever since.'

Chapman appeared in the 1962 Footlights Revue, *Double Take* – it was his last year at Cambridge before going on to medical school –with Tim Brooke-Taylor, John Cleese, Humphrey Barclay, Tony Hendra (who later went to

FOOTLIGHTS 1962

DOUBLE TAKE

America and edited the magazine *National Lampoon*), Alan George, Nigel Brown, Miriam Margolyes (who later became a professional actress) and Robert Atkins, that year's president. Humphrey Barclay remembers: 'He had a terrific nostalgia for sentimental, music-hall . . . that sort of feeling started to come into it, which hadn't been there before at all. It made a very strange mixture for the revue.' The show was directed by Trevor Nunn, who went on to become Artistic Director of the Royal Shakespeare Company.

Double Take: 'I Buffoni' – Tony Hendra and Graham Chapman; and 'Duello' – Graham Chapman, John Cleese, Alan George, Humphrey Barclay and the wrought-iron set

Brooke-Taylor: 'We had this very twee set – Trevor Nunn, who was, I don't know, Marlowe Society or whatever, had to produce *Much Ado About Nothing*, and the only way he could get the set he wanted was to take half the budget from the Footlights – so we were appearing on this wrought-iron thing – none of us felt very comfortable about it. There were some very good things in the show – and it was very successful at the Edinburgh Festival – but it wasn't very "gutsy". It was the first complete runaway from satire. There were one or two "point numbers" in it which were a hangover from old-style revue, which make my toes *curl* with embarrassment when I think about them. I would love to see the "caveman" number now – the thought of us all coming on in these terrible skins and singing "We're a most important Caveman . . ." and, oh, *dreadful* dance routines – awful. Awful. Sends me into a terrible cold sweat, the thought of it.'

Several of the items resurfaced later – Cleese's solo 'Startistics' appeared in *That Was the Week That Was*, read by David Frost – it is a send-up of the sort of broadcast astronomy talk which replaces incomprehensible astronomical statistics with even more incomprehensible similes; 'Don't touch the Duke' and 'Meek Week' appeared later in *I'm Sorry I'll Read That Again*; and a karate sketch with Brooke-Taylor, Chapman and Cleese was later reworked by them in *At Last the 1948 Show*.

One of the musical items in *Double Take* – a skit on pop singer Adam Faith which also later appeared in *That Was the Week That Was* – was written by Bill Oddie, who was a friend of Cleese and Brooke-Taylor, and had entered Cambridge at the same time – 1960. He did not actually appear in a Footlights revue until their last year, 1963.

Tim Brooke-Taylor

Trevor Nunn

Oddie was born on 7 July 1941 in Rochdale, Lancashire – and his North-of-England bluntness, suitably exaggerated, has become part of his stock-in-trade. He says: 'I think I've been fairly lucky all along the line, in having other people around who set up some kind of tradition into which I could fall; which is important, I think, if you don't have a showbiz background and you're not blessed with great confidence, which I'm not. At school – King Edward's, Birmingham – there was a guy there called Nat Joseph (who went on to be the head of Transatlantic Records) and he wrote a revue and for some odd reason I was in it. I can't think why. After he'd done that, and established the idea that there was a school revue – and it wasn't entirely parochial, either – it became a tradition, and I did the second one. It was always the musical side that I was most involved in – I remember putting silly words to the boring old rugby songs.'

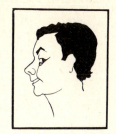

Humphrey Barclay (the artist)

Oddie went to Cambridge having no real idea of what his career might be, and read English. When he arrived in 1960, people like David Frost were still there: 'I was terrified by the urbanity of all the other people there – I was there at that funny cross-over period when some of them had done National Service and were much older than I was – and also some of them had London connections, Cambridge seemed a bit of .an interruption for them – they rather frightened me, and I didn't get into a continuation of what I'd started at school until quite late on. It was the music that gave me my particular "in", because I really was the only person writing that sort of thing – funny songs which sound like contemporary pop or rock-and-roll.'

Tony Hendra

Up to that time, musical items in revues had tended to be 'rather jolly', in a Flanders-and-Swann sort of style, or Gilbert-and-Sullivan send-ups, which Oddie describes as being 'fifty-five a penny'. (It was a basic joke that any hopeful auditioner for the Footlights would do either a Gilbert-and-Sullivan song with new words, or a news sketch.) Oddie never much cared for the style, let alone wanted to parody it, and instead his musical items lampooned contemporary pop songs. One of the first was the Adam Faith skit used in *Double Take*, which arose from Faith having an audience with the Archbishop of Canterbury, and was written in his style. This new departure in musical style went down very well with the audience. Oddie: 'That sort of audience like to feel that they're very sophisticated, but of course rock-and-roll has a slightly "naughty" edge to it, and I think they were enjoying the fact that they could enjoy that sort of music as well as thinking how clever it was.'

John Cleese

Oddie's songs were excellent, even at this early stage (most of the early ones later resurfaced in *I'm Sorry I'll Read That Again*) and it is surprising to find that he has had no formal musical training. 'The tape recorder is my instrument – over the years I've got over feeling inadequate because I can't write the parts out or do the arrangements.'

Graham Chapman

Although women had appeared in the revues – Eleanor Bron in *The Last Laugh* and Miriam Margolyes in *Double Take*, for example – the Footlights Club itself was very much a male preserve, much to Oddie's irritation. 'We used to do smoking concerts which were appallingly sexist at the time. That annoyed me very much. It was only men – and they had a sort of "ladies night", like the bloody Masons; and one or two people, who *shall* be named – Tim – actually voted against having women in the club. Something like "they wouldn't be any good".'

Tim Brooke-Taylor defends his position, at least in terms of that period. 'It wasn't a sexist thing – the actresses at Cambridge were *actresses* – they took over the Amateur Dramatic Society, and they were suddenly going to make the Footlights a very theatrical club. It was really to block the theatre people coming in and taking over. It was a wrong decision, in a way – but at that particular time, it's hard to believe, but people got slightly self-conscious when there were women around. We were all green – and suddenly everybody would behave totally differently. Women were not on the whole the creative forces – not willing to make complete and utter fools of themselves.'

One of the members of the cast for the 1963 revue was David Hatch. He was born in May 1939, and had gone to Cambridge in 1959 to read history. 'I originally went to Cambridge to read theology – I had a brother reading theology, but when I got there I decided I couldn't do the Hebrew, so I decided to do history. Having done my degree, and having done a certain amount of college revue and acting, I stayed on for an extra year to do a teaching diploma, the "Dip. Ed.". It was during that year, my fourth year in Cambridge, that there was an audition for the Footlights, which Humphrey Barclay held – and I was actually teaching across in Oxford at the time – and I tossed up whether to go in for the audition or not – and I did the audition, and Humphrey decided I should be in the show.'

Another member of the cast who almost didn't bother to audition was John Cleese: 'I was rather Weston-Super-Mare about it all, and I took the work really quite seriously. I seriously considered not doing the revue the third year, because I was a bit behind on my work and I suddenly thought, "Well, I don't really need this revue," and it was only at the end when I thought, "Well, what the hell, it's not *that* much work, I'll do it" – and it was an appalling winter, so there was no football, so that gave me a bit more time.'

Under the continuing feudalism applicable to the presidency of the Footlights Club, Robert Atkins had handed the post on to Tim Brooke-Taylor, who now had to choose a director for the 1963 revue. He invited Humphrey Barclay – who was most surprised, as he had decided that he had to work for his degree, and had given away his make-up in a 'grand gesture'. Barclay: 'I said "Why me? I've never directed anyone in my life." Tim said, "I know, but there's nobody else, so you'd better do it." I thought maybe I could allow myself the treat of doing that ... I was very lucky in the terrific coaching I'd had from Trevor Nunn the year before, in how to handle revue material.'

The show was given the somewhat unpronounceable title *A Clump of Plinths*, which inspired the designer to provide a number of large box-like objects which could be opened up and rearranged to form a wide variety of settings. Even with that set as an excuse, it was still a very odd title. Tim Brooke-Taylor: 'Either John Cleese liked the word *Plinth* and I liked *Clump*, or vice versa – I can't remember. It was a recount, actually, because the original title that came up – it was done on a secret ballot – was *You Can't Call a Show "Cornflakes"*. A lot of people demanded recounts on that, and it was discovered that it had been fiddled by Humphrey Barclay, very ineptly. He was probably right – it was better than *A Clump of Plinths*.'

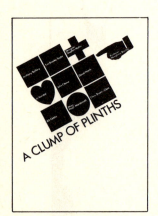

The revue's musical director was once again Hugh MacDonald, and the cast was Bill Oddie, David Hatch, Tim Brooke-Taylor, Chris Stuart-Clark, Tony Buffery, Jo Kendall as the one girl, and 'John Otto Cleese'. Otto is not, and never has been, his middle name. Many years later his mother told the *Sunday Times*: 'John's middle name is Marwood, but he never used it. It is a shame. I don't know why. He used to call himself Otto at one time. I don't know why. It was when he went a bit mad. My husband and I used to say he was always going a bit mad, with that *Python* programme especially, but he's done all right for himself. He grew very quickly as a boy. His clothes and his feet were a great worry. I don't think his feet are as big these days. They must have shrunk.'[11]

Cleese remembers: 'It was very difficult for Mum to quite take it in. She came up to Cambridge to see the revue, and I think she thought it was just a lot of students prancing around a church hall – so when she was taken into the Cambridge Arts Theatre, which is a very nice theatre, with plush curtains and nice boxes and really clean seats, and she was given a programme that was properly printed just like other theatres she'd been to, I think she was a bit thrown by it.'

The programme consisted of thirty-four items, mostly written by the performers, though there were also contributions from Peter Pagnamenta, 'McEwan et al', and, according to the programme, Cardinal Richelieu. Tony Buffery performed a farmyard impersonations sketch; Tim Brooke-Taylor and Chris Stuart-Clark demonstrated how a music-hall double-act might have been in Elizabethan times: 'My spouse, my spouse, she's been unfaithful.' – 'Does she play the *strumpet*?' – 'Yes, and she's no *virginal*, either!' Bill Oddie contributed a number of lively songs, including a negro spiritual for three city gents travelling on a Green Line Bus. He also co-wrote with Cleese a 'self-consciously literary' Somerset Maugham skit, 'It Can't End Like This', with the first appearance of the John and Mary characters who later featured in several sketches in *I'm Sorry I'll Read That Again*. Barclay says: 'I remember rehearsing that with John and Jo; it wasn't quite working for a stage presentation, and I had to try and get across to them that essential feature of the sketch, which was strangled emotion – not being able to say things – because – you were too moved. I remember that my clue was the marvellous record of the balcony scene from *Private Lives* with Nöel Coward and Gertrude Lawrence.'

KENDALL:	Ah – it's a magnificent country – it's so *big*. I should never have thought that a country could have such a – such an irresistible attraction for me. Ah – the Dark Continent – ah, Africa!
CLEESE:	Malaya, darling.
KENDALL:	Malaya, Africa – they're all *British*.
CLEESE:	Mary, darling.
KENDALL:	Yes, John darling?
CLEESE:	Mary, there's something I must – tell you.
KENDALL:	Yes, John darling . . .
CLEESE:	Mary, please don't make it any more difficult for me, it's – hard enough as it is You see, it's been going on for some – time, now.
KENDALL:	What has, John?
CLEESE:	Mary, please try to understand.
KENDALL:	But I *do* . . .
CLEESE:	No! You think that you do, but you don't. You see –
KENDALL:	John! Do you mean – it's all over? Between us, I mean?
CLEESE:	I . . . I . . .
KENDALL:	Oh, God!

The revue would probably have gone on to the Fringe of the Edinburgh Festival, as the previous year's had done, but it was seen in Cambridge by Michael White – described by Bill Oddie as 'the most consistently interesting producer in the London theatre' – who arranged for it to play for three weeks at the New Arts Theatre. En route for London, they played for a week at the Robin Hood Theatre, Averham (near Newark), and then a week at the York Festival; it opened at the New Arts Theatre on 10 July 1963.

Before following the Cambridge Footlights team in their translation into the West End, it is worth looking at the rival university, Oxford. Although the Cambridge Footlights Club has always attracted most of the attention, and indeed the whole tradition of revue seems to have been stronger at Cambridge, there was a strong theatrical tradition at Oxford, represented by the Experimental Theatre Club as well as the Oxford University Dramatic Society, and Oxford, like Cambridge, had its tradition of summer revues and also sent shows to the Edinburgh Festival Fringe. Two important people in the development of the story of the 'Oxbridge Mafia' emerged in the 1963 and 1964 Oxford revues – Michael Palin and Terry Jones.

Terry Jones was born on 1 February 1942. 'I always wanted to write poetry – from the age of about five to the age of about fifteen I always regarded myself as a bit of a poet. I got into a sort of academic mould at school and university – I was going to be an academic, I suppose, but then I suddenly Saw the Light in the Bodleian Library – I thought, "I don't want to spend my life writing words about words that somebody else wrote about what somebody else wrote about what somebody else wrote . . . I'd rather actually write the original words." But I never intended to make funny things at all.' He had no opportunity at school to show any dramatic talent: 'Our school didn't really have any outlet for that kind of thing – our headmaster was an adherent of Moral Rearmament, I think drama was a synonym for homosexuality and all that is bestial in human nature.'

He read English at Oxford. 'Tantamount to reading nothing, really. I worked on *Isis* (the university magazine) for a bit – I've just read that I was distribution editor for *Isis*! – I got involved with the Experimental Theatre Club, doing a Brecht play. I came to revue through Brecht, really, because it was through doing Brecht that I got into the ETC, and they always did a revue in the summer term.' One of the items he wrote was the sketch with the dead-pan commentary on custard-pie jokes which was later performed at the 1976 Amnesty show. 'The idea for the sketch wasn't mine, really – it actually came from Bernard Braden, I believe – but then I worked it out with Michael Palin, who I didn't really know at the time.'

Michael Palin was a year junior to Terry Jones, being born on 5 May 1943. Apart from improvising irreverent monologues about the coronation when at preparatory school – 'how they ran out of toilet paper during the service, silly things like that' – his early dramatic experiences were limited to reading Shakespeare plays to his mother, playing all the parts – 'until she managed to prevail upon me to shut up'.

Palin was actively discouraged from taking any major part in school dramatics by his parents, who had seen his elder sister go into repertory theatre and become disillusioned with it. He played minor parts in school productions

ETCETERA ▶
◀ ETCETERA

A WEEKEND REVUE
DIRECTED BY MICHAEL PALIN

**WITH THE FOURBEATS
AND THE BALLET CLUB**

**PLAYHOUSE: SUN NOV 15TH
5.00 AND 8.15 PM**
SEATS 3 6 FROM YOUR COLLEGE REPRESENTATIVE
WHO WILL BE AT:

THE FIRST OF A SERIES OF
ETCETERAS' PRODUCTIONS IN THE
PLAYHOUSE DESIGNED TO ENCOURAGE
CABARET AND REVUE IN OXFORD

of Shakespeare, but it was not until he went to Oxford that he got involved in any form of revue or cabaret. He formed a friendship with Robert Hewison, who was in his history class, and together they started doing short double acts in a club run by the Oxford Union. This led on to their performing at a number of amateur-run cabarets and similar functions.

Palin: 'We did a sketch which was a documentary about banana addiction, which ended up with the presenter eating more and more bananas to illustrate his point, and gradually his eyes becoming rather set and fixed. Whoever did that part had to eat about twenty bananas in fifteen seconds, which was a most horrible thing to do. We also did a little quickie, which was somebody, in foreign gibberish, with a big packet of "Tide" (the washing powder), advertising it; then saying "Tide, lovely Tide – very good", pouring it into a bowl and eating it. Blackout – laugh, you hope; whilst the performer retires behind screens to regurgitate "Tide". Doing bananas *and* "Tide" in one cabaret was really the ultimate in masochistic comedy, because this vile mixture of tastes was there for the rest of the evening. Sometimes you'd do a cabaret and be given a slap-up meal instead of money – and it always tasted of "Tide" and bananas.'

Palin and Hewison also did sketches spoofing Armand and Michaela Denis (at that time popular presenters of television nature films) and wartime RAF briefings (common targets at the time). Palin: 'I was always more conventional in that I thought a sketch should be two people talking at each other all the time. Robert Hewison had ideas like a sketch which was a mime, really, about two people looking into a bucket, and we had a tape of different noises which went with it – vast amounts of water, and plugs being pulled out at the bottom of the bucket.'

At the end of Terry Jones's second year at Oxford, in the summer of 1963, he appeared in an Oxford revue which went to the Edinburgh Festival. 'Ian Davidson was producing it – Doug Fisher was in the cast, and I was brought in as a last-minute replacement for Paul MacDowell. We always felt we were a bit ahead of the Cambridge revues – they were always very slick, it was all part of a formula, I suppose – and the Oxford revue, there was no organisation at all, how they decided who did the revue I just don't know. I suppose that particular revue was rather intellectual, and rather in the satirical mode. It wowed them in Edinburgh, and then it did two weeks in the West End, at the Phoenix Theatre.' The revue was given the rather daft title of '****'. The theatre critic Harold Hobson mentioned it briefly, commenting that Terry Jones was 'a first-class mimic'.

Early in 1964, during the second term of Terry Jones's final year at Oxford, he, Palin and Hewison collaborated on a revue called *Hang Down Your Head and Die*, another Experimental Theatre Club production, which ran for six weeks at the Comedy Theatre in London, and was 'a revue against capital punishment'.

Then, in the summer of 1964, Palin and Jones worked together in a revue simply called *The Oxford Revue*, with Doug Fisher, Nigel Pegram and Annabel Levinton. Terry Jones says: 'That revue was very different to the previous year's – whereas "****" had been very much in the *That Was the Week That Was* satirical comment style, this one was more like antecedents of *Monty Python* – "zany", people were calling it. It was more bizarre. One had the feeling one was doing something new and slightly different. It had a tremen-

Hang Down Your Head and Die: Michael Palin and Terry Jones

dous effect on the papers – the critical reaction was "Wow! Something new has happened!".'

Jones left Oxford in the summer of 1964; Palin, being a year junior, in 1965. That year Palin appeared again at Edinburgh in the revue *The Oxford Line*, which he also directed, and which was apparently even more like an ancestor of *Monty Python*.

Their next few years consisted mostly of small writing and acting jobs, until they collaborated to write gags for *The Frost Report* – as did Cleese and Chapman – and subsequently went on to their own television shows. The story of their careers is resumed in Chapter 8.

When the Cambridge Footlights revue, *A Clump of Plinths*, opened at the New Arts Theatre in London on 10 July 1963, the title had been changed to *Cambridge Circus* – a purely commercial title that caused a lot of confusion, because the Cambridge Theatre isn't at the street junction which is called Cambridge Circus, and anyway the show wasn't at the Cambridge Theatre. The 'circus' part also caused trouble – later, when the show went on a tour of New Zealand, people used to come and complain that there were no elephants. Critical reaction was on the whole favourable, although lacking in foresight. George Seddon wrote in *The Observer*:

> You cannot expect every Cambridge Footlights Revue to start a new wave or spew up a vast amount of talent. But of course you do, and of course they don't. *Cambridge Circus* ... will start nothing, but it does the expected rather well; while there is no whole new original conception, there are some original twists to give an air of freshness.

The high spot of the evening was the final sketch, called 'Judge Not', written by John Cleese. Brooke-Taylor says: 'John wrote the format and then we ad-libbed various things into it. I remember working on it when we didn't really know the lines. For example, I played a music-hall comedian at one stage, and that literally was ad-libbed as it went along, and it got stuck.'

The scene is, of course, a British court of law. The judge was played by David Hatch; the prosecuting counsel by John Cleese; the defending counsel by Chris Stuart-Clark; the defendant, one Arnold Fitch, was played by Tony Buffery; Tim Brooke-Taylor played Percy Molar and the geriatric usher; and Bill Oddie played another usher and Sidney Bottle.

CLEESE: M'Lud, in this case m'learned friend Mr Maltravers appears for the defence and I appear for the money. The case would appear to be a simple one, m'lud – the prosecution will endeavour to prove that the snivelling, depraved, cowardly wretch whom you see cowering before you –
(The judge and the defendant look vaguely behind them for the wretch)
– returned home on the night of the fourteenth of July in a particularly vicious and unpleasant frame of mind; had words with his wife and then deliberately assaulted his pet ostrich by throwing a watering can at it.

HATCH: A what?

CLEESE: A watering can, m'lud – a large cylindrical tin-plated vessel with a perforated pouring piece, much used by the lower classes for the purpose of artificially moistening the surface soil.

HATCH: Thank you, Mr Bartlett, your knowledge is inexhaustible.

CLEESE: You are very gracious, m'lud. Now if I may continue, the ostrich, taking fright –

HATCH: The what?

CLEESE: Ostrich, m'lud. Ostrich, a large hairy flightless bird resident in Africa, remarkable for its speed in running and much prized for its feathers.

HATCH: Ah, a kind of kookaburra.

CLEESE: *No*, m'lud. The ostrich, taking fright, flew through a window and landed on a passing ice-cream cart.

HATCH: A *what* cart?

CLEESE: Ice-cream, m'lud. Ice-cream, an artificial cream substitute, sweetened, flavoured and frozen, originally invented by the Mohican Indians as an antidote to trench-foot.

HATCH: Remarkable, remarkable.

CLEESE: Thank you, m'lud; if I may be *allowed* to continue – landed on a passing ice-cream cart, thereby causing a dollop of ice-cream –

HATCH: A what?

CLEESE: *A DOLLOP!!!*
(Hatch, Stuart-Clark and Buffery fall off their chairs)
I beg your pardon, m'lud, I'm afraid I was trying to clear my throat – thereby causing a small – er, *portion* of ice-cream to fall on the plaintiff, Mr Sidney Bottle – a dwarf – who was hopping past at the time, thereby soiling Mr Bottle's new suit. And those, quite simply, are the facts of the case, m'lud.

The first witness is Sidney Molar (Tim Brooke-Taylor), a company director of no fixed abode, and also a music-hall comedian.

Cambridge Circus in London:
'Judge Not' – John Cleese
prosecutes, Chris
Stewart-Clark defends, Tim
Brooke-Taylor cowers

CLEESE: Would I be correct in thinking that your wife has comparatively
          recently visited the West Indies?
B-TAYLOR: Yes!
CLEESE: *Jamaica?*
S-CLARK: Objection!
CLEESE: I'm sorry, m'lud, I withdraw that question. Mr Molar – did you
          meet your wife in a revolving door?
B-TAYLOR: No, she *went of her own accord*! I thank you!

The defendant, Arnold Fitch (Buffery) is called, and after a reworking of
the old joke about the off-stage usher who persists in 'calling Mr Arnold Fitch'
and has to be forcibly silenced, the prosecuting counsel gives a masterly
demonstration of the techniques of legal cross-examination.

CLEESE: You are Arnold Fitch, alias Arnold Fitch?
BUFFERY: Yes.
CLEESE: Why is your alias the same as your real name?
BUFFERY: Because, when I do use my alias, no-one would expect it to be the
          same as my real name.
CLEESE: You are a company director?
BUFFERY: Of course.
CLEESE: Did you throw the watering can?
BUFFERY: No.
CLEESE: I suggest that you threw the watering can.
BUFFERY: I did not.

CLEESE:	I put it to you that you threw the watering can.
BUFFERY:	I didn't!
CLEESE:	I submit that you threw the watering can!
BUFFERY:	No!
CLEESE:	*Did you or did you not throw the watering can!*
BUFFERY:	I did not!
CLEESE:	YES OR NO? DID YOU THROW THE WATERING CAN?
BUFFERY:	No!
CLEESE:	*ANSWER THE QUESTION!!*
BUFFERY:	I – I didn't throw it!
CLEESE:	So – he *denies* it! Very well – would you be surprised to hear that you'd thrown the watering can?
	(pause)
BUFFERY:	Yes.
CLEESE:	And do you deny *not* throwing the watering can?
BUFFERY:	Yes.
CLEESE:	HAH!
BUFFERY:	No!
CLEESE:	Very well, Mr Fitch – would it be true to say that you were lying if you denied that it was false to affirm that it belied you to deny that it was untrue that you were lying?
BUFFERY:	Ulp . . . Er. . . .
CLEESE:	You hesitate, Mr Fitch! An answer, please, the court is waiting! Ah ha ha hah! Ah ha ha hah! . . .
BUFFERY:	Yes!
CLEESE:	What?
BUFFERY:	Yes!
	(Cleese desperately tries to work out if it is the right answer or not)
CLEESE:	No further questions, m'lud.

The unfortunate defendant is next confronted with 'Exhibit A', brought on by Tim Brooke-Taylor as an usher. He says: 'I had come on with Exhibit A, which was a portable bidet, although I was too naïve to know that at the time. I thought it was a baby's bath. I brought it on and took it off – but after a little time I made the man older and older and older, and more and more doddery – just to make the others laugh, really, which was totally irresponsible, but it was going down with the audience.' Oddie: 'I promise you, he took a minute to get across the stage; he'd take a minute to get to the middle with the exhibit, and then there were no questions about it and he'd take a minute to get off again.' Brooke-Taylor: 'Then they got me by saying, "wait a minute", so it was called back, and I had to come back again. This was terribly exhausting, but it worked supremely well. It just built and built. *The Critics* on radio said: "Tim Brooke-Taylor did a masterly parody of Jean Martin's 'Lucky' in the original French production of *Waiting for Godot*." I hardly dared to go on the next night.'

Finally, the plaintiff, Sidney Bottle (Bill Oddie), is called.

CLEESE:	Call Sidney Bottle, just once.
USHER	*(Oddie, off):* Call Sidney Bottle . . . just once!
	(There is a long pause. Nobody seems to appear)

CLEESE: You are Sidney Bottle. You are presumably a company director. You are also a dwarf.

At this point the audience would explode with the realization why the witness box appeared to be empty. Oddie: 'Actually to get a laugh on not doing anything at all was very satisfying. That would go on for a minute because the longer you wait, the sillier it gets.'

CLEESE: Now would you tell the court in your own words, on the night of the 14th of July, as you were returning –
        (Cleese does a double take on the witness box)
CLEESE: Mr Bottle? *(calls)* Mr Bottle!
        (A desperate hand appears above the wall of the witness box)
CLEESE: Ah, there he is, m'lud. Could we give Mr Bottle something to stand on, m'lud, for the benefit of the jury?
HATCH: Yes, yes, of course.
        (He beckons into the wings. Enter Brooke-Taylor into the witness box, seeming to carry a stool or something which he places beneath the unseen dwarf. He exits. One hand appears over the edge of the box, then the other, and Mr Bottle pulls himself up until his nose is visible. He is very cheerful, as dwarves go.)
CLEESE: Now, Mr Bottle –
        (Bottle falls out of sight. Painfully he clambers back, settles himself, grins at the two counsel, and looks over his shoulder and gives a wave at the judge. This of course removes one of his supporting hands from the edge of the box and he disappears out of sight again. Once more his left hand appears over the edge of the box, then his right hand.)
CLEESE   *(nastily):* There you are, Mr Bottle – how nice to see you.

Bill Oddie: 'You could see fingers appear and keep slipping off – on a good night I could go on for hours on that one, just getting a hand up there, then two hands, then falling off, then wait for somebody to speak and fall off again.' Hatch: 'It was really quite cruel, I suppose, but it used to drive people fairly mad, and of course it got enlarged when we went on tour. Eventually a third hand would come up; and one night a fourth hand came up and it was a black one.'

The sketch ends in total confusion – what nowadays the Muppets call 'a rave-up ending' – as the dwarf shouts (or rather squeaks), the counsels argue, a dwarf policeman whose helmet and truncheon are all that are visible comes into the witness box and belabours the unfortunate Mr Bottle, and the judge flings over the edge of his box a large sign declaring 'Lunch'.

The reviews were so good that the original three weeks at the New Arts were extended to five, and then on 14 August 1963 the show transferred to the Lyric Theatre, where it ran for over a hundred performances. Brooke-Taylor: 'It was very splendidly successful in that none of us expected any of it.'

When the show transferred, Tony Buffery dropped out the cast in order to take up his career as a research psychologist. His place was taken by Graham Chapman, then at medical school. 'St Bartholomew's Hospital – bless it! a marvellous place – has always been one of the few medical institutions that favours the loony, the oddball character – which has often had very good results medically; there's a rather impressive list of innovative characters associated with the place – as far as activities outside medicine were concerned, they rather encouraged them, provided they were mentioned in the programme notes. Of course, appearing in *Cambridge Circus* every night for three or four months, it was rather difficult getting up at eight in the morning to rush in for a ward round.'

In the last month of the run at the Lyric Chris Stuart-Clark left the cast – and show-business. He went into teaching, and his place was taken by Humphrey Barclay. It was this revised cast which recorded a radio version of some of the sketches – including a highly truncated version of 'Judge Not' – in November, for transmission in the BBC Home Service on 30 December 1963.

When the run ended on 9 November, the cast went their separate ways for a time. Cleese was offered a job writing and producing for BBC Radio, although, as it turned out, he did no production. He says: 'Bill Oddie had picked up 60 per cent of the reviews, I would have said – Tim got about 25–30 per cent – and I picked up 10–15 per cent. I was surprised, because I thought I was good – and I thought that Bill was very good although in a sense he had plum parts; but after this sort of abundance of reviews, I thought to myself, "Well, obviously I'm not as good as I thought" – it really didn't worry me very much, and I was happy to join radio as a writer.' Right up to the time he accepted the job with the BBC he had intended to go on into law – and he had in fact been accepted by a very good firm of solicitors – but he thought about it and asked them to release him.

David Hatch had been intending to go into teaching. He had a job lined up in Basingstoke, which he first managed to postpone so that he could stay in the West End, and finally opted out of altogether. He worked for *Radio Times* for a short period, and then as a research assistant on *In Town Today*.

Tim Brooke-Taylor had by this time abandoned any idea of going into law, and applied for a BBC general traineeship, which he failed to get. He joined the commercial television company, ATV, as a researcher.

Humphrey Barclay, despite his hopes of getting into television administration, had also failed to get a BBC general traineeship even before *A Clump of Plinths* opened in Cambridge. He was introduced, by Brooke-Taylor, to Peter Titheradge, who had come down from the BBC on a recruiting mission. (Titheradge had at that time been with the BBC for some years, and before that had experience of writing for Variety. He was a bit of an oddball, given to writing long memos in verse.) Barclay was reluctant to see him, but eventually was persuaded to come down to London.

'I had no idea I was coming down for a job – and I was offered £1200 a year to be an assistant producer – I couldn't believe it! It had never occurred to me to go into radio – my parents thought it was all right because it was the BBC. I must say, I always thought that I was very very lucky to have been carried on the crest of this particular wave. I think I was lucky to be the person that these creative people were happy to trust to do the "bones".'

Barclay is under-rating himself – he was and is a perceptive producer of comedy as well as being a talented artist; his scrapbooks of the various incarnations of *Cambridge Circus* are adorned with numerous witty and elegant caricatures of his colleagues (see also pages 34, 35 and 51).[12]

The broadcast of *Cambridge Circus*, plus Barclay's presence in the BBC, led to a short series of half-hour programmes made up partly of material from

Cambridge Circus and earlier revues which had not been broadcast, and partly of new material. The cast was Tim Brooke-Taylor, Tony Buffery, John Cleese, David Hatch, Jo Kendall and Bill Oddie. Humphrey Barclay produced, in conjunction with a more experienced BBC producer, Ted Taylor. The title was the standard newsreaders' apology – *I'm Sorry, I'll Read That Again.* The show went on, in later years, to be something of a cult. At this stage though, it sounds distinctly patchy – some of the material is good, but there are a number of less successful items – and the audience seem uncertain about it all, although they respond well to the best jokes. The music, in comparison with the later shows, is surprisingly 'straight'; and the main weakness of the shows is that they are constructed entirely on a revue basis, with no attempt at linking between items – a format which does not work too well on radio, particularly when the performers are little-known as well as invisible.[13]

The three shows which formed this first, preparatory series of *I'm Sorry, I'll Read That Again* were recorded on 10, 17 and 24 March 1964, and broadcast – out of order, not an unusual technique – on 3, 10 and 17 April. They acted almost as a warm-up for the reappearance of *Cambridge Circus* on a tour of New Zealand arranged by Michael White, who had brought them to London in the first place.

By this time, Graham Chapman was the only member of the team who was still thinking of following his original career. 'My parents were very much against my taking time off medicine to do this rather flippant thing; but the Queen Mother was opening a new biochemistry building at St Bartholomew's, and I was secretary of the Students Union, so I was invited to have tea with her. I mentioned this decision of mine, that I'd have to take time off medicine if I went to New Zealand – she said that it was a beautiful place and I must go. I used that as a kind of Royal Command to my parents, so I was able to go with their blessing. I'd have gone anyway, but that made them feel very much better about the whole deal.'

Barclay was released by the BBC to go on the tour; he rehearsed the cast, which now consisted of Brooke-Taylor, Chapman, Cleese, Hatch, Kendall and Oddie, with Jonathan Lynn (another Footlights member, but a year younger) replacing Chris Stuart-Clark. The best items were all still in the programme, but several items were replaced with new material. One item, which was new at least to this cast, was Terry Jones's custard pie sketch from *The Oxford Revue*, presented under the title 'Humour Without Tears'.

The tour, which lasted for six weeks, started in May 1964. It is difficult to say whether the New Zealanders were more entertained by the cast than the cast were by the New Zealanders. Humphrey Barclay: 'Most of the audiences didn't really know that they were coming to see a live show, they thought they were coming to see a film – and the old-age pensioners would trot up to the manager and ask if he could turn the sound up. They didn't know what to make of us, really – we were billed as "Masters of Mirth" because of coming from university. In fact the reviews were splendid, and the audiences gradually picked up.

'We arrived in Christchurch in the middle of winter, and we were put in a temperance hotel – which didn't please us – and there was no heating; it was so cold that Graham Chapman was reduced to running hot water in his basin and saying embarrassing things to himself to make himself blush! Jo Kendall complained to the manageress, and *she* said "If you're cold, dear, run up and

Cambridge Circus in New Zealand: John Cleese in the 'Cloak and Dagger' sketch; Tim Brooke-Taylor and Jonathan Lynn as Elizabethan comics

down the corridor."

'We did four radio shows there, using up a lot of old material; one was *The Cardinal Richelieu Show*, another was *The Peter Titheridge Show*; one was called *The Mrs Muir Show* – that was just to give the poor old dear a fright. When we were in a guest house in Wellington – *Cambridge Circus* had arrived in the same week as the film *Zulu* – we were ushered into this boarding house, and in the main living room was a little old lady to whom we were introduced – this was Mrs Muir. So we all said "hello", standing there – gawky undergraduates with our suitcases – and she said: "Oh, hello – are you the Zulus?" We had to disillusion her – but it didn't convince her, and she kept saying things like, "I've got a brother in Africa, do you know him?" So we called one of the shows *The Mrs Muir Show*.'

There had been rumours about a possible trip to America before they left for New Zealand, but nothing had seemed to come of them. Then, one day while they were in New Zealand, a cable arrived announcing that they were opening on Broadway. Barclay: 'So we thought, OK, Broadway next, in a blasé kind of way.' They had been booked by leading American impresario Sol Hurok – which they found rather puzzling, because he was best known for putting on the Russian ballet, and operas; *Cambridge Circus* hardly seemed his sort of material.

They opened 'cold' on Broadway without touring first. Barclay: 'We arrived with a show which we'd polished a great deal by now, having played for four months in London and toured for six weeks in New Zealand. We started learning our way round America backstage, which is different – the stage manager was a *frightfully* elegant gentleman, who always wore a suit, and gold rings and things – and they didn't really know what we were about, but they were very tolerant. We ran the show through for a lot of nameless people sitting in the stalls. I went down afterwards and said, "There you are, there's the show – how is it?" – and this man said, "Well, yes, I see what you've got there – tell me, the number you use to close the first half, have you got anything else you could use there?" – I said "Er, no, that's our first half close, we don't have anything else" – and he said, "The number that opens the second half isn't too good, is it?" I thought, "Christ, that's the Oscar Wilde parody, we can't lose that, that's Tim Brooke-Taylor as Edith Evans." And he went right through the show, and proceeded to demolish *everything*! Leaving us in a total state of tears and desperation – if they wanted us, why were they trying to change everything? Some dearly-loved numbers bit the dust, like the Oscar Wilde parody – they said the Americans wouldn't understand it. We dredged up a few numbers that were old things that we'd forgotten about, and certainly weren't in the original *Cambridge Circus* – like a number that Tony Hendra wrote, which was Mark Anthony delivering "Friends, Romans, Countrymen" with a body that started to get too heavy for him. We were all sitting there, racking our brains in hotel rooms at three o'clock in the morning, and then somebody remembered a number that had been done in the revue after us at Cambridge, by people like Eric Idle, and Johnny Lynn who of course was with us. This was the Beatles singing a cross between the "Hallelujah Chorus" and "I Want to Hold Your Hand". We had to go rushing out into Broadway to buy Beatle wigs, which you could at that time.'

Tim Brooke-Taylor: 'We couldn't learn it in time, because it was literally the next day; my only bit of inspiration was to make us choirboys, so that we could have hymnbooks in our hands – and on opening night it was encored! We didn't do it again – we didn't dare!'

Cambridge Circus opened at the Plymouth Theatre, New York, on 6 October 1964. After the performance, the cast sat around nervously and waited for the reviews in the morning papers. Barclay: 'Tim Brooke-Taylor's mother was there, who's a lovely lady – and she and her sister had come over – I remember her patting Sol Hurok, this eminent eminent gentleman, on the wrist and saying, "I'm sure it'll be all right, Mr Hurok, because Tim's quite worried, and when he's worried he's always done well – just the same with his exams at school."'

When the reviews came out, they were almost all favourable, except for the *New York Times* – Barclay describes Tauberman's review as 'a bit so-so'. This was apparently enough to convince the backers that it was not worth putting money into advertising the show – an odd attitude, since almost all the other reviews were favourable. This policy of not advertising led to dark suspicions on the part of the cast that they were a tax loss which had misfired – although John Cleese thinks that Sol Hurok, being used to prestige shows which advertised themselves by word of mouth, didn't realize that he ought to advertise this one.

The show closed on Saturday 24 October, after twenty-three performances. Barclay: 'The closing night was traumatic – the Sunday papers come out early, and the *New York Herald Tribune* colour magazine had a whole page article by Walter Kerr, the most percipient American critic, and a great authority on comedy; a whole page article on how glorious the humour of *Cambridge Circus* was.'

Kerr's review was highly enthusiastic, and is worth quoting at some length because he gave a description of the custard pie sketch which could hardly be bettered. He began by pointing out that normally analysing comedy *while* trying to be funny doesn't work. He cited the case of the Charlie Chaplin comedy *The Circus*, in which Chaplin's tramp arranges for accidents to happen during his circus performances, because he has discovered that it is the accidents which are earning him laughs. Kerr found that, having had the joke 'signalled' in this way, he did not then find Chaplin's performance funny.

Having quoted this example, he then briefly described the custard pie

Cambridge Circus in New Zealand: the Custard Pie Sketch – Bill Oddie, Tim Brooke-Taylor and Jonathan Lynn demonstrate; David Hatch narrates

sketch – the dead-pan commentary analysing the pratfalls, the accidents with a long plank, and the various methods of delivering custard pies – and went on:

If we had never seen Laurel and Hardy, we could still dictate the moves. By this time we are laughing so hard that we are in no mood to dictate anything. We saw the trap baited and we have still walked into it, where we are very, very happy.

How is the trick worked? How have we been conned into laughing when we were warned that we would be? I suppose I shouldn't try to analyse it. But if you will watch very closely you will see how intelligent the entertainers of *Cambridge Circus* are. For they are extremely careful to indicate that what is happening is not in the least bit funny – not for the people who are supposed to *be* funny. The three men who illustrate each successive law begin to notice that falling on the floor is not altogether pleasant. Their palms hurt and their overalls get dirty. A whack on the back of the head with a plank is a nuisance – the whop hurts. As for the mess of the tarts – well, they do not speak of it, but their jaws set and their teeth show. Someone has thought this *funny*? Indignation seethes, silent but unmistakable; one more joke like this and it is going to turn into outrage.

And that is how the trap is baited – with pain. Having been told that something is hilarious we are shown that it is just plain unbearable, thank you, and as a result it becomes hilarious. That is a very nice parlay, and I couldn't be more admiring.

(The comparison with the performance of the custard pie sketch in the 1976 Amnesty show is interesting, because there the demonstrators attacked their job with a sort of malicious glee which was effective enough, but not as hilarious as the approach Kerr has described.)

To be told that they had succeeded where Chaplin had failed was a most amazing compliment for the cast – and particularly for Barclay's direction. Barclay: 'And there I was reading this – which was really saying "These boys are the greatest we've seen in years" – and the show was closing upstairs! We were all streaming with tears – ludicrous – we were very soppy that night!'

49

The show transferred to Greenwich Village, to a small theatre called 'Square East' at 15 West 4th Street. Cleese: 'It was very pleasant – the audience ate as they watched the shows, but the waiters didn't serve during the show much, or if they did they did it very nicely – it was small and intimate, and I was able to *act*, which I always rather preferred to the projection that was necessary on stage. I was very happy there.' Barclay, on the other hand, was beginning to lose interest because the cabaret-style setting made the performances much less susceptible to direction.

They performed a few items from the show in a one-off concert called *In Pursuit of Excellence – an afternoon for the John F. Kennedy Library* on 15 November 1964, in Connecticut, and performed two sketches on television in *The Ed Sullivan Show*.

Around the end of the year they broke up by mutual agreement. Barclay and Hatch came back to the BBC as producers – Hatch produced *Roundabout*, amongst other things, and both were involved in *I'm Sorry I'll Read That Again*, as was Jo Kendall. Cleese, Oddie and Brooke-Taylor stayed in the USA for a time. Jonathan Lynn came back to England to a career in stage and television writing, and went on to become the Artistic Director of the Cambridge Theatre Company and in 1979 directed the successful satirical musical *Song Book*. In 1980 he co-wrote the BBC-2 television comedy series *Yes Minister* with Antony Jay. Chapman also returned to England, going back into medicine for a time before going on into television in collaboration with Cleese and the others.

The story of the *Cambridge Circus* team is resumed in Chapter 7. The show itself ran for a short time with an American cast. Tim Brooke-Taylor saw it: 'It was awful. I'd been in on the auditions, and they were very funny, they were very good – but the director very stupidly had told them to copy everything we'd done; and so nervous tics and so on were brought in, which were totally irrelevant. None of them were able to relax at all. It was like waxworks. Awful, and it died almost immediately.'

Despite the attention that *Cambridge Circus* had attracted, particularly in the States, the British public were far more concerned with the 'satire boom', which had come to a head during this time. In order to catch up with them, we have to return to 1961, to the time when *Beyond the Fringe* had only just become the brightest light on the London stage.

LEFT TO RIGHT: Bill Oddie, John Cleese. David Hatch, Jo Kendall, Graham Chapman, Jonathan Lynn, Tim Brooke-Taylor.

This is a drawing (made especially for this celebration edition of Varsity) of the London-New York cast of "Cambridge Circus" by their director Humphrey Barclay. This was the record-breaking Footlights Revue of 1963, which spawned a group of comedians who have made an enormous mark on the entertainment scene since then. Between them they have created BBC Radio's "I'm Sorry, I'll Read That Again", BBC TV's "Twice A Fortnight", and Rediffusion's "At Last The 1948 Show" and "Do Not Adjust Your Set", four comedy shows which have broken completely new ground. Humphrey Barclay used to draw for Varsity and is now a TV producer (with Rediffusion).

3.
The Establishment Club; 'Private Eye'; 'That Was The Week That Was'

The so-called 'satire boom' is an essential part of the story of the 'Oxbridge Mafia', even though most of them took little part in it, but merely stood on the sidelines and threw it scraps occasionally. *Beyond the Fringe* prepared the way for the vogue for satirical comedy that itself prepared the way for the much freer comedy which the Oxbridge Mafia were later to create.

'Satire' is defined by *Webster's Twentieth Century Dictionary* as: 'a literary work in which vices, follies, stupidities, abuses, etc. are held up to ridicule and contempt' and 'the use of ridicule, sarcasm, irony, etc. to expose, attack or deride vices, follies, etc.'. The important thing about this definition is that satire is not *necessarily* funny, although humour is one of its principal weapons. For this reason, in coming from *Beyond the Fringe* and *Cambridge Circus* to the 'satire boom', we turn a sharp corner of style and purpose. Up to now, we have been dealing with performers who set out principally to be funny, using a variety of styles of humour of which satire is only one, and by no means the most important. They also, in effect, shared their own humour with the audience, allowing it to eavesdrop on performances which they had written to please themselves. Now, with the various manifestations of the 'satire boom' we are dealing with people who had a definite standpoint; wishing to question the established order, and to ridicule what they saw as folly, they regarded humour as only one of a number of weapons, albeit the most important.

The time was ripe for something along these lines. The Conservative government had been in power since 1951; and under the prime ministership of Harold Macmillan, leader of the party since 1957, it was seen by many people as a bastion of reactionary government by privileged people. It was *Beyond the Fringe* that prepared the public for satire – most specifically Peter Cook's lampoon of Macmillan. Alone of the *Beyond the Fringe* team, Cook had a conscious desire to be satirical. His visit to Germany and France in 1957, and his memory of the political cabarets there, had given him the desire to open his own satirical cabaret club. Having made some money from writing for *Pieces of Eight* and *One Over the Eight*, he set things in motion even before *Beyond the Fringe* opened in London.

'I got together with the treasurer of the Footlights, a guy called Nick Luard – not a performer – as he was treasurer, I imagined he was a financial wizard. He also had a bit of money. I was panicking that somebody would do it first; we eventually found premises in Greek Street [one of the shadier areas of Soho, in London's West End – the premises had previously been a striptease club] and Sean Kenny agreed to design it; we negotiated a lease – it was all quite chaotic. Because of the advance publicity, about seven thousand people joined before it

On Thursday a club of an entirely new kind opens in London, one that may restore our national life an element that has long been in abeyance—theatrical satire. It is called 'The Establishment.' The name itself is ironical, as established authority will be the chief target of its attack. It will be run by Peter Cook, one of the "Beyond the Fringe" quartet, and Nicholas Luard, a young writer recently returned from America and will provide—besides a jazz orchestra and the usual club facilities—a nightly cabaret by resident and visiting performers, its premises devised by Sean Kenny. Free from the Lord Chamberlain's control and managerial restraint, the accent of the show will be on scurrilous vigour, daring and invention. Below, Jonathan Miller, another of the "Beyond the Fringe" team who will himself appear from time to time in the cabaret, discusses the background of the venture.

CAN ENGLISH SATIRE DRAW BLOOD?

by Jonathan Miller

had even opened: they joined on the idea, at two guineas a time, which roughly financed the building of it.'

On 1 October 1961, shortly before the club opened under the name *The Establishment*, Jonathan Miller wrote a long article in *The Observer*. He explained how the savage political satire of the eighteenth century had dwindled to 'a whimsical form of self-congratulation' under the influence of nineteenth-century good manners and the 'philistine values of an industrial élite'. He also blamed the rise of the public schools (i.e. private, fee-paying schools for the upper classes) and their emphasis on loyalty and unquestioning service:

'Theirs not to reason why' is here an expression of praise and approval rather than a signal for a rain of scorching contempt which such blinkered loyalty richly deserves. 'Bloody fools' is the only healthy reply on hearing the news of the Light Brigade fiasco. It is to be hoped that when *The Establishment* opens its doors the cry of 'bloody fools' will ring loud and clear through Soho and down the courtly reaches of Whitehall.

He concluded by saying: 'The ranks are drawn up and the air resounds with the armourer's hammer. When battle is joined one can only hope that blood will be drawn.'

Peter Cook says: 'That article was very flattering, but in a way it wound up as being a disservice. The only blood that flew was from my mouth when somebody hit me round the head with a handbag.'

Cook persuaded an excellent cast to appear – David Walsh, John Fortune, John Bird, Jeremy Geidt and Hazel Wright were in the first show, and later Eleanor Bron joined the cast. (John Fortune had been in the 1961 Footlights revue under his real name, John Wood. He had to change it because there was already an actor called John Wood.)

Eleanor Bron had left Cambridge in 1960, but had been in hospital for about a year after a spine operation; she then worked in the personnel department of the De La Rue company for a short time, which she didn't like. In joining *The Establishment* she took up the career which she had originally wanted – acting – and which she has followed ever since. The cast was a very strong one, Bird having a sharp political eye, and Fortune and Bron being very good at elliptical social comment; Bron in particular showed herself to be an excellent actress, the mistress of the subtle inflexion and the expressive pause.

Cook: 'I was very very lucky in the cast I got. I also persuaded Dudley Moore to play with his trio down in the basement, at slave labour rates, but he just enjoyed himself a lot and had a fantastic opportunity to meet young women. For two years it was a great place, which I still look back on with tremendous fondness. There was all the excitement of bringing Lenny Bruce over ... those were tremendous times. Some of the things we did are as outrageous as anything that has been done subsequently. I think more so ... extremely bad taste flourished at *The Establishment*. I remember a crucifixion scene, with John Fortune as Christ, and Jeremy Geidt and John Bird as the robbers objecting that Jesus was (*a*) higher up than they were, and (*b*) getting all the attention.'

Another sketch, which started something of a cottage industry, was John Bird as Jomo Kenyatta being interviewed about football but persisting in going on about taking over the office of Queen of England. This characterization became the standard imitation of black African politicians.

Cook: 'There were lots of rows . . . What I liked about those days was that *The Establishment* and *Beyond the Fringe* didn't fit into a fashionable way of thinking. What really annoyed people were attacks on the liberal left. If there *were* sacred cows at that time, they weren't Macmillan, or the Church – the real sacred cows, to some people, were ladies like Pat Arrowsmith. If *The Establishment* did an attack on Pat Arrowsmith (worthy though her thinking might be), people used to get physically violent – they'd say, "That's not what you're here for"!' This is how Cook came to be clouted round the head with a handbag.

Most of the sketches, however, were aimed at the government, the bureaucrats, the rich upper classes – in fact 'the Establishment' themselves. Oddly, a very large proportion of the club's membership consisted of just those people. John Bird: 'What we did wrong was to attack them there and then – not physically – we were very hostile towards the audience. We assumed that a lot of the audience would not agree with what we said . . . which actually, you can't do. That was the thing that Lenny Bruce told me – he said, "You've simply got to believe that everybody in that room is sharing something with you – it may be true that they don't, but if you play it as if you and they are together, then you'll come over better." That's exactly how he did it; in spite of his reputation he was a tremendously warm performer. Even if audiences disliked intensely what he was doing, they couldn't help liking him.'

At about the same time that *The Establishment* opened, another manifestation of the 'satire movement' also made its first appearance – the magazine *Private Eye*, a joint venture between Richard Ingrams, Christopher Booker and William Rushton. Ingrams and Rushton met at Shrewsbury School, where they contributed to the school magazine, *The Salopian*. After leaving school and doing National Service, Ingrams went to Oxford, where he and another Old Salopian, Paul Foot, took over the running of the magazine *Parson's Pleasure*. The name of the magazine came from a stretch of the River Isis where men were allowed to bathe in the nude, and, according to Ingrams, it was 'entirely given over to savage insults and abuse of everyone in the university'. When *Parson's Pleasure* folded for lack of funds, Ingrams and Foot contributed to another humorous magazine, *Mesopotamia*, run by 'embryonic whizz-kid' Peter Usborne, and also incorporating the talents of Andrew Osmond, John Wells and non-university contributor William Rushton.

Rushton was born in 1937, and established himself as a cartoonist of some talent while still at Shrewsbury School. He then did National Service: 'I went into the Army for two years – Trooper 23354249 Rushton, W. G. – I hadn't got to university due to my failing maths seven times at "O" Level. I didn't know what to do – everyone said, "Get a qualification", so I became an articled clerk to a solicitor. After about a year, exams loomed . . . During that time I did a political cartoon for *The Tribune*, and then went to work for the *Liberal News*, which goes to show that I was basically a mercenary.' So he dropped articled clerking and became a full-time political cartoonist, with a regular strip in *Liberal News*.

Liberal News would seem an unlikely breeding-ground for satire, but the remaining third of the *Private Eye* triumvirate, Christopher Booker, also worked there at this time. He had also been to Shrewsbury School, but, being younger than Ingrams, had not actually worked with him on the school magazine. As he did not do National Service, he came down from Cambridge in 1960, a year before Ingrams. About the middle of 1961, Booker had a letter from Peter Usborne, who had been the business manager of *Mesopotamia*. Usborne had been in America, and had come back full of bright ideas for a satirical magazine, which had been the subject of several long but inconclusive discussions between himself and Booker. This time more serious discussions were held. Booker: 'We were talking about the almost unthinkable prospect of raising £300 – we'd done one or two surveys about printing costs and so on, and thought that £300 would just about start the thing off. That's how Andrew Osmond, who had been associated with *Mesopotamia*, came to be called up in Paris where he was working for the Foreign Office, and asked whether from his bottomless pit of money he could spare £300. With that, Osmond flew back, and got very actively involved; in a sense the business side of the magazine was worked out between Usborne and Osmond, with myself as the third party holding the ring.'

Ingrams, Booker and Rushton held meetings to try to decide what should go into the magazine – and also to think up a title. Suggestions ranged from *Bladder*, *Finger* and *Tumbril* to *The Flesh is Weekly* and *The British Letter*. In the end Osmond suggested *Private Eye* and everybody else acquiesced out of sheer exhaustion.

The first, experimental, issue of *Private Eye* appeared in October 1961, and was followed by two more during the following few weeks. They were sold by hand in a few places such as 'Nick's Diner' and a coffee-bar haunted by members of the Campaign for Nuclear Disarmament. The printing was done, on yellow paper, by the offset litho system just becoming available from Rank Xerox. Booker: 'The early issues were driven by Osmond and myself in his little Mini-Minor up through Neasden; which is how Neasden came to be the great *Private Eye* God-awful place, because, as we drove through Cricklewood and Neasden we thought, "This is a God-awful place".'

The experiment was sufficiently successful to encourage them to go ahead with the magazine on a regular basis, and the first 'proper' issue of *Private Eye* (on white paper) came out in February 1962. By April 1962, however, Osmond was coming under pressure from his family, and pulled out to return to the Foreign Office, and *Private Eye* looked to be in danger of sinking for lack of financial support. Rescue came in the person of Peter Cook, who had hoped to start a magazine after *The Establishment* became successful, but had been beaten to it by *Private Eye*. He had already made one useful contribution to the magazine by suggesting their front-page format of news photographs with bubble captions; now he and Luard became majority shareholders. After a few uneasy meetings the staff settled down to the new regime. They moved to a deserted warehouse in Neal Street, being among the first of the new generation to move into the area as preparations went ahead for the old Covent Garden fruit market to move. Then they worked under rather squalid conditions in the waiters' changing room in The Establishment Club before moving to their permanent premises in Greek Street. The magazine went from strength to strength through 1962, reaching a circulation of about twenty thousand.

Peter Cook was now the proprietor of the two main wings of the fast-growing satire movement, but he was about to be rivalled by sponsorship for it from quite a different quarter – the British Broadcasting Corporation. Cook and Bird had originally put to the BBC an idea for a television series.

Bird: 'We tried to sell it as a "package" – it was supposed to be done as if coming from *The Establishment*. We had long discussions with various people; we put great detailed formats into it, over a period of several months, and they eventually said "no". Within an indecently short space of time I was asked to be the link-man in this new late-night satire show they were putting on, which was not entirely dissimilar to the one we had put to them.' This was the programme which more than anything else is remembered as the leader of the satire boom – *That Was the Week That Was*, which was almost immediately abbreviated, mercifully, to *TWTWTW* or *TW3* by anyone writing about it – a convention which will be adopted in this book.

At first sight it appears very strange that such a pillar of society as the BBC should get itself involved in an exercise of this nature. This view is reinforced by the popular view of the BBC as a great granite monolith, internally and externally consistent in word, thought and deed. It is, of course (and fortunately), nothing of the sort. It is more like a Roman galley with several people trying to steer in different directions, the galley-slaves out of synchronization on the oars, and the hortator issuing memos instead of banging a drum. In practical terms the BBC's construction is semi-feudal, with many of the advantages of the feudal system in terms of protection for members of one department from the wrath of another, and even from higher up. The several hierarchies are each responsible to the BBC's chief executive, the Director-General, who is himself responsible to the Board of Governors, which takes no direct part in programme-making decisions under normal circumstances, but in a way carries out the functions of a constitutional monarch – 'to advise, to encourage, and to warn'.

The Director-General at this time was Hugh Carleton Greene (now Sir Hugh Greene), who had been in office since 1960 and brought to the post a liberal-minded outlook which accorded well with the BBC's increasing break away from the cosy image of the 1950s. In its earlier days, the BBC had steered very clear of any involvement in politics – it is, of course, required by its charter to be absolutely impartial – and had more recently found that, with an increasing importance attached to the official broadcasts by the political parties (which the BBC has no hand in writing), it was under all kinds of pressure from politicians who felt misrepresented or under-represented. (Once again, the expression 'the BBC' tends to give the wrong impression, when different departments might have quite different relationships with the outside political world; but in the interests of brevity the term 'the BBC' will continue to be used, meaning in fact 'the relevant BBC official, acting either with or without instructions from further up the hierarchy'.)

The history of *TW3* needs really to be considered in the broader context of the BBC's relationship to politics in general. A much fuller idea of the situation than can be given here can be gleaned from two useful books: *Facing the Nation* by Grace Wyndham Goldie (Bodley Head, 1977) and *The Production of Political Television* by Michael Tracey (Routledge and Kegan Paul, 1978). The latter book, though rather indigestibly written, examines the present-day balancing-act that the BBC has to perform in order to keep out of trouble; Mrs Goldie, who was closely involved with *TW3* as Hugh Greene's representative in the programme discussions, gives a fascinating picture of the growth of the BBC's position in the political world. What emerges, quite clearly, is that almost every government since the war (and some before it) has felt that the BBC's function ought to be to present the official viewpoint of the government, not to confuse matters by allowing the opposition to broadcast *their* views; and that it is only the certain knowledge that one day they will themselves be in opposition that has prevented each government from taking steps to end the BBC's political independence. Add to this the fact that almost every general election since the war has been distinguished by the spectacle of whichever party lost trying to blame the BBC's election coverage for its own failure, and it can be seen that the BBC walks a very tricky tightrope. In this situation, for the BBC to mount a programme which is politically satirical is tantamount to a tightrope walker inviting a troupe of jesters to bounce up and down on his tightrope. It is to the eternal credit of the BBC that *TW3* ever happened, and the eventual confused outcome of it and its successors should be seen in the light of the BBC's peculiarly exposed position. Much the same applies to any hint of 'suggestiveness' or 'bad language' – in fact, the BBC is everybody's favourite Aunt Sally, and any alleged misdemeanours, whether religious, political, or of bad taste, have always brought the self-righteous out of the woodwork.

The beginnings of *TW3* lie back in 1957, in the magazine programme *Tonight*, first broadcast on 18 February to fill the period between children's television and the evening programmes which up to then had been left empty, because it was supposed that parents would not otherwise be able to get small children to go to bed; this was known as the 'Toddlers' Truce'. *Tonight* innovated in more ways than by filling the six o'clock to seven o'clock gap; it also had a freshness of outlook which made an immediate impact after years of broadcasts which tended to treat politicians with reverence and workers with condescension. The principal architects of the programme were Donald Baverstock and Alasdair Milne, and it was to them that the responsibility for mounting *TW3* was given, to the fury of the Light Entertainment Department who felt that it should not have been given to Current Affairs.

Hugh Greene had been sounding out some members of Light Entertainment Department about the idea: 'I had the idea that it was a good time in history to have a programme that would do something to prick the pomposity of public figures; I've always had a considerable degree of confidence in the power of laughter. I thought it would be healthy for the general standard of public affairs in the country to have a programme which did that. *How* it did that was, to my mind, not my affair. All I did was to start talking about this idea, to start putting it in people's minds. So far as programme format was concerned I didn't have anything in my mind – I *did* have in my mind the political cabaret in Germany; I hadn't known it in the Weimar Republic, but it did still exist in the first years of the Nazi regime.'

Greene's decision to take the programme away from Light Entertainment came when a programme featuring the American satirist Mort Sahl was mounted by Light Entertainment, in which introductory remarks were made along the lines of 'Fancy Auntie BBC putting this on'. This so annoyed Greene that he gave the new idea to Current Affairs to mount; Light Entertainment Department never forgave him.

The director of *TW3* was *Tonight* producer, Ned Sherrin, who set about finding a cast. He found several people by visiting a revue presented by Stephen Vinaver at 'The Room at the Top', Ilford – a small theatre positioned halfway up a furniture store. William Rushton, who had previously appeared in a Richard Ingrams production of Spike Milligan's play *The Bed Sitting Room*, was in the cast: 'It was John Wells, Richard Ingrams, me and, of all persons, Barbara Windsor [who stars in many of the *Carry On* films]. Ingrams did his John Geilgud impersonation and said "fuck" – which he wouldn't do today, but he did then – and I did Harold Macmillan. Ned Sherrin came one night – he was looking for a Harold Macmillan – and he said, would I like to appear in the pilot for this show he was doing – he'd had this idea of a satire show which was sold to dear old Hugh "Carleton-Towers" as being redolent of Berlin in the thirties. Whenever he was asked about satire, he always said, "I remember Berlin in the thirties", which was obviously the big experience of his life.'

Sherrin asked John Bird to be link-man, but plans had been made to take the cast of *The Establishment* to America, and Bird was more interested in going with them than fronting a hypothetical television series. Still on the hunt for a link-man, Sherrin went to a nightclub, the Blue Angel, where David Frost was performing – the most important item in his repertoire being a Harold Macmillan impersonation not entirely dissimilar to Peter Cook's. Frost had left Cambridge in 1961 and gone to work for one of the commercial television companies, Associated-Rediffusion. He was attached, as a very junior assistant, to the magazine programme *This Week*; and subsequently presented a dreadful series called *Let's Twist*, featuring the current dance craze. He made a point of learning the techniques of television, which stood him in good stead later, but nobody at Rediffusion was interested in giving him anything particularly interesting to do. He made a few odd appearances at the Establishment Club, as a stand-in for members of the cast who were indisposed, before doing the two-month stand at the Blue Angel which led to his 'discovery'.

According to the producer of *Beyond the Fringe*, William Donaldson, Frost almost went in quite another direction: 'While I'm not responsible in any way for the success of *Beyond the Fringe*, I'm *entirely* responsible – by default – for the success of David Frost. He desperately wanted to take over from Peter Cook in *Beyond the Fringe* when Peter Cook went to America; and I was quite keen on the idea, but Peter Cook said, over his dead body. And the other person, who was desperate to take over from Dudley Moore, was Richard Ingrams ... the team I was going to have take over was, Richard Ingrams, David Frost, John Wells and the only person who did go into it – Joe Melia. They all auditioned – they had to audition for everybody, first for me, then the others – the humiliation! Cook and the others used their veto ... And if they'd got those parts, one would never have heard of any of them again – and that would have been the end of Frost, and the end of Ingrams. If I'd stood up to Peter Cook, and had Frost, Ingrams and Wells, we would never have heard another word from any of those people. Ingrams is the one who doesn't like to be reminded of that ... I'm always reminding him!'

Allowing for Donaldson's considerable gift for embroidery, the story simply emphasizes the accidental nature of so much of the story of the Oxbridge Mafia – except that Frost, having a tremendous drive, would probably have risen to fame eventually.

Sherrin signed Frost up to do the pilot programme, which Frost introduced with the assistance of Brian Redhead, one of the *Tonight* presenters; this idea of having two link-men was dropped after the first pilot, as were a number of other ideas which didn't quite come off. All sorts of ideas were tried out – in fact the pilot ran for about two-and-a-half hours; Millicent Martin sang the opening number and then left to go on holiday, and Rushton claims that she was in Spain before the recording finished. The format of the show was, according to John Bird, more like the suggestions put up by the cast of *The Establishment* than the format eventually adopted.

One of the highlights of the recording came in a debate between drama critic and political columnist Bernard Levin and a group of Conservative ladies. According to Sherrin, writing in the *Sunday Mirror* in 1966, the debate took on almost surreal proportions, with one of the ladies reiterating, 'Mr Macmillan has always satisfied me' and asking: 'Mr Levin, how would you like it if your daughter was out in a dark lane at night and nothing done about it?'

The recording was played back to a group of television executives, who felt that it was hardly suitable material for broadcasting. However, Sherrin says that the programme was saved, strangely enough, by the Conservative ladies; they protested to the Conservative Central Office, who complained to the BBC, as a result of which Kenneth Adam, the Director of Television, had to see the recording. He saw potential in it, and the programme went ahead. (Grace Wyndham Goldie, in *Facing the Nation*, does not refer to this incident, and seems to think that the Conservative ladies were 'good-humoured, but made it clear that they would not want, on any future occasion, to be associated with a programme of this kind'.)

It is a great pity that this original pilot recording does not exist, particularly as Bird, Bron and Fortune made appearances before going on to America with *The Establishment*. A second pilot was made, however, and this does exist. It was recorded on 29 September 1962, and this time ran to a rather more practical length – an hour and a half. The format is much closer to the final version, with Frost as the sole presenter, linking a number of sketches with brief jokes and topical comments. Most of the items in this show turned up later in the actual transmission; they included John Cleese's 'Startistics' monologue, performed by Frost under the title 'Regella (a new star)'; and a carefully researched attack on Norrie Paramor, Artists and Repertoire Manager for Columbia Records, which pointed out that he arranged for singers of hit records to sing one of *his* compositions on the *back* of the record in order to get half the royalties (actually a not uncommon practice, but this was the first time it had been exposed to public view). This last item rather upset Mr Paramor when it was broadcast a few weeks later, but, like many of the later *TW3* 'exposés', it was simply a collection of easily observable facts.

TW3 was first broadcast on 24 November 1962, the first of a twenty-three-week series (there was a subsequent fourteen-week series at the end of the following year, of which more later). Hugh Greene, who had deliberately not seen the dummy runs, watched the first transmission somewhat nervously: 'I was delighted; the programme sprang fully armed into life – almost every item seemed to be absolutely on the ball, and I thought, really we have achieved something.'

The show was certainly something new in its whole approach, and gained very large viewing figures as the series progressed. The regular cast consisted of David Kernan, Roy Kinnear, William Rushton, Kenneth Cope, Lance Percival, *diseuse* Millicent Martin, with Frost as link-man and actor in some sketches; Bernard Levin appeared most weeks in often acrimonious discussions with various people. One of the most immediately noticeable things about the programme was that it made no attempt to hide the mechanics of the television studio; Sherrin had decided that, as the show was so fast-paced and put together in a hurry, it would be impossible to guarantee to keep cameras out of shot; he therefore made a virtue of necessity and used minimal sets, and frequently showed the audience, the overall layout of the studio, the cameras and other technical paraphernalia. The sharpness of the writing (or at least some of it) and the enthusiasm of the performers produced a further 'edge' to the show which made it compulsive viewing even on the occasions when it was not particularly well written.

William Rushton adds another reason for the show's success: 'It was produced under Talks, which meant that we were protected from the very jealous members of Light Entertainment who didn't like us at all. But we also got trolleyloads of drinks, being Talks – there was a wonderful piss-up before and after the show, which you wouldn't have got with Light Entertainment. Mrs Reynolds was the magnificent lady in green who served the drinks before and afterwards, and knew everybody and looked after them, and was, I think, a major influence – she did make sure you were relatively sober by the time you got on! And the studio audience were served with the most appalling mulled wine, served by girls in black fishnet stockings . . . And it was "live" as hell . . . it was very exciting.'

With *TW3* David Frost suddenly found his feet, and indeed became a star overnight – an interesting phenomenon, considering his track record up to then. Christopher Booker: 'The most interesting thing about how all this started is the extraordinary charisma that Peter Cook had as an undergraduate, and the extraordinary lack of charisma that old Frostie had. He really was a dogged little tryer, a sort of joke figure, because he tried so hard and seemed to

That Was the Week That Was:
David Frost, William
Rushton, Millicent Martin,
Roy Kinnear and Lance
Percival

have so little talent . . . but he was never disliked . . . He's a riddle – who is the real Frost? Is there one? He just was born as a phenomenon, and came fully fledged as a rather unappetizing phenomenon to Cambridge; somehow he just had this one tremendous driving force, which was his ambition to be famous for being David Frost.'

Frost's real achievement seems to have been to have had the intelligence to recognize his limitations, and to compensate for them with a very high organizational ability and a tireless energy. The work he had put into learning the techniques of television while working for Rediffusion – who had made little enough use of him, but had been unreasonably angry when he abandoned them for the BBC – stood him in good stead in *TW3*. Booker: 'Everything to do with television really brought out the hidden shallows in Frost – he had a gift for the telly; as soon as he came into a television studio something happened, he just was at home. It was the one place where he really could be fully himself; he had an intuitive gift for the power of television.'

Booker collaborated with Frost in writing much of the linking material, and usually two sketches in each show. Booker: 'I enjoyed doing scripts with him – it was a quite uncanny process, whereby I would have some idea for a sketch, and we would then talk it through for an hour or two; most of the jokes came from me, but where Frostie's skill came was that at a certain point he'd say, "Right – I think we've got enough now"; and I would just go to a typewriter and sit down, and he would virtually dictate a script – he had an amazing gift for putting a sketch together in such a way that it would work on the air.'

Like many of the *TW3* items, the Frost/Booker sketches and monologues have now lost their sparkle, because they were highly topical, and in any case do not look nearly as effective when written down as when spoken in the context of the programme.[14] This brief item, from the transmission of 2 March 1963, has at least the advantage of being relatively untopical:

FROST: Last week Adam Faith and the BMA; this week, more investigations, more reports, more pop singers exposing their less flip sides. But, quite honestly, who are all these sex investigations for? For the old? – but they're bathed in memories and growing old gratefully. For the very young – who don't think about it? For the teens and twenties – who don't think twice about it? In short, we don't know who these articles are for, but we're against. Love should be obscene and not heard.

RUSHTON: All these wretched articles on sex, old chap – do you read them often?

PERCIVAL: Oh, good gracious no – three or four times at the most.

FROST: You've been listening to the BBC Sex Appeal.

The quality of the writing was extremely variable, as might be expected considering the pressure under which much of it was done. Public accusations of 'smut' and 'sexiness' are difficult to assess nowadays; any so-called sexiness is so slight as to be barely noticeable, and much of the 'smut' is really very harmless, although there were some unnecessarily childish exhibitions from time to time.

On the other hand, much of the writing is excellent and to the point. Some of the best material is in fact investigative journalism, to the extent that it takes facts from a number of sources and ties them together to build up an often damning portrait of the victim. The Norrie Paramor exposé is a good example of this; and another excellent sketch, broadcast on 23 March, excoriated the much-hated Home Secretary, Henry Brooke. It was written by Frost and Booker in a style parodying the biographically maudlin television series *This Is Your Life*. Frost, in the style of Eamonn Andrews, lists some of Brooke's activities, beginning with the incident in which he decided to deport a Jamaican girl guilty of shoplifting £2 worth of goods, and then changed his mind:

FROST: Your word, Henry, isn't very constant, is it? But you were going to deport her, weren't you, originally?

RUSHTON: Yes, we were going to send her back where she came from.

FROST: And where was that?

RUSHTON: Brixton.

FROST: But you did it, Henry, to protect your country's interests.

RUSHTON: Oh yes – my country, white and wrong.

FROST: And then, on July 29th, this voice was heard in a field in Gloucestershire:

VOICE: Seig Heil.

FROST: Yes, Henry, the voice of George Lincoln Rockwell, the American Nazi leader, recorded in Britain on July 29th. Henry, you acted. Two days later you announced that George Lincoln Rockwell would be officially banned from entering Britain. But August 1962 was a busy time for you, Henry. Do you remember this voice?

VOICE: Save me, save me!

FROST: Yes, you have a broad back, Henry, and you turned it on Robert Soblen. Unfortunately Dr Soblen cannot be with us but – you remember Henry – he was a convicted spy and a dying man. The Americans demanded his return, and he fled here from Israel and asked for the traditional right of political asylum. But to you, Henry, there were more important things than tradition.

RUSHTON: Yes, I am sure that when the full facts are revealed, you will agree that I was acting in the best interests of this country. By acting in the best interests of the United States of America.

FROST: That meant that you not only decided that he couldn't stay, but even where he'd got to go. You told the House of Commons:

RUSHTON: 'Directions have been given to the airline for Dr Soblen's removal to the United States. He is fit to travel and I must act as I have said I will.'

FROST: Which is rare. Alas, Henry, Dr Soblen took an overdose of drugs – and let you down.

Music played a very important part in the style of the programmes. Each show began with the signature tune, composed by Ron Grainer and sung by Millicent Martin, with different words every week, written by Caryl Brahms, suitable to the week's events . . . 'That was the week, that was – it's over, let it go . . .', and apart from the topical and satirical use of songs, many of the programmes featured jazz songs with words – usually by Stephen Vinaver – fitted to transcribed jazz improvisations, which were performed superbly by

Millicent Martin. The musical direction throughout the two series was by Dave Lee. Lance Percival also made his own musical contribution by improvising calypsos on subjects suggested by the audience.

TW3: Lance Percival;
Timothy Birdsall

Apart from the standard cast, there were fairly regular appearances by Timothy Birdsall and Bernard Levin. Birdsall, another ex-member of the Cambridge Footlights Club and a brilliant cartoonist, did quick on-the-spot drawings with somewhat surreal commentaries which were very funny. Levin engaged in spirited argument with various people or groups of people, and also did a number of very sharp reports on Parliament. He rapidly became the most hated person on the programme in the eyes of some viewers, who saw him as abusive, unpleasant and subversive. The fact is that on seeing his pieces and interviews today, he emerges as intelligent and with strong and sensible viewpoints; what is most noticeable – and this is what probably caused most of the complaints – is that he will not accept evasions.

There were also many complaints about the sketches. An item on 'Silent MPs', broadcast on 19 January, listed a number of members of Parliament who had made no contribution to the proceedings of the House for a considerable period of time. Greene: 'When one of them opened his mouth for the first time for many years in the Commons claiming it was a breach of privilege he was laughed out of court, with both front benches rolling about with laughter.'[15]

On the whole, politicians took the programme's lampoons of them in good part – although the Conservative Central Office became rather touchy. Inevitably there were accusations that the programme had a left-wing bias; but, since it was largely lambasting the government of the day, which was Conservative, this was unavoidable – it didn't stop the team from attacking Labour politicians on occasion.

Obviously, the programme frequently called on Rushton for his impersonation of the prime minister, Harold Macmillan. Rushton: 'I did do it quite well – I will admit, it's my only impersonation that people have ever actually recognized – so I'm very grateful to the old bugger . . . but then I had voted for him, so I think he owed me something!' By all reports, Macmillan found Rushton's impersonation highly amusing. Greene: 'Macmillan I'm sure was amused by the programme . . . Wilson used to *say* that he was – Dick Crossman at one time was going round saying that if a Labour Government came into power they couldn't put up with that sort of thing, and Harold Wilson told me not to worry in the least – Crossman was talking a lot of nonsense.'

TW3: William Rushton

As a change from Rushton's imitations of Macmillan, the show of 8 December 1962 included newsreel film of the genuine article – but edited in such a way as to make Macmillan appear to repeat phrases and generally look foolish.[16] This caused protests from the Conservative Party which caused the BBC to ban any future tampering with newsfilm – a ruling which remains in force, although it is invoked only occasionally.

Greene says that most of the complaints about items lampooning members of Parliament came from the party offices rather than from the members themselves – in fact on more than one occasion members of Parliament defended the programme. Members of the public, on the other hand, were not slow to protest about anything they disliked. (The surviving letters to the BBC about *TW3* show, very approximately, a proportion of two-thirds complaining to one-third in favour.)[17]

One factor common to many protests, both in letters to the BBC and to the newspapers, is that complainants have missed the point of the item. One of those which caused most complaints was the 'Consumer's Guide to Religions', broadcast on 12 January 1963. Most complainants interpreted the monologue, written by Robert Gillespie and Charles Lewson, and read by Frost, as a direct attack on religion itself. However, the introduction, spoken by Rushton, made the standpoint clear from the start – that with more and more religions making their appeal from a worldly point of view, there was a danger of their being judged by the standards of the world. As a demonstration, the item imagined a report on religions by the consumer magazine *Which?*. As one of the newspaper reviewers shrewdly pointed out, the ensuing report was not so much an assessment of religions as their adherents. Far from attempting to undermine religions, as many viewers indignantly imagined, the item mocked the over-casual attitude of many churchgoers. The Church of England emerged as 'Best Buy', with the comment: 'It's a jolly friendly faith – if you are one there's no onus on you to make anyone else join – in fact no-one need ever know. And it's pretty fair, on the whole, too – with some of these products we've mentioned . . . you start guilty from the off. But the Church of England is *English*. On the whole you start pretty well innocent, and they've got to prove you guilty.' The other religions were also examined sharply – Roman Catholicism, for example, drew the comment: 'The confessional mechanism here is standard. The rule here is don't, but if you must, confess as soon as possible afterwards. We found this very useful.' Again, the barb is aimed not at the Church, but at those who pay only lip-service to its requirements.

Inevitably, internal dissensions arose over what the limits of the programme's approach should be. Because of the topicality of the programme, some of the items were not completed until the afternoon before transmission, and this was sometimes used as an excuse to try to avoid possibly offensive material being seen by anyone in authority until it was too late. On the other hand, restrictions imposed by the BBC were often resented. Grace Wyndham Goldie quotes Donald Baverstock as saying, very understandingly, 'If a group of people are expected to go to the limits of what is permissible, they must have it within them to go beyond those limits.'

The last few weeks of *TW3*'s first series were enlivened by the breaking of the Profumo scandal – a complicated and discreditable affair involving the Minister of War, two call-girls, rumours of 'orgies' and accusations of leaked government secrets; and the unfortunate Dr Stephen Ward, whose ill-advised attempts to blackmail the government on the behaviour of Profumo brought the whole thing to a messy and much-publicized head and led to his suicide. *TW3* indulged in numerous jokes about Christine Keeler (one of the call-girls), but *Private Eye* did rather better. Rushton remembers Stephen Ward coming into the *Private Eye* office, saying, 'Obviously you know everything' – to which they of course said 'yes' – and spilling the whole story; a marvellous scoop for them.

The first series of *TW3* ended on 27 April 1963. Hugh Greene had no doubts that it should return in the autumn; the Board of Governors was rather concerned about it – not so much from the political aspect as from the problems of 'smut' and 'sex', and directives were issued that the autumn series should be better controlled in these areas.

The first series had certainly been a resounding success in terms of audience figures, and in the amount of attention paid to it by the press. The publicity was not necessarily a good thing, at least in Christopher Booker's view: 'The fact that it became such an overnight success did undoubtedly go to the heads of all the people who were involved – which wasn't surprising, because until November 1962 they were all pretty obscure – and so there was an air of self-congratulation about *TW3* which reinforced the lack of discrimination in the show.' Booker also viewed with a jaundiced eye the way the press elevated the actors involved into being 'great searing social commentators'. If any of the *TW3* team were what the press claimed, it was the writers – people such as Peter Lewis and Peter Dobereiner, David Nathan and Dennis Potter, Gerald Kaufman, or Keith Waterhouse and Willis Hall. In a way it is a tribute to the atmosphere of the show that the performers should become identified with the material, but, as a writer, Booker is understandably a little irritated by the lack of credit where it was due.

While *TW3* took its summer break, *Private Eye* went from strength to strength – its circulation rose to about ninety thousand on the strength of the Profumo affair. There was some internal dissension – Rushton says that Booker was 'a nit-picker' whereas Ingrams would tend to want to get finished

and go home. When Booker went off to get married that summer Ingrams and Rushton sent him what they now admit was a rather rude letter saying, 'Don't come back'. The magazine went on without him for a time, although he returned to the fold eventually.

In June, *TW3* lost one of its best and most original contributors when Timothy Birdsall died of leukaemia at the age of twenty-six. He was a cartoonist of considerable imagination and ability – his 'quick-sketch' appearances on *TW3* gave little idea of his abilities – and was widely liked; his death came as a blow to those who knew him.

While *TW3* had been promoting 'satire' in England, the cast of *The Establishment* had been playing very successfully in America, where they had arrived just after *Beyond the Fringe*. They found the American audiences very receptive, and easier to play to than their British counterparts. John Bird: 'In England there's no tradition of the kind of cabaret theatre where people go, and have a meal, and actually *listen*. If you're doing a completely verbal thing – which we were doing, there wasn't any staging, the stage wasn't big enough – then *any* kind of interruption is upsetting.' They played Chicago and Washington, then took the lease of the old El Morocco club in New York. Bird: 'It's a lovely old club, with a theatre – a stage, with curtains – and we were tremendously successful. It became a very social, even intellectual centre – people used to go there every night!'

Their material ranged from political satire to Eleanor Bron and John Fortune's superbly acted – and often improvised – dialogues which observed English social conventions with a very sharp eye. In this example, they play a young couple who have gone back to the girl's flat after an evening out. Each really wants to ask the other to go to bed but is unable quite to get round to it (this was 1963, when the 'sexual revolution' was hardly yet under way).

FORTUNE: I mean, if two people are attracted to each other, I mean, why on earth can't they just go up to each other and say, you know – for example, 'You're an attractive girl, you know, and I'm – an attractive man, I suppose, you know, and why don't we go to bed?' . . . I mean, that's the . . .

BRON: Well yes, of course – I mean, of course, that's how it ought to be – but somehow, it never is . . . Well – it's so silly, really . . .

FORTUNE: Stupid, yes . . .

BRON: Although, in fact, what you're saying isn't *strictly* true . . .

FORTUNE: Oh, go on, yes . . .

BRON: It's just, in fact, a man *can* go up to a girl and say . . . that . . . but a girl, you know, poor thing, just has to sort of sit, and . . . sit, and . . . well, wait, really.

FORTUNE: Well, I suppose that's true, up to a point, yes . . . (*pause*) Where are you going for your holidays this year – have you decided at all?

BRON: Oh, well, I'm still sort of hovering between Portugal and Poland, in fact. It's really just a question of visas. Whichever one I get first, I suppose.[18]

As the awkward and embarrassed conversation proceeds, it emerges that

Fortune is planning to go to Sweden for his holiday.

BRON: Actually, what we were saying before, you know, about relation-ships – there, the whole thing is so frank, and open, and *easy* . . .

FORTUNE: Yes, it's one of the reasons I'm going, actually.

BRON: It really is – for example, they have one of these wonderful places in the open air, you know, with tables and so on, and you can just be sitting at one of these tables, and one of these wonderful blond men . . . will come up, and – and ask you to dance; and you dance, and talk, and they all talk English, which is marvellous . . .

FORTUNE: Yes, they do, don't they – extraordinary . . .

BRON: . . . and they will say, quite openly – without any of this awful sort of – well, you know . . .

FORTUNE: Yes, I know, yes, quite . . .

BRON: . . . 'Will you come to bed with me?' – and, you know, you could – you know, if one had wanted to . . .

FORTUNE: It's a great place, Sweden, I think – I mean, honestly, to think of an experiment on that scale is so fantastic, don't you think? Actually, funnily enough, I really feel I know something about Sweden, you know, apart from reading about it and listening to Sibelius – I've actually been corresponding with a pen-friend for about a year now – he's a Canadian at the university – and he told me such a lot about the social mores and this – this sexual – thing, you know, which is – so important . . . Actually, he told me one story, I think you may love this, because it does sort of reflect upon this whole business – he said, apparently, that last summer he was going to a party in Stockholm, and there were going to be lots of – er, broads there, you know – and he actually went so far, before going to the party, as to get hold of an orange – just an ordinary sort of domestic orange – and stuff it into his fly! I mean, fantastic thing to do – just imagine, this great – bulge – really – fantastic thing, I thought . . .
(He lapses into embarrassed silence)

BRON: Fantastic.

FORTUNE: Yes, really it was, fantastic . . .
(pause)

BRON: There are some oranges over there.

Needless to say, the situation never develops into anything.

Peter Cook was not too busy with *Beyond the Fringe*, which was still running on Broadway, to organize a little unorthodox publicity when *The Establishment* opened in New York. Cook: 'David Merrick – one of the other impresarios who'd wanted to put on *Beyond the Fringe* – had opened a show called *Subways are for Sleeping*, and got terrible reviews. He got genuine people, who had exactly the same names as all the theatre critics, and made them write out 'raves' for this – so it said, "The Best Show in Town". For example, he found a Richard Watts, for Richard Watts of *The Post*. When I opened *The Establishment*, I found a David Merrick, who was a black postman from Philadelphia. He came to see the show, and he liked it – and so he wrote all these rave reviews, saying *The Establishment* was better than *Oliver*, *Stop The World* . . . and whatever David Merrick shows were on, rolled into one.

This infuriated David Merrick and he threatened a lawsuit – against me for doing *exactly* what he'd done with the critics.' Merrick did not put his threats into practice.

The success of *The Establishment* led to an offer from Ed Sullivan; Bird and Cook were to write and appear in a satirical television show, with some American actors also appearing, and Jonathan Miller was to direct. They approached the task with enthusiasm, preparing a half-hour show to be broadcast on 10 May 1963 under the title *What's Going On Here?* John Bird was under no illusions about the exercise: 'I knew what American television was like – I knew we had no chance whatever of doing anything remotely like what we wanted to do. We actually lasted two shows . . . Sullivan hadn't actually been to see *The Establishment*, he'd just been told we were the biggest thing in New York. His son-in-law – the producer – had been to see the show, but all he knew about was success – he kind of didn't see what he saw.' They prepared a television show which was witty, and deliberately avoided bad language.

Bird: 'I shall never forget when Sullivan came to see the run-through – he couldn't believe his eyes or ears. The enormity of it was so great to him that he couldn't focus on any one thing . . . we'd picked up a news item about a town in Maryland; we hadn't mentioned the town, but we did say Maryland . . . the first thing Sullivan said was, "You can't say 'Maryland'!" – the reason being he had a number of viewers in Maryland, and they would be offended. That wasn't the worst thing, but it was something his mind could focus on. Jonathan thought that was his only objection – whereas it was quite clear he couldn't believe the whole thing! I knew there was no way we could possibly make it – we could never have changed ourselves so radically . . . But Jonathan took it fantastically seriously – he kept walking out. Everything became a matter of principle. But it was just hopeless, and so they paid us off.' The strict controls on American television – operated by the networks to avoid upsetting the sponsors – ensured that the *Establishment*'s television show was quite impossible to mount; and later American attempts to copy *TW3* ran into the same difficulties.

Meanwhile the original Establishment Club in London was sinking into a quagmire, owing to a combination of financial difficulties within the owning company and the absence in America of key members of the cast. Cook did manage to obtain the company's shares in *Private Eye* in addition to his own: 'That was what I salvaged from the wreck, and still have – not that it's a money-making thing, but I'm pleased to have it.' With Cook as majority shareholder *Private Eye* at last had a firm backing, and went from strength to strength despite the frequent libel actions which were beginning to be a way of life for the magazine. The Establishment was taken over and rapidly became rather seedy. On his return from America Cook was offered his half-interest, as before, by the new owners. 'I took one look at the club and said "No". The whole atmosphere had gone – the place was filled with rather large men, and I didn't think it was salvagable; and I think the entire cast – who had returned from the States – felt exactly the same way. And so I got out – that was the end of the Establishment for me.' Not long afterwards it became a typical Soho nightclub, and is now a blue-movie cinema.

All this had happened by the time *TW3* returned on 28 September 1963 for its second series. Whether because of the BBC's Board of Governors' strictures on the content of the shows, or for other reasons, there is no doubt that most of the sparkle had gone. There were still some good items, but a much greater incidence of threshing about for want of ideas. Adverse public reaction was by now something of a reflex action – although once again the strongest reactions were caused by a misunderstanding of sketches.

A record number of complaints was reached on the occasion when *TW3* commented on the new prime minister. Macmillan's failing health having been made worse by the Profumo affair and other problems, he annoyed many people by choosing as his successor Sir Alec Douglas-Home, who resigned his peerage to take up the post. This was seen in many quarters as a further example of privilege. Douglas-Home had to stand at a by-election in order to take a seat in Parliament; among those who opposed him was William Rushton, in a gesture of magnificent futility. He polled forty-five votes.

TW3's comment came, on 19 October 1963, in the form of a monologue written by Christopher Booker, and spoken by Frost in the *persona* of a previous Prime Minister, Disraeli. He began:

> 'My lord: when I say that your acceptance of the Queen's Commission to form an administration has proved, and will prove, an unmitigated catastrophe for the Conservative Party, for the Constitution, for the Nation, and for yourself, it must not be thought that I bear you any personal ill-will. Indeed, I must regard you as simply the pathetic victim of circumstances too great for your understanding. Let it not be thought either that your inheritance of an ancient and anachronistic title, through no intention of your own, should in itself be regarded as in any way an obstacle to your possession of an even higher honour – the highest that the people of this country can bestow. Were you large enough a man, such trivial encumbrance would pass without controversy. No – from all accounts, you are a pleasant man, of even and determined disposition, blessed with many qualities that would in any case mark you out above your fellow men – as a private individual. But just as you are the holder of an ancient earldom through no intention of your own, so stage by stage you have been raised up the ladder of our public life – again, through no intention of your own – until at last you have been lifted above the heads of the multitude as a bloody and archaic sacrifice. Your bleak, deathly smile is the smile not of a victor but of a victim. You are the dupe and unwitting tool of a conspiracy – the conspiracy of a tiny band of desperate men who have seen in you their last slippery chance of keeping the levers of power and influence within their privileged circle. For the sake of that prize, which can at best be transitory, those men are prepared to dash all the hopes of the Party they profess to love, and of the Nation which they profess to serve; or rather the two nations which by their actions they seek to perpetuate.'

The monologue continued by comparing Douglas-Home unfavourably with Macmillan, particularly in his lack of knowledge of economics, the tide of history and the lives of the ordinary people who must now submit as his subjects without consent.

This piece was intelligently written and closely reasoned; even so, it was by far the most savage attack on a political figure that the BBC had ever broadcast – so much so that Sherrin had to refer it upwards to the Director-General. Booker: 'I remember standing in the hospitality room, with the show due to go on the air in two hours time; and getting a call from Hugh Greene put through to me, as the writer, explaining why he thought certain passages ought to be taken out – which is an extraordinary thing; I was twenty-six – where nowadays do you find the Director-General of the BBC ringing up twenty-six-year-olds saying, "I think perhaps we ought to take this out"?'

Even in the toned-down version quoted above, the item provoked a storm of protest from viewers – a staggering 599 telephone calls, and 310 letters of complaint. Many people seemed more upset by Frost's tag, with which he closed the show: 'And so, there is the choice for the electorate: on the one hand, Lord Home – on the other hand, Mr Harold Wilson. Dull Alec versus smart-alec.'

With an increasing number of protests from the public, and a general election inevitable in the following year, Hugh Greene came to the decision that the programme ought not to continue past the end of the year. When the announcement was made to this effect on 13 November, there were howls of protest from many people who saw this as a victory for the forces of reaction. Many letters were received in support of the programme; Randolph Churchill sent a telegram describing the BBC's Advisory Council as the 'biggest body of spoil-sports in the country'.

The decision, however, was entirely Greene's. He says: 'Sir Arthur fforde, the chairman of the Board of Governors, was a sick man; he was a very liberal-minded man, but didn't have the strength to keep as close a hold on the feelings of the Board as he would have done otherwise. Sir James Duff, the vice-chairman – an excellent man – was a bit old-fashioned in his attitudes on the "smut" angle, and I knew that he was getting particularly worried about it. I began to be worried lest there should really be a row on the Board of Governors, and lest Sir James Duff might resign. I came to the conclusion that it was in the interests of the BBC that the programme should come to a premature end.' The reason given publicly – that there was expected to be a general election in the spring – was also in Greene's mind; the BBC is required to provide balanced coverage, particularly in a pre-election period, and as Greene says, 'You can't balance laughter'. In the circumstances it is difficult to see what else Greene could have done but take it off – in an election year the BBC would have been placed in very tricky political cross-fire had it continued anywhere near the actual date.

It is said that imminent execution 'concentrates the mind wonderfully'; certainly the last few editions of *TW3* were rather better than the earlier shows in the second series. The last show was broadcast on 28 December 1963.

For a programme which ran to a total of only thirty-seven editions *TW3* made an amazing impact; indeed it still has a considerable reputation, although perhaps there is something of a nostalgic glow which has caused people to forget how amateurish it could be on occasions. When one watches the tele-recordings today, it is noticeable that there is nothing on modern television with anything like the 'edge', even if the edge was a bit ragged at times. *TW3* paved the way for several more so-called 'satirical' shows, which will be covered in the next chapter, but it remains the only television show ever to blow a fresh breeze through the hypocrisy and deference which characterized much of broadcasting's attitude to politics.

Bill Oddie sees its principal contribution as the widening of the acceptable range of jokes: 'Instead of doing, "I say, I say, my mother-in-law" you could do "I say, I say, Harold Macmillan", and it could be the same joke – and very often *was* the same joke.'

TW3 also pioneered a broadening in the range of acceptable vocabulary on television, which made comedy shows such as *Steptoe and Son* and *Till Death Us Do Part* possible. Some of the viewing audience might not see that as a desirable thing; but in a changing world television would have been very foolish to cling to the cosy outlook of the 1950s.

With *TW3* off the air and the Establishment Club on its last legs, only *Private Eye* was left. It had by 1964 taken on very much the style which it retains to this day – and it is a considerable achievement that the magazine has survived and has never missed an issue. With Booker no longer the main driving force, the outlook of *Private Eye* changed, becoming, in Ingram's own words, more 'strident, abusive and left-wing'. The most usual accusation against *Private Eye* is that of nihilism – a purposeless thrashing about. Kenneth Tynan sent them a letter saying 'When are you going to get a point of view'; Ingrams says, 'What Tynan means is, when are we going to get *his* point of view – I don't want to have Tynan's point of view. In a certain sense I think *Private Eye* has to be anti-everything and everybody if it is to have any point.'

The general scope of the magazine widened – they were able to include more actual reportage as they built up better contacts, and in fact have gained a reputation for scurrilous reporting – no bad thing, because in doing so they often report things which most newspapers will not touch, but which ought to be reported. The other side of this coin, of course, is the regular incidence of libel suits. Ingrams: 'It's one thing to write something, and another to prove it in a court of law . . . Malcolm Muggeridge once said that he wasn't interested in facts, he was interested in the truth. A lot of people wouldn't print the stuff in *Private Eye* because they would say, "We can't check this". I would say, "Am I fairly sure this is true?" When you come to assess that, checking is irrelevant – it's a matter of whether a particular story has the ring of truth. This applies to a whole lot of things which you read, in the newspapers, or in history – it applies to the Bible, actually – you can't check it out.'

Booker returned to the magazine in 1965, and collaborated with Ingrams

The Late Show: Barry Humphries as Mrs Everage

on the 'joke pages'; Rushton drifted away, becoming more interested in television. One newcomer was Australian Barry Humphries (who later performed in the guise of 'Dame Edna Everage'); he contributed a comic strip detailing the adventures of an Australian character, Barry McKenzie. Humphries says: 'My upbringing was rather prim; [at university] everything I did was very deliberately moralistic. I was consciously trying to chastise the Australian community for its complacency – I felt around me there was a terrible comfortable smugness, and I was the person to puncture this. I was pleased to be invited to write a comic strip for *Private Eye* in which I was able at last to invent a very vulgar working-class character – Barry McKenzie. I could use all those extraordinary Australian euphemisms for vomiting – the kind of vernacular of incontinence – parking the tiger, yodelling on the lawn, the Technicolor yawn, the liquid laugh – all those terrible terms that I'd been genuinely disgusted by as a prim youth.'[19]

One of *Private Eye*'s most successful regular items was 'Mrs Wilson's Diary', purporting to be an every-day story of an ordinary prime minister's wife; this was the basis for a 1967 stage show by Richard Ingrams and John Wells, produced by Joan Littlewood.

Under Peter Cook's influence *Private Eye* also issued a number of flimsy gramophone records with the magazine, starring Cook himself with Dudley Moore, Rushton and Ingrams. The humour (like that of *Private Eye* itself) ranges from the witty to the childish; one of the best is the earliest, purporting to be an election address on behalf of Douglas-Home. (Rushton as Home: 'Only under a Conservative government could an incompetent old fart such as yours truly get into high office.')

Much of the humour in *Private Eye* has continued to be very repetitive – Ingrams says that he likes repetition and old jokes – and one of their principal satirical weapons seems to be the liberal if unsupported use of the adjective 'appalling'. Ingrams: 'The epithet "appalling" I would defend in all those cases – those people who are referred to as "appalling" *are* appalling, to me. You have to give us the benefit – before we call someone appalling we have looked into the matter in some detail. In other words, we don't liberally scatter the adjective "appalling" on just anyone – we don't want to bore the reader by saying, "This is the reason why we find so-and-so appalling".' Ingrams thinks that it is not the function of *Private Eye* to praise people – other than by simply not mentioning them – and so inevitably the magazine appears to be anti-everything. Nevertheless, if more backing were given to some of *Private Eye*'s assertions – even at the risk of being boring – it is possible that it would give less appearance of thrashing about nihilistically in a quagmire of fourth-form abuse. To its credit, it tends to assume a fairly high level of intelligence and informed-ness among its readers – and it is quite prepared to be as rude about itself as anyone else.

Private Eye is the sole survivor of the 1962–3 'satire boom' which also comprised *TW3* and *The Establishment*; the boom was a strange phenomenon partly inspired by *Beyond the Fringe*, and existed in parallel with the ultimately more important main stream of anarchic university humour. Satire was not entirely dead, however, although when it returned to the BBC it had taken on a rather different aspect, in some ways more akin to the original ideas of *The Establishment*; and it was members of the cast of *The Establishment* who brought to television satire a less frenzied and more intelligent approach.

4.
'Not So Much a Programme'; 'BBC-3'; 'The Late Show'; the John Bird, John Fortune and Eleanor Bron series

Although its run on BBC Television ended at the end of 1963, *TW3* was not quite dead; William Rushton and another member of the team, Al Mancini, went on tour in America in company with Bill Oddie, Oddie's wife Jean Hart, and Tim Brooke-Taylor. Oddie and Brooke-Taylor had just finished their run in *Cambridge Circus,* and were using some of the same material on this tour, while Rushton and Mancini performed some of the *TW3* material. Bill Oddie: 'It was billed as "David Frost's" – in letters about twenty-five feet high – "That Was The Week That Was" – in letters a little bit smaller – involving the rest of us, in letters absolutely non-existent. The small flaw in this billing was that David Frost wasn't actually in it, so we would go round the country virtually getting lynched in some areas because he wasn't there.' Occasionally Frost joined them. Tim Brooke-Taylor: 'One night I caught him telling the man who was going to announce us, "You do know I'm the star, don't you" . . . which he was.'

Oddie and Brooke-Taylor found the tour great fun, playing one night to three hundred people and another night to six thousand. They did one-night stands across Canada, down the West Coast, across the South and generally through a very wide range of American towns. Brooke-Taylor: 'I have always reckoned that American audiences are the best audiences we ever had – we had of course pruned the material so that they didn't see the *very* English sketches, which they wouldn't have understood; but the style of English humour – like the courtroom scene – went down as well as anything. We got very chickeny when we got to the South, because we had one or two satirical numbers – Governor Wallace sketches suddenly seemed to find themselves not included!'

In Britain, meanwhile, there was a cessation of satirical hostilities until after the general election on 15 October 1964, in which the Labour Party came to power with a small majority; the new prime minister was Harold Wilson, a pragmatic Yorkshireman who was a complete contrast to Douglas-Home. With the electoral stumbling-block out of the way, the BBC were able to resurrect satire, although they deliberately avoided imitating the style and format of *TW3*.

The new show was given the rather indigestible title of *Not So Much A Programme, More A Way Of Life – NSMAP* for short – and was once again directed by Ned Sherrin, with David Frost as chief anchor-man. The programme departed from its predecessor's style by alternating sketches with live discussions. This was one of the first appearances in England of the now-ubiquitous 'chat show'.

The biggest mistake made in the planning of *NSMAP* was to schedule the show for three nights a week – Friday, Saturday and Sunday – which put rather a strain on everyone concerned. This obsession with threes originally extended to the presentation as well. Christopher Booker: 'There were going to be three link-men, and three guests, and three lots of satirists making jokes, and so on. It was a total shambles to start with, but it did settle down – to a large extent due to Frost, he did pull the thing together.' The other supposed link-men were P. J. Kavanagh and William Rushton, who says: 'I was going to have nothing to do with the programme whatsoever; Frost couldn't do the last of the pilots – I was flown back from a wedding in Munich pissed as a fart – I was absolutely out of my skull, no idea what was going on – arrived back for the Sunday night, and did a Frost. I must admit, it's the best thing I ever did in my life. I knew who nobody was – I was turning to people on the guest panel and saying "What's your name?" . . . I was offered a permanent post, which was a disaster, because Frost was determined in his heart of hearts that it should be his; and Kavanagh and I really didn't mind. Neither of us wanted to be on the programme. So we got elbowed to one side a bit; and in the end we were being paid £80 a show for doing nothing – it was the best job I ever had, except that it was driving me absolutely up the spout!' So after a few weeks Rushton left the programme.

The first edition of *NSMAP* was broadcast on 13 November 1964 (Friday 13, as several newspapers gleefully pointed out) and ran, three nights a week, until 11 April 1965 – a total of sixty-three programmes; of which sixty still exist, recorded, like *TW3*, on 16mm film as a reference in case of complaints or queries. Since most of the shows devote longer to the discussions between the guests than to the sketches, this amounts to an awful lot of film devoted to talking heads. The more interesting guests include Bernard Levin, Harvey Orkin and Patrick Campbell – the only television personality to become famous by capitalizing on a stutter. The secret of his success is that what he has to say is usually well worth waiting for. Frost is clearly in his element in these discussions. Indeed in many ways he comes over better than in some sections of *TW3*, where he merely demonstrates that he is not cut out to take part in sketches. In *NSMAP* he controls the discussions very well on the whole, having the sense – denied to many chairmen – to keep quiet when the discussion is going well under its own steam, and only interfering to keep the ring if arguments start to get out of hand.

However, *NSMAP* is mostly of interest because of the sketches, the best of which are by John Bird, Eleanor Bron (her first television appearances), John Fortune and John Wells. Bron made a number of appearances as Lady Pamela Stitty, a Conservative lady of quite remarkable vapidity. Bron: 'They weren't a very strong political statement – they weren't very subtle or knowledgeable jokes. The television political comment was somewhat different from *The Establishment* material; but I think they had political value in that audiences had not hitherto seen politics as part of the fabric of their lives.'

In the first edition of *NSMAP*, 'Lady Pamela' is interviewed by P. J. Kavanagh about the discussions then going on in the Conservative Party over a possible change of leadership.[20]

KAVANAGH: There's been a certain amount of criticism of Sir Alec – do you think this is a sign that he's going to stand down from the leadership?

BRON: Good heavens, no, I don't at all. I think he ought to go on as leader, and I think he will. I think people have been jolly unkind about Alec, you know, I think they tend to underestimate him. I suppose you've probably seen him on television, and in the House of Commons – well I do rather wish that people could get a chance to see him in Committee, because he is absolutely staggering there – he's forceful and dynamic, and vigorous and decisive – you really wouldn't recognize him.

KAVANAGH: But you did mention his television appearances – some people have said these contributed to the Tory defeat. Would you agree?

BRON: No, I don't agree.

KAVANAGH: But if there were to be a change of leadership, is it going to be easy to choose Sir Alec's successor?

BRON: Not easy at all, no – it's never easy to choose a leader. You see, leaders are not made in a day – of course, Alec was, he's rather the exception, that's why we're trying to find another method of trying to choose, you see . . .

KAVANAGH: But who will the choice be between?

BRON: Well, thank goodness we have lots and lots of very good men in the party – I always do think it's disastrous politically for a party to have only one really good man.

KAVANAGH: Well people of course have criticized the government for being a one-man-band – you seem to think that?

BRON: Goodness, no – it seems a most extraordinary thing to say – it is of course so terribly easy to criticize and so terribly hard to govern, but that remark seems to me to be extraordinary – I should think it's the last thing you could possibly say about Alec.

KAVANAGH: But – surely you mean Mr Wilson?

BRON: Oh, good heavens – I'm sorry – I keep on doing that. I'm awfully sorry – I find it so terribly difficult to adjust, it's been such a long time . . .

It had been the BBC's intention that *NSMAP* should be more tightly controlled than *TW3*, in the hope of avoiding any further howls of complaint from upset viewers. This turned out to be a forlorn hope; in the first show a monologue by John Bird, imitating President Jomo Kenyatta of Kenya (expanded from the one he had done at the Establishment), drew bitter and angry complaints from the Kenyan High Commission. The BBC very rightly stood firm, because, as so often happened, the complaints arose partly from a failure to understand the sketch. In this case, the Kenyan High Commission were so incensed by the spectacle of Bird waving a fly-whisk (Kenyatta's trade-mark) and doing his standard African accent that they failed to see that the monologue combined its irreverence towards African politicians with a sharp dig at British colonial practices.

'So then, let us be surgin' forward under de leadership of de party. We have seen the evils of the two-party system under other governments. We have seen the mad scramble for power in Britain, with the Homes and de Wilsons, and their corner-in-de-hole plottin', and their callin' each other tadpoles and leapers, while the country is slidin' to de dogs. And what about Grimond, stickin' both ends up de middle? Nevertheless, we must not condemn them, condemn their system just because it is not like ours. What is right for Africa may not be right for Britain. We, in Africa, cannot shirk our responsibilities to the under-developed nations, and I have taken certain secret measures regardin' this which I can now reveal to you. Tomorrow mornin', while all England is snorin' and slumberin', thousands of highly trained soldiers of the Kenya Army will be landin' on de beaches. Crack units of de Fourth Battalion de Nairobi Poison Spears will be creepin' about and seizin' key government buildin's, with the aid of their fatal plungin' movements of their machete knives, arrestin' de chief officers of state – the Queen, the Prime Minister, the Archbishop of Canterbury, and de most powerful of dem all, the greasy eminence behind de Throne – the notorious Warden of All Souls. Britain will be ours. No doubt there will be the occasional blood-bath. But, I always say, you can't make an omelette without layin' eggs. I myself will temporarily assume the office of Queen until a reliable native replacement can be found.'

Not So Much a Programme:
John Bird as Jomo Kenyatta

Almost without exception, the press disliked *NSMAP* – many of them referred back to *TW3* almost as to a golden age, despite the fact that they had published vitriolic assessments of *TW3* in its time. *Private Eye* also flung a few well-aimed brickbats in the form of a flimsy gramophone record in which Peter Cook does a devastating imitation of Frost, while the other members of the *Private Eye* editorial team make rude noises in the background suggestive of an uncontrolled live discussion (among other things).

As the series progressed, the balance of talk to sketches worsened. The edition of 14 February 1965, for example, runs fifty-eight minutes, and has only two sketches and one song.

Then, on 27 February, *NSMAP* plunged the BBC into the biggest row of all those arising from the 'satire' programmes with a sketch, written by Donald Webster, showing a dialogue between a Roman Catholic priest and an Irish mother (played by Patricia Routledge) in a Liverpool slum. The priest (played by Roy Hudd, a regular member of the cast, who was just beginning his career in television) solicits a donation for the Church, and enquires after the woman's children – it emerges that she has over twenty-five. As she is not pregnant, he asks if she has sinned (i.e., used contraceptives), but is told that her husband is not 'doing his duty' every night because he cannot afford to get drunk. The priest gives her back ten shillings, to enable her husband to afford his beer and thus rise to the occasion.

The sketch is satire with a blunt instrument – quite a contrast from the Bird and Bron style – and had already been included in the first pilot. It is not surprising that it caused complaints, although one wonders whether it was really necessary for members of Parliament to work themselves into a lather and, even after receiving a written apology from Hugh Greene, demand that Frost should apologize publicly (which he did not do). One of the relatively few letters to the press which supported the BBC suggested that it was the discussion which followed the sketch which had upset people. In it, Norman St John Stevas complained about the sketch and refuted its premise, while Dee Wells made an impassioned speech accusing the Roman Catholic Church of exacerbating world population problems by refusing to allow the United Nations to supply the Third World countries with contraceptives. It was certainly the best discussion of the series.

The show of 28 March included a sketch which precipitated yet another row. This time the sketch itself was harmless enough, but its timing was misplaced. It presented the story of the abdication of King Edward VIII in the style of a musical comedy; it was not unsympathetic to him – he was then still alive, as the Duke of Windsor – but the fact that it was shown less than four hours after the announcement of the death of the Duke's sister, the Princess Royal, betrayed a remarkable lack of sensitivity on somebody's part. Again, complaints were made – this time rather more justified.

It was the last straw. The series was due to end on 11 April, but it had been expected that it would return in the autumn. It was now announced that it would not do so, but that a different satirical format would be used. What this all amounted to was the removal of David Frost as the most obvious scapegoat.

This sudden exclusion from the sphere in which he had made his name might have been the end of Frost's fame, but he bounced back and within a very short time was appearing in pseudo-topical shows such as *The Frost Report*. Although he impinges again on the story of the Oxbridge Mafia, both in *The Frost Report* and as a producer, his departure from the satire scene also marks his transformation into a Television Personality. Christopher Booker: 'He had an intuitive gift for the power of television, right up to the point where he reached the Everest of his universe ... the American "Chat Show". I remember the first time he saw American chat shows. It was the first time I'd really seen Frost starry-eyed – he had at last seen the thing that he wanted to do, which was to be Carson, or Parr, sitting in the middle of that unreal little world that is the chat show. He set himself this goal, and all the way through the late sixties he just didn't put a foot wrong.'

The phenomenon of Frost – a success story for the sixties if ever there was one – has caused him to be the recipient of much good-natured (and some not so good-natured) abuse. Though not witty of himself he is a great provoker of wit in others – a feeling in some quarters that he has 'lifted' ideas from others led Jonathan Miller, medical to the last, to refer to him as 'the bubonic plagiarist'. Among the wit and occasional rancour, the most sensible and calm assessment of Frost comes from John Cleese: 'If he had an American accent, nobody would see anything odd about him. He is, in a sort of psychological jargon sense, the most extrovert person you'll ever meet. His standards are very much the standards of the outside world – a success for David is what is judged successful. The criticism I make is that he doesn't have sufficient commitment to quality – that he sees so many shows as things to be done, and he does them as neatly and as quickly and in many ways as efficiently as he can.'

William Rushton likes to cap any discussion of Frost with his favourite story, conveying (to him) the essence of Frost the Enigma. He was on one occasion working with a girl who was Frost's current girlfriend: 'She was in a terrible state – kept bursting into tears, so I said, "What's the matter – has Frost done something terrible to you?" – vaguely hoping that she would reveal that he had – she said, "Yes – he won't give me the telephone number of his car".'

With the end of *NSMAP*, Eleanor Bron spent a time working with various theatrical repertory companies – 'I felt that as I hadn't had any training I ought to go away and learn my craft'. Her appearances in *NSMAP* had given her a certain fame which led to her being invited to take over Honor Blackman's rôle as the female sidekick to Patrick McNee in ITV's glossy sub-James-Bond thriller series *The Avengers* – a part requiring much use of judo and fast cars, which she felt not to be her style. One of the roles she did take up at this period was that of the High Priestess Ahme in the Beatles' film, *Help!*

Help!: Eleanor Bron as High Priestess Ahme

During the summer of 1965, Bron, John Fortune and Alan Bennett appeared with John Bird in Bird's television film *My Father Knew Lloyd George*, which was broadcast on BBC-1 on 18 December 1965. Bird: 'Ned Sherrin said, "What would you like to do in the summer?" – that's how you should do television! I had this idea of doing a historical thing, with just a few of us playing all the parts. I wrote out a detailed synopsis, which depended on the idea that what happens in history is not "history" until later on – when historians get hold of events. We shot it all on location; I never wrote a complete script – I would often write the next day's pages the night before. Jack Gold, the director, was wonderful – he directed with great style and didn't worry about what the ending was going to be.'

The highly complex plot revolves round the efforts of a character, played by Fortune, to clear his grandfather (also played by Fortune) of a scandal involving the wife of the prime minister. It eventually emerges that the one shred of definite evidence in favour of the scandal – a compromising letter – was in fact written under the instructions of the prime minister in an attempt to cover up a total mishandling of some diplomatic affairs by the grandfather; in fact, although the scandal had a genuine basis, the evidence for it is a fabrication. The film is beautifully shot and directed, and full of quiet humour. Fortune plays about three characters, while Bird, Bron and Bennett each play about thirteen parts – including an impersonation by Bird of Queen Victoria. Alan Bennett displays more acting range in this film than in any of his other work; his oily Victorian villain is a characterization quite unlike the more usual dry Bennett creations.

John Bird won the Society of Film and Television Arts award for the 'Television Personality of the year, 1966' for *My Father Knew Lloyd George* and his appearances in the next emanation of satire to come from the BBC – *BBC-3*. (The title was a dig at the BBC's new second channel, BBC-2, opened the previous year.) The show, which was produced once again by Ned Sherrin, went out (on BBC-1) late on Saturday evenings from 2 October 1965 to 2 April 1966. Fourteen of the telerecordings – made for the same reasons as the previous shows – still exist, from which it can be seen that the structure of the show is similar to *NSMAP*, except that Frost is replaced by Robert Robinson, an older and more urbane broadcaster who has since become well known for chairing panel games such as *Call My Bluff*.

Bill Oddie appeared in a number of the shows, as a singer. He says: 'It was a period I didn't enjoy very much, because I didn't think the show knew what it was meant to be; one of the ironies about that period is that it was very much dominated by Ned Sherrin, who basically seems much happier, to me, doing nice little theatre shows about lesser-known songwriters. Those satire shows got worse and worse, as far as I could see, as his influence became greater and greater – you got more and more dancing; whereas Frost was tough – he's nothing if not tough – he had that strange ability to *appear* to be a man of the people. God knows he isn't.'

BBC-3 certainly suffers from a lack of 'bite', and one of its problems is that most of the items go on for far too long and become tiresome. Its greatest asset is the presence of Bird, Bron and occasionally Alan Bennett. Some of their material goes on for too long, but even so it is far better than much of the surrounding soggy fog. In the first programme, on 2 October 1965, John Bird continued a tradition he had started in *NSMAP* of giving little homilies in the character of Harold Wilson, the prime minister – who had been making quite a few television appearances himself in an attempt to maintain the 'dynamic new Britain' idea which had been his election platform. Bird's impression of Wilson, aided by a wig and a suitable pipe, was a worthy addition to the gallery of prime ministerial impersonations that Peter Cook had started.

> 'Now I imagine you'll think it a bit peculiar for me to appear on such a gay and light-hearted programme as this. But, you know, I don't have to go on being prime minister for a living – I could always go back to being a socialist. But seriously, though – I think all of you working here on *Sunday Night at the London Hippodrome* have a dynamic rôle to play in the new Britain. Now, as you know, the Department of Economic Affairs last week published its National Plan for 1970. And this means that we in the government are faced with two overwhelmingly urgent tasks. First of all, we must think of another pointless project to keep George Brown quiet for the next ten years. Secondly, we must all see that the targets in the plan are fulfilled. Now, I'll be frank with you; I admit, in the privacy of this television studio, that all is not well within the government. Some of my colleagues have not performed as I expected them to. Even worse, some of them have. But there are better prospects to come. This morning, for example, George Brown told me he had seen the Queen. Well, there it is – some people see snakes, some people see elephants; George sees the Queen.'

Bird: 'I used to try to think myself into his mind – which was quite easy to do after a time. The rule was never to use anything which the audience couldn't have read about in the papers – I would never use any material which journalists knew about, but nobody else. Because you're on for twenty-six weeks you can keep up a running commentary on the government in a way which a show at a theatre couldn't possibly do – and the great thing about television is that you are using exactly the same medium as the people themselves. Lady Falkender (Wilson's secretary) has since said to my ex-wife that they would turn on the television set sometimes to see me; and the number of times that I would actually articulate what they had been thinking about, under wraps, was quite uncanny. She said that Wilson got rather paranoid about it.'

BBC-3 did manage to emulate its predecessors by causing one major row when, on 13 November 1965, Kenneth Tynan said THAT WORD. He was taking part in a live discussion on stage censorship, and when asked whether he would allow a play to be put on at the National Theatre in which sexual intercourse was represented on the stage, replied: 'Well, I think so, certainly. I doubt if there are any rational people to whom the word "fuck" would be particularly diabolical, revolting or totally forbidden. I think that anything that can be printed or said can also be seen.'[21]

The incident brought a storm of protest, following all the usual patterns, and aimed, of course, at the BBC rather than him. Nowadays the whole thing seems rather silly; although the word is still not common on television, it has been used – when relevant – in the responsible newspapers. 1965 was a bit early for public use of it, however, and in fact Tynan probably set the cause of liberated speech on television back about five years.

Alan Bennett's handful of appearances on *BBC-3* are well worth watching in the films which exist. He says: 'I got into the way of writing occasional sketches with John Fortune or John Bird. We would meet towards the end of the week and try to knock out a script. I had a contract which allowed me to withdraw if no satisfactory idea emerged. I wasn't used to working to such a tight schedule or to performing live on television, but I got to enjoy it. It was also well paid – by the minute, I remember, which gave one an incentive to pad it out.' The existing appearances include several clever, though rather long, sketches with Bird, and one or two monologues, including his description of a literary party held by Virginia Woolf, broadcast on 29 January.

'. . . and was that the Pope? Or was it me? But it *was* the Pope – and then I remembered – for Arsenal were playing Vatican City at Highbury the next day. And always, there would be Virginia herself, elegant and quizzical, her great nostrils quivering, the sunlight playing over that long, pale face. She never used cosmetics, except to powder her nose; but then she had her father's nose. She would be talking perhaps of her contemporaries – of how she had met Hemingway, and how Ernest had said "When I reach for my gun, I hear the word 'culture'". How easy it was for them, she thought, how easy it was for them but how hard it was for her. For she must always be asking, "What is life like? . . . Life is like . . . Life is just . . . a bowl of cherries, was that it?" But no, for someone had said that before. And besides, it was false to the whole nature of reality. But of all the honours that fell upon Virginia's head, none I think pleased her more than the *Evening Standard* Award for the Tallest Woman Writer of 1933, an award she took by a short neck from Elizabeth Bowen, and rightly, I think, because she was in a very real sense the tallest writer I've ever known. Which is not of course to say that her stories were tall – they were not. They were short.'[22]

A number of Bron and Bird's sketches in *BBC-3* were improvised, with remarkably good results, considering the tension of improvising on live television; and it is really only their material, with a few exceptions, which makes the last of this lineage of satire shows of any interest. Called *The Late Show*, and running for twenty-three weeks from 15 October 1966, this series really is the dying gasp of the movement which began with *TW3*. The chat show side of the preceding programmes has been dropped, but so has Sherrin who, for all Oddie's comments, could at least give a show some sort of style. *The Late Show* does have a handful of short film inserts by Michael Palin and Terry Jones, and a couple of appearances by Barry Humphries in drag in his character of Mrs (later 'Dame') Edna Everage – the audience are obviously unfamiliar with Edna, and unsure how to react, but his monologues are well written and performed. Humphries can inject a world of meaning into a phrase such as 'My husband Norm is *very clever with his hands*'.

The edition of 29 October is fairly typical of the series, and includes a sketch about Suez which makes an interesting comparison with similar items in *TW3*; the representations of the politicians involved are so preposterous that the valid points being made by the sketch become badly blurred by the over-acting.

Of more interest in this edition is one of Bird and Bron's improvised sketches, which takes as its starting point a number of recent escapes from prisons. With a touch of the 'wouldn't-it-be-funny-ifs' that *Beyond the Fringe* was supposed to have killed off, they speculate on what would happen if a prisoner's mother was asked by the police to make a television appeal to him to give himself up.

BRON   (*reading prepared script*): 'Hello, Bill. Wherever you are. This is your mum' – I'll say 'mum' – 'speaking. I hope you are watching' – here, he hasn't seen me for six years, he might not even recognize me. I've got new teeth.

BIRD: Lovely, yes . . .

BRON: Sorry . . . (*reads*) 'Please be sensible, and give yourself up, for your own sake, and the sake of all your loved ones . . .' (*giggling*) He hasn't got any, that's his trouble . . . sorry – 'We are all sick with worry at home – it's nearly killing your father'? – I can't say *that* – that's what he went inside for, nearly killing his father! He hit him over the head with an iron bar, you should know that.

BIRD: Of course, I'd forgotten.

BRON: It wasn't his fault, you know – I don't blame him entirely – it was his Dad's fault, some of it. He was too strict with him – he always was, you know, he ruled him with a rod of iron, you know, well, I told him, 'You can't, he's a growing-up boy, you got to be a bit lenient, you can't always rule him with a rod of iron'. And of course, one day, the inevitable happened, and Bill grabbed hold of his rod of iron and started hitting his dad over the head with it. And since that day, Bill's never looked back. Nor of course has his dad, because he got hit on the back of the neck . . .

The Late Show: Andrew Duncan, John Bird, Eleanor Bron, Anthony Holland, Barry Humphries and (seated) John Wells

The last edition of *The Late Show*, broadcast on 1 April 1967, includes a silly musical sketch about James Joyce in which the cast keep saying 'satire is dead'; they are right. There were to be two further descendants of this troubled lineage, but neither is stylistically connected with the original phenomenon. *Quiz of The Week*, which ran for nine weeks from 5 July 1969 and for eight weeks from 20 June 1970, arose from a *Quiz of the Year*, broadcast on Christmas Day 1968, in which a team from *Private Eye* (Ingrams, John Wells and William Rushton) were pitted against a team consisting of Mary Kenny, Neil Shand and Linda Blandford in a topical quiz presided over by a mandarin-like Ned Sherrin. The *Private Eye* team faced a different opposing team every week in the second series, while only Rushton was regularly in the first series.

The other last manifestation of satire came in *Up Sunday*, with Rushton and Wells, backgrounds by courtesy of technical trickery, and no budget. It ran from 6 February to 16 July 1972 and 5 November 1972 to 28 January 1973 in a late-night slot on BBC-2, the minority channel; Rushton describes it as 'pretty tough and hairy', but they received no complaints because nobody much was watching. Two more short series followed during 1973.

After the ending of *The Late Show* John Bird went on to his own television series, *A Series of Birds*, which ran for eight weeks from 3 October 1967. Each episode told a completely different story, apart from one story which, having been over-written, was spread across two editions. Bird wrote the scripts in association with John Fortune; the producer, Dennis Main Wilson, brought in Michael Palin and Terry Jones to write 'additional material'. The fact that the series had a number of unconnected stories seemed to confuse the public (and the BBC) and the most successful in terms of audience appreciation was the two-part narrative, 'The Eric Giddings Story', because in the second half the audience knew from the start what to expect. The shows tell the story of a BBC documentary team who are making a film about an unemployed man, Eric Giddings.

In the first episode we see the machinations necessary to obtain realistic-seeming shots – simple things like pouring a cup of tea have to be done over and over again until the director and the cameraman are satisfied. In the second episode, the BBC have decided to make the documentary into a series; unfortunately for them, the publicity results in their subject being offered a job. Having committed themselves to a series, the BBC has to employ him to remain unemployed. Both shows are cleverly written and make their points quietly – 'satire by the back door' in Bird's words. Michael Palin says: 'It gave Terry and me some of the best writing opportunities we'd had – I think the best since we'd started. It was an attempt to break away from sketches and write narrative; and also learning to work with people like John Bird and Dennis Main Wilson was good experience.'

Bird was deliberately trying to break away from the formula series, which did not endear him to the BBC: 'I was given carte blanche because I was "a star", to do anything I liked. I made the mistake – which I've only just come to realize was a complete and fundamental error – of thinking that originality, of material and approach, is a good thing; whereas in fact it is an anathema to television. It's the thing which they like least. What they would like to do for a new comedy series is to have the same cast as a currently popular series, and for all thirteen scripts to be the same every week – so that in the end the audience can chant the script in unison with the performers. That's their ideal television show. And, to an extent because they've been conditioned to it, that's the audience's ideal, too. I didn't realize this . . . The last show of the series, which was bitterly hated in the Light Entertainment section of the BBC, was very much the sort of thing that I wanted to do. It was just a conversation between John Fortune and me about England, done in different sets, but the conversation was continuous.'

This show, called *Lucid Intervals*, was broadcast on 21 November 1967. The conversation between Bird and Fortune is punctuated by some scenes of Bird as a council official trying to intervene in a landlord-tenant dispute; Fortune is a government official who is so fed up with England that he is thinking of emigrating.

BIRD: Emigrate? Anything wrong?
FORTUNE: No, nothing you could sort of put your finger on, no.
BIRD: It wasn't anything I said, was it?
FORTUNE: Well – oh, I see, no, nothing in that way, no . . .
BIRD: Nor women, I suppose?
FORTUNE: Women? No – no, the Foreign Office thinks a great deal of the British woman. She's better designed and more efficient and easier to make than any other woman in the world. It's nothing in particular, really – I'd be quite sorry to leave England – I like it here, it's a splendid place, England.
BIRD: Why do you want to emigrate, then?
FORTUNE: It's such an awful country. I know I said I like it, and I do, but sometimes I think that I'm wrong in liking it, you know – sometimes I begin to feel that the things I like most about it I in fact, er, dislike.
BIRD: Well, I can understand this about – taxation, and all that sort of thing, but – I mean, for heaven's sake, you've done fantastically well in the Foreign Office, especially for somebody our age. It's a very good job you've got here – very influential.
FORTUNE: I suppose it is a good job, and I suppose it is influential, in a way, but it's just so *silly*. I mean there's no challenge, you know.
BIRD: Oh, there's a terrific challenge – it's very difficult.
FORTUNE: Oh, it's difficult, yes – it's difficult in the same way that being English is difficult.
BIRD: Yes . . . no, I'm sorry, you lost me there – in what way difficult?
FORTUNE: Because it's so easy. You know – I find it fantastically difficult to be English, and also to work here, because it's so terrifyingly, appallingly easy.

John Bird says: 'I was actually given a dressing down by Tom Sloane, the then Head of Light Entertainment, about three months afterwards, for doing that kind of show. He said, "It's not what I call Light Entertainment." And I'd used tiny little bits of Brahms as linking music – no more than a few bars – and he said, "What was that music?" I said, "Brahms." He said, "We don't have things like Brahms in Light Entertainment."'

Bird then made a series for the Independent Television company ATV, called *With Bird Will Travel*, which started on 28 June 1968. Again, he brought in different situations each week, and, again, it was not appreciated. The format was that Bird and Carmen Monroe were seen in a television control room – complete with a working radio-controlled camera looming large in the centre of the set – from which they could call up various reports and interviews; this was arranged to enable Bird both to link the show and indulge in his impressions. The humour is nicely oblique – perhaps too much so for commercial television – although there is a little too much reliance on the 'something going wrong on the air' routine. Bird: 'I was very into technology at the time, and it was supposed to be an advanced nerve centre; I made a lot of notes which justified technically all the things which happened – the technology was either there or just round the corner. I wasted a lot of time on that. But the show disappeared without trace . . . the only comment Ned Sherrin made on it was, he said it was rather under-lit.'

Eleanor Bron and John Fortune, meanwhile, wrote a one-off programme, *What Did You Say This Thing Was Called, Love?*, broadcast on BBC-2 on 9 June 1968; this led to a series called *Where Was Spring?* which ran for five weeks on BBC-2 from 27 January 1969 (and was followed by a repeat of *What Did You Say . . .*) and then a second series of seven from 12 July 1970. The programmes were produced by Ned Sherrin and directed by Terry Hughes, and consisted of man-woman dialogues in stylized settings.

The most interesting thing about *Where Was Spring?* is that some of the dialogues make assumptions about sexual behaviour which, whatever may have been the case in the outside world, were not common on the BBC in 1969. In this example, we eavesdrop on a couple in bed on the morning before the wedding.

Where was Spring?: Eleanor Bron and John Fortune

BRON: Did I tell you Mummy phoned last night? She's so sentimental. She was very worried.

FORTUNE: Why?

BRON: Oh, she said she didn't like the idea of my spending my 'last night alone' alone. (*They laugh*) If she could see us now! I've heard so many of my friends who've been living together say that as soon as they decided to get married everything went wrong . . . but it seems to have made us – much better. Hasn't it?

FORTUNE: Mm. Much.

BRON: Mmm . . . do you want to see my wedding dress? I'm going to try it on!

FORTUNE: Hey! I thought it was supposed to be unlucky to see the bride in her dress.

BRON: Silly, that only applies to the groom.

FORTUNE: Oh yes.

BRON: It is a bore. I wish we could have got married on the same day.

FORTUNE: Never mind. At least I'll be there. Besides, I wanted to be Edward's best man. I couldn't do both.

BRON: He insisted on a white wedding, you know. I was surprised.

FORTUNE: Ah well, it's all for the best . . .

BRON: All for the best man, actually. (*They laugh*) It's worked out terribly well, hasn't it?

FORTUNE: Well, of course. It's what I said: if we hadn't decided to get married we'd never have stayed together. We were going from bad to worse! Physically and mentally: it was humdrum, man. That's the only word for it. We might just as well have been married . . . Now – well! We'll have all the excitement: the danger, the thrills, letters, clandestine meetings . . . All the advantages of Adultery.

BRON: Ooh, that word . . . it gives me goose pimples . . . look!

FORTUNE: I mean, it's already so much better.

BRON: Yes . . . and this is just *pre*marital infidelity!

FORTUNE: Yes! And think – when we're married, even at your home, even in office hours, there's always a chance that Edward will turn up unexpectedly. Does he get migraine or anything like that?

BRON: I don't know. You probably know him better than I do. He's terribly conventional.

FORTUNE: That's all to the good. He'll be jealous, then. Such a big man, all that red hair. I should imagine he's given to uncontrollable rages.

BRON: Mmm . . . I'm a bit afraid he'll be rather possessive. What if he did come back and find us?

FORTUNE: But that's just it!

BRON: Darling! He might shoot you, and I couldn't bear it!
(*She hugs him*)

FORTUNE: Has he got a gun?

BRON: Yes.

FORTUNE: Marvellous. What kind?

BRON: Ooh, I don't know. It's a . . . Russian, I think . . . begins with an S . . . Sawnoff?

FORTUNE: Sawnoff . . . Sawnoff shotgun!

BRON: Yes, I think so. Are they any good?

FORTUNE: What on earth does he want with one of those?

BRON: He goes out at night, he says, hunting.

FORTUNE: What?

BRON: Owls, he said, or something.

FORTUNE: In the middle of Mayfair?

BRON: I don't know. Maybe. There are nightingales in Berkeley Square. I'm counting the days to your wedding. She's a lucky girl, Cynthia.

FORTUNE: Edward's a lucky man.

BRON: She's awfully pretty, Cynthia. She and my sister Angela were at school together.

FORTUNE: Yes, she told me.

BRON: Which do you think is the more beautiful? Cynthia or Angie?
FORTUNE: There's not much in it . . .
BRON: I've always been jealous of Angela, you know.
FORTUNE: Why?!
BRON: She is so lovely. The odd thing is she doesn't have any man at all, that I know of. I suppose because she's always on the move; she never has time.
FORTUNE: Oh, I don't know. It doesn't take all that long.

Bron and Bird appeared in a BBC-2 series, written by N. F. Simpson, called *World in Ferment*; it ran for six episodes from 23 June 1969 and was a rather bizarre parody of current affairs programmes such as *Panorama* and *World in Action*. They also appeared in the series *Beyond a Joke*, written by Bron with Michael Frayn; this ran for six weeks from 21 April 1972 on BBC-2.

Making Faces: Eleanor Bron and Tim Preece

Frayn then wrote a series for Bron, called *Making Faces*, which started on 25 September 1975. Bron: 'I thought it was wonderful, but the BBC didn't; it was six programmes about the same girl at different times in her life. It wasn't consecutive situation comedy, so they didn't know what to call it – whether it was series, or drama – so they got into a terrible flap. Then they wiped them all, and I'm very sorry about that.'

Because of the BBC's apparent lack of enthusiasm for her work Bron has since largely concentrated on straight acting; she has also written a book, *Life and Other Punctures* (André Deutsch, 1978) in which she disguises a number of autobiographical revelations as an account of her cycling holidays in France and Holland. It is a warm and witty book, and less oblique than her style of performed humour.

While *Making Faces* was failing to impress the BBC, John Bird's relationship with the moguls of Television Centre was also becoming a bit strained. He and John Fortune did a series of seven called *Well Anyway*, running from 24 September 1976 on BBC-2. Bird: 'It was obviously our last chance at the BBC . . . We didn't get any proper direction, which we needed – having written it, we gave the most boring performances – particularly me, I gave an awful performance. Having written something, and concentrating so much on the writing of it, you tend to imagine what the performance will be like – so you

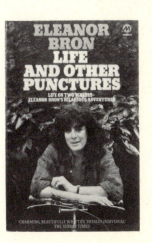

forget to do it! We did get better, and the scripts got better. They commissioned us to write the first two of the second series – and then they wouldn't do them. They commissioned us separately to write pilots – which I didn't take seriously; I wrote a script – I just thought it was blood money – I wrote something called *Brahms, You Bastard*, which would have been quite a good script. Jimmy Gilbert rejected it – he said to my agent, "It's very funny – but it's a play." Well, all situation comedies are plays – they aren't anything else – but he wanted me to take it to Drama. Presumably he had heard a rumour that they did plays there.'

This has marked a stopping place in Bird's television writing for a time, although he has interesting plans for a programme based on a journey across southern England by train.

He has in recent years achieved a certain notoriety for his imitations of Idi Amin: 'They started at *The Establishment* as impressions of Jomo Kenyatta – the voice has never changed, only the names of the leaders. It's actually Peter Cook's version of Jonathan Miller's idea of an African accent – and the interesting thing is that when Alan Coren started writing his Idi Amin pieces for *Punch*, the sort of florid rhetoric that I used for my Jomo Kenyatta pieces had become so associated with it that he actually wrote in my style. I don't think he realized that he was copying me, and not the actual man himself, who doesn't talk either like Coren writes or like I speak.' Bird voiced some of Coren's pieces, adding a few of his own, on gramophone records and in some public appearances.

Bird, Bron and Fortune's humour is always delightfully subtle and oblique – perhaps too much so for the popular taste – and it is to be hoped that their present enforced abandonment of it for straight acting will be only temporary. The principal difficulty seems to arise from the fact that they can really only exercise it on BBC-2, as the minority channel; and that while they prefer not to work within rigid boundaries of 'situation comedy' or 'sketch comedy', the BBC tends to prefer to be able to categorize them safely. *My Father Knew Lloyd George* is an excellent example of what they can do when they are not constrained by categorization.

In the last two chapters we have followed the programmes which descended, directly or indirectly, from *The Establishment*. While all this was going on, other members of the Oxbridge Mafia were also producing interesting results. In order to follow the next of these parallel lines of descent we need to return to 1965, and the end of the second American run of *Beyond the Fringe*.

5.
Alan Bennett; 'On the Margin'; 'Forty Years On'

We left the cast of *Beyond the Fringe*, at the end of Chapter 1, with the dissolution of their partnership. As we have seen, Miller went on into theatre direction; and Cook and Moore went on as a double-act, which will be examined in the next chapter.

Alan Bennett, however, had at this time not really decided what he was going to do. While *Beyond the Fringe* was still running in London he had been doing some research and a little teaching at Magdalen College, Oxford. His shyness made him nervous of both his pupils and the other dons. He remembers the first time he dined at the High Table, wearing the long gown which is the badge of an Oxford (or Cambridge) academic: 'As I sat down at this long table, the sleeves of my gown got caught under the legs of my chair, so that I was actually very restricted. I was too shy to get up and move the chair back. The servants brought the dishes round – if they brought them very close I could reach, but I could help myself to very few things, and the man on my right said, "Are you a vegetarian?" '[23]

It was while he was wondering what to do after his return from America that Ned Sherrin asked him to contribute to *BBC-3*. This experience convinced him that the academic life was not for him: 'I think probably there's a streak of pure tinsel in my character, which didn't really find much expression in Oxford.' Having enjoyed working on *BBC-3* he started assembling suitable material for a television series; this eventually emerged as *On the Margin*, a series of six half-hour programmes broadcast on BBC-2 weekly from 9 November 1966 starring Bennett with a supporting cast of professional actors.

Apart from Bennett's sketches, each programme included a straight poem by John Betjeman or Philip Larkin; and a film clip of an old-time music-hall comedian. These clips, which included songs by Marie Kendall and the incomparable Lily Morris, as well as Wilson, Keppel and Betty's hilarious 'sand dance', are such classics of broad comedy that they might well have overshadowed Bennett's own work if he were a less subtle writer.

As in *Beyond the Fringe*, Bennett revealed himself as a master of pin-point accuracy of observation. Then, as now, his economy of style produced believable characters whose weaknesses and follies could be mocked with a precision attained by all too few comic writers. It is perhaps illustrative – if a little obscure – to compare his writing with the graphic style of the turn-of-the-century cartoonist Phil May, whose ability to create a character from just a few well-placed pencil lines came like a fresh breeze into the Victorian convention of complex, fussy detail which all but smothered the joke of the cartoon in an over-engraved fog. Indeed, when the proprietors of the comic magazine *Punch* complained that he used too few lines, May retorted that when he could use half as many, he would charge twice as much.

As with May, there is nothing wasted in Bennett's work. In place of the highly coloured writings of other contributors to the genre, he offers a charcoal sketch, every line with a meaning and almost uncomfortable in its accuracy. However, he is rarely unkind, and never bitter. Writing as one who stands outside the world he gently satirizes, he is content to observe without passing judgement.

Direct parody of a style is not one of his most common techniques, but programme 4 of *On the Margin*, broadcast on 30 November 1966, included this neat parody of John Betjeman which had already appeared in *BBC-3* and which, as read by Bennett in a sad, elderly voice, fully justified its reappearance.[24]

On Going to the Excuse–me

Bolding Vedas, Shanks New Nisa
The Trusty Lichfield swirls it down
To filter beds on Ruislip Marshes
From my loo in Kentish Town.

The Burlington, the Rochester –
Oh, those names of childhood loos;
Nursie knocking at the door –
'Have you done your number twos?'

Lady typist – office party –
Golly, all that gassy beer –
Tripping home down Hendon Parkway
To her Improved Windermere.

Chelsea buns and lounge bar pasties
All swilled down with Benskin's Pale;
Purified and cleansed with charcoal
Fill the taps in Colindale.

Here I sit, alone and sixty;
Bald, and fat, and full of sin.
Cold the seat and loud the cistern
As I read the Harpic tin.

Jonathan Miller appeared in one of the programmes, and John Fortune in another; the regular company of supporting players included John Sergeant, Virginia Stride and Yvonne Gilan – straight actors who fitted very well into Bennett's style.

Bennett had complained that in *Beyond the Fringe* he was never allowed to 'camp it up'. In *On the Margin* he promptly demonstrated his ability to flaunt a limp wrist with the best of them. This particular character appeared in a number of sketches; in the first programme he was the aesthetic proprietor of an antiques shop. One would never have suspected that a Yorkshire accent could be so camp.

SERGEANT: Well, actually, I was looking for something rather along the lines of a teapot stand. It's a birthday present for my wife. I bought her a teapot for her Christmas present, so I thought I'd follow it up with a teapot stand.

BENNETT: Oo! The last of the big spenders. Teapot stand . . . Well . . . *(moves to Welsh dresser)* you could stand a teapot on here very nicely.

On the Margin: Alan Bennett and John Sergeant in the antique shop sketch (9 November 1966)

SERGEANT: Yes – but it's a little bit bigger than what I had in mind, really.

BENNETT: Oo! It *is* big . . . it *is* big . . . but only an expert would have spotted it. But you know, if you'd be advised, you can't go wrong with these, you know *(still fingering Welsh dresser)* because these are going to *rocket*. The Americans are buying them up, you know. If you had six or seven of these tucked away, you'd never starve. I mean, you wouldn't have room to eat, but you'd never starve.

SERGEANT: How much do they run to?

BENNETT: Well, I'll have to look in my little book. I wouldn't want it to go to anybody who wasn't going to cosset it – but I think you're a cosseter, aren't you? Now then – it's seventy-five pounds, but I could stretch it and let you have it for seventy-four guineas.

SERGEANT: I prefer to pay less, really.

BENNETT: Do you know, it's funny you should say that, love, because most people prefer to pay less, whereas I prefer to charge more, you know. I think it's just a matter of taste.

SERGEANT: This is nice. (*Touching a table*)
BENNETT: Oh, I can see I'm going to have to watch you – you really have the eye, don't you? Can you keep a secret?
SERGEANT: What?
BENNETT (*taps table*): Wedgwood.
SERGEANT: But I thought that Wedgwood only did pottery?
BENNETT: That's the secret. It's a very unique piece. There's only one other in existence, and it's on trust for the nation. It's fifty-five pounds, and if you pass that up, you want your bottom smacking.
SERGEANT (*pointing at old money box*): That's not an antique. They had these when I was a boy.
BENNETT: Oo, you said it, dear, not me. (*Picks up chamber pot filled with hyacinths*) Have you ever thought of going in for these? I like to think that this is Worcester.
SERGEANT: What is it?
BENNETT: Well, it's an eighteenth-century breakfast cup, is that. I mean, in the eighteenth century they used to have these great big breakfasts – I mean, none of your two prunes and a Weetabix – so they had such big cups. (*Picks up an old policeman's truncheon*) Do you know what they're using these for nowadays?
SERGEANT: Well I know one thing – it's not teapot stands.
BENNETT: Oo, get in the knife box, you're too sharp to live.
SERGEANT: I was reading in one of the Sunday newspapers that the latest trend is this 'camp' thing. Have you anything 'camp'?
BENNETT: *Now* he tells us!
SERGEANT: Have you any camp teapot stands?
BENNETT: Do you know, if you'd come in here a week ago, I was knee deep in camp teapot stands. I've had teapot stands in this shop as camp as a row of pink tents.
SERGEANT: Really?
BENNETT: I tell a lie – as camp as a row of pink *frilly* tents.

A regular feature throughout the series was 'Streets Ahead', or, 'Life and Times in NW1' – NW1 being the London postal district which includes Marylebone, Euston and Camden Town. Originally this area had been defiantly Cockney. (Bernard Shaw's Eliza Doolittle – in *Pygmalion* – was born in Lisson Grove, near Marylebone; and Camden Town, though unsung, was also a working-class community.) However, in the mid-sixties this area was rapidly being taken over by trendy upper-middle-class professional people.

Bennett's sketches follow one such household – Nigel and Jane Knocker-Threw. In the third episode they are holding a children's party. Nigel is played by Bennett, Jane by Yvonne Gilan, and their friends Sam and Clarissa by John Sergeant and Virginia Stride. Nigel and Clarissa are in the kitchen:

CLARISSA: How old is Tristram now?
NIGEL: Oh, now, I can always remember – he's very close to your James, isn't he. Er – because Tristram is Suez, and James is Hungary. And Belinda is the first sort of dynamic feeler put out by Moscow when everything started, you know, to ease up a bit.

(*Sam comes in*)

SAM: Clarissa, hate to say this, love, but James is being rather coarse with little Cordelia Innskip. Can you come in?

CLARISSA: Oh, my darling – is he really? I'm so sorry. (*Exits*)

NIGEL: Clarissa, love, ho shouldn't go, you're pregnant.

SAM: James never takes any notice of me at all. He's worse than all the rest of them put together.

NIGEL: You know why, don't you, Sam?

SAM: No?

NIGEL: Well, he was trained far too early. I mean, six months . . .

SAM: Well, *I* was trained at six months, and it never did me any harm.

NIGEL: Well, I don't know – you can't start holding a baby out at three weeks and expect it to do anything else except harm. I mean, take Tristram – I mean, Tristram's eight now, and he's – more or less nominally trained, but I mean, he's still capable of turning in a very Chaucerian nappy. Jane just doesn't bother.

SAM: Yes, actually, I noticed her not bothering next door.

NIGEL: Really?

SAM: Yes – that rather nice Afghan rug.

NIGEL: Oh, Lord . . . Are you going down to the hospital to see it born?

SAM:.   I suppose so – I did with James.

NIGEL: It is perhaps the most beautiful experience in all the world – and also the most nauseating. I remember, when Jane was having Belinda I was in rather a quandary because the night she started having the pains there was this repeat of a Ken Russell film on, and I'd missed it the first time. Just a question of priorities, really. I watched the film. Well, I mean – you know, we were going to have more kids, and it's not every night you can see a Ken Russell film.

In the next week's episode, Nigel and Jane are upset to discover that their au pair, Heidi (Margaret Nolan), is pregnant.

NIGEL: Of course, I don't want to say 'I told you so', Jane, but – I told you so. I mean, this is why I wanted her in by eleven – you would let her stay out till twelve.

JANE: Look, love, if Heidi wanted anything she'd get it by eleven.

NIGEL: Yes, and she'd get it again by twelve.

JANE: Just because Heidi's pregnant doesn't mean to say *you* can be vulgar as well.

NIGEL: I wonder who's child it is?

JANE: You don't think it was that awful Nigerian?

NIGEL: Jane, sometimes I think your socialism isn't even skin deep. . . . Heidi – the person, the, er, swine who did this to you – was he, um – (*taps black book*) was he black?
          (*Heidi shakes her head*)

NIGEL   (*relieved*): So he was (*taps white object*) white?
          (*Heidi shakes her head*)

NIGEL: Oh my God, it's a Chinese waiter.

JANE: You see, Heidi, we have to put the children first.

NIGEL: Moral point, Jane – Heidi's having a child, too.

JANE:	Yes, love – but we've *got* ours. She's only *having* hers. First come, first served.
NIGEL:	Well, so far as I can see there are three courses open to us; one, she goes back to Sweden forthwith; two, she marries the blighter, but if it's Hoo Flung Dung from the Chinese restaurant I honestly don't think that's a good idea; or three, we compromise and put her out on the street.
JANE:	Or four, she has it adopted over here.
NIGEL:	No, that wouldn't do – poor little thing, it would never speak a word of English.
JANE:	You see, Heidi, we in England are very narrow-minded – when I say we of course I don't mean *us* –
NIGEL:	Not *us*, Heidi, I mean we're very broad –
JANE:	We're very narrow-minded about children born out of wedlock.
NIGEL:	Yes – children born out of wedlock – bastards, Heidi, that is – bastards have a stigma – ugh! – you see – whereas, in Sweden, you see, what with all the sauna, and the –
HEIDI:	Sauna, *ja, ja, ja* . . .
NIGEL:	Yes, Heidi – and the suicides right, left and centre, and the nude bathing, and the Royal Family waiting at bus stops, I mean a tiny little stigma like that would probably never be noticed – so why don't you go upstairs and pack?
JANE:	Oh, I've done that for her already.
NIGEL:	Now, isn't that kind, Mrs Knocker-Threw's already packed for you, Heidi. Goodbye – *auf wiedersehn* – (*Jane ushers Heidi out*)
NIGEL:	Jane – shall I ring the agency, love?
JANE:	Oh yes, do that – and get an ugly one this time.

The programmes are full of neat sketches – a 'film profile' on a northern writer stands out as being more acid than is usual for Bennett ('I don't think the State does enough for artists and writers generally in the way of subsidy and tax relief and so on – I mean, as an artist and a writer, I have to be surrounded by beautiful things and beautiful people – and beautiful people cost *money*'); and a spoof of a group of over-serious critics discussing a mythical play called *Yes, We Have No Pyjamas* has been overtaken by the fact that there has since been a stage presentation with such a title.

Although he has made television appearances since, *On the Margin* marked the end of Bennett's period of activity in television comedy. Subsequent appearances, both on TV and on stage, have been in subsidiary roles in his own plays; in *On the Margin* we can see the transition between Bennett the comedian, and Bennett the playwright – or rather, we *could* see the transition had not the BBC, in an act of criminal vandalism, allowed the recordings to be destroyed.

While he was working on the series, Bennett was also compiling a stage show which he at first thought of in terms of a literary revue. It was to include the Virginia Woolf monologue (already quoted from its appearance in *BBC 3*) as well as a lampoon of a literary criticism of Lawrence of Arabia. Gradually the idea took shape of setting these and the other sketches into the framework of a school play, presided over by a headmaster of, in both senses, the Old School.

Bennett says: 'Originally titled *The Last of England*, it was offered first to the National Theatre, but without much response. Then Frith Banbury put wheels in motion to get it produced by Stoll Theatres – though like John Bassett with *Beyond the Fringe*, Frith got very little credit for his efforts in the end. The play seemed to me much closer to what I wanted to do in the theatre than *Beyond the Fringe*.'

Re-titled *Forty Years On*,[25] the play opened at the Apollo Theatre, London, on 31 October 1968. Bennett himself appeared as a junior schoolmaster, and John Gielgud as the headmaster presiding over an impression of the sweep of recent history by the masters and boys of the school. With a magnificent detachment from his surroundings, the headmaster addresses the school before the start of the play. In this extract he is remembering the two world wars.

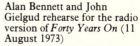

HEADMASTER: Some of the older ones among you will remember Bombadier Tiffin, our Corps Commandant and Gym Instructor, lately retired. The more observant ones among you will have noticed that one of Bombadier Tiffin's legs was not his own. The other one, God bless him, was lost in the Great War. Some people lost other things, less tangible perhaps than legs but no less worthwhile – they lost illusions, they lost hope, they lost faith. That is why . . . chewing, Charteris. That is why the twenties and thirties were such a muddled and grubby time, for lack of all the hopes and ideals that perished on the fields of France. And don't put it in your handkerchief. Hopes and ideals which, in this school, and in schools like it all over the country, we have always striven to keep alive in order to be worthy of those who died. I think it was Baden-Powell who said that a public schoolboy must be acceptable at a dance, and invaluable in a shipwreck. But I don't think you'd be much use in either, Skinner, if you were playing with the hair of the boy in front. See me afterwards.

Alan Bennett and John Gielgud rehearse for the radio version of *Forty Years On* (11 August 1973)

Bennett's subsequent plays seem to fall beyond the strict scope of this book, although the same pointed humour is present in many of them. The series of television plays broadcast by London Weekend Television in the winter of 1978–9 showed the range to which Bennett has expanded his writing. It included several quiet comedies, and one rather odd play – *The Old Crowd* – which was made even odder by its director, Lindsay Anderson. This was Anderson's first TV work for many years. In his films, such as *If* and *O Lucky Man*, he had shown an interest in alienation techniques – in *O Lucky Man* this took the form of 'distancing' the audience from the story by having a character (Alan Price) who both appeared in the action and sang songs, on and off-screen, which commented upon the action as it progressed. In *The Old Crowd*, Anderson allowed the cameras and other technical paraphernalia of the television studio to be seen several times; he also, according to Bennett, took out a lot of the jokes. The result was very unlike Bennett's usual style.

Bennett has only very rarely been interviewed on television – he claims he makes a bad interviewee – but Russell Harty, his old friend from Oxford, managed to persuade him to be a guest on *Russell Harty Plus . . .*, one of ITV's premier chat shows. The show was broadcast on 21 October 1977. Bennett was inclined to be reticent, although he performed one of his monologues and suddenly came to life in the process; but what he had to say as an interviewee turned out to be as entertaining as one might have expected.

Talking about the pleasure he got from having his work performed, Bennett said: 'The nice thing is to hear people laugh when you've caught the way people actually speak. The laughter is laughter of recognition.' Much of his writing, of course, centres on the north of England, which accounts for his preoccupation with subjects not normally considered funny, such as funerals and illness. 'I think it's just being northern – northern women's lives are slung between three poles; dirt, disease and the lavatory. It is funny, but it's also sad. They batten onto illness – people always make out that their case is very interesting: "Our Clifford went into hospital and he *baffled* the surgeons . . . They had Mr Venables in to look at him – he's one of the top people – he looked at Clifford's stomach and he said, 'Well, this could go either way' . . . Frankly, I think it's *nerves*."'

He revealed one of his secrets – that he carries a small notebook in which he writes down remarks that people make which might be suitable for future use. He read out some gems:

'I thought that was a fellow in a raincoat bending down – it's two sheep!'

'I see the President of Romania's mother is dead – there's always trouble for somebody.'

A headline: 'Rumple-suited pragmatist is Quebec's new leader.'

On a shop front: 'It's Floggo time at Trouserama.'

'They came to fit a new coat-hook in the toilet last week – they were four days doing it – I'm ashamed to be British sometimes.'

And one gloriously dotty quote which he surely must save to be the title for his autobiography: 'That fool of a tortoise is out again.'

Bennett's summation of *Forty Years On* might well be applied to his work as a whole: 'Within the framework of *Forty Years On* I was able to be both sad and funny. Critics prefer you to be one or the other, but audiences have no objection if you manage to be both.' By making the transition from humorous writer to playwright he has stepped out of the area covered by the present book. He has brought to his recent work the same sharp insight which characterized his comic writing. He is still developing his technique, and remains his own sternest critic.

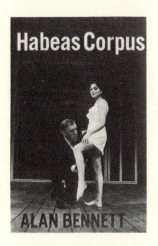

6.
Peter Cook and Dudley Moore; 'Not Only But Also'; 'Goodbye Again'; 'Behind the Fridge'; 'Derek and Clive'

When the cast of *Beyond the Fringe* went to the USA in 1962, the show continued running in London with the substitute cast. Peter Cook says: 'I, with utter arrogance, said that it should stop after we left, because it would be a pity for it to dribble away. I felt that once we'd all left, nobody would come and see it. Of course, it was still running when I got back from the States and was looking for a job! I came back expecting to be enormously well known, and of course nobody knew me from Adam.'

Having been out of the country for three years, with the two runs of *Beyond the Fringe* in New York and his activities with *The Establishment*, it is hardly surprising that he had been eclipsed in the public eye by *TW3* and its descendants. However, he was not long in re-establishing himself. Bernard Braden, the Canadian-born comedian, was at that time doing a series for ITV called *On the Braden Beat*. He invited Cook to appear regularly in the character of the miner who wanted to be a judge. Cook did about twenty monologues, sitting on a park bench and staring straight into the camera with a glazed look in his eyes. The character, now given the name E. L. Wisty, made an immediate impression on the viewers. The striking thing about E. L. Wisty was that he never smiled – Cook managed to keep a straight face throughout, despite the audience laughter. The monologues were improvised into a tape recorder on the night before the show, and transcribed onto a teleprompter so that Cook could read them while looking directly into the camera. This technique went well with the glazed look.

E. L. Wisty is a classic comic creation. Uneducated, uninformed, but full of totally imaginary 'facts', repressed, but with a strong fantasy life, he simply sat in a dirty raincoat on his park bench and, in a near monotone, held forth on his subject for the week.

'If there's one thing I can't bear, it's when hundreds of old men come creeping in through the window in the middle of the night and throw all manner of garbage all over me. I can't bear that. I think that's unbearable. Ghastly old men, with great pails of garbage, throwing it all over me. I don't think it should be allowed, I think there should be a place for those people to go. And I don't think it should be my room. I'd vote for any party that would say "I won't allow people to throw garbage all over me". But none of the parties seem to be particularly interested. That's why I formed the World Domination League. It's a wonderful league, the World Domination League. The aims, as published in the manifesto, are total domination of the world by 1958. That's what we're planning to do. We've had to revise it – we're hoping to bring a new manifesto out with a more realistic target. How we aim to go about it is as follows: we shall move about into people's rooms and say, "Excuse me, we are the World Domination League – may we dominate you?" Then, if they say "Get out", of course we give up. There's been some wonderful dominators in history, you know. Attila was one. He was a wonderful dominator. Attila the Nun. He was an amazing dominator. He had a Gothic Horde, you know. A wonderful Gothic Horde, and he used to move about entire countries and strangle people completely to death. And then, when everybody woke up, they'd see a little note pinned to their chest, saying: "You've been dominated. Ha, ha. Attila the Nun." Hitler was a very peculiar person, wasn't he. He was another dominator, you know, Hitler. And he was a wonderful ballroom dancer. Not many people know that, he was a wonderful little dancer, he used to waltz around with a number "8" on his back. The only trouble was, he was very short, and people used to shout out to him when he was dancing, and say, *"Wie kurz du bist* – how short you are!" And this of course enraged Hitler. He flew into a tantrum, and he gave up ballroom dancing, and took up wholesale raping and pillaging instead. Of course, Mrs Hitler was a charming woman, wasn't she – Mrs Hitler, a lovely woman – she's still alive, you know. I saw her down the Edgware Road only the other day. She'd just popped into the chemist's to buy something, and I saw her sign the cheque, "Mrs Hitler". So I knew it was she. I tried to go up and talk to her, but she slipped away into the crowd. I was hoping she'd be able to come to the next meeting of the World Domination League.'[26]

Dudley Moore, being primarily a musician, had made few contributions to the text of *Beyond the Fringe*, although he wrote and performed several musical lampoons. He also seems to have been slightly overshadowed by the other three in the earlier days of the show, but became more self-confident during the New York run. Several new items were added as the American run progressed, one of them being a sketch Cook had written several years previously. Entitled 'One Leg Too Few', it presented the plight of a one-legged actor auditioning for the part of Tarzan. Moore is of course the 'unidexter', as Cook describes him.

COOK: Need I point out to you where your deficiency lies as regards landing the rôle?

MOORE: Yes, I think you ought to.

COOK: Need I say with over-much emphasis that it is in the leg division that you are deficient.

MOORE: The leg division?

COOK: Yes, the leg division, Mr Spiggott. You are deficient in it to the tune of one. Your right leg I like. I like your right leg. A lovely leg for the rôle. That's what I said when I saw it come in. I said, "A lovely leg for the rôle." I've got nothing against your right leg. The trouble is – neither have you.

Around the time of *On the Braden Beat* the BBC asked Moore to do a one-off special television show. Moore invited Cook to be on the show, and Cook wrote two sketches; one with two idiots in cloth caps discussing imaginary and unlikely adventures involving famous film stars, and one about an upper-class idiot whose life's work consisted of teaching ravens to fly underwater.

This show led the BBC to ask Cook and Moore to team up for a series. It was called *Not Only . . . But Also*; the first series was produced (i.e. directed) by Joe McGrath, a loony Scotsman with whom Cook and Moore got on very well, except that Cook thought that McGrath was too enthusiastic – he found everything very funny, where Cook would perhaps have preferred some constructive criticism.

The planning of the programmes was a little on the loose side. Cook says: 'The things we thought out were the filmed items. We were always late on deadlines (for the studio material) – we always had enough material for the show, but practically inevitably we'd change it – we'd become dissatisfied with the stuff we'd written, and do something at the last minute. One of the nicest things I found about working for the BBC was their adaptability. They'd ask two months in advance what sets we'd need. We wound up saying, let's have one which could be an office, or a living room, just by changing the furniture.' In the end the sets were only the slightest suggestions – an odd door or window, and a small amount of furniture – which gave a slightly unusual and rather effective 'feel' to the show.

The first series went out on BBC-2, fortnightly from 9 January 1965, the

Not Only But Also: Pete and Dud

105

seven shows each lasting forty-five minutes. They consisted of several sketches, at least one filmed item, and one or two guest items – some comic, some straight music. The second series, produced by Dick Clement, whom Cook found 'more objective', consisted of seven half-hour programmes, broadcast weekly from 15 January 1966; and four years later there was a further series of seven – the first to be transmitted in colour – produced by Jimmy Gilbert. These third series shows were also forty-five minutes each, fortnightly from 18 February 1970.

The general style of the shows remained unchanged, although some of the ideas of the first series were expanded in the later ones, and some of the regular characters began to develop strong identities. The most famous characters to emerge from *Not Only . . . But Also* were the two cloth-capped idiots – Dud and Pete. Cook says: 'As far as I'm concerned "Pete" is a slightly more active extension of E. L. Wisty. The relationship between Dud and Pete is, Pete is the informed idiot, and Dud is the uninformed idiot. They're both idiots, but Pete is always slightly superior. In fact, he knows nothing either. They discuss the same lofty subjects as E. L. Wisty. If I remember right, the first series of Dud-and-Petes we didn't have scripts as such, we had a lot of headings – we'd rehearsed a lot, and we roughly knew what we were going to say, but not word for word. It came across as if we were improvising it, which was not strictly true, but we had a lot of latitude.'

Dud and Pete obviously hail from the Dagenham area – Moore came from this area originally, and apparently contributed a lot of autobiographical material to the sketches. Cook says that most of the names Moore mentions are of real people. The pair make a very good combination – Cook says: 'Dudley can root out a lot of things from his working-class past, and I can root out a lot of things from my basically middle-class upbringing. Again there's an obvious advantage in my being tall and his being short; him being cuddly and me being stone-faced.'

The sketches are unusually long – normally eight to ten minutes – which makes it impossible to quote one in its entirety; also their construction precludes taking single excerpts. In the following example, broadcast on 6 March 1965, three extracts are put together in order to give an idea of the whole sketch. What is missing is largely a sort of wandering speculation, most of it concerned with the technical difficulties involved in flying to the moon on gossamer wings. The sketch was published in 1971 in the book *Dud and Pete – the Dagenham Dialogues* (Eyre Methuen); what follows, however, is a transcript from the original broadcast, which differs in a number of ways from the published version.

Dud and Pete have just boarded a bus which is waiting at the depot. Dud is complaining about his lack of success with women, and Pete, with his wide experience of the subject, is advising him.

PETE: Did I ever give you the account of my tempestuous affair on the 42B?

DUD: They've discontinued that route, haven't they, Pete?

PETE: Yes, due to the incident I'm about to relate. I used to go on the 42B, I think it was spring of 1948, anyway, one day I got on the bus – you know, perfectly normally – sat down, uneventfully, the bus started up, went on a stop, stopped, nobody got on, nobody got off, bell rang, the bus started up again, went to another stop, nobody got on, nobody got off, the bell rang, the bus went on another stop, nobody got on, nobody got off . . .

DUD: How long's that go on for, Pete?

PETE: About five stops, Dud – it was a fairly uneventful journey until the incident. I won't bore you with the details –

DUD: You already have, Pete.

PETE: Anyway, after about six stops, suddenly this uncannily beautiful woman, with incredibly sensuous looks about her, got onto the platform of the bus.

DUD: Tempestuous beauty?

PETE: A tempestuous beauty, Dud, of a type rarely seen. Anyway, I thought, hello, you know –

DUD: What, you said hello to her, did you?

PETE: No, I thought hello. I thought I'd play it very cool, Dud.

DUD (*sings*): Play it cool, boy.

PETE: You have to play it very cool with women if you're going to get anywhere, you see. Anyway, I could immediately see what she was after – it stood out a mile, what she was after – 'cos she gave me a fleeting glance.

DUD (*giving him a fleeting glance*): Like that?

PETE: No, slightly more fleeting that what you've just done.

DUD (*giving him a rapid fleeting glance*): Like that? . . . I've ricked my neck, Pete.

PETE: Yes, similar to what you did, without the ricking. Anyway, she gave me this fleeting glance, and I was immediately aware of what she wanted, so I looked the other way. So she went upstairs immediately. I thought, funny –

DUD: Funny, yes –

PETE: Her going upstairs, me sitting downstairs –

BOTH: Funny, her upstairs, me downstairs, funny . . . (*etc. etc.*)

PETE: I knew what she wanted. So, sure enough, about five stops later, she come down the stairs, got off the bus without even looking at me. I thought I'd play it very cool, so I went on another four stops, got off down at Green Lane, and I never seen her again.

DUD: 'Course, you know Pete, you got a way with birds that I haven't got.

PETE: Yes, I have, yes.

DUD: Did I tell you about that girl Joan Harold, who I used to know? She used to travel on the 148 bus route a lot.

PETE: Wasn't she the tempestuous gypsy beauty with raven hair down to her waist?

DUD: Yes, delicately boned hands.

PETE: Alabaster body, perfectly formed . . .

DUD: Thrusting through her dress.

PETE: Yes, Joan Harold, thrusting through the dress, yes . . .

DUD: Well anyway, as you know, or as you don't know, she used to travel on the 148 bus.

PETE: 'Course she did, Dud.

DUD: Six o'clock every evening she used to get the 148 bus home. I used to leave work about five o'clock, as you know, about ten miles from where she was, anyway, but I always felt I had to see her, so what I used to do, I used to come out of work, I used to get the 62B up to Chadwell Heath Merry Fiddlers, then I used to go down the hill and get the 514 trolley down to Rainham Crescent. Then I used to go over by the railway bridge and go across those fields by the dye works. There's a parsnip field and then there's another one with cabbages.

PETE: 'Course there is, Dud, I remember that.

DUD: I'd come out the other side by the hedge, by which time the 148 bus, the six o'clock one, was coming round that corner, Hobb's Hill. Now, it used to come round very slowly, 'cos it was a very sharp turn, and there's no bus-stop there, but it used to be very slow. If it was going too fast I used to lay down in the middle of the road. But what I used to do, I used to leap on the platform as it went past, 'cos I knew she was on that bus.

PETE: Well, what happened then, Dud?

DUD: Well, I used to lay panting on the platform for about ten minutes.

PETE: Well, that's no bloody good. Did you ever get to speak to her at all, this Joan Harold woman?

DUD: Yes – once when I got off the bus she got off behind me, and I thought, you know, I'd play it a bit funny with her, and I dug her in the elbow and I said ''Ere, Joan, chase me', and I ran off across Bonham Gardens, and halfway across Tiverton Square, before I realized she hadn't budged an inch.

PETE: Well, that's no bloody good, you got to play it cool with these women, Dud, if you want to get anywhere – did you ever get anywhere at all with her, take her out or anything?

DUD: I did take her out once, Pete – I took her out to West Ham Speedway, once – I bought her two cups of tea, a box of Pontefract cakes and a takeaway pizza. Nothing.

PETE: Nothing?

DUD: Nothing, boy.

PETE: How much did you spend on her?

DUD: Six-and-three.

PETE: Six-and-three, and nothing?

DUD: Nothing, boy.

PETE: Not a touch?

DUD: Not a sniff, mate.

PETE: Blimey, you've been done, Dud, that's no good to treat women like that – you've got to be extremely rough and tempestuous with women.

Two girls get on, and Dud, egged on by Pete, tries to play the great lover with one of them.

DUD   (*to the girl*): How about a . . . what? (*forgets his line*)

PETE   (*prompting him*): 'How about a bit of passionate love with me?'

DUD: How about a bit of passionate love with me, then?
    (*The girl slaps his face*)

PETE: What happened, Dud?
DUD: She slapped my face, Pete.
PETE: Well, you're away, aren't you.
DUD: Am I?
PETE: Physical contact after such a brief meeting? That's the way to do it,
         Dud – now you got to play it extremely cool. Why don't we go
         upstairs and ignore them for about ten stops.

As time went on, Dud degenerated slightly – he started to twitch, and to
become even more stupid. Pete, on the other hand, stayed as imperturbably
misinformed as ever.

Each show opened with a filmed and spectacular version of the signature
tune – Moore playing it on a cinema organ, or in various surroundings which
eventually included Tower Bridge. There were also some carefully worked out
film sequences, including a First World War spoof (which caused a few viewers
to complain about the subject matter) and a clever profile of a film star with a
suspicious resemblance to Greta Garbo. The item ended with Cook made up as
Garbo, mimicking the closing shot of *Queen Christina*. He says: 'I thought I
looked incredibly beautiful – I fancied myself rotten! I thought I looked rather
better than she did!'

Not Only But Also: Peter
Cook as Greta Garbo (18
February 1970)

The musical items helped to break up the comedy, and were retained in the
later series; but Cook and Moore found that the use of guest comedians made
difficulties because of their particular way of working, and the second and third
series sketches mostly consisted of dialogues between them. An exception to
this was 'Poets Cornered', a regular feature of the third series. Cook and Moore
joined forces with a guest speaker – the guests included Spike Milligan,
William Rushton, Frank Muir and Barry Humphries – in a rhyming contest.
The object was to continue, without hesitation, in the composition of a simple
poem, picking up from the previous speaker at the sound of a buzzer operated
by the producer, Jimmy Gilbert. Cook: 'We were poised on these chairs, and
the first person not to rhyme fell into this terrible pool of gunge – which was
just a way of lengthening the show or shortening it, it was completely arbitrary
– we none of us knew when we were going to go, Jimmy would press a button

and we'd fall in the foam.'

In the earlier shows the sketches were either first improvised into a tape recorder by the two of them, and then transcribed; or, if they were written in the normal way, Cook would do most of the work. Cook: 'Gradually Dudley developed far more of a rôle in the writing. I tend to flutter off very quickly, and improvise, and ignore illogicalities – I'd rather get through a whole sketch quickly, and then come back and deal with whatever is wrong. Dudley began, when we had an idea, to examine what was logically incorrect, right at the beginning. I would regard this as pernickety, and he would regard it as logical. So the writing process became slower.'

The quality of the writing (and improvising) certainly maintained a very high standard over the three series; there were the occasional ideas which did not entirely come off, but there were also many classic comedy sketches. The best remembered are of course the Dud and Pete dialogues, but there were also a number of sketches in which Cook could create his 'stolid, imperturbable, upper-class fools'. One of these was the sketch about teaching ravens to fly underwater which had been written for the first show they did together. The same character, Sir Arthur Streeb-Greebling, reappeared in the fourth show of the second series. He was interviewed by Moore, in what sounds like a largely improvised sketch, about his latest unfortunate venture – a restaurant called 'The Frog and Peach'.

MOORE:	Don't you feel that you're at a disadvantage because of your menu?
COOK:	The menu! Oh dear, yes, this has been a terrible hinderance to us, building up a business. The menu – have you seen it?
MOORE:	Well I have, yes.
COOK:	It's a most appalling thing – there's so little to choose from. You start with – what's that?
MOORE:	Spawn cocktail.
COOK:	Spawn cocktail! One of the most revolting dishes known to man. Then there's .only two other dishes, really – there's frog *à la pêche*, which is frog done in Cointreau with a peach stuffed in its mouth – and then of course there's *pêche à la* frog, which is really not much to write home about . . . The waiter comes to your table, it's got this huge peach on it which is covered in boiling liqueur, you see, and then he slices it open to reveal about two thousand little black tadpoles squiggling about . . . it's one of the most disgusting sights I've ever seen. It turns me over to think of it.
MOORE:	It is rather nauseating.
COOK:	Squiggle, squiggle, they go – ugh!
MOORE:	Who does the cooking?
COOK:	My wife does the cooking, and luckily she does the eating as well. An amazing creature – of course she's not a well woman. Not a well woman at all, so she very much resents having to go down the well every morning to sprinkle 'Swoop' on the toads. An amazing creature, my wife – an amazing creature. I met her during the war, actually –
MOORE:	You did?
COOK:	Yes, she blew in through the drawing room window with a bit of

shrapnel, became embedded in the sofa – and you know, one thing led to her mother, and we were married in the hour.

The Very Best of Peter Cook & Dudley Moore

Not Only . . . But Also established Cook and Moore as an effective, well-balanced team. The programmes were entertaining, with many excellent sketches which gave Cook ample opportunity to indulge in the 'spiralling absurdity' which is his stock-in-trade. The closing number of every show – 'Goodbye', sung in a sort of well-oiled twenties manner – became the signature tune of the duo for their subsequent appearances; their record of it reached number eighteen in the hit parade in July 1965.

Cook and Moore made their first appearance in a cinema film shortly after the first series of *Not Only . . . But Also*. They took lead rôles in *The Wrong Box*, a film version of the novel by Robert Louis Stevenson and Lloyd Osbourne, which details the complications arising between the families of the last two survivors of a tontine (a form of lottery in which the total investment eventually goes to the last surviving subscriber). The scriptwriters unfortunately succumbed to the temptation to try to 'improve' the original by overloading it with star names and a wide variety of intrusive comic devices, but even so it has a number of good moments, and Cook and Moore emerge from the chaos as well as anyone in a distinguished cast including Ralph Richardson, John Mills, Peter Sellers, Wilfrid Lawson and Tony Hancock.

Their next film appearance was in *Bedazzled*, scripted by Cook from an idea by himself and Moore. Cook describes it as the only film he's ever worked in that he's remotely satisfied with. It received a poor critical reception in Britain – the general comment was along the lines of 'Cook and Moore have failed to make the transition from the small screen' – but in other countries, which had not seen *Not Only . . . But Also*, the film was much better received.

The story is a reworking of the Faust legend in a form which allows what are in effect a series of sketches to be linked by a dramatic framework. Moore plays Stanley Moon, a sad little failure of a man who is a short-order cook in a Wimpy bar, and who is infatuated with a waitress but too timid to speak to her. Failing in an attempt to kill himself, he is befriended by one George Spiggott (Cook) who turns out to be the Devil. He offers Stanley seven wishes in exchange for eternal damnation; Stanley agrees in the hope of attaining his waitress.

Cook's Devil is something of a sad character himself, reduced to petty evils such as scratching gramophone records and cutting off telephone calls. The irony of the story is that he is the only person who has ever shown any interest in Stanley, who grows to like him despite the less attractive side of his character – and despite the fact that he is able to spoil each of Stanley's wishes by finding a loophole. For example, when Stanley specifies a happy existence with his waitress in a cottage in the country, each in love with the other, children, and roses round the door, he finds that she is married to a saintly husband (played by the Devil) and that neither of them can indulge in adultery because they admire the husband too much.

Each of the wishes acts as a sketch in which Moore, Cook and Eleanor Bron as the waitress can indulge in a variety of characterizations.

The linking sections consist largely of scenes between the Devil and Stanley as their relationship deepens. Insisting on his more attractive modern name of Spiggott, he explains the history of his downfall to Stanley.

SPIGGOTT: It was Pride that got me into this. I used to be an Angel, you know, up in Heaven.

STANLEY: Oh yes, you used to be God's favourite, didn't you.

SPIGGOTT: That's right. 'I love Lucifer' it was in those days.

STANLEY: What was it like, up in Heaven?

SPIGGOTT: Very nice, really – we used to sit around all day, and adore Him. Believe me, He was adorable – just about the most adorable thing you ever did see.

STANLEY: Well what went wrong, then?

SPIGGOTT: I'll show you. Here we are – give me a leg up, would you?
(*He climbs onto a pillar-box*)

SPIGGOTT: Now then – I'm God. This is my throne, see. All around me are the cherubim, seraphim, continually crying 'Holy, Holy, Holy' – the Angels, Archangels, that sort of thing. Now, you be me, Lucifer, the loveliest Angel of them all.

STANLEY: What do I do?

SPIGGOTT: Well, sort of dance around praising me, mostly.

STANLEY: What sort of things do I say?

SPIGGOTT: Anything that comes into your head that's nice – how beautiful I am, how wise I am, how handsome – that sort of thing. Come on, start dancing.
(*Stanley starts tap-dancing and singing*)

STANLEY: You're wise, you're beautiful, you're handsome ...

SPIGGOTT: Thank you very much.

STANLEY: The Universe – what a wonderful idea, take my hat off to you.

SPIGGOTT: Thank you.

STANLEY: Trees – terrific! Water – another good one!

SPIGGOTT: That *was* a good one.

STANLEY: Yes – sex, top marks!

SPIGGOTT: Now, make it more personal, a bit more fulsome, please. Come on.

STANLEY: Immortal, invisible – you're handsome, you're – er – you're glorious, you're the most beautiful person in the world. Here – I'm getting a bit bored with this – can't we change places?

SPIGGOTT: That's exactly how I felt.

Spiggott also introduces Stanley to the Seven Deadly Sins, of which the most notable is Raquel Welch as 'Lust', bringing Stanley his breakfast in bed, and tantalizing him with hidden meanings in phrases such as 'buttered bun'.

The film works on the whole very well, although both Cook and Moore give rather subdued performances in places – in particular, Cook's performance as Spiggott is strangely flat. Cook says: 'I think we were acutely aware that film was costing money ... The film wouldn't have been made if Stanley Donen hadn't directed it. In fact, he turned down – I think it was *Hello Dolly*, for which he would have been paid more than the entire budget of *Bedazzled*. I'm extremely grateful to Stanley Donen for making the movie; but I think we were too overawed. I don't think we relaxed enough in performing and we did takes which we weren't satisfied with which were too "tight".'

One particularly felicitous idea in the film was lifted straight from a sketch in *Not Only ... But Also*. Stanley, having specified that he and his loved one should enjoy eternal love in quiet surroundings, and that she should have no men in her life, forgets to specify that they should be of opposite sexes, and finds that they are both nuns – to be precise, members of the Order of Leaping Berelians, who perform their devotions on a trampoline. The sight of nuns in full habit leaping up and down – and doing somersaults – on a trampoline is really extraordinarily funny. Cook was at first unhappy at the idea of reusing television material, but Donen pointed out that the shows had only been seen in Britain, and that the sketch would be new to the rest of the world. Cook: 'I was particularly pleased – I saw it in Rome, dubbed into Italian – it was fabulous in Italian, I had the most beautiful voice – it was the number three box-office film in Italy.'

Bedazzled: Cook and Moore

The film ends happily – the Devil, having reached his target number of souls, kindly returns Stanley's, and demands readmission to Heaven. He is rejected – for Pride – but on trying to retempt Stanley he finds that Stanley has learnt his lesson and is not interested in any more one-sided bargains.

Cook and Moore appeared in three hour-long programmes for ITV in August 1968, called *Goodbye Again*, which were intended to be saleable to the American market, and had an American guest every week as a consequence; but they were not entirely successful at recapturing the spirit of *Not Only . . . But Also*. They were unhappy with the hour-long format, and also had something of a personality clash with the director. Cook thinks that their scripts were not up to their usual standard. Certainly the sketches were for the most part less memorable than in *Not Only . . . But Also*, although there were several effective additions to the Dud and Pete saga, including this discussion, which takes place in a doctor's waiting room, about a lady fortune-teller of their acquaintance:

PETE: I went down there the other Friday for one of her combined Bingo and Black Magic sessions.

DUD: Down to her basement?

PETE: Yes, she has them down the basement. It's quite cosy. I went down there with a group of people, including Mr Prendergast, you know, just as curious human beings, just to see if there was anything in it. And sure enough, there was something in it.

DUD: What was that?

PETE: Mrs Woolley, sitting in the end of the basement, at the table. She had a tea-cosy, all over her head.

DUD: All over it?

PETE: Not *all* over it, just the eyes peeping out. Just down to here, you see. And in her left hand, she had a fish-fork. And in her right hand, she had a frozen fish-finger, for sacrificial purposes, you see – for summoning up the Devil. Normally she slits a cockerel's throat over an upturned tea-chest, and says 'Land of Hope and Glory' backwards; but she'd been out on the booze a bit the night before, and she was a bit short of cash, so she made do with a fish finger.

DUD: A sacrificial fish finger?

PETE: A sacrificial fish finger.

DUD: Say that six times quickly! (*He starts to*)

PETE: I'd rather you didn't, if you don't mind. Then suddenly, she switched off the light.

DUD: Click.

PETE: Very similar to the noise you just made then. And a strange chill come over the room, due in no small measure to the fact that she'd left the fridge door open when she was going for the fish finger. And the room was lit only by a guttering candle which flicked eerie shadows everywhere.

DUD: Gutter, gutter.

PETE: Gutter, gutter. And suddenly she began to moan and tremble, as if seized by an alien force.

DUD: More like Mr Prendergast – he gets a bit itchy at nine, doesn't he.

PETE: Well, she was sitting next to Mr P. And she moaned, and she trembled – and suddenly out of her mouth come a strange tongue.

DUD: Somebody else's tongue, Pete?

PETE: No, her own tongue come out, but she spoke in a strange ethereal mystic voice that was not her own. And suddenly she said –

NURSE   (*behind Dud*): The doctor will see you now.

DUD: That's uncanny! I didn't see your lips move!

PETE: Well, as in most of these cases, Dud, there is a rational explanation for that fact. The reason my lips didn't move was I wasn't speaking.

Between *Goodbye Again* and the third series of *Not Only . . . But Also* in 1970 Cook and Moore pursued their careers in films, both separately and together. Moore also continued to establish himself as a witty and elegant jazz pianist – his playing embellished all the television programmes, and he also composed the score for *Bedazzled*.

Cook appeared in the 1968 thriller *A Dandy in Aspic*, playing a straight part. He now thinks it was 'a mad decision – my agent at the time thought I should change my image. Stanley Donen was always saying that I should become the new Cary Grant – which I would have been delighted to do. I was supposed to become a straight actor. I don't think I was *that* embarrassing, but I was slightly embarrassed by it. The director, Anthony Mann, died three-quarters of the way through the movie . . . and luckily not many people saw it.'

Dudley Moore starred in the film *Thirty is a Dangerous Age, Cynthia*, written by himself, John Wells and Joe McGrath who also directed (or rather overdirected; his taste in jump cuts, wipes, and montages tended to swamp the already thin material).

Both Cook and Moore appeared in a French-Italian co-production, *Quei*

Temerari sulle loro Pazze, Scatenate, Scalcinate Carriole – known in America as *Those Daring Young Men in their Jaunty Jalopies* and, more tersely, in Britain as *Monte Carlo or Bust!* The film was directed by Ken Annakin, and was an ill-advised attempt to follow up the same director's *Those Magnificent Men in their Flying Machines*. The original was bad enough, but the sequel outdid it in sheer heavy-handedness.

Cook and Moore also appeared in Richard Lester's 1969 film *The Bed Sitting Room*, based on the bizarre play by Spike Milligan and John Antrobus. The film is set in a post-nuclear-war Britain; Cook and Moore are two police-men whose contribution to the scene of disaster consists largely of an injunction to 'keep moving'. The most bizarre event, however, took place off-screen. Cook and Moore had to go up in a balloon. Cook: 'It was very windy – we really shouldn't have gone up, but it was the last day at that particular location. There was a balloon expert with us, crouched; and when we got up there, he said, "*I* wouldn't go up on a day like this." I said, "You *are* up on a day like this, what do you mean?" He said, "Well, it's just for Mr Lester, but I wouldn't normally go up – we're at the mercy of the winds." Whereupon we fell violently to the ground and I had to have my cartilage out. I was planning a four-week holiday – I spent it in hospital.'

The last of this batch of films, all made within a two-year period, was *The Rise and Rise of Michael Rimmer*, originally written by Graham Chapman (who was taking a rest from medicine after passing his exams) and John Cleese. They had been asked to write it by David Frost, but the script gathered dust on his shelf for about two years before Cook saw it and expressed an interest. The script was rewritten by Cook, Kevin Billington, Cleese and Chapman, and the film was directed by Kevin Billington.

The film tells the story of Michael Rimmer, an unscrupulous business efficiency expert who works his way into Parliament and manages to become prime minister (by quietly assassinating the existing one). He proceeds to submit every parliamentary decision to a referendum, to the point where the public get so fed up with them that a referendum on whether there should be any more referenda is greeted with an overwhelming 'no' vote. Rimmer is consequently installed as a democratically elected dictator, and the film ends with the only two decent characters killing each other in independent attempts to assassinate Rimmer.

Cook remembers: 'David Frost was the executive producer. He got quite paranoid in that he thought that we were exactly mirroring his career – which to an extent we were, some of the character was based on David. The ultimate irony was that the set designer, who had never seen David's living room, and which we'd never talked about to her, produced an almost exact replica of David's room.'

The film was not successful, partly due to Billington's directing it in too pretty a style, and partly because the satirical element was rather smothered in an atmosphere which was more farce-like than was suitable to the subject.

Early in 1971 Cook returned to television, and involved himself in a total, unmitigated and fascinating disaster called *Where Do I Sit?*. This arose because the BBC asked him to chair a chat show on BBC-2. He was uncertain of his ability to handle such a show, and asked if he could do a pilot. The BBC, with a touching and totally misplaced confidence in his abilities in that area, were quite happy to go straight ahead with a series of thirteen, although they were slightly worried by Cook's insistence on doing the shows 'live'. Cook: 'I said, the whole thing is, there's so little live television, people will enjoy disasters if they happen. And sure enough, disasters did happen. I found out on the first programme that I was no good at talking to people on television.'

The chat sections were alternated with sketches, something which further reduced Cook's ability to concentrate on the guests. He found that he couldn't think of anything to ask them, much less cope with the tricky art of running a chat show, which involves not only talking intelligently to the guests but thinking ahead to the next question and trying to keep some sort of structure to the show. Once he telephoned a viewer who had rung in to object to the previous week's show. Since the call was placed 'on camera' during the course of the transmission and without preparation, this involved a wait while the viewer was fetched from another room (where he was sensibly watching the other channel) in order to have a rather meaningless conversation with Cook. Cook also asked the audience whether they objected to an improvised sketch he had done with Spike Milligan, in which Cook, playing God, claimed (among other things) that the Universe fell off the back of a lorry. When one member of the audience did object, Cook was a little rough with him – not intentionally, but it is hardly fair to ask someone in a television studio audience to stand up to an experienced performer.[27]

The shows got really dreadful reviews in the papers, but good viewing figures, which tended to confirm Cook's feeling that people enjoy seeing disasters on television. He would have liked to go on with the series, but the BBC got a severe attack of cold feet and cancelled the series after three shows.

In the summer of 1971 Cook and Moore went to Australia (where it was of course winter) to do two television programmes for the Australian Broadcasting Commission; these were shown in Britain under the title *Pete and Dud Down Under*. The shows were on the whole a trifle confused, although some of the items were quite good – they included the 'Colonel Bogey' send-up and 'One Leg Too Few' from *Beyond the Fringe*. One sketch involved Pete and Dud with some genuine Australian cricketers; Sir Arthur Streeb-Greebling explained his plans for domesticating the funnel-web spider; and 'Bollards' reappeared in an expanded version.

They also compiled a new stage show, called *Behind the Fridge*, which ran successfully in Australia, and then opened in London in October 1972. Cook: 'We did it rather lazily in the West End – we didn't work hard enough at it. When we took it to the States we had Alexander Cohen producing, and he made us work. It was a much, much better show on Broadway.'

The show contained a number of quite good sketches, including one odd and very 'black' one about a passenger in a minicab who thinks that he is trapped with a homicidal driver.

COOK	(*opening door*): All right, sir – get out!
MOORE:	For God's sake, man – be reasonable!
COOK:	I've got a job to do, sir.
MOORE:	For God's sake, don't do anything rash!
COOK:	This is it, sir.
MOORE	(*grovelling*): No, listen – look, I'm a rich man! Take my money, for God's sake, anything –
COOK:	Just two pounds, sir.

MOORE:	Please, don't do it! Take the whole lot!
COOK:	We're here, sir. At the House of Lords.
	(*Big Ben is heard chiming*)
MOORE:	So we are ...
COOK:	Your final destination.
MOORE	(*calming down*): I'm awfully sorry – I slipped out of the car. My legs aren't what they used to be at all.
COOK:	Accidents can happen to anyone, can't they, sir.
MOORE:	Oh now, listen – I know this sounds pretty stupid, but I thought for one moment you were going to ... shoot me!
COOK:	Shoot you, sir? Shoot *you*? Why, the idea never crossed my mind! I mean, you're not famous enough, are you. Page two, column three – who needs that? It's the front page we're after, isn't it, sir.
MOORE:	Yes, of course – I hadn't thought of it that ...
COOK:	Cheerio, sir. Good luck! Pip, pip!
	(*Gets into the car and drives off: speaks into radio*)
COOK:	Four five.
RADIO VOICE:	Four five.
COOK:	Proceeding torso job.[28]

The sketch created a distinctly uneasy atmosphere, quite unlike most of their earlier work, but other sketches in the show were more in their usual style, including another Dud and Pete dialogue.

The show went to America under the title *Good Evening*, opening in Boston on 12 October 1973 on its way to New York, where it ran from 29 October 1973 to 30 November 1974. It was much more successful than it had been in London, getting good reviews both on Broadway and on the subsequent tour, which started in Washington in February 1975 and ended in Los Angeles in August.

In 1978 Cook and Moore starred in a film version of *The Hound of the Baskervilles*, directed by Paul Morrisey, the protégé of Andy Warhol. Cook: 'It was one of those ideas – let's combine Peter Cook and Dudley Moore with "far-out" Paul Morrisey and see what happens. What happened was a mess, with some funny moments. Asking Paul Morrisey to direct English comedy – which he loves – is like asking me to direct an improvised movie about junkies in L.A. Not compatible at all. The script is a very bad compromise between Dudley, myself and Paul. At the last minute, Paul thought of the idea that throughout all our sketches runs the common theme that I am the informed idiot and Dudley is the uninformed idiot. We transferred our sketches to Holmes and Watson, and they played very well, but none of them remain in the film, except for the perennial "One Leg Too Few". Paul edited one version of the film which we showed to an audience; I thought it was very bad. Dudley and I edited the version which is now out, which I regard as marginally better, but there's still no making it any good.'

Another departure in Cook and Moore's style is the development of their characters Derek and Clive. These dialogues started as privately recorded tapes, which 'escaped' and multiplied as such tapes have a habit of doing. Three years after the originals had been made, by which time there were many pirated copies around, Cook and Moore issued them on a long-playing record. The reason for their initial reluctance was that the sketches depended on the

117

use of language and choice of subject matter which rendered them quite unsuitable for broadcasting or general distribution. Derek and Clive have been described as 'Pete and Dud on "speed"'; in fact they are really more punk versions of the original characters. Inevitably the tapes had a wide underground circulation because of their use of bad language; but once the initial shock value has worn off they are less funny than one could have hoped from such a source.

There have been several more Derek and Clive records issued since, the most recent at the time of writing being *Derek and Clive – Ad Nauseam*. Obviously, this sort of humour can only be done on gramophone records; as Cook points out, anyone who buys a gramophone record which is supplied complete with a bag to be sick into cannot complain that they were not warned.

The extension of comedy into previously unacceptable and sometimes distasteful areas is a perfectly laudable ambition; but unfortunately Cook and Moore have fallen into the trap of assuming that these areas are funny in themselves. In fact, the use of such subjects needs to be counterbalanced by comedy of an even higher standard than usual.

To be fair to Cook and Moore, they make no claims for their Derek and Clive material, nor do they insist on its acceptance. Quite simply, they find it funny, and invite anyone who cares to eavesdrop on them to take it or leave it. In the last item on the record they play a couple of stuffy critics who disapprove of the language used in the sketches – and indeed demonstrate it at some length in a manner which for once is quite funny.

Both Cook and Moore have taken on something of a rôle as broadcasting 'personalities'. Moore, besides continuing as a jazz pianist and writing some film music – he also occasionally makes dark threats to write a symphony – briefly assisted Jonathan Miller in the television series *The Body in Question* and helped narrate a television documentary about the nature of Time. Cook has shown his ability at quick improvisation in *The News Quiz* on radio, and also in a programme called *Why Vote, It Only Encourages Them*, the second half of which, broadcast once the polls had closed, brought a welcome touch of levity to the 1979 general election.

Moore has also been striking out on his own in the field of cinema comedy, and establishing himself as a star in America with his performance in Blake (*Pink Panther*) Edwards's film *10*. Cook appeared in the 1979 Amnesty Gala, *The Secret Policeman's Ball*, and showed that he had lost nothing of his skill in his savage parody of the judge's summing up in the recent trial of Jeremy Thorpe for conspiracy to murder. Cook's version of the summing-up overtly instructs the jury to find the defendant not guilty, and describes one key prosecution witness as 'A piece of ordure – a piece of excrement – unable to carry out a simple murder plot without cocking the whole thing up'.

From his pre-*Beyond the Fringe* days to much of his later work, Cook has shown himself a superbly imaginative comedian – a master of lunatic lines of reasoning which burgeon into a jungle of illogical fantasy. Moore, when teamed with Cook, tends to view these jungles from a low eye-level which reduces him to immediate bewilderment; and so the idiot who knows nothing and the idiot who knows everything have established themselves as a richly comic team.

Peter Cook and Dudley Moore

7.
'I'm Sorry, I'll Read That Again'

When *Cambridge Circus* finished its run in Greenwich Village, New York, at the end of 1964, the cast went their separate ways for a time. Humphrey Barclay and David Hatch went back to jobs at the BBC, and Bill Oddie and Tim Brooke-Taylor went round America with the touring version of *TW3*. Graham Chapman went back to his medical training for a time, while Jo Kendall pursued her acting career.

John Cleese stayed in America, and auditioned successfully for the Broadway version of the musical show *Half a Sixpence*, which starred Tommy Steele. Cleese still finds it amusing to think that he was able to get into the show, in view of the non-existence of his dancing and singing abilities: 'It is very funny to think that Mr Hickley, who used to teach at my prep. school, would not allow me to do singing classes – partly because I was subversive, but mainly on sheer lack of talent. I'm sure I was the only man he ever taught who ever finished up singing in a Broadway musical!'

When he got tired of *Half a Sixpence*, he joined the magazine *Newsweek* for a short time: 'But I failed to write what they wanted – the guy that I'd met from the magazine, who was my mentor, went off somewhere and was therefore unable to ment me, and I was rather lost.'

He then joined the cast of the touring version of *The Establishment*, which was still in the States, and went with it to Chicago and Washington. This took him through to Christmas 1965, when he returned to England.

Tim Brooke-Taylor, meanwhile, had returned to England and, after working as editor and writer for a Spike Milligan series on ATV, appeared for three months in *On the Braden Beat* in the slot recently vacated by Peter Cook's E. L. Wisty. Brooke-Taylor appeared as a bowler-hatted city gent. He says the character was 'amazingly right-wing. It was great fun – I used to take something that had happened in the week and be *really* prejudiced about it. It was a bit frightening – I did one about colour prejudice, being amazingly prejudiced, but thinking I was a liberal – that was the idea of the character – and then I went into a pub and found people talking about it and my attitude, and saying, "Yes, quite right, wasn't he?" I suddenly realized they'd taken it straight – that really did frighten me.' This of course is exactly what happened to Johnny Speight's series *Till Death Us Do Part*; the main character, Alf Garnett, intended as a satire upon bigotry, came to be taken by some sections of the population as a spokesman.

Humphrey Barclay, by now back in his post as a BBC Light Entertainment Radio producer, was casting around to see whether he could compile a revue format programme to carry on from where the preparatory three programmes

of *I'm Sorry I'll Read That Again* left off. He says: 'I blush to think of it now – it was going to be called *Get Off My Foot*.' However, the original title was retained, as were many of the original cast. Tony Buffery was no longer available, and Cleese was still in the States – he joined the cast for the second series – so the cast consisted of Brooke-Taylor, Oddie, Jo Kendall and David Hatch, who by now was also a Light Entertainment producer.

In place of Graham Chapman, Barclay hired Graeme Garden, who like Chapman was studying medicine. Garden was born on 18 February 1943, and so was a year behind Cleese and Brooke-Taylor at Cambridge; when Brooke-Taylor left Cambridge and the Footlights Club in 1963 he handed the presidency on to Garden.

Although he had taken part in one or two dramatic activities at school, Garden was really more interested in art – like Barclay, he has a neat touch with a pencil – and it was only when he went to Cambridge in 1961 that he started to take more interest in drama. He joined CULES – 'the Cambridge University Light Entertainment Society; not to be confused with the Cambridge University National Trust Society which I remember had a short-lived existence.' The standards of CULES were less demanding than those of the Footlights Club (although many members of the Footlights were also in CULES) and Garden derived a good deal of enjoyment from their shows – in particular touring the West Country during the long vacation and giving free shows to hospitals, orphanages and prisons. In his second year he was encouraged to join the Footlights Club: 'I'd seen the Footlights shows, and I'd thought "I'm not going to take them on at their own game" so I did something that nobody else was doing, which was a quick-sketch act. That got me into the Footlights.'

Once in, he started getting more and more interested in the sort of material that they were doing – witty sketches and songs. 'I suppose the people you meet and like and get to know influence you as much as what you would like to do yourself. I would have imagined that I would have got more involved in art societies, and drawing and painting; but at the time I didn't care for the odd one or two people I met who were involved in that sort of thing.'

He auditioned for the 1963 Footlights Revue (which became *Cambridge Circus*) but failed to get into the cast. He left Cambridge in 1964, and it was while he was in the first of his three years at medical school that Humphrey Barclay invited him to participate in *I'm Sorry I'll Read That Again*.

ISIRTA, as it will be more convenient to call it, has become something of a legend. Its inventiveness and exuberance – and its delight in really awful old jokes for their own sake – has made it one of the most popular radio shows in the public memory. It had a long run – ten years altogether if one counts the original broadcast of *Cambridge Circus* – with eight series, plus the short preparatory one and the 'specials', making a grand total of 103 shows.

The first series proper began recording on 28 May 1965, and began transmissions on 4 October. John Cleese was back from America in time to join the cast for the second series, which began transmissions on 14 March 1966. Graeme Garden was granted leave of absence from the third series, which ran from 3 October 1966, because he was on a midwifery course in Plymouth at the time. However, he managed to deliver scripts for the show in between delivering babies.

After this the casting settled down to Brooke-Taylor, Cleese, Garden, Hatch, Kendall and Oddie; and the show ran to seven series, with an eighth series in 1973 after a break of three years.[29]

The earlier series were written by a wide variety of people – apart from the cast, names such as John Esmonde and Bob Larby (who later wrote *The Good Life*) or Brian Cooke and Johnny Mortimer (who later wrote *Man About The House* and *Father Dear Father*). As with the preparatory series, the shows were in a straightforward revue format, with little or no continuity. Many of the sketches were very well written and performed; and a new departure was that some of the characters became 'regulars'. Two such characters were John and Mary, from the Malaya sketch in *Cambridge Circus*, still played by Cleese and Kendall. In this appearance in the twelfth show of the second series, their relationship is still in a state of permanent disintegration.

JOHN: Ah, how I love to be alone in the country.

MARY: John?

JOHN: Yes?

MARY: *I'm* with you.

JOHN: How I love to be alone in the country.

MARY: But John – *you* brought me with you!

JOHN: I didn't. You hid in the back.

MARY: But you must have noticed.

JOHN: Not at all – it's a very large tandem.

MARY: But John – when we fell off going down the stairs – you *must* have seen me.

JOHN: I thought you were a hitch-hiker.

MARY: But I'm your wife. You must have recognized me.

JOHN: I didn't, Mary.

MARY: Why not?

JOHN: Well, because you were disguised as a cactus.

MARY: Oh, John – why don't you admit it? You don't love me any more. (*pause*)

JOHN: All right, I admit it.

MARY: John – once we had something that was pure, and wonderful, and – and good ... what's happened to it?

JOHN: You spent it all.

That extract was from a sketch written by John Cleese; by the following series, the combination of Cleese and Oddie had followed John and Mary further into their strange – and by now distinctly surrealistic – existence. In this example, drawn from the third show of the third series, their pillow talk is still conducted with the same tension of suppressed emotion that Barclay had taught them in the original sketch.

MARY: Goodnight, darling.

JOHN: Goodnight.
    (*effects of bed creaking and bedsprings twanging*)

MARY: John – how much longer is this going to go on? This lying awake at night, tossing and turning, talking and arguing, never knowing what you're thinking – what's on your mind, John? Why can't you sleep? Why can't you rest? Oh John – where's the sleep that knits up the ravelled sleeve of care? Oh John – if there's anything I can do or say that'll help you rest a little – John? – *wake up*!

JOHN: What is it – what is it?

MARY: Oh, John – can't you see what I'm doing to you? . . . Why are you laughing?

JOHN: I always laugh when you do that to me.

MARY: Oh John – talk to me!

JOHN: I'm sorry, I've got things on my mind – I'm tired – I'm worried about the chickweed – it was thoughtless of me, I know, but God knows I haven't had much sleep skinning that bison last night . . .

MARY: Which bison – not George?

JOHN: No, Henry.

MARY: So Henry's dead.

JOHN: Yes.

MARY: I can't say I'm sorry, he was mean, even for a bison.

JOHN: I'm going to sleep.

MARY: John – talk to me – say something to me – say you hate me, say I'm ugly . . .

JOHN: Which?

MARY: Say I'm ugly.

JOHN: You're ugly.

MARY: You're only saying that – you don't really mean it! You don't care – you never think about me – up and down all night, warming the milk, mashing the rusks, all the crying and the bedwetting –

JOHN: Yes, I know . . .

MARY: I wouldn't mind if we had a baby.

JOHN: I'm sorry, but I prefer bisons – good night.

MARY: John – what's happening to us?

JOHN: I know you know.

MARY: You know?

JOHN: Yes.

MARY: Oh God. John –

JOHN: Yes?

MARY: What do you know?

JOHN: Well, I could be wrong.

MARY: You mean about me and Nigel?

JOHN: Oh, I *was* wrong! I thought it was Rupert.

MARY: You're right – it is Rupert – I can never remember names.

JOHN: Anyway, I do know about last Friday.

MARY: Last Friday?

JOHN: Yes – he was in my bed, wasn't he.

MARY: How did you know?

JOHN: He kept pushing me out.

MARY: You mean you were there too?

JOHN: You didn't even notice? Oh, God!

MARY: Well, you've been having your little bit of fun, too. I noticed the lipstick on your cheek, and I suppose it was you who took my mascara.

JOHN: I was playing circuses.

MARY: All right – but I've something else to say – I don't want Mother in the front room any longer.

JOHN:	But, Mary –
MARY:	It's no good – you've got to bury her.
JOHN:	But she's still useful – she still feeds the dogs.
MARY:	No, no – they haven't touched her for weeks.
JOHN:	But, Mary – can't you see ...
MARY:	She's not *my* mother.
JOHN:	Well, she's not *my* mother.
MARY:	Oh!
JOHN:	Mary?
MARY:	Yes?
JOHN:	What's your second name?
MARY:	Cleethorpes.
JOHN:	Oh, I'm terribly sorry, I seem to have made some sort of silly mistake – I'm awfully sorry about this ...

Humphrey Barclay produced the first four series, before defecting to Independent Television. It is not usual for the name of a comedy programme's producer to be familiar to the general public, but because the credits at the end were always presented in joke form – for example, 'The show was produced by Humphrey Barclay, who was produced by Mrs Barclay' – Barclay found that his name was recognized in shops; and indeed he is still remembered in connection with the programme.

The policy of keeping the jokes going extended not only to the credits but also to the music. Up to that time most comedy shows had 'straight' musical items as a relief from the jokes. Because they had Bill Oddie in the cast, they were able to make the songs funny as well. Oddie's contribution to the shows is considerable; he has discovered the secret of writing parody songs, which is that the parodies should be good songs in their own right. As a consequence, the songs are still fun to listen to even when the style they lampoon is only a dim memory. Altogether in the eight series there are over a hundred and forty songs – no mean achievement. Among them are the policeman's song, 'My Identikit Girl'; the music-hall comedian's song, 'No, No, But Seriously Though'; the catchy, 'Here Comes The One-Man Band'; the street directions song, 'Marcella's Lane' in which several different sets of route instructions are sung in polyphony; and many more. Oddie: 'A great compliment goes to Dave Lee and Leon Cohen, who used to run the orchestral side, because we didn't get much rehearsal – and the sound-effects people, because we often did things which were like Spike Jones, and we had to do them live, no pre-recording.'

Not quite all the music is by Oddie. John Cleese sings the 'Ballad of Oliver Cromwell' to music by Chopin, and presents the melody 'Rose of England' with a set of new words bemoaning the plight of someone with a ferret up his nose. These two items demonstrate just exactly why Cleese was not allowed to sing at school.

Gradually the number of contributors to the show reduced. In the early stages Barclay had to compile the scripts from the various items submitted, and the first rehearsal would consist largely of an editing session as much of the material was rewritten by dissatisfied customers. After a while it was found much easier for the writing to devolve largely on Oddie and Garden, although as late as the fourth series other members of the cast were still contributing items. David Hatch wrote a series of sketches in the second, third and fourth series, which present the conversations between three babies left in their prams outside a supermarket.

The babies don't always have the same names, nor is the casting consistent. In the ninth show of the fourth series (broadcast on 18 June 1967), Hugh is John Cleese, Rupert is David Hatch, and Cyril is Tim Brooke-Taylor. Cyril's Mum, normally played by Jo Kendall, is Jean Hart on this occasion.

RUPERT:	Morning, Cyril – what's the trouble?
CYRIL:	Just bewailing my lost youth.
RUPERT:	But you're only one.
CYRIL:	Yes – but in forty-nine years I shall be fifty. Imagine – I'm nearly fifty! Then it's but a step 'till I'm a hundred and three. And then I won't be able to walk.
RUPERT:	Well, you can't walk now!
CYRIL:	Yes, but when I'm old I won't even be able to crawl along the mantelpiece and be sick in the clock.
RUPERT:	I don't see why not – my grandfather does.
HUGH:	Oh, go on – cheer up – would you like some milk from my bottle?
CYRIL:	No thanks – I'm trying to give it up. I've got three chins already. How ever many will I have when I'm fifty?
HUGH:	You shouldn't eat so much.
CYRIL:	It's my only vice. I don't smoke – I don't drink – and I can't.
RUPERT:	Here comes your old bag again, Cyril.
CYRIL:	Let's give her Test Three.
ALL THREE:	Moo, moo, moo!
CYRIL'S MUM:	Well, what's the game, children – can you see a moo-cow, den?
CYRIL:	She is so *stupid*!

Gradually the shows developed more of an identity than the pure revue format of the earliest ones. In the third series there was even a serial, 'The Curse of the Flying Wombat', co-written by Oddie and Garden (whose inter-natal contributions tended to come up from Plymouth on the backs of envelopes). It had some sort of a plot, but was principally notable for introducing Tim Brooke-Taylor's Lady Constance de Coverlet, a highly exaggerated version of his Edith Evans impression from *Cambridge Circus*. By the end of the series, Lady Constance had become a favourite; grossly over-sized, over-sexed, over-acted, and greeted with a tremendous ovation.

In fact, by the fifth series (which started on 14 April 1963), the audience were giving tremendous ovations – and cheers, groans and boos – to almost anything. Cleese, for one, found this rather disconcerting. 'Suddenly the audience changed – it started getting like playing at the cup final. Instead of having a nice audience that laughed, suddenly there was a football crowd atmosphere. We suddenly realized that something was catching on. To be perfectly honest, I didn't care much for what was catching on. I found all the groaning and the shouts from the audience was on the whole not the sort of humour I cared much for.'

Oddie: 'It's wonderful to think the audience was so carried away that they would turn up every week in vast numbers, but at the same time there was unquestionably a period when they did take over. To a certain extent we encouraged the booing and hissing of really bad jokes, but then they would do that to what was a good joke – they really just wanted the catch-phrases and the dirty bits. And they became over-conscious of their actual rôle – they were looking for times for them to get in; the audience wanted to be the star of the show. We all felt like telling them to shut up and go home at times.'

Cleese used to do just that sometimes; he also tended to dislike some of the more obvious humour. Garden: 'The way he used to despise the scripts and the audience added a new dimension to his character. He used to stand there and scream "easy!" at them every time we got a belly laugh.' Cleese really prefers to avoid puns and very broad humour, and so was not always happy with the quality of the scripts. He says: 'I remember once or twice criticizing the script, and I realized that this obviously didn't make me very popular – so though I doubtless made my odd sarky remark, which is in my nature, I don't know that I criticized the shows that much thereafter. If I was given something that I *really* didn't like, I *did* change it, because I wasn't going to "die" in front of an audience if I could help it. Getting up in front of an audience, trying to be funny and "dying" is the most excruciatingly embarrassing experience, and it's one I'm prepared to make myself quite awkward in order to avoid!'

The writers traded on Cleese's personality. Oddie: 'There were elements about him which were endearingly arrogant . . . Like, eventually he refused to come into rehearsal. He had it written into his contract that he didn't have to come to rehearsal.' In fact, Cleese was getting a bit irritated with the amount of time spent sitting about while the musicians rehearsed; he had married the American actress Connie Booth shortly before, and was a little reluctant to be away from home for the entire day every Sunday. In the end the rehearsal time was shortened, without any detriment to the show. Obviously, Cleese's slightly abrasive attitude was a gift to the writers; the version of *Othello* in the eleventh show of the fourth series is one of many occasions on which Cleese is given a scripted opportunity to harangue the audience.

CLEESE: Oh, Iago, you're a brick!
B-TAYLOR: No, I'm just a little stoned, that's all.
    (*the audience groans*)
CLEESE: Look – now look, if you don't think that's funny, how about this one?
ODDIE: I say, I say, I say – 'I sent thee sixpence for thy leman. Hadst it?'
B-TAYLOR: 'I did impeticos thy gratility; for Malvolio's nose is no whipstock. My lady has a white hand, and the Myrmidons are no bottle-ale houses.'
ODDIE }
B-TAYLOR } Oi!
CLEESE: Yes – that's *real* Shakespeare. *Twelfth Night*, actually. So just you be thankful for *our* jokes, or else we shall do *all* the Shakespearean comedies, one by one, very slowly, *twice*. Right – carry on.
BAND: LINK
HATCH: So, next afternoon, Cassio went to it, to woo Desdemona.
B-TAYLOR (*pansy voice*): Ooh, tu-whit, tu-whoo, Desdemona.

At the end of the fourth series the production was taken over by David Hatch. Since he was actually performing, and therefore unable to hear the finished product until afterwards, he always had an assistant producer to keep an ear on things in the control cubicle. At first this was Peter Titheradge, then later on various junior producers helped out.

The sixth series saw the return of the idea of a serial running throughout the series. This time it was 'Professor Prune and the Electric Time Trousers', which had a more than passing resemblance to BBC Television's long-running science fiction series *Doctor Who*. The choice of name for the lead character arose from the theory that the typical *ISIRTA* listener would be a dimwit called Angus Prune – and indeed the lively signature tune had collected some words which led to it being called the 'Angus Prune Tune'.

In the first episode (broadcast 12 January 1969), the various parts were handed out to the cast. Nothing was left for Brooke-Taylor but the ignominious part of Spot, the dog, whose sole contribution to the dialogue was an occasional 'woof'. The audience immediately started going 'aah' whenever Spot appeared, and within a short time any mention of Spot would get a huge cheer. This had not been intended by the writers, but it was too good an opportunity to throw away. In the fourth episode Cleese (in character, not in reality) finally erupts.

HATCH: Well now, we're certainly in a tight spot.
B-TAYLOR: Woof!
(*cheers from the audience*)
KENDALL: Uncle – what's that noise?
GARDEN: Oh, just Spot getting another cheap round of applause.
(*'Oh' from the audience*)
CLEESE: All right, that does it – I'm fed up with Brooke-Taylor getting applause for going 'woof'. We have to work for it, you know – I spent years learning how to act. I don't just get up in front of a microphone and go 'baa' or 'eek'.
HATCH: John – you mustn't resent it. After all, you've got a nice big motor-car, and a flat in fashionable Knightsbridge, and six kittens, and a stuffed leather rhino – I mean, all Timothy's got is his 'woof'. You don't begrudge him that, do you?
CLEESE: Yes.
(*The audience go 'ahhh'*)
HATCH: Well, what more do you want?
CLEESE: I want to go 'woof'.
B-TAYLOR: All right – you can have it – I crave not the acclaim of the masses (*the band plays 'Land of Hope and Glory'*) – the sound of raucous applause means nothing to me – after all, I am at heart an Actor. To Be Or Not To Be ...
(*everybody else yawns*)
B-TAYLOR: That Is The Question; Whether Tis Nobler In The Mind To Suffer The Slings And Arrows Of Outrageous Fortune, Or To Take Arms Against A Sea Of Troubles, And By Opposing – *WOOF*!
(*Tremendous cheers and applause from the audience*)

In the end, Spot became something of a monster as far as the cast were concerned – a fact reflected in the ever more disastrous fates he meets in the later episodes. In a later series, Brooke-Taylor introduced a news item by saying 'Sport' – and even that got a round of applause.

Despite Cleese's dislike of puns, they became a regular feature of the show. For some reason, fish seem to provide a particularly good subject, and in many shows the plot of the serial is held up while the cast indulge themselves with Fish and Quips. This example comes from the same episode as the excerpt above, and was perpetrated by Bill Oddie.

HATCH: All around them were all manner of sea creatures, and they sat watching them on a coral reef.
            (*Several voices sing 'God Rest You Merry, Gentlemen'*)
GARDEN: Oh, coral singers.
HATCH: And one by one they named the fish they saw.
CLEESE: There now follows an attempt on the world Fish Joke record. Are you ready? On your marks . . . Set . . .
FX: SHOT
GARDEN: Look – a fish playing a guitar.
B-TAYLOR: Julian Bream.
KENDALL: And on drums:
GARDEN: Max Roach.
KENDALL: And one on Bass fiddle.
HATCH: And they're playing 'Salmon'.
CLEESE: 'Salmon'?
HATCH: 'Salmon-chanted evening'.
B-TAYLOR: Or it could be 'I Met Her In Manta-Ray'.
KENDALL: And there's a little sole.
GARDEN: Oh yeah, Baby.
CLEESE: I didn't ketch that.
GARDEN: You must need a herring aid.
CLEESE: Don't shout – you'll give me a head-hake.
KENDALL: Don't carp.
CLEESE: Here comes the oyster parade.
B-TAYLOR: Ah, happy dace are here again.
KENDALL: And what are those scruffy little boys?
CLEESE: Sea-urchins.
HATCH: What were those?
KENDALL: Smelt.
HATCH: They still do.
KENDALL: And there's one that looks like Julie Andrews.
CLEESE: A star-fish.
B-TAYLOR: And another carrying today's newspaper.
GARDEN: Topical fish.
B-TAYLOR: That was a sharking one.
KENDALL: Don't be shellfish.
CLEESE: You're losing your sense of porpoise.
B-TAYLOR: I feel eel.
HATCH: Don't flounder.
CLEESE: Then whelk-ome to a sardine end.
BAND: CHORD.

Because David Hatch was producing as well as performing, it was an obvious move for the writers to capitalize on the fact by building him up as an announcer/producer who was vainly trying to control the cast. This was part of an increasing tendency for the cast to play themselves, so that any 'dramatic performances' were not presented simply as a single-level interpretation, but on two levels – that characters in sketches and serials were played by the exaggerated versions of the genuine personalities of the performers. In the case of Hatch, Oddie kept on making him extend his range simply because Hatch was modest about his abilities. The illusion that Hatch was unable to control his colleagues was only based on reality to the extent that he had to make sure that the whole thing didn't become *too* wild; but in many of the shows he is presented as failing to keep much order – despite help from Cleese.

In his script for the opening of the eleventh show of the seventh series (broadcast 26 April 1970), Bill Oddie demonstrates, quite independently, a theory which Spike Milligan had also evolved some nineteen years earlier in *The Goon Show* – that an audience will laugh at anything, no matter how meaningless, if it is only repeated often enough. The cast sets out to do this with the word 'teapot' – and having driven themselves, rather than the audience, into a state of giggles over it, attempt to proceed with the show.

HATCH: Yes, welcome to the eleventh week of Full Frontal Radio, and right away . . .

GARDEN: 'ere, 'ere – this'll make you laugh –

HATCH: Don't interrupt.

GARDEN: No, listen to this – my wife – my wife has gone to the West Indies.

HATCH   (*resignedly*): Jamaica?

GARDEN: No, she went of her own . . .

HATCH: That's not funny.

GARDEN: Teapot!

HATCH   (*laughs hysterically*): Now, that *is* funny! Anyway, anyway, as I was saying . . .

ODDIE: My wife, my wife, my wife . . . my wife, she's so fat . . .

HATCH: Not again –

ODDIE: No, it's good this – my wife, she's so fat, when she walks down the street, she looks like three dogs, fighting in a . . .

HATCH: Teapot? (*general hilarity*) . . . Look, that's quite enough now, quite enough now . . .

B-TAYLOR: My wife . . .

HATCH: Now, stop it.

B-TAYLOR: My wife –

HATCH: Now push off, you silly old . . . teapot!
(*Hatch, Brooke-Taylor, Oddie & Garden laugh helplessly*)

KENDALL: Oh dear, I do most sincerely apologize – whilst those buffoons are getting over their silly fixation with teapots (*more laughter*) – it's not funny!

GARDEN: What isn't?

KENDALL: Teapot. (*Breaks down giggling*)

CLEESE: Now, that is quite enough. That word is banned from now on.

THE OTHERS: What word?

CLEESE: I'm not saying it – you'll only start giggling if I do.

THE OTHERS: Say what?

CLEESE: Say it. . . . No . . . Nobody's to say it . . . it's forbidden. Nobody must use the word teapo . . . po . . . po . . . (that was close) – you must not use that word except in very desperate circumstances, as in the case when the audience hasn't laughed at one of your jokes, right? Now no more giggling.

THE OTHERS: No, all right.

CLEESE: Good. So now, on with the teapots. Oh! Show! Oh, blast the teapots.

The circumstance which Cleese had foreseen arises at the end of the show. Frantically the cast man the emergency life-jokes ('That was no lady', etc.), to no avail.

KENDALL: They're not working! Abandon script!

GARDEN: There's one last chance. Get on the radio and broadcast the International Distress Call To Summon Appreciation When All Else Fails!

HATCH: Teapot! Teapot! Teapot!

THE AUDIENCE (*in unison*): Ha, Bloody Ha!

Hatch inevitably found himself, as had Barclay, having to say 'no' to some jokes which were a trifle too broad to be broadcast; but there were also periodic objections from higher up the hierarchy to the use of certain words and expressions. Some of these were very odd; the American slang expression 'cow-poke' for cowboy has been around for a long time, but apparently it suddenly conjured up a rather graphic picture in some official's mind . . . On the other hand, in the same series that 'cow-poke' was censored there was a character called Martha Farquar, to whose name no objections were raised at all.

Garden denies deliberately trying to push doubtful material through: 'I don't find shocking people, in itself, admirable – for a start it's very easy. I don't find that pushing the boundaries back is particularly worth while. But, if achieving your effect – whatever that effect may be – involves pushing the boundaries back, then you have to look fairly closely at the boundaries and decide if you really believe that it's worth it.'

Oddie: 'Radio comedy has almost *always* been filthy – I mean, *Round The Horne* was non-stop, and ours was pretty bad sometimes – but the people who are responsible for censoring it don't always understand the clever bits, so you put in something really obvious; they cross that out, and miss the next one, which is a little bit subtler. But by and large we didn't have a fantastic amount of trouble with censorship, and it got easier as the years went by. I think we were very well protected by our producers.'

The seventh series was the last to follow closely on the preceding ones – there was a three-year gap before the eighth and last series – and by this time the cast were fully confident of their material and characterizations, and had also learnt to control the audience. Each of them had developed a strong radio personality, quite apart from the impersonations – Garden does an excellent Walter Gabriel and a devastating Eddie Waring[30] – and the regular characters such as Oddie's elderly servant Grimbling and of course Brooke-Taylor's increasingly grotesque Lady Constance. The scripts were never claimed to be intellectual, but extracted a good deal of lively fun out of the ridiculing of idiomatic English and the pursuit of excessive literal-mindedness. The series has a stronger identity of its own than the others because of the introduction of an idea which acted as a linking device – that the programmes were in fact being broadcast by a pirate station, called, inevitably, Radio Prune.

ISIRTA: recording session

The seventh series ended on 10 May 1970, and there was one special edition on 31 December. The last series, which started on 4 November 1973, was something of a bonus, because by now the cast were engaged on other things – Hatch in straight production; Brooke-Taylor, Garden and Oddie in *The Goodies*; and Cleese in *Monty Python's Flying Circus*. Hatch thinks that it only came about because there chanced to be 'windows' in everyone's schedules which happened to align.

Great play is made in the first programme with the time which has passed – in fact Tim Brooke-Taylor has 'forgotten' how to do Lady Constance and has to undergo an operation before he can once again produce the voice. One thing which evidently has not changed is Cleese's in-character objections to his roles, as is witnessed by the adaptation of *Star Trek* in the third show.

B-TAYLOR (*camp voice*): Well, anyway, heart – what is our position, Mr Zulu?
CLEESE: Velly uncomfo'table, Claptain.
KENDALL (*on distort*): Emergency – Captain Kink to the bridge immediately – emergency.
B-TAYLOR: Never a dull moment.
CLEESE: Quite light, Claptain.
HATCH: And so Captain Kink . . .
CLEESE (*normal voice*): Just a minute – is that all?
HATCH: What?
CLEESE: Is that all I've got this week? 'Velly uncomfo'table' and 'quite light Claptain' – is that it? (*goes on complaining*)
HATCH: Yes. And so Captain Kink . . . quiet please . . . and so Captain Kink sprang into the lift.
GRAMS: STEEL SPRING TWANGS.
HATCH: Nice one! (*A voice in the background shouts 'Was it worth it?'*) The lift took him swiftly up to the bridge.
GRAMS: LIFT DOORS CLOSE.
BAND: 'GOING UP' MUSIC.
GRAMS: LIFT DOORS OPEN.
B-TAYLOR: Oh – lift full of ruddy musicians as usual.

The Scottish Chief Engineer (Scott, Scotty for short, from Scotland) tells the Captain that there is a serious emergency.

B-TAYLOR: Scotty – you take the lift down to the engine room . . .

GARDEN: But it's awfu' heavy, Captain.

HATCH: With the Starship Enterprise completely out of control, things were bad.

ODDIE (*slap, slap*): Naughty things!

HATCH: The Captain leapt boldly to the controls and furiously started pushing buttons.

ODDIE: Get off!

KENDALL: Oh, Buttons – if only I could go to the ball . . .

HATCH: Just a minute, just a minute . . .

ODDIE: After all . . .

ODDIE & KENDALL (*singing*): 'When you wish upon a star . . .'

HATCH (*hurriedly*): And speaking of stars, that brings us back to the plot – the door opened and in came Mr Zulu.

CLEESE (*off*): Oh – that's me again – about time too.

HATCH: Zulu staggered across to Captain Kink . . .

CLEESE: Yes yes –

HATCH: Then suddenly and dramatically . . .

CLEESE: Yes yes yes –

HATCH: He collapsed without a sound.
(*The audience go 'Ahhh'*)

CLEESE: Without a sound!

HATCH: Yes! Kink knew there was . . .

CLEESE: I'm sorry, this is disgraceful!

HATCH: Look, do stop complaining, John.

CLEESE: No, no – I think this is very shabby treatment. Good Lord, I mean, I give up my Sunday afternoon to come in here just for the sake of a lousy 'quite light Claptain' – I could have been at home mowing the kittens – no, I'm sorry, . . .

HATCH: Look, this is a jolly exciting story – if you're just going to spoil it by moaning, then you might as well go home.

CLEESE: Yes, but –

HATCH: No, no – I've had enough, you see – I mean, just go on home. Here's your satchel – go on.

CLEESE: All right, I will.

And he does – but he soon returns. After he has been allowed to be Mr Spock, the ship crashes on an asteroid at precisely 6 p.m. Asteroid Time. ('Ah well, if asteroid time the pubs will be open.')

ISIRTA spans a long time in the story of the 'Oxbridge Mafia'. Growing originally out of *Cambridge Circus*, it acted as a forcing-ground for the three members of the cast who went on into television together and eventually became *The Goodies* – Brooke-Taylor, Garden and Oddie – as well as giving both Barclay and Hatch valuable experience from which they went on to be, respectively, Head of Comedy for London Weekend Television and Head of Light Entertainment for BBC Radio. Cleese, in a way, never really belonged in *ISIRTA* – although it benefited immeasurably from his presence. As he says, it is not really his type of humour; and although he enjoyed doing it, largely because it gave him a chance to meet his friends regularly, he never felt very deeply involved with it.

Above all, *ISIRTA* is fun to listen to. Certainly it is undisciplined and frequently self-indulgent, but the exuberance and sheer enjoyment of the cast communicates itself clearly to the listener. Barclay: 'We were very lucky to get away with it, because we were still basically amateurs – there was always a quality of young adventurers rather than professional actors. We were lucky that there was a vogue for all this at the time, and the listeners were willing to follow us and support us through a great deal of public experiment.'

The experiment can be classed as an unqualified success; seen in perspective, *ISIRTA* belongs in the top handful of radio comedy shows.

ISIRTA, 1968: Bill Oddie, John Cleese, Tim Brooke-Taylor, Jo Kendall, Graeme Garden and David Hatch 'rehearsing'

Graham Chapman

John Cleese

Frank Muir

Marty Feldman

Peter Tinniswood

David Nobbs

David Frost

Denis Norden

Barry Took

Barry Cryer

Willis Hall

Dick Vosburgh

Keith Waterhouse

8.
'The Frost Report', 'At Last the 1948 Show'; 'Twice a Fortnight'; 'Broaden Your Mind'

At about the time that the Cambridge Footlights graduates were beginning their long run in *ISIRTA*, the two escapees from Oxford – Michael Palin and Terry Jones – were looking around for suitable careers. Terry Jones left Oxford in 1964, and found himself drifting into show business almost by default of something better to do. He had appeared in the Oxford Experimental Theatre Club's revue *Hang Down Your Head And Die*, and then he and Palin took an Oxford revue to the Establishment Club, only finding out when they got there that it was by then very run-down and seedy. Even so, the experience seems to have given Jones a taste for the Theatre.

He was asked by William Donaldson to write a show for which only the title – *The Love Show* – existed at that stage. He enlisted Palin's help, and they produced a revue which was more or less about the 'sexual revolution'; revolutionary or not, it established the idea of a Palin-Jones writing team. Meanwhile Jones entered the portals of the BBC, which was as always on the lookout for likely young graduates. After a brief period as a script editor for television, he worked on *Late Night Line-Up*, a lively end-of-the-evening arts magazine on BBC-2. The programme went out nightly, except weekends, and the head of the producing department, Rowan Ayres, wanted to vary the routine by making the Friday night editions lightly satirical in tone. Jones, with Palin, Robert Hewison and Barry Cryer, wrote suitable sketches for a few weeks until inter-departmental jealousy caused the idea to be killed off.

Palin, meanwhile, had left Oxford in 1965. At first he had feared that he would have to make a living in advertising, but this terrible fate was averted as he gradually became established as a writer – with help from a six-month period spent hosting a low-budget pop programme called *Now*, produced by TWW, the Independent Television company serving Wales and the West Country. The programme eventually foundered because pop music and small budgets tend to be incompatible concepts, but if nothing else it justified its existence by keeping Palin out of the soft-focus world of Martini and soap powders.

Palin and Jones did a week with an Oxford revue at a small theatre club, the Rehearsal Club, above the Royal Court Theatre. The club had an excellent atmosphere and first-class food, but suffered from a drought of audiences. However, one of the 'eight or so' people who did come during the week they ran there was David Frost; and as far as Palin and Jones were concerned the whole exercise was justified by the fact that he asked them to write for a new television series he was setting up – *The Frost Report*.

The programme was going to require a large team of writers, and Frost had been keeping an eye on his successors in the Footlights Club. John Cleese, who near the end of 1965 was planning to return to England from the USA, was both delighted and surprised to receive a phone call from Frost. Cleese remembers that Frost called from Kennedy Airport, filling in the few seconds before his plane left – inviting him both to write for and appear in *The Frost Report*. Cleese agreed, and was left feeling rather stunned by the opportunity while Frost rushed off to catch his plane.

The writing team was both large and impressive. Several came from the *TW3* stable, including Keith Waterhouse (the author of *Billy Liar*), Willis Hall (writer of various screenplays), David Nobbs (who later wrote BBC television's *The Fall and Rise of Reginald Perrin* and the novels on which it was based) and Peter Tinniswood (author of the novel and television series *I Didn't Know You Cared*). The field of radio comedy was represented by Frank Muir and Denis Norden (co-writers of *Take It From Here* and stars of *My Word!*), writer and performer Dick Vosburgh, Barry Cryer (who later collaborated on *Hello Cheeky!* and scripts for Morecambe and Wise) and Barry Took (co-writer of *Beyond Our Ken*). Graham Chapman, who was at this stage in his last eighteen months at medical school, was having to take his training seriously because of looming examinations; however, he managed to find time to co-write a few items with Cleese.

The head of this motley collection was Marty Feldman, whose experience included writing for *Educating Archie* in the 1950s and touring the variety theatres as part of a really rather primitive music-hall act called Morris, Marty and Mitch. He also wrote many editions of *Round The Horne* in collaboration with Barry Took. Feldman has a rather odd face, with protuberant eyes (which he later exaggerated for comic effect in his television appearances). At this time he had put performing behind him and was firmly established as a comedy writer.

As each *Frost Report* had a central theme, a 'theme script' to which the other writers could work was written by Antony Jay (who had worked on *Tonight* and *TW3*), although it was not always adhered to. The writing factory would then produce a number of little pseudo-topical sketches, linked in what was grandly known as a 'Continuous Developing Monologue' (CDM for short) by Frost and 'Cadbury's Dairy Milk' by some of the writers. John Cleese remembers: 'At the end of the show, before this huge list of names, the credits always used to say "Written by David Frost", which was really a bit naughty. *Chosen* by David Frost, fair enough!'

What is particularly interesting about the writing team is that it brought together for the first time the future Monty Python team – Cleese, Chapman, Palin, Jones; and, a newcomer to the field, Eric Idle.

Idle was born on 29 March 1943, and went to a boarding school in Wolverhampton of which he says (in an article in his *Rutland Dirty Weekend Book*): 'It was in addition an ex-orphanage, having only recently gained the "ex" when it ran out of orphans. The war had, however, given the half-orphan trade just the shot in the arm it needed, and at this time the school was largely stocked with boys like me who had lost a parent in the Forces, and were having their education paid for by the RAF and other guilty bodies.'

He went on to Cambridge in 1962, so that his first year there was also Cleese, Oddie and Brooke-Taylor's last. He made his way into the Footlights Club via the usual route of college smoking-concerts – Tim Brooke-Taylor remembers auditioning him and two others who had been at the same school, doing material with which they had obviously had a great success in a sixth-form concert. 'They were the most arrogant threesome we'd ever come across! It *beamed* over their faces as they did their sketches. Eric beamed least, and looked a little sheepish occasionally – and of course he was the best.' History does not record what happened to the other two, but Idle went on to take over the presidency of the Footlights Club in his final year, 1964–5 – inheriting it from Graeme Garden as Garden had inherited it from Brooke-Taylor.

It is interesting that the infiltration of the show-business world by the Cambridge Footlights Club ends with Eric Idle. Since then the connection has been broken, and the Footlights Club seems to have produced no revues which generated any outside interest, although occasionally its members still make brief appearances at the Edinburgh Festival and on radio. It is quite possible that Idle would not have gone into show business but for his connection with Brooke-Taylor and thus with the sudden burst of success the Footlights Club had with *Cambridge Circus*.

Idle left Cambridge in 1965, with a degree in English, just in time to contribute to *The Frost Report*. At this early stage he mostly contributed short gags to the CDM. Tim Brooke-Taylor remembers writing what he calls a 'computer joke' with Idle – not that it was about a computer, but that it might well have been written by one. 'We thought, "What's happened this week? Harold Wilson . . . let's do a God joke . . . Harold Wilson and God . . . There's been a dock strike . . . so no food coming in . . . Harold Wilson, God and no food . . . right: Harold Wilson, when faced with the dock strike, said 'All I need is five loaves and two small fishes'." We sent this in – it was written like a computer, I've never written anything like that before – and I thought the audience would never stop laughing! It was one of the most depressing evenings of my life. Eric and I went to the bar and got really quite drunk.'

Idle appears to have been something of a late starter, and indeed it was only really with *Monty Python's Flying Circus* three years later that he showed his full abilities; but of course he is three years younger than Cleese and Brooke-Taylor. He wrote one or two sketches for *The Frost Report*; one was a monologue for Ronnie Barker, on the idea that Christmas could be staggered, which shows the beginnings of his particular style. Although it is rudimentary compared with his more complex later writing, this early work demonstrates something akin to Peter Cook's ability to build a spiral of absurdity, together with a skill – and indeed a fascination – with words for their own sake.

So, if for no other reason, *The Frost Report* is interesting as the first meeting-ground for the future Python team; but it also stands up well as an amusing programme in its own right. Part of the reason is that, despite a superficial appearance of being satirical, it is in fact nothing of the sort. Frost was far too astute to actually link himself any further with the 'satire boom', which by this time had had the plug pulled out of it and was sinking fast. *The Frost Report* is topical to some extent, but much of the material is funny for its own sake.

Altogether there were twenty-six editions of *The Frost Report*, in two series of thirteen, starting on 10 March 1966 and 6 April 1967 respectively. Each programme set itself a definite topic, such as 'Youth', or 'Women', or 'Crime' etc.; the several short sketches and two longer ones which were the norm for each programme were linked by Frost and his Continuous Developing Monologue, and there was a song in each edition from Julie Felix. Because the programmes were 'live' viewers could be invited to write in with 'pet peeves' on the subject of the following week's programme; some of these were read out and were really quite witty.

Feldman would normally write one of the two main sketches, and Cleese and Chapman the other. One of Cleese and Chapman's creations was an awful woman, played by Sheila Steafel, who appeared in several of the programmes. This example is from the programme on 'Youth' in the second series, broadcast on 22 June 1967. Cleese is an undergraduate, home on holiday, whose mother refuses to admit that he is growing up. The sketch is brilliantly observed, and one can only hope that it did not derive from personal experience.

SHEILA:	It *is* nice to have you home, dear – how long is your holiday?
CLEESE:	Till September.
SHEILA:	Oh good – it will be nice having you here all that time.
CLEESE:	Yes, well ...
SHEILA:	Your father and I see so little of you – it will be nice having you all to ourselves for three months.
CLEESE:	Yes, well, I shall be going away for a *part* of it.
SHEILA:	Because your father's got three weeks off at the end of August, and I thought how nice it would be for all of us if we all went up to Bridlington to stay with Auntie Jo-Jo.
CLEESE:	Yes, well I'm afraid I don't think I'll be able to manage that.
SHEILA:	Because I remember how much you used to like Bridlington.
CLEESE:	Because I'm going to Crete.
SHEILA:	Your father and I are so looking forward to it.
CLEESE:	Mother –
SHEILA:	Because it's the only holiday he gets during the year and I know you wouldn't want to disappoint him.
CLEESE:	Mother – I'm afraid that I've decided that I'm going to Crete.
SHEILA:	Well, I remember how much you enjoyed Bridlington last year. It did your father and I so much good, because we're not as young as we used to be, and we don't see very much of you nowadays, well not as much as we'd like to. We're getting on. We don't know how much longer we're going to – be here. So it would be such a treat for all of us.
CLEESE:	Mother, don't you *remember* last year? It was sheer misery for all of us. Two weeks of sitting in the car on the sea front with the windows up, bickering.
SHEILA:	What a wicked thing to say – you said you enjoyed it.
CLEESE:	That's a lie.
SHEILA:	How dare you speak to your mother like that – it's horrid!
CLEESE *(firmly)*:	Well, don't lie.
SHEILA:	*I* don't know what's happened to you. You've changed since you've been to university. All you want to do is spend all your time with your *friends*. Or *reading*.
CLEESE:	Mother ...
SHEILA:	You blackguard!
CLEESE:	Mother ...
SHEILA:	Anyway, why do you want to go to *Crete*?

CLEESE: Oh, you *did* hear. Because Crete is beautiful, has a wonderful climate, and historically is one of the most interesting, fascinating, and important places in the world. Unlike Bridlington.

The principal performers in the series were Ronnie Corbett and Ronnie Barker, who have since worked as a team in their television series *The Two Ronnies* (which retains something of the format of *The Frost Report* in its use of sketches linked by a gag-narration). Cleese thoroughly enjoyed working with them, because not only were they very professional but also very unselfish, and never minded other people taking the lead in sketches.

Cleese and the two Ronnies were teamed in a series of short sketches in which the three of them stood in a line facing the camera and gave different viewpoints on various subjects. This is particularly effective in Marty Feldman and John Law's sketch on class, in which the demonstration of class relationships is given additional point by Cleese's six foot five inches, Barker's five foot eight-and-a-half inches, and Corbett's five foot one inch.

CLEESE: I look down on him *(indicating Barker)* because I am upper-class.
BARKER: I look up to him *(indicating Cleese)* because he is upper-class; but I look down on him *(indicating Corbett)* because he is lower-class. I am middle-class.
CORBETT: I know my place. I look up to them both. But I don't look up to him *(Barker)* as much as I look up to him *(Cleese)*, because he has got innate breeding.
CLEESE: I have got innate breeding, but I have not got any money. So sometimes I look up *(bending knees and doing so)* to him *(Barker)*.
BARKER: I still look up to him *(Cleese)* because although I have money, I am vulgar. But I am not as vulgar as him *(Corbett)*, so I still look down on him *(Corbett)*.
CORBETT: I know my place. I look up to them both; but while I am poor, I am honest, industrious and trustworthy. Had I the inclination, I could look down on them. But I don't.
BARKER: We all know our place, but what do we get out of it?
CLEESE: I get a feeling of superiority over them.
BARKER: I get a feeling of inferiority from him *(Cleese)*, but a feeling of superiority over him *(Corbett)*.
CORBETT: I get a pain in the back of my neck.

John Cleese says: 'I still acknowledge that without David Frost I would have taken a very long time to get off the ground – I always assume I would have done eventually, but God knows how long it would have taken – and literally since then I've never had a day out of work.'

Palin and Jones were junior writers on the first series, mostly generating CDM, but they did have a set of rather neat visual jokes in the show that won the Golden Rose at the Montreux Festival in 1967 – they showed how karate champions might approach cutting a wedding cake, and a karate knock on a door by Ronnie Barker caused the whole house to collapse. Because they were only earning about £14 per week between the two of them, the producer, Jimmy Gilbert, occasionally let them do walk-on parts, for which they were paid extra.

Between the two series of *The Frost Report* Frost did a series for the commercial television company Rediffusion, called *The Frost Programme*. Brooke-Taylor and Cleese were also involved, but because the programme was not shown in the West Country (owing to TWW's rather obscure networking policy) Cleese's father came to the not unnatural assumption that his son was now out of work. Cleese: 'I got a letter saying, was I interested in becoming a personnel director at Marks and Spencers. When I told this story in an interview two or three years ago, some lovely spark at Marks and Spencers actually sent me a form to fill in!'

When the second series of *The Frost Report* started in April 1967 Palin and Jones felt more confident about their work; they took more part in the preparatory discussions for each programme, and developed a niche for themselves in doing short film inserts. They had material in every programme in the second series, including a number of sketches performed in the studio. This example comes from a one-off follow-up to the series, broadcast on 26 December 1967, under the title *Frost Over Christmas*. Cleese and Corbett play strangers who meet at a party.

CORBETT: What do you do?
CLEESE: I'm the world's leading authority on Impressionist paintings.
CORBETT: Oh, really? I'm an accountant. Chartered accountant. Where do you live?
CLEESE: I live in a converted monastery in the Outer Hebrides.
CORBETT: Oh really? I live in Hendon.[31] Is your wife here tonight?
CLEESE: No – she's in Vietnam. Fighting.
CORBETT: Do you know Hendon at all?
CLEESE: Er – yes, I think I passed through it once, yes – when I was being kidnapped by Russian agents.
CORBETT: Oh, really – where were they taking you?
CLEESE: They had a frigate waiting for me in the Thames Estuary.
CORBETT: Oh, really? You must have come down Alveston Road, then, past our house. It's just near the Baths, there.
CLEESE: Yes, well, I wouldn't really know, I'm afraid – they drugged me rather heavily with Hypertalsin Metrathecane.
CORBETT: Oh, really. What does that do to you?
CLEESE: Paralyses the mind.
CORBETT: Oh – does it affect the eyesight at all?
CLEESE: Oh, yes – you're totally unconscious.
CORBETT: Oh well, you wouldn't have seen our house, then – number thirty-seven. It's just on the corner – it's very nice. You must pop in sometime.
CLEESE: Well, that's very kind, but not for a time – I'm afraid I'm going to prison.
CORBETT: Oh, really? Not anywhere in Hendon, is it?
CLEESE: No, no – in Guatemala. A currency offence I committed when I was over there investigating a man-eating cactus they'd discovered.
CORBETT: You went all the way to Guatemala just to see cactuses?
CLEESE: Yes – it was quite interesting actually, while I was there I was nearly trampled on by a herd of wild buffalo.
CORBETT: Oh, really – just to see cactuses. I wish I'd known, 'cos they've got a

display of them at Hendon Central Library. It's very interesting talking to someone like you, because it's not everyone who's interested in Hendon.

CLEESE: I'll show you something that will interest you – now, have you ever seen one of those before?

CORBETT: No.

CLEESE: Do you know what it is?

CORBETT: No, I don't.

CLEESE: It's a Tibetan prayer shawl. Do you know how I got it?

CORBETT: No, I don't.

CLEESE: It was given to me by the chief slave-girl of the sacred High Commander of the Tibetan Army. God, she was a beauty. Hair black as a raven's wings. One evening, during the feast of Ramsit Asi, the all-powerful God of Light, when ten thousand bullocks are sacrificed on the mountainside, she crept into my tent, filling the air with a delicious fragrance – and casting aside her tribal gown, her black hair spilled over her delicate pale skin as she climbed into my bed.

CORBETT: Really?

CLEESE: She came from Hendon.

By the second series Cleese was beginning to feel dissatisfied with the whole exercise – he describes this as the pattern of his life. He also found the live television rather worrying; it was the last live television he did, apart from interviews. (In fact it was practically the last live television that anybody ever did, at least in the light entertainment field.)

Meanwhile as a result of their work on the first series of *The Frost Report*, Frost had invited Cleese and Chapman to write the film *The Rise and Rise of Michael Rimmer* (See page 115). Since they were to go to Ibiza to write it, Chapman jumped at the chance to sit in the sun. The script took three months to write, after which Chapman had a three month delay before it was possible for him to go back into medicine. He filled this in by writing for Roy Hudd – which demonstrated to him that he could make a living writing on his own, if he wanted to. Here Fate, in the form of the Inland Revenue, intervened: 'I found after my first year in writing that if I'd gone back into medicine I wouldn't have been able to pay the tax for that year, so I've been at it ever since. And I still can't pay my tax, so I'm forced to carry on writing.'[32] He is in fact qualified medically, but would have to do a year in hospital before he could go into practice.

While Cleese and Chapman were working on the *Michael Rimmer* script Marty Feldman and his wife, and Tim Brooke-Taylor came out to Ibiza on holiday. David Frost also flew out – possibly to make sure that Cleese and Chapman had actually written something – and suggested that Brooke-Taylor and Cleese might like to appear in a television series which Frost would produce and sell to ITV. It was a natural next step to include Graham Chapman, and then Brooke-Taylor and Cleese independently thought of including Feldman. Frost was the first to object – largely on account of Feldman's peculiar eyes – but he saw the error of his ways and pushed the show through, over the objections of the television company, Associated-Rediffusion, who didn't much care for Feldman's eyes either. Feldman himself was rather nervous about the whole idea, as it was some years since he had performed; but in the event he stole the show, and went on to his own series and a subsequent career in Hollywood, which just shows how wrong a television company can be.

The series was given the title: *At Last the 1948 Show*. Cleese says: 'The whole title was a joke about BBC television executives – *At Last the 1948 Show*, arriving in 1967, the whole idea was that it had been on the shelf for nineteen years while the TV executives decided whether to run it or not!' The first series ran for six weeks from 15 February 1967 (in the London area) and was followed by a second series of seven, starting on 26 September 1967.

In a deliberate move to get away from the feeling of *The Frost Report* (the second series of which ran between the two *1948 Show* series) the shows had no individual themes, and were just a collection of unrelated sketches with the deliberately primitive linking device of a pretty but silly girl who thought that it was really *her* show. Brooke-Taylor: 'John and I went to a night-club to look at dancing girls . . . we were so embarrassed! We'd gone through an amazing number of auditions . . . and word had got around that we were looking for a girl for a television show. We were so out of our depth . . . call-girls all around! Acutely embarrassing!'

The girl they chose was Aimi Macdonald; she linked the sketches by launching a 'make the lovely Aimi Macdonald a Rich Lady' appeal, and sending messages to her admirers. In the first series she was helped by other girls, so that in the second programme there were two hostesses, in the third programme there were three hostesses, and so on. Very few other ITV companies took the series, which was not networked.[33] One of those which did was ATV (Midlands) and they ran the shows a few weeks later – in the wrong order, thereby completely sinking the multiplying hostesses joke. ATV did not take the second series; Granada (for the North of England) did, having not taken the first series. Many parts of the country never saw the show at all, although by the second series it was in the top ten for the London area.

At Last the 1948 Show: publicity pose with Tim Brooke-Taylor, John Cleese, Graham Chapman and Marty Feldman admiring the lovely Aimi Macdonald

The sketches starred Cleese, Chapman, Brooke-Taylor and Feldman in various combinations, with walk-on assistance from Dick Vosburgh, Barry Cryer and Eric Idle, among others. Bill Oddie and Jo Kendall also made guest appearances, in sketches which had originally appeared in *Cambridge Circus*.

At Last the 1948 Show is chiefly remarkable for the range of its material. Unlike any of the previous shows mentioned in this book, the items do not adhere to a particular style; but vary between normally constructed sketches – with a beginning, a middle and a punch-line – and totally surrealistic sketches. A good example of the latter is one in which a dentist clambers into the mouth of his patient and prepares to blast a bad tooth with dynamite. Not unnaturally, this causes objections from a group of Welsh miners who appear at the back of the throat. All this activity causes the patient to swallow, leaving the dentist and his nurse frantically clinging to the uvula before being swept away down the patient's gullet. More than any other sketch in the show, this one foreshadows the savage surrealism of *Monty Python*, but there are other indications of the sort of ideas which were germinating. A fascination with television presentation is shown in many of the openings to the programmes; these often consist of noisy trailers for unlikely dramas, but one of the more interesting is a summary of 'the story so far'. Again, the use of captions (the term here includes both written captions and still photographs) foreshadows *Monty Python*.

> *Caption: THE STORY SO FAR*
> VOICE: The story so far.
> *Picture: Cleese as Erich von Stroheim.*
> VOICE: Winsome state-registered nurse Otto von Nail-Scissors ...
> *Picture: Map of Sardinia.*
> VOICE: ... whilst on a midget-spotting holiday in Sardinia ...
> *Picture: Brooke-Taylor as Archbishop Makarios.*
> VOICE: ... meets the sinister stoat-heiress Andromeda Manby Flutes-waller posing as a dilettante Archbishop and YWCA Butterfly champion.
> *Picture: Feldman as a viking*
> VOICE: Otto's swarthy cousin bread pudding farmer Milton Stag-bottler ...
> *Picture: Chapman as an Air Marshal*
> VOICE: ... and his wife Air Marshal Sir Abdul Buglepellet ...
> *Picture: Chapman as a wrestler*
> VOICE: ... née Reg Pubes the international piano wrestler ...
> *Picture: Donald Peers*
> VOICE: ... and one-time personal pig-sticker to Donald Peers ...
> *Picture: An all-night goat wash*
> VOICE: ... are lured into the all-night goat wash and the electric Turkish Bath in the Edgware Road ...
> *Picture: Feldman as a nun*
> VOICE: ... where Grummett, ...
> *Picture: Feldman as a cat*
> VOICE: ... Strimbongler, ...
> *Picture: Brooke-Taylor in a nightshirt*
> VOICE: ... Polk, ...
> *Picture: Rawicz and Landauer*

VOICE: ... Rawicz and Landauer, ...
Picture: The cast of 'The Desert Song'
VOICE: ... and the full West End cast of 'The Desert Song' are lying in wait for them disguised as a ...
Picture: Close-up of a typewriter
VOICE: ... typewriter. Meanwhile in a Chilean slaughter-house half-way up the Eiffel Tower –
Medium shot: Cleese at desk
CLEESE: I'm sorry – there seems to have been some mistake. Here is the news.

Another use of captions, in a manner foreshadowing *Monty Python*, happens when a sketch about a joke shop, which becomes progressively more surrealistic, ends with a caption saying 'HOW ABOUT THAT?'.

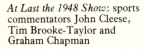

At Last the 1948 Show: sports commentators John Cleese, Tim Brooke-Taylor and Graham Chapman

Most of the sketches, however, are more conventional; and almost without exception of a very high quality. They are certainly appreciated by the audience, whose laughter almost smothers some of the lines – and also the cast tends to take some of the sketches too fast, which, coupled with the enthusiasm of the audience, does not always aid intelligibility. The four main protagonists take turns at being straight men when the occasion demands it – and even Feldman, whose cast of feature makes him ideal as a mischief-maker, is convincing as a straight man beset by lunatics in several of the sketches. In one such sketch, written (late one night) by all four, he is a harmless little man waiting at a bus stop who gets unwillingly drawn into a conversation with a maniac (Cleese) who is fascinated by ants, and who insists on demonstrating their mating calls and sign language.

CLEESE: What's this, then? What's this then? (*Waves his arms about*)
FELDMAN: I don't know!
CLEESE: Go on – do it, do it!
FELDMAN: No, I feel silly!
CLEESE: Go on – do it – it's easy!
FELDMAN: Please don't make me.
CLEESE: All right – guess what it is, then. (*Waves arms*)

FELDMAN: An ant.
CLEESE: Good, good – it's an ant! What's he doing?
FELDMAN: I don't know what it's doing!
CLEESE: It's signalling! It's signalling! He's saying – 'Give us a hand with this small vole!'
FELDMAN: He's *what*?
CLEESE: He's saying, 'Give us a hand with this small vole!'
FELDMAN: Wait a minute, wait a minute.
CLEESE: What?
FELDMAN: How do you know he's saying 'Give us a hand with this small vole'? I mean, it's so *specific*.
CLEESE: Come on matey – 'Give us a hand with this small vole.'
FELDMAN: How do you know he's saying Give us a hand with this small vole?
CLEESE: Well, I don't *know* – it might be anything!
FELDMAN: You what?
CLEESE: It might be anything! Well, I'm not a bloody ant, am I? *How should I know what a bloody ant says* – WHO CARES WHAT A BLOODY ANT SAYS!
FELDMAN: Well, you brought it up in the first place!
CLEESE: SHUT UP, OR I'LL EAT YOU! (*Screams*) That is the death cry of a worker ant! Now – you do it!
FELDMAN: No!
CLEESE: Go on – you do it!
FELDMAN: (*Pathetic scream*)
CLEESE: Rotten! What a rotten death cry of a worker ant! Rotten! (*Very loud scream*) Whereas a queen ant, which is a thousand times larger, goes: (*Very very loud scream*). You do it!
(*Feldman rushes off: off-screen squeal of brakes and scream*)
CLEESE: That's it! That's it – that's quite good!

This is one of Cleese's most spectacular performances, as he screams himself hoarse. Many of the sketches involve Cleese in being aggressive in some measure; one such as Cleese and Chapman's psychiatrist sketch, with Cleese as an unsympathetic psychiatrist and Brooke-Taylor in one of his regular characterizations as a scared little rabbit of a man.

CLEESE: You haven't been here before, have you?
B-TAYLOR: No.
CLEESE: Fine. I'm Doctor Gilbert.
B-TAYLOR: How do you do. My name's Gibbonposture.
CLEESE: Ha ha ha ha ha – Oh dear, excuse me . . . Now, (*walking towards couch*) are you a bed-wetter?
B-TAYLOR: What?
CLEESE: Are you a bed-wetter?
B-TAYLOR: Well . . . Er . . . I . . .
CLEESE: Well, I'll lie on the couch. You sit on the chair. Better safe than sorry. (*Does so*) Ah, that's better. Ha ha ha, Gibbonposture, ha ha ha . . . Now, you're not under the impression that you're Kenneth Wolstenholme, are you?
B-TAYLOR: What?

CLEESE: Do you think you're Kenneth Wolstenholme?
B-TAYLOR: No.
CLEESE: Good. I've got five of them already, and it's getting tricky keeping their appointments apart. Coming in here with their dirty macs, shouting irrelevant information . . . Why Kenneth Wolstenholme, that's what I want to know . . . Still, if you're mad . . .

The psychiatrist's attitude, not surprisingly, deters the patient from broaching any confidences. But Brooke-Taylor remembers: 'In the rehearsal, John was going through an "acting" phase – everything had to be underplayed, with little nuances – I went off despairingly to Marty Feldman and said, "It's not working – I've got nothing to be frightened of." Marty, very shrewdly, said "Stamp on his toe after about thirty seconds." So I did. The look of *fury* in his face – the words kept going, but he couldn't understand why I'd done it. The sketch was very funny – it was wonderful to see the playback, and know "That was when I stamped".'

CLEESE: Look! What's the matter – you come in here, you won't tell me what's up, it's all bloody mumble . . . I can't hear a word. You're all tensed up like all the other nuts who come in here. It's not much fun listening to your type of loony drivel eight hours a day, you know. It's so bloody *boring*, for one thing. My God, it's boring! So will you just tell me once and for all, in God's name what is wrong with you!
B-TAYLOR: I think I'm a rabbit.
CLEESE: You stupid loony! Of course you're not a rabbit! Pull yourself together!
B-TAYLOR: I *am* a rabbit.
CLEESE: If you were a rabbit you'd have great big long ears!
B-TAYLOR: They must have dropped off!
CLEESE: Don't be so stupid! If you say you're a rabbit once more, I'll smash your teeth in! Now – what are you?
B-TAYLOR: I'm . . . er . . . er . . . a dog!
CLEESE: That's better! We'll take it from there next week.

Both series of *At Last the 1948 Show* abound in excellent sketches – so much so that making a selection of them is extremely frustrating, because something good inevitably has to be left out. High spots are Chapman as a government minister who falls to pieces (literally) while he is being interviewed; a karate demonstration in which the various 'chops' have a delayed – and devastatingly cumulative – effect; a Chinese restaurant sketch which is a masterly exercise in non-communication; a farming sketch which contains some superb mock-rural dialect ('Ignorum! Im barn troodle morn stupid an a pot in a kloot!'); and several old friends including Chapman's self-wrestling, the first John and Mary sketch, and 'Judge Not' from *Cambridge Circus*.

Some of the sketches are rather more sadistic in tone than had been normal in television comedy up to then; these include Feldman as a gypsy 'selling' lucky favours ('Gypsy boot through your hat – nothing luckier than that – old Gypsy saying, sir'), and Cleese and Chapman's interview with a shepherd (Chapman) at a sheepdog trial. Brooke-Taylor is the interviewer.

B-TAYLOR: How do they drive the sheep?

CHAPMAN: You are a nosy old turnip, aren't you. Well, I tell 'ee, my old dear ... The dogs bark at the sheep, then they crawls up to them on their bellies, then they nudges them with their noses, then they buries their fangs in 'em.

B-TAYLOR: Oh ... and then the dogs herd the sheep into the pens?

CHAPMAN: Ar. Sometimes the sheep drive *them* into the pen, and then the dogs just sit there looking embarrassed, and everyone laughs at 'em, and I laughs at 'em too – I think it's very funny. My wife – she thinks it's funny.

B-TAYLOR: Does she really.

CHAPMAN: Got a great sense of humour, my wife.

B-TAYLOR: I'd like to meet her some time.

CHAPMAN: Ever since her accident.

B-TAYLOR: I'm sorry to hear that.... How many sheep-dogs have you?

CHAPMAN: 'Tis a secret, I'm not telling you ... 'tis a most holy secret that cannot and must not be divulged. Two.

B-TAYLOR: Oh, you have two dogs?

CHAPMAN: Shh!

B-TAYLOR (*whispering*): You have two dogs?

CHAPMAN: Yes.

B-TAYLOR: Where are they now?

CHAPMAN: Oh ar, well one of them's over – now where is he? Ar – over there by that pile of dead sheep. Magnificent brute – treacherous to a fault. Just has this little weakness for mutton.

B-TAYLOR: Do the dogs kill the sheep?

CHAPMAN: Only in fun. Still, that's better than burying them in the ground and pulling their heads off – it's more humane.

B-TAYLOR: Yes – well, perhaps you could get your dogs to give us a demonstration.

CHAPMAN: Oh, you don't need the dogs for that, you just bury the sheep in the ground ...

B-TAYLOR: No, no – could you get the dogs to drive the sheep into the pen?

CHAPMAN: I've only got old Butcher here at the moment – I don't know where Crippen's gone to. He must be off after the judges – he senses they're his natural enemies.

B-TAYLOR: Well, could you just put Butcher through his paces, then?

CHAPMAN: All right – I'll get him to drive that sheep into that pen over there. Right ... (*whistles*)
(*Frantic baa-ing noises from off-screen*)

B-TAYLOR: urely, Mr Leigh, he shouldn't be ... Mr Leigh, what *is* he doing? Surely he shouldn't be *eating* that sheep?!

CHAPMAN: You shut your mouth!

B-TAYLOR: Oh, goodness me – how awful! Oh, this is embarrassing!

CHAPMAN (*shouting at the off-screen dog*): STOP THAT, YOU THIEVIN' CUR, OR I'LL TEAR YOU APART WITH MY BARE HANDS! (*To B-Taylor*) Ar, look at that – I swear he understands every word I say!

Other excellent sketches include Cleese as the proprietor of a tourist agency for a totalitarian country ('You will be able to visit one of our collective farms and see some of our world-famous politically-orientated cows'); Feldman as a man who cannot keep awake making an appeal on behalf of people suffering from sleep starvation; and a sketch in which four English tourists meeting in Spain discover that they are all called Sydney Lotterby (the name of a real-life television producer) which paves the way for several later sketches in which the Lotterbys appear as boring nuisances.

Throughout the shows runs the linking thread of the lovely Aimi Macdonald's inconsequential performances:

AIMI: Some people have complained that this show is not satirical. So the
            lovely Aimi Macdonald is going to be hard-hitting and outspoken
            and prick the sacred cows of British pomposity. Here goes – Mr
            Heath's got a glass leg! Next week – Mr Wilson's legs!

The first series ends in magnificent style with Cleese's rendition of 'The Ferret Song' in an even more grandiose style than its appearance in *ISIRTA*; and the second series ends with another *ISIRTA* song – Cleese's 'The Rhubarb Tart Song', to the tune of Sousa's 'Washington Post'.

The shows are remembered with great affection by those who were geographically lucky enough to see them; and a gramophone record (since deleted) was made from the sound tracks of some of the items.

At Last the 1948 Show is one of the most important steps on the road to *Monty Python's Flying Circus*. It has a variety of approach which has been matched by few other television shows, and a large number of very entertaining sketches – some of which have subsequently resurfaced in *The Two Ronnies*. In view of the importance of the series, Cleese was understandably annoyed to discover that Paradine Productions (Frost's producing company) has wiped eleven of the thirteen video tapes; this is a great pity because the programmes would stand up well to a repeat even today. The participants got on well together, and found the production people helpful – this was one of the few shows involving the *Cambridge Circus* people which seems to have had no censorship problems – and the happy atmosphere led to the blending of talents which made *At Last the 1948 Show* one of the most successful television comedy shows of the 1960s.

At the beginning of 1968 Cleese married Connie Booth, the actress he had met while in America, and for the next eighteen months, he concentrated on writing. He and Chapman were major contributors to the series which arose directly from *At Last the 1948 Show*. BBC Television, watching with envious eyes, had recognized a considerable comic talent in Feldman, whom up to then they had seen only as a scriptwriter. The new series, *Marty*, was built round the more disruptive side of the character he had portrayed in the *1948 Show*, and Tim Brooke-Taylor and John Junkin appeared in the supporting cast. The writers included Feldman and Barry Took; and Michael Palin and Terry Jones, who also made a few brief appearances.

Marty was shown on BBC-2; there were two series of six programmes, beginning respectively on 29 April and 9 December 1968, plus a 'special' made as an entry for the Montreux Light Entertainment Festival, where it won the Silver Rose; this edition was transmitted on 17 March 1969.

Many of the sketches in the first series were well written – some were lifted from the *1948 Show* – and made good use of Feldman's peculiar looks and slightly anarchic characterization. Several of them picked up ideas already started in the *1948 Show*. For example, there had been several sketches in which Feldman appeared as a miscreant in the employ of an organization such as British Railways, whose crimes emerged gradually as he was subjected to a disciplinary interview – rather in the manner of a Bob Newhart monologue. This idea re-emerged in *Marty* – for example, as a BBC newsreader who has made up the news as he goes along.

The show was produced by Dennis Main Wilson, who had been in radio production since the late 1940s (he started the radio version of *Hancock's Half-Hour*) and in television from 1957; he produced, among other things, *Till Death Us Do Part*. Cleese: 'Dennis was hopeless on organization, but very, very good on flair, and doing wild things. The first series was very good, it had a lot of very good material in it. The second series changed radically. Graham and I were commissioned, and I think we sent in eight scripts; of which, to our astonishment, after initial floods of thanks, six were returned. (We subsequently did five of them on *Monty Python*, so there was nothing wrong with them.) It became obvious that what Marty really wanted was star vehicle sketches, whereas we were still writing sketches with three or four equal parts. Marty is a quite exceptionally good performer, and I don't think we've seen the best of his performing skills in what he's done since. He was very good at character; but most of it now is Marty as himself, breaking places up.'

Certainly the shows place a rather heavy reliance on sketches involving a sort of mindless disruption of any situation by Feldman. There are a few good sketches in the later shows, but even in the one which won the Montreux Silver Rose much of the material is rather thin. The best sketch has Feldman upsetting the occupants of a vet's waiting room by bringing in a large basket containing a beast which we never see, but which is obviously quite fearsome.

Marty: worried budgie owner and Feldman with beast in basket

('I looked him up in the *Cattle-breeder's Guide* – he wasn't in there; I looked him up in the *Standard Book of British Birds* – he wasn't in there either; I finally found him in the Book of Revelations.') Apart from this there is a general over-use of speeded-up film, although this is partly because, being a Montreux entry, the show is deliberately more visual than would normally be the case.

Feldman subsequently went on to Hollywood, and made successful appearances in several films from the Mel Brooks stable, notably *Young Frankenstein* and *Silent Movie*.

Young Frankenstein: Marty Feldman

Cleese made a brief foray into straight cinema, appearing as a TV public relations man, which was a piece of light relief in the romantic film *Interlude*,[34] made in England in 1968. It is Cleese's only more-or-less straight rôle to date: 'It's something I'd like to do more of, but the number of scripts I get which are any good is absolutely infinitesimal.'

Chapman, meanwhile, was writing for Ronnie Corbett's series *No, That's Me Over Here*, together with Barry Cryer and Eric Idle. Cleese and Chapman were then asked to rewrite a film called *The Magic Christian* which had been through several unsatisfactory screenplays. Cleese: 'The script we were sent really was rubbish. It had gone through about seven drafts, and the last person to have a go was somebody who wrote the most eloquent stage directions I've ever read, and the most completely atrocious dialogue.' Money was raised for the film on the basis of their rewrite; then Terry Southern – who had written the novel on which the film was based – was imported from the United States and the script was rewritten yet again. The final result is a mess, despite having a quite extraordinary cast headed by Peter Sellers, and including, apart from Cleese and Chapman themselves, Richard Attenborough, Laurence Harvey, Christopher Lee, Spike Milligan, Ringo Starr, Roman Polanski, Wilfrid Hyde White, Patrick Cargill and Dennis Price. The director was Joe McGrath. Cleese and Chapman feel, not unnaturally, that the film would have been a lot better if their script had been adhered to.

The Magic Christian crawled into the daylight early in 1970, by which time Cleese and Chapman were taking part in *Monty Python's Flying Circus*. They were briefly involved in a comedy series for ITV under the aegis of Humphrey Barclay, which will be mentioned in Chapter 10, while *Monty Python* itself will occupy – and indeed overflow – Chapter 11.

The Frost Report gave Michael Palin and Terry Jones their first real chance to establish themselves as writers; indeed their karate gags, which were in the Montreux edition in 1967, gave them quite a reputation within the BBC as specialists in filmed items. Even before that, they had actually appeared in filmed items on *The Late Show*. One of the assistant directors, Ian Davidson, had been at Oxford with Terry Jones (he had left before Palin's arrival); he invited them to perform in a samurai spoof called 'Hibachi' which was transmitted on 21 January 1967. This led to several more appearances in the series; one was in a sketch they wrote about commuters who made their way to work through a jungle, complete with crocodiles and other hazards; another was a slapstick joke filmed in the style of Antonioni – this had big close-ups of the banana skin, and echoing footsteps as the victim approached, and was all very 'significant'.

Palin's parents had by now dropped any objections they might have once had to their son taking up a career in acting; they were happy to see him earning a living, and rather proud of his being on television – even if it was only *The Late Show*. Palin also made a brief appearance in Ken Russell's television film *Isadora* – he and Eric Idle appeared as members of a jazz band playing on the roof of a hearse. (Idle also made a very brief appearance in Jonathan Miller's *Alice in Wonderland*.)

Palin and Jones then contributed a number of film items to a television series which grew out of *ISIRTA*, called *Twice a Fortnight*, which starred Bill Oddie, Jonathan Lynn, and Graeme Garden.

Twice a Fortnight (21 October 1967): Jonathan Lynn, Tony Buffery and Graeme Garden

Graeme Garden, who was still writing for *ISIRTA*, passed his medical examinations in 1967. He should then have gone on to do a year as resident in a hospital, and in fact had a job lined up; but Eric Idle, with whom he was sharing a flat, introduced him to Roger Hancock, who was Idle's agent. Garden: 'Roger sat me down – he was very stern about it, and he said, "You can't just muck about at it, you've got to decide whether you just want to go on writing for a hobby, or whether you're prepared to go out and get the work, because nobody's going to ring up and ask for you." Without a word of a lie, literally at that moment the phone went, and it was Tony Palmer, who said, "I understand you represent Graeme Garden – would he like to appear in *Twice a Fortnight*?" I've held that over Roger's head ever since.' (Roger Hancock says: 'I dine out on that story, which is quite true, so it's hardly something he holds over my head!')

So Garden deferred going into medicine while he tried going into television; it has remained deferred.

Twice a Fortnight, which ran for ten weeks from 21 October 1967 on BBC-1, arose from Tony Palmer's wish to direct something including Graeme Garden, whom he had known at Cambridge. Despite opposition from his head of department – oddly, the programme was produced under the aegis of the Music and Arts Department – Palmer went about setting up the programme, including Bill Oddie and, at Garden's suggestion, Michael Palin and Terry Jones. Palmer says that Oddie was very keen to bring over to the series the audience-participation atmosphere of *ISIRTA* – something which Palmer opposed, although he did attempt to create a different feeling of audience participation by grouping them closer to the performers than had been usual up to then. Oddie and Palmer were periodically in dispute about various aspects of the show. Oddie: 'Tony Palmer used to be known as the *"enfant terrible"* of directing. Graeme said that the strict meaning of *"enfant terrible"* is "awful child", and that just about sums it up. I'm afraid – and I think he would own up to it now – he was quite appalling most of the time. He used to stamp around saying "I don't understand this!" He did bizarre things like getting us to do it as if it was live, and then making it virtually impossible – that feeling that somehow if people are panicking it's going to be funny; and it isn't. It was nervous breakdown time, really.'

Palmer says: 'What they forget is that they knew nothing about television. One was faced with a group of people who were very skilful in their way – full of good ideas – but with absolutely no idea how to translate those ideas into pictures. Their way of dealing with me would be always to assume that I hadn't understood the script; and all I was trying to point out to them was what they were proposing simply would not work. They'd come up with a film idea, and I'd say, "Fine – that'll take a week; we've got about two hours."'

One of the problems with *Twice a Fortnight* was that the audience participation tended to get out of hand. There is disagreement over the reason for this. Oddie: 'Palmer literally issued that audience with drinks, squeakers and motor-horns when they came in, and should have had his head chopped off for doing it. They were totally uncontrollable.' Palmer firmly denies issuing anybody with squeakers or motor-horns, and points out that giving the audience a drink is not an invention of his – *TW3* did it. Whoever was to blame, the second show in particular is almost unintelligible because of the noise the audience is making, and all the programmes suffer from a surfeit of groaning and cheering.

A number of the items were recycled *ISIRTA* sketches, included against Palmer's advice; as he predicted, they tend not to transfer well to television. Much of the material, whether ex-*ISIRTA* or not, is messy in the extreme. On the plus side, Palmer – who wanted some music to break up the comedy but who was reluctant to have too many Oddie songs – managed to persuade a number of leading pop groups and musicians to appear. These included Cream, Scaffold, Cat Stevens, The Small Faces and The Who. This alone gave the show something of a reputation among rock fans, since it would normally have been quite impossible for any comedy show to include such groups – they appeared as favours to Palmer.

Palin and Jones wrote film inserts rather than studio material, which were rather more successful, in that they had to be carefully planned rather than performed in the studio with its participating audience. Terry Jones: 'I think those films were the first time I realized how much good filming could add to

Twice a Fortnight: Terry Jones and Michael Palin (in bathing costumes) and a bemused Jonathan Lynn

comedy. Palmer wasn't very sensitive in a way to what we were doing, but he had a tremendous visual sense – he knew how to get a good picture, and it looked terrific. I became aware then that you could marry beautiful pictures to comedy and get something really amazing.' This attention to the sheer 'look' of the material became a characteristic of Palin and Jones's later work. Several of their films for *Twice a Fortnight* are very effective; in particular a version of the Battle of Hastings (1066) presented as a home movie.

Palmer encouraged the use of film inserts for the programme because he felt they made a break from the noisy audience, although he says that he was always having a fight for them against Oddie's disapproval. Oddie in fact wrote one or two film sequences; up to this time he had been writing very verbal material, but the experience of doing these films developed his interest to include visual gags, which proved very useful later on in *The Goodies*. Palin and Jones's material, however, tended to be atmospheric rather than jokey, which was not to Oddie's taste. He says: 'It taught me that you have to provide laugh points; otherwise you get what we now call a "so-what" sequence – it's quite spectacular, but is it funny?' Oddie and Garden insisted on inserting some gags into a croquet game sequence which Oddie considered that Palmer was filming as if it was an advertisement (Oddie: 'Which is where he should have been, shooting commercials') and which was, again, atmospheric rather than having laugh points. Later on, Palin and Jones were able to develop their own style of quiet atmospheric humour in less frantic context.

One very effective film grew from an idea of Oddie's, which Palmer developed. It started from the premise that miniaturized policemen would in some way be an advantageous thing. This turned into a sketch about mini-cops, whose police dogs were chihuahuas, and who instead of horses rode alsatians. Palmer cleverly filmed the main action sequences in reverse, with the performers also acting in reverse, so that when projected the actions are in the right direction, but look strangely and indefinably odd. Oddie found the actual filming as hilarious as the finished product: 'I turned up for the filming, and I couldn't get out of the car for laughing – from behind a bush that didn't look as if it could hide anybody, six three-foot policemen trotted out – and I couldn't get out – I just found the whole image creepy and yet funny. It was the abandon with which these midgets threw themselves into it . . . a police car would drive up, and the boot would open, and six little policemen leap out of the boot! It's very much a Goodies-type sequence.'

Despite its faults, *Twice a Fortnight* served the useful purpose of getting both the Palin–Jones team and Bill Oddie interested in highly visual comedy, which they were able to exploit later to a considerable extent. Although there were – and still are – differences of viewpoint on the programme, the disputes were neither continuous nor deep enough to discourage the participants from wanting to do a second series (even though this did not in the end materialize). Palmer: 'The interesting thing about *Twice a Fortnight*, looking back on it, was not that it gave these guys an opportunity to get on television; but that you saw within it, very clearly and within quite a short space of time, the flowering of two quite different kinds of humour which clearly would never be in the same bed together again. My great mistake was in allowing it to go on – I should have said, "We must do more of these films", *or*, "The films are too expensive, let's go the whole hog with Bill". It should either have become *The Goodies* as it were, or it should have become a rather more surrealist visual humour, which was my original idea.'

It is fortunate that Palmer allowed the two styles to continue to 'share the same bed', since they went on to develop into two diverse and enjoyable branches of Oxbridge Mafia comedy. The series also weaned Garden and Oddie away from radio and into television; although *ISIRTA* continued for some time, they were getting a bit fed up with radio work because they felt that BBC Radio was not giving them sufficient backing, and indeed was sometimes being actually obstructive. Oddie: 'I remember somebody saying to us, "There once was a show called *The Goon Show*, and they don't work for us any more, so don't get uppity with us"!'

Garden's next foray into television was in partnership with Tim Brooke-Taylor. The idea for the show was put into Brooke-Taylor's mind by a number of 'encyclopaedias' then being issued in the form of weekly parts, which could be collected and bound to produce a sort of alphabetically arranged oversized colour supplement. The show which emerged from this was called *Broaden Your Mind*, and subtitled *An Encyclopaedia of the Air*. Basically it provided a loose format into which almost any idea for a sketch could be fitted; the usual approach was to take a mock-educational line, and there were also short spoof quizzes and mini-lectures.

The programmes were produced by the real Sydney Lotterby, whose name had been taken in vain in *At Last the 1948 Show*. The first series ran for six weeks on BBC-2, starting on 28 October 1968. Garden and Brooke-Taylor bore the brunt of the performing, and were assisted by John Junkin and Jo Kendall, with guest appearances by Graham Chapman, Michael Palin and Terry Jones. Some of the sketches were lifted from *I'm Sorry I'll Read That Again*, which had often included '*ISIRTA* Looks at . . .'-type sketches in its first halves; the Elizabethan music-hall sketch from *Cambridge Circus* was resurrected; and Cleese and Chapman contributed a sketch which was a reworking of 'The Wonderful World of the Ant' from the *1948 Show*, this time in terms of birds who drop pointed stones on their prey. Garden thinks that the reuse of *ISIRTA* material may have been a mistake: 'I remember that the things which were least successful were the things which hadn't been totally conceived for television. You'd suddenly realize that all the humour was in the dialogue, and that there was no sort of character you could do.'

The humour in the shows is for the most part surprisingly gentle. Among the regular features of the first series were sketches involving two old men

called Teddy and Freddy, played by Garden and Brooke-Taylor respectively.
Brooke-Taylor: 'Perhaps we fell in love with them too much ... I think
Graeme and I would always be doing Teddy and Freddy sketches if we weren't
careful – we both liked them, they were slightly dotty and great friends – there
was a danger of it getting too soft.'

Teddy and Freddy's first appearance found them lecturing on the signing
of Magna Carta, in a very slow and doddering style.

GARDEN: Hello.
B-TAYLOR: Hello.
GARDEN: In our history section tonight, Professor Frederick Pottermore
          here, and myself ...
B-TAYLOR: Sir Edward Windward.
GARDEN: Yes, what is it, Freddy?
B-TAYLOR: I was just telling them who you were, Teddy.
GARDEN: Ah, most kind. Well, tonight we look at the Magna Carta.
B-TAYLOR *(holding it up)*: This is just a facsimile.
GARDEN: Not the real thing.
B-TAYLOR: Not the real thing at all.
GARDEN: However, we shan't just be telling you about it ...
B-TAYLOR: Won't we, Freddy?
GARDEN: No, no, no – by way of an educational experiment, we shall be
          acting out for you ...
B-TAYLOR: In dramatic form ...
GARDEN: In dramatic form ...
B-TAYLOR: Very dramatic ...
GARDEN: The signing of the Magna Carta by King John at Runnymede –
BOTH: In 1215.
          (They put on crown and helmet)
B-TAYLOR: I am the leader of the Barons, hooray.
GARDEN: And I, d'you see, am King John.
B-TAYLOR: And this is a facsimile of the Magna Carta.
GARDEN: Not the real one.
B-TAYLOR: Not the real one.
GARDEN: And away we go.
B-TAYLOR: King John.
GARDEN: Yes?
B-TAYLOR: Sign here please.
GARDEN: Certainly. *(He signs)*
B-TAYLOR: You know, Teddy, I've a feeling there should be a little more to it
          than that.
GARDEN: We've missed out the first bit.
B-TAYLOR: Oh, so we have – better start again.
GARDEN: We're going to start again, d'you see.
B-TAYLOR: Knock, knock.
GARDEN: Come in ... what do you mean, 'knock knock'?
B-TAYLOR: That was a sound effect. Knock knock.
GARDEN: No, no, there were no doors at Runnymede, Freddy. It was in the
          open air.
B-TAYLOR: Sorry, Teddy.

GARDEN: Start again.
B-TAYLOR: Knock knock.
GARDEN: Start again without knocking, Freddy.
B-TAYLOR: Right ho, Teddy.
             (Pause)
GARDEN: What are you waiting for, Freddy?
B-TAYLOR: I was waiting for you to ask me to come in.
GARDEN: Come in?
B-TAYLOR: Ah, thank you. Here I am.
GARDEN: Who are you?
B-TAYLOR: It's *me*, Teddy.
GARDEN: I can see that. I'm now speaking as King John.
B-TAYLOR: I follow you – I am Baron Fitzwalter of ... do you like the
             accent? ... I am Baron Fitzwalter of Dunmow and Baynard's
             Castle, yeay.
GARDEN: Oh, I like it. And what do you want?
B-TAYLOR: We barons are revolting. Ha ha.
GARDEN: That's a very old joke, Freddy.
B-TAYLOR: I'm a very old man, Teddy.

Broaden Your Mind returned for a second series, running for seven weeks
from 17 November 1969. Bill Oddie, who had made one guest appearance in
the first series, appeared regularly in the second series, performing some of his
songs. He did not altogether like the first series of *Broaden Your Mind:* 'I
thought it was a bit cosy, and a bit safe – I do like a nasty edge to humour, I do
like things to be a bit distasteful and to annoy a few people. I got called in on
Barry Took's instructions, I think – he felt that Tim and Graeme were a bit
urbane, and rather nice. He wanted somebody unpleasant – that was the way
he put it, "Come in and be unpleasant"!'
    Graeme Garden says: 'Bill has wonderful ideas about "toughening things
up" ... He possibly thinks that farting jokes are "adult", and I don't – I think
they're juvenile. They may or may not be "toughening up" and "pushing back
barriers" but I don't think they're necessarily more "adult" than what you're
allowed to get away with. He was brought in because we couldn't really keep
him out much longer!'
    Certainly the second series of *Broaden Your Mind* is noticeably less cosy
than the first, although whether this was due to Oddie's contributions is open
to debate. Some of the sketches which had first appeared in *ISIRTA* had been
written by him, but all the new material was written by Garden and Brooke-
Taylor. Teddy and Freddy do not appear, but Garden and Brooke-Taylor are
joined by actor Roland MacLeod as three elderly gentlemen known as the
'Buffies'. They usually appear against the background of a gentlemen's club,
and are far less gentle and likeable than Teddy and Freddy.

MACLEOD: Long-haired fellas! When we were their age we were ...
B-TAYLOR: Fighting in France.
MACLEOD: No, no, we were fighting in France. You don't find these long-
             haired fellas fighting in France, do you.
B-TAYLOR: No imagination, that's it. When I was their age I joined up, went
             off to the war, and got killed.

GARDEN: Not like these long-haired intellectuals.
MACLEOD: Had all my hair blown off in the war. Had to wear a wooden wig.
GARDEN: I lost three legs.
B-TAYLOR: Three legs.
GARDEN: And a gramophone.
MACLEOD: Had my gramophone blown off.
B-TAYLOR: I had my hat blown off.
GARDEN }
MACLEOD } Good God.
B-TAYLOR: I had to get a wooden one.
GARDEN: I had everything blown off, I'm completely wooden you know.
MACLEOD: Tell that to these modern long-haired fellas and would they believe you?
B-TAYLOR: No, they're not so damned stupid.

Another regular and unpleasant character in the second series is the fiendish Doctor Findish, of the British Institute of Applied Science and Not Germ Warfare. He is played by Garden with a German accent, and delivers short scientifically educational lectures.

GARDEN: Heat. Let us consider the application of this simple physical phenomenon in our everyday lives. Now I have here a bunsenburner and a pan of water. I place the water on the pan, so . . . this makes the water 'hot'. 'Hot.' And when it is hot, we can use it for all sorts of things – for making tea, for washing up, and for hurting people. The possibilities are endless. Now, have you all got your pencil and paper ready? Is your pencil nice and sharp? Good! Keep it behind you at all times, and remember – go for the eyes.

Many of the items are more visual – most of the second series programmes start with Garden and Brooke-Taylor marooned on a high rostrum of the sort beloved by television designers ('How the hell do we get down?'); and there are also some film items. The film editor on the series was Jim Franklin, who was just beginning a long and fruitful association with Garden, Brooke-Taylor and Oddie. He had worked as film editor on *The Frost Report,* and before that on Robert Robinson's *Points of View* where, among other exercises, he had helped to overdub an excerpt from the cowboy series *Laramie* with upper-class English accents, to great comic effect. He contributed the idea for a very clever piece of film in the final edition of *Broaden Your Mind:* 'It intrigued me one day when my wife gave our dog a toffee. It got stuck on her molars, and she put her head up in the air and made these strange mouth movements. I thought, that would be nice to set that to music, and make her "sing".'

He filmed his dog and another one at five times normal speed as they wrestled with their toffees, and then carefully fitted the film, working frame by frame and using loops, repeats and still frames, to two voices singing 'Anything You Can Do, I Can Do Better'. This technique was not new – Franklin had used it in *The Frost Report* to make Harold Wilson and George Brown appear to do the hokey-cokey, and it dates back to the 1930s when a newsreel company made Hitler's storm-troopers appear to dance to 'The Lambeth Walk'. The singing dogs film for *Broaden Your Mind* is superbly done, with the dogs' movements very closely synchronized to the singing. Franklin: 'It cost about £500 to do that piece of film. Syd Lotterby, who was producing, said to me, "You're spending all my budget! It had better be a good piece of film." I'm glad to say that that particular piece of film has been transmitted at least fourteen times, so we've had our money's worth from it.'

Despite the comparative gentleness and the occasional self-indulgence in the writing, *Broaden Your Mind* is a likeable and very amusing show. Garden found the writing process almost too enjoyable: 'I can write with somebody, as long as it's somebody like Bill Oddie, who I have very little in common with temperamentally – sense of humour, yes, but we're very different people – Tim and I are temperamentally far too suited together, and it's far too easy for us to just chatter and waste time. I need somebody to chivvy me up a bit.'

The BBC would have been happy to have had a third series, but by this time *Monty Python's Flying Circus* had started and Garden felt that its anarchic presence pushed them into either becoming even more soft and gentle, or trying to compete with the Pythons in outrageous sketches. Neither idea seemed sensible, and so he, Oddie and Brooke-Taylor put their heads together and planned the new television series which was to establish them firmly as a team – *The Goodies*.

9.
'The Goodies'

Television loves a formula. Any idea which produces good ratings is certain to promote a flock of imitations, all conceived within a tight predictable format, which can easily be written, directed and acted by a team of experienced hacks who appear to be working in their sleep. In 1970 the current formula was 'caper'-type crime series, with teams of criminals or semi-official law enforcers, lots of action and little plot. It was partly to send up this idea that Garden, Brooke-Taylor and Oddie created the formula for their own series – except that, wisely, they kept the format as unspecific as possible. Garden: 'Michael Mills is one of our great patrons and benefactors . . . he was Head of BBC Television Comedy at the time. We went to him, and said, "We want to do an agency of three blokes, who do anything, any time." He said, "Well, I get that idea on my desk twice a week, but if that's what you want to do, I'm prepared to believe that you can do it." The purpose was to use the sort of humour that everybody had been using in sketches, in a sustained half-hour programme.'

The beauty of this very loose idea was that it left them free to do almost anything – a tight format is the prime enemy of sustained invention – and they fully justified the trust that Michael Mills had placed in their abilities. They were contracted to do a series under the title *Narrow Your Mind*, which they changed to *The Goodies*. Oddie: 'It's to the credit of the BBC – and also one of the reasons why by and large it is more satisfying to work for the BBC – that they very often will take a chance on a series, rather than making you do a pilot, and judging the first script, and going through all that stuff, which is nearly always counterproductive.'

The first series, of seven programmes, began transmissions on 8 November 1970. The first programme, 'The Tower of London', was very carefully written in order to set up the characters and the situation; it is worth examining closely because it contains much of the atmosphere and attitudes of *The Goodies*. The three play themselves – or rather, they play three characters with the same names who share some characteristics with the real people – 'Tim', the well-brought-up patriotic coward; 'Graeme', the mad scientist and inventor; and 'Bill', a sort of manic bearded gooseberry. Actually, in this first series Bill has a moustache but no beard – the beard came a little later; Tim has yet to acquire the Union Jack waistcoat which is later his pride and joy; and Graeme wears ordinary spectacles instead of the large-framed ones which have become the trademark of his *Goodies* persona (minus lenses – in real life and other appearances Garden now wears contact lenses).

Even in this first show, the influence of the Hollywood animated cartoon is evident, although it became stronger later on, to the extent that many of the shows are very like a *Tom and Jerry* or *Bugs Bunny* cartoon but with flesh-and-blood characters. This approach is evident in the filmed sequences of the first show, while the studio sequences rely on the interplay between the personalities as well as visual gags.

We first see the three moving into their new office. It appears that Tim's auntie has left him lots of money, which has been spent by Graeme in setting up the office for their new agency. It has a computer, a year's supply of food (a picture of a supermarket behind a door); by an electronic trick (colour separation overlay, to be precise) the same door also opens to reveal a bathroom and a bedroom. The same trick enables the window to look out on a variety of views.

TIM: It's great!

BILL: Fantastic!

GRAEME: Everything we could possibly need.

TIM: Everything we could possibly need.

BILL: What for?

GRAEME: Well . . .

TIM: Well . . .

GRAEME: Yes, that's a point – what *is* it for?

TIM: Well . . .

GRAEME: Well . . .

TIM: Well . . .

BILL: Yes? What are we going to do?

GRAEME: Well, come on – it was your idea.

BILL: Yes – whatever it is.

TIM: That's it. Exactly. Exactly. It *was* my idea. Um . . . We are the Goodies.

GRAEME }
BILL } : Yes, we know that.

TIM: And we are – er – going – to – do good – to people.

BILL: How *wet*!

GRAEME: How are we going to do that?

TIM: We'll just have to wait and see. When people need us – and they're bound to need us – then we'll know what we're needed for. All we have to do is advertise we exist, and we'll soon get people needing us – now *you* should have arranged the advertising.

BILL: It's all right, it's all right – I've done that. Now look – I put one in *The Times*.

TIM: That's good.

BILL: I put one in there. (*He holds up a copy of 'Penthouse'*)

TIM: That's not so good.

BILL: I put one in *Man's Thing*, one in *Woman's Thing*, one in *Rubber News* and one in *Beano*.

GRAEME: You're casting the net a bit wide, aren't you?

BILL: Well, I don't know what we do, do I.

GRAEME: What did you say? . . . 'The Goodies. Phone 083-1234. Anything, any time.' That's a bit vague, isn't it?

BILL: We'll get plenty of enquiries.

TIM: That's fine. Phone 083-1234. Is that our number? Where's the phone?

GRAEME: Ah. Er, well – I'm afraid I sort of forgot that, a bit.

TIM: No phone.

BILL: It's all right – now look, there's an old lady downstairs – that's her number, she takes in messages for us.

TIM: That's not very good for our image.

(Knock on door. Old lady enters with message, gives it to Bill, exits)

TIM: Can't she speak?

BILL: She can't even write – 'Dear Giddies – this is very urgent. You are officially requested to report at precisely two o'clock at the Tower of London. Admission two-and-six.'

In a film insert, we now see outside the office block. The Goodies approach a large flashy car – and wheel out from behind it a three-seater bicycle. (This model is a normal tandem with an extra seat over the back wheel for Bill. Later on they acquired their 'trandem', which has three seats and three sets of pedals.) They fix a police-car-style flashing lamp on to Tim's head, put up a flag saying 'The Goodies', count to three and mount the bike in unison. They promptly fall off. Finally getting going, they wobble down the road in very uncertain control, until they arrive at the Tower of London. They park the bike and Bill pumps up an inflatable model watchdog, complete with a notice saying 'It Bites'.

The Goodies: Bill, Graeme and Tim with trandem

In the Tower, they are welcomed by the Chief Plain-Clothes Beefeater, played sepulchrally by George Baker. It appears that someone has been stealing the Beefeaters' beef, with the result that they are wasting away – in fact there are only two left, and, as we see, they are only three feet tall. Baker has been feeding them on corned beef – the torture chamber has been converted into a kitchen, complete with thumbscrews as garlic-crushers, and a huge swinging pendulum (*à la* Edgar Allan Poe) to slice the corned beef. It nearly slices Tim, as well.

Back in the office, Bill is having 'visions' as a result of being turned on by lemon sherbert – visions which Graeme is able to pick up and display on the computer. These sherbert visions were a regular feature in the first series, but were later dropped because they were becoming too much of an obvious device, and were rather limiting. Oddie: 'I quite liked it, actually; I think if we were an American series that would have been very much kept, and every week you would have had that, whatever happened. We never tried to do that – we tried different things as much as possible.'

In this case, Bill's visions produce a puzzle picture on the computer, which they decipher to mean the Crown Jewels – presumably the next target for the thief. They use another of Graeme's inventions to dress themselves as Beefeaters – a wardrobe, seen side on, into which they walk from one side, emerging on the other in full costume (a very neat piece of video tape editing). Off they go again on the bicycle, using a pike as a balancing pole to the danger of innocent bystanders.

After a 'natural break' with some spoof advertisements (another regular feature in the first few series) we see that Graeme has equipped the Crown Jewels with a highly complicated burglar alarm – it works its way in easy stages from notices saying 'Please do not steal' and 'Burglars will be prosecuted' through various burglar-terrorizing devices to a large cannon labelled 'Hands up'. No sooner have they set the trap than they encounter a Real Burglar – complete with a bag labelled 'Swag'. They chase him, in a speeded-up film sequence which is typical of most of their programmes. There are a number of very neat gags, as their prey uses a polo mallet to 'fire' a cannon-ball at them. (We are invited to infer from the polo-stick that the burglar is His Royal Highness the Duke of Edinburgh – the first of a number of digs at the royal family.) Pursuing him to Buckingham Palace, they realize when he enters unhindered that it *was* him. They are horror-struck. Tim bursts into tears.

All turns out well, however. Back at the office – Tim is packing to leave for Canada – a fanfare heralds the arrival of 'Black Rod', the messenger of the House of Lords. He delivers a Royal Message and, pausing only to solicit a tip, departs. The message explains that the Crown Jewels had been pawned, owing to royal financial difficulties, and what the Goodies had interrupted was actually an attempt to put them *back*.

BILL: So the ones in the Tower are really fakes?

TIM: That's right, they put the replicas there. But now they're back in the money, what with their television appearances and selling Balmoral to the Burtons, they decided to get the real ones out of pawn, and then they tried to put them back . . . (*realization*) and – and *we stopped them*!

GRAEME: What happens to us?

TIM (*reads*): 'We found the whole incident most embarrassing, and to save a public scandal we should be obliged if you would treat the matter as an Official Secret. Your own actions throughout, however, were quite loyal and proper, and it only remains to assure you that when the time comes for our next Birthday Honours List, we shall see you right. All the best, Elizabeth R.'

The Goodies are still in business.

The show is interesting in that it demonstrates, even at the very beginning, many of the Goodies' obsessions – the royal family, clever gadgetry, and highly visual film sequences. *The Goodies* is the only show from the Oxbridge Mafia to rely very largely for its effect on visual gags rather than dialogue. Often there are good gags in the spoken sections – sometimes very old gags, which are put over very well and so are still funny – but the principal influence of the show is the world of the Hollywood cartoons.

It is untypical of the majority of later shows in its use of a guest star – a number of other early shows used guest stars, usually as villains, but this idea was fairly rapidly abandoned. Oddie: 'It got a bit of a hang-up because you were always looking for that situation where you had somebody who was your enemy all the time – and, from the purely practical point of view, we kept giving them the best lines. We got very cross about that, and we got very fed up with the basic image of the programme being the guest villain, with the three of us standing in a line, having almost become one. It very much cut down the area of possible interplay between the three of us.' Instead, they developed a basic plot idea where one of the three would go quite mad on some idea – often to the extent of threatening the whole country with it – and the other two have to intervene. Oddie: 'We provide our own villainy – basically, one of being allowed to become quite horrendous. From that point of view we trampled right across any idea of being "good".'

The last programme of the first series is an early example of this technique. Arising from the then-recent 'pirate' radio stations illicitly broadcasting pop music from just outside the three-mile limit, the Goodies run their own pirate radio ship – in fact a submarine (disguised as a rowing boat). Unfortunately they have only one record – the popular melody 'A Walk In The Black Forest'. As if pirate radio was not enough, they also set up a pirate post office, collecting letters by a variety of ruses which mostly involve mobile letter-boxes containing Bill and Tim. The letters are tied to balloons, which float over the ship and are shot down by Graeme. He sorts them, puts them in bottles and throws them into the sea. When they are washed up on the shore, Bill and Tim rescue them and set about their delivery rounds. Their methods include letters fixed to arrows and pigeon post – a very large parcel instantly drags a very small pigeon to the ground.

After the 'commercial break', Tim and Bill are back in the radio station – still playing 'A Walk in the Black Forest'. Graeme, however, has 'flipped'. First he proposes a pirate bus service – a ring route running round the British Isles outside the five-mile limit[35] – and then, assuming the dress of a Gestapo officer, attempts to use the boat to tow the whole of Britain outside the five-mile limit. Jumping up and down in the boat in a fine Germanic fury, he puts his foot through the bottom and sinks with a military salute. At this point it occurs to him that he may have been wrong.

Back in their office, all three Goodies sit with their feet in bowls of hot water, fighting off chills as they tease Graeme about the impossibility of towing the British Isles away. Meanwhile, through the window behind them we see the Statue of Liberty float past . . .

That show is one of the few episodes of *The Goodies* to be written by all three. Brooke-Taylor was closely involved with the other two during the original setting-up of the first series, but was unable to be involved in the actual writing because of other work. Earlier shows carry the credits 'Written by Graeme Garden and Bill Oddie, with Tim Brooke-Taylor' but the 'with Tim Brooke-Taylor' was eventually dropped. Brooke-Taylor: 'If we were in America, we would all be demanding things like "series created by . . ." but the three of us did create the series. Bill and Graeme write very fast; I find I can't keep up with that sort of speed. They also like to go away and write on their own – they tend to divide the show into two halves and write half each. One half is usually completely different from the other – in odd little bits of style – and it's easier for me than anyone else to say "That doesn't quite work".'

The second series, which ran for thirteen editions, began on 1 October 1971. Many of the shows perpetuated the guest star format, but the best example pitted the Goodies against a new kind of villain – a giant kitten. The show worked so well that it was remade, with additional film sequences, and entered for the Montreux Light Entertainment Festival, where it won the Silver Rose. (Tim can be seen in the first programme of the following series painting the trophy gold.) The remade version was broadcast on 9 April 1972.

Bill has set up business as a vet, and has filled the office with strange animals needing attention. These include a vampire bat, which leaps straight for Graeme's jugular vein when he opens its box, and a bush baby which is just a small ball of fur which persists in attaching itself to his finger. Both these are of course just studio props, but handled by Garden in a very convincing way so that they really seem alive. Spurred on by Graeme, Tim and Bill go out collecting loony animals, which are all packed into the same basket – these include a kitten, a dog (both real) and a fifteen-foot python. Back at the office, an excuse is found for running Jim Franklin's film of the singing dogs *again*, before the Goodies take their animals out for a walk.

This sequence, like many of the film inserts in *The Goodies*, is backed by some very effective music by Bill Oddie – in this case a song, 'Dumb Animals'. Oddie's music plays an important part in creating the atmosphere of the shows, although the audience's attention is of course mostly fixed on the visuals. In the Montreux show film, various film editing techniques, including loops, make a dog flap its ears in time with the music and a tortoise jump up and down; while Tim, who has a tiny white kitten on a lead, finds it first doing press-ups and then (thanks to speeded-up film) racing round the park dragging him after it.

Inadvisedly, Graeme feeds the kitten on some special hormones, with the result that it grows to giant size. It escapes, and terrorizes London in some beautifully faked film shots. By very careful choice of camera lenses, and slowing the film down by precisely the right amount, the kitten makes a very convincing giant. The shot of it climbing (and demolishing) the London Post Office Tower is still used as part of the montage behind the opening titles. In the end, the Goodies have to go aloft by slinging their bike – now a genuine three-seater, or 'trandem' – from a balloon, in order to inject an antidote into the kitten.

Much of the credit for the effectiveness of this and other *Goodies* film sequences must go to Jim Franklin, who directed the filming for the first two series; thereafter he also did the studio direction, taking it over from John Howard Davies. With his previous experience as a comedy film editor, he was the ideal choice to direct *The Goodies'* film sequences. He says: 'I found it very challenging, very exciting – damned expensive, of course, but the BBC is one of those organizations for whom you *can* try experiments. Right from the word go, we were experimenting and we were enthusiasts.'

A wide range of techniques is used for *The Goodies* – not only tricks with the film camera and editing, and the equivalent tricks done in the actual television studio, but also what are called 'visual effects'. The BBC maintains a special visual effects department, which has over the years created monsters and spaceships for *Doctor Who* and *Quatermass* and other science fiction plays, as well as explosions, models, and so on. Their considerable ingenuity has often been stretched to the limit by *The Goodies*.

Garden and Oddie deliberately set out to make the fullest possible use of the medium when they started writing the show. Garden: 'We wrote scripts very often to make use of a particular technique. In general, when we write anything we already have an idea of how that effect can be achieved.' Oddie: 'We're very conscious of not doing things just for the sake of it – it's got to have that laugh point in there, otherwise it becomes a "so what" sequence. We make a point of understanding the technical side; we never put anything into a script where we can't suggest a way that it could be done, technically.'

In fact, most of the effects are in the end not done in the way that the writers have suggested, because their method would be too expensive or not good enough. Garden: 'But if you've said that you can do it, it's up to them to do it better, or cheaper. Anything *is* possible – you can achieve anything on television or film, if you're prepared to pay for it.' *The Goodies* is very unusual from the production point of view, in that the writers sit in at the planning and budgeting meetings, and haggle over the cost of the stunts. They may, for example, be told that they can have two gags at £250 each or one at £500; or that they can have two at £500 if they are prepared to lose another one which will cost £1,000 to mount. In this way, the team can balance the cost of each gag against its probable effectiveness on screen; obviously, they would not hang on to a gag which would be very expensive but might not be very funny. Oddie: 'We try and learn every single side of it – which is very hard work, and means that somebody's got to be "on duty" all the time. When we're filming, we always make a point of *one* of us being awake, even if we're not in a sequence. It's not lack of trust in anybody – it's just the only way, because reading one of our scripts is impossible.'

With the third series – now fully directed by Jim Franklin – the Goodies move to a new office. The first programme (broadcast on 4 February 1973) begins with some builders, who are supposed to be redecorating their old office, merely wrecking it. Finding that prices are not only too high for them, but visibly mounting (the estate agent's advertisements are equipped with price labels that increase as we watch) they decide that the only solution is to renovate a deserted railway station. Failing to find one, they build their own movable railway station (in the style of the small Victorian country stations which consist of little more than a stationmaster's cottage). Inside, they have an office very similar to their old one, complete with driving controls beneath the window. Searching for somewhere to park it, they find a deserted area which looks suitable, until they are menaced by a number of earth-shifting machines which, through clever driving and speeded-up film, behave like prehistoric monsters. Giant mechanical diggers, their scoops gnashing, pursue the Goodies like long-necked dinosaurs. The whole sequence is brilliantly staged, and is in many ways based on the 'Rite of Spring' sequence from Walt Disney's *Fantasia*. Indeed Stravinsky's music is used as a backing for the Goodies' film.

The railway station office remains throughout the third and fourth series. It is interesting to notice that in the third series the hallway outside the door to the office displays, very properly, a framed abstract of the Offices, Shops and Railway Premises Act (required by law to be posted on such premises).

The first programme of the fourth series, 'Camelot', takes place mostly away from the office, as the Goodies are called to take care of a castle belonging to a relative of Tim's who thinks he is King Arthur. Although situated in an ordinary suburban street, it is indeed a real castle, complete with drawbridge – and an ordinary front garden gate labelled 'Camelot'. As Tim's relative leaves for his holiday – complete with mediaevally dressed family – a narration identifies them all, ending with 'the dog, Spot'. This of course produces a cheer from the fairly high proportion of *ISIRTA* fans in the audience. The show continues with a number of verbal and visual digs at Arthurian legend as portrayed in Hollywood films.

The third and fourth series contains a mixture of good and less effective programmes; indeed, throughout all the series there are programmes which do not come off as well as the team had hoped. Oddie: 'I've always maintained that our programmes may or may not be funny, but they're always interesting. If it's a failure, well, it was a good try. I think in comparison with *Monty Python's Flying Circus*, their "highs" are higher than ours, their "lows" are lower than ours. I think we're more consistent.' These series suffered from being placed too early in the evening. Whereas the first two series went out at times ranging between half-past nine and half-past ten, the third and fourth series shows were broadcast at about eight-fifteen, with the last two being as early as six forty-five. Oddie: 'Consequently, the BBC started labelling us as a kid's show, because they realized kids did like it. Then they started getting up-tight about the content.'

During the fourth series, on Christmas Eve 1973, the Goodies broadcast a special programme which was aimed rather more at children than their usual shows. It was called *The Goodies and the Beanstalk*, and was the first time they had gone over the half-hour length; it ran forty-three minutes and was made entirely on film. The traditional story got a bit bent in its encounter with the Goodies. The giant, for example, is small and played by Alfie Bass (the archetypal Jewish tailor); and on the way up the mountain they encounter an edition of *It's A Knockout* (the popular series in which teams from various towns compete in spectacular and often hilarious semi-athletic games) – another excuse for Garden's Eddie Waring impression. There are also some flying geese – mechanical models with flapping wings 'flying' down an invisible wire – and some flying pantomime geese.

As well as visual effects, stunts are a major part of the Goodies' style. The three do most of their own stunts, except when specialized skills such as horse-riding are called for, or when dummies are used for spectacular falls. Though many of the stunts look dangerous, obviously every precaution is taken to prevent accidents. Garden: 'You go to do something – like sliding down a chute into the sea – and you're happy to do it, and you sit there, and it's about to go when somebody says, "That thing down at the bottom, he might catch his leg on that . . ." So they go and move that, and meanwhile you're sitting there wondering about it. And then people start talking about insurance and responsibilities; and before you started, you were happy – but an hour later, when everyone's said, "Well, I dunno, in this wind . . ." you're absolutely terrified out of your wits. So by the time anyone actually gets round to doing a stunt, every possible precaution has been taken.'

There are stunts a-plenty in the sixth and last of the fourth series, 'The Race', broadcast on 12 January 1974. The Goodies are still in their railway station office (the notice outside the door now announces the withdrawal of freight services from Strathclyde station). Having entered Le Mans, Graeme is teaching Tim to drive. In the absence of a car, Bill has to pretend to be one by lying on his back with his raised feet acting as accelerator and brake pedals. When Tim presses the accelerator-foot, Bill makes appropriate engine-noises; and when Tim passes his test, he does so by driving Bill, who is lying on his back harnessed to two chairs which he pulls along.

The actual race is run between a wicked Baron in a black car and the Goodies in their mobile office (a lorry, suitably disguised for the filming). After several hair-raising incidents, and some attempts at sabotage by their adversary, they lose control of the office as the brakes fail. Clambering on to the top of it as it travels, they attempt to stop by lassoing a French 'pissoir'; inevitably, they drag it along behind them for a time. After falling off the building and getting briefly involved in a can-can competition, they drop back on to the office from a railway bridge, go through the roof and land once again in their room. This is a typically complex Goodies' stunt, using dummies, speeded-up film and carefully-integrated studio work. After further frantic and unavailing attempts to control the building, it heads straight over a cliff, sprouts wings and flies off into the sunset.

The fifth series, which ran for thirteen weeks, started on 10 February 1975. After the unsatisfactory placing of the previous two series, this one fared rather better for being placed at nine o'clock, a timing which was maintained until the eighth series. By the fifth series *Monty Python's Flying Circus* had come and gone, and Oddie thinks that this also helped their viewing figures: 'We do have a bigger audience now, and a much more tolerant audience, especially since *Monty Python*'s not on ... people suddenly realized we were all right, and we've been allowed into this group. Also, we asked the BBC to put us on at nine o'clock on BBC-2; we got hundreds of letters from kids complaining that they couldn't watch it any more, and the audience shot up from three million to ten – so we were right, there! People do tend to be very conscious of their image as viewers – especially in this kind of an area where they know, for example, that we appeal to kids. A fully-blown *Time Out*, *Sounds* and *New Musical Express* reader will not be seen dead watching *The Goodies* at that point. You've got to be a *Python* fan, because that's clever, and we're not, we're childish ... it's as stupid as that. But we've got that bigger audience now.' Brooke-Taylor: 'Suddenly *The Goodies* became "socially acceptable", and we won the *Sun* awards, with Morecambe and Wise second and *The Two Ronnies* third! Suddenly our records were selling, and our books were selling – it all happened in that one year.'

These books, *The Goodies File* (Weidenfeld & Nicholson, 1974) and *The Goodies Book of Criminal Records* (1976), are ingeniously laid out, with a variety of subjects and presentations; the Goodies and their designer Anthony Cohen have put a good deal of care into them. They are highly entertaining for 'dipping into', though perhaps it would be a brave reader who would try to go through either of them cover-to-cover. The gramophone records are mostly of musical items, written by Oddie and performed by all three; some of them are lifted from *ISIRTA*.

The fifth series certainly has a number of well-made and amusing shows. In the second programme, 'Clown Virus', the original idea of the Goodies actually being sent for for some purpose makes one of its rare reappearances. The plot is even more weird than usual, involving a virus which turns people into clowns – a good enough excuse for a number of slapstick gags.

The fifth programme, 'Frankenfido', is rather better integrated. Graeme has taken to breeding strange dogs. Bill and Tim, who hope to win Cruft's dog show, have ordered one, but it turns out to be nothing but a white fluffy object. Bill and Tim can't even tell which end is which until it pees on the table; Bill dries it out by putting it through the mangle. In Graeme's laboratory, a converted tiny castle, he demonstrates some of his results. Having bred a dog with a mouse, he has ended up with a two-foot high mousehole and something that won't come out of it. Left unobserved for a moment, Tim's 'dog' succeeds in mating with a feather duster – it produces a number of small white furry sausages. This encourages Graeme to go rather overboard on the whole idea, which leads to 'Cruft's Ideal Dog Exhibition' including such monstrosities as a North Sea Gas Dalmation (a gas cooker with spots). Tim, despairing of winning a prize, has entered Bill disguised as a dog (as the dog Spot, actually). Bill walks off with all the day's prizes, because of his abilities to follow instruction (and play a tin-whistle) whereas all Graeme's dalmation cooker can do is obey the order 'stay'.

Stung by his failure, Graeme finally 'flips' and retires to his laboratory to produce his masterpiece – Frankenfido. This turns out to be a six-legged peculiarity with a long neck and a long snout (it is in principle a sort of three-layer pantomime horse with appendages). The obligatory chase sequence which ensues culminates in the hilarious sight of this sextupedal syntheticate frantically pedalling along on the Goodies' trandem. In the final scene, the monster has produced an offspring – the result of closeting with the Oddie-dog. It has a similar body to the monster's, but Bill's face – with whiskers.

The stunts and gags in the fifth series are of a very high standard. Several of them were used as illustrations for a programme about special effects in the cinema, called *How On Earth Did They Do That?*, broadcast on 23 December 1974. It included a number of optical effects: sequences from *The Golden Voyage of Sinbad* and many earlier films; and, since many of the techniques

The Goodies: 'Rome Antics' (7 April 1975) – Tim losing a gladiatoral combat with a sheep; 'Kung Fu Kapers' (24 March 1975) – Tim and model Graeme; 'Kung Fu Kapers' – Bill, Grand Master of Ecky Thump, is about to attack Tim with a black pudding; also Bill, Graeme and Tim with Stone Age tandem

used by the BBC for *The Goodies* date back to the days of silent films, the programme showed various trick shots being filmed.

However, *The Goodies* does not depend entirely for its success on these visual jokes. The interplay of the three participants is very important, although it is not always as obvious as the more spectacular side of the shows. By the fifth series, each of the three had developed a persona which was fully rounded, and with a depth gained from the links with the actual person in each case. The three people we see on the screen are not the three performers as they actually are, but the characterizations tend to be exaggerations of them as they appear to be.

The 'Tim' of the shows is a patriotic coward, complete with Union Jack waistcoat and a gilded throne, much given to declaiming his views to the accompaniment of 'Land of Hope and Glory'. Oddie: 'Tim quite rightly claims that he hardly ever is seen in a suit and tie – but somehow you feel he should be! There's no question that he is patriotic – on the very simple level, he is basically pro-royalty and I'm not.' Brooke-Taylor: 'We've taken little sides of ourselves . . . I *am* a coward . . . Once, I was doing my "Land of Hope and Glory" speech – "We must fight them," et cetera – that originally was all it was, but I said, "I'd never do that, I might actually *say* it all, but at the end I'd run away." Which is in fact how it finished – the other two went out, and I went and hid in a cupboard.'

'Graeme' is presented in the shows as a loony scientist. Oddie: 'He's cleverer than either of us – he's certainly got that air of a recluse, that professorial thing – he's a qualified doctor, for a start, so he knows what to do with bits and pieces and test-tubes.'

'Bill' is something of a contrast to the others. In a way he keeps their characters down to earth, and yet he is the most fantastic of the three. There is something rather Pan-like about him. Oddie: 'Within the show, in a strange sort of way I'm usually the most reasonable one – which is odd, because visually I'm the *least* reasonable one. But I'm the one who's a righteous conservationist, and those two are made to be absolutely bloodthirsty loonies . . . very often the stories are built round that idea.' Brooke-Taylor: 'I think we all identify with Bill's character – he's the spokesman for what we're trying to say. In a *way* it's a true reflection of him.'

The corporate image built up by the three of them is a very strong one, with the characterizations well balanced. Inevitably, this has had the effect of confusing other people, who think the three of them live together and are going to ride up on the trandem. Garden: 'It's not just members of the public, either – very often television companies or publishers will think that because they've given a message to one of us, they've told "The Goodies". The fact that we all live in different houses, with different families, and do different things, doesn't appear to enter people's heads! Even the BBC we've had this with. They just assume we sit round the table in the office, and say "Oh, we've got to go to the Beeb tomorrow" and get on the bike . . . And I think people do expect you to be funny the whole time. Some people of course are relieved to find that you're not.'

It is the interplay of these carefully developed characters that gives *The Goodies* its strength and prevents it from degenerating into a collection of 'sight gags'. As Brooke-Taylor says, the programmes are best when the three are interrelating – the show is not really about kittens and Post Office Towers.

The last show of the fifth series gave them an ideal opportunity to inter-relate, for the simple reason that they had run out of money and couldn't afford any film sequences. This was not the first edition of *The Goodies* to avoid the use of film – they had done one in the third series which was about Bill becoming a pop star – but on this occasion they scripted a situation where they are entombed in their office under tons of concrete. Facing the fact that there will be no rescue, and with the 'phone and television cut off, they attempt to construct an ordered society.

GRAEME: Gentlemen – I'm sure that you will all agree that the stable and successful civilizations of the world have all been composed of three basic groups – the ruling class, the scientific and technical class – and the workers.

BILL: Cobblers!

GRAEME: And the cobblers. And I feel that we, here, are particularly fortunate in that we have, in our midst, representatives of all these three basic types; and if you will allow me ...

BILL: Hang about a bit – whom is which?

GRAEME: I should have thought that was quite obvious.

TIM: Heah heah!

BILL: Wait a minute, come on – name the names.

GRAEME: Now Bill, please, you're just wasting time.

BILL: Time? We have enough to waste, you four-eyed git! Name the names!

GRAEME: All right, then – well clearly, *I* am the scientist.

BILL: Just 'cos you wear glasses.

TIM: I am the ruling class.

BILL: Just 'cos you've got poncey blond hair and no chin.

TIM: Precisely.

GRAEME: And you are the worker.

TIM: Because you're smaller than us. And because somebody's got to clean the shoes.

BILL: *Why can't you clean the shoes?*

TIM: Because I'm quite clearly and obviously a lord! And lords don't clean shoes – it's a well-known fact.

BILL: It's not a well known fact! Now listen here, mate – (*shouting*) in this new society we're going to have equal division of labour, *and every single one of us is going to clean the shoes!*

TIM (*shouting*): YOU SNIVELLING LITTLE COMMIE!

BILL: YOU ÉLITIST FASCIST PIG!

GRAEME: This is good – political discussion, a healthy thing.

BILL: This isn't political discussion, we're just shouting at one another.

GRAEME: Same thing. Anyway – here is my solution: Tim, you can be a lord. But you've got to clean the shoes.

TIM: Oh, all right. I suppose we all have to strive together to create a new society. (*Plays 'Land of Hope and Glory' on the wind-up gramophone*) We shall build –
(*Bill takes the record off and smashes it*)

TIM: What did you do that for?

BILL: Silent revolution, my Lord Timbo.

TIM: We shall build a fine life – a better tomorrow – a finer world for our children to live in . . .

BILL: What do you mean, 'children'? We're not going to have any children, are we, think about it, you know – let's face it, for the next three years, we three are doomed to be bachelors gay . . . That's an idea, isn't it . . .

TIM: Get off!

BILL: Hey – I don't mind shaving, you know. Underneath this lot I look a bit like Liza Minelli.

TIM: I've often wondered why you grew it.

BILL: You bitch!

TIM: But no children – I hadn't thought of that – that's terrible. I want a son – *I must have a son!* Graeme – you're a doctor . . .

GRAEME: Sorry, can't be done.

TIM: But a man isn't a man unless he exercises his right to fatherhood!

BILL: You can exercise it all you like, but you won't find much use for it here!

Between the fifth and sixth series, the Goodies indulged in their longest sustained performance so far – forty-eight minutes of it, in *Goodies Rule – OK*, transmitted on 21 December 1975. The programme was entirely on film and positively bristles with invention – perhaps too much so for its own good, because forty-eight minutes of it is a bit remorseless. After various failures as a pop group, Tim, Bill and Graeme hit on a winning formula involving pinching odd characteristics from various famous groups. They are such a success that they play to a packed audience at Wembley Stadium. In order to prevent riots, the audience consists entirely of policemen and policewomen. As a result of their success the Goodies receive OBEs, at a garden party so waterlogged that it takes place *under* water; in fact the Queen has to dive under the water to pin on the medals. After a complicated plot sequence involving the Goodies opposing attempted governmental suppression of enjoyment, they find themselves opposing a new kind of government – a puppet government. Literally. The Prime Minister is Sooty, the Home Secretary is Sweep (popular glove puppets

Goodies Rule OK (21 December 1975): the waterlogged garden party

from the heyday of children's television, and still going strong); and the
Cabinet consists of almost every puppet character that has ever appeared on
British television. Having dressed up as oversized marionettes in order to
infiltrate the Cabinet meeting, the Goodies find themselves doing battle with
six foot tall Pinky and Perky, Andy Pandy and the Flowerpot Men – and finally
make their escape, spectacularly pursued by a giant Dougal and Zebedee from
The Magic Roundabout. The show has many really excellent stunts and gags,
and the only problem with it is that it is fifteen minutes too long.

The sixth series, which ran for seven weeks from 21 September 1976,
contains several very inventive shows. In 'Daylight Robbery on the Orient
Express' the Goodies have to combat three fake Goodies (presumably Bad-
dies?), who spend a long sequence being Marcel Marceau – all three of them. In
'It Might As Well Be String' the Goodies market string as if it was a new
invention; and in '2001 and a Bit' we are privileged to see into the future, to the
time when the Goodies are elderly. The final show, 'The Goodies – Almost
Live', is really more of a pop concert, in which the three perform some of their
songs, including their best selling 'Funky Gibbon'.

The seventh series consisted of six episodes, starting on 1 November 1977,
but with one of them delayed to 22 December. In the second programme,
'Dodonuts', Bill is seen in his conservationist rôle, protecting a dodo – Graeme
had found it in a pet shop. ('Was it going cheap?' – 'No – SQUAAAWK!!!')
The others, being portrayed as unrestrained hunters, would be quite prepared
to shoot it, but Bill takes a liking to it – even after Tim has very inadvisedly fed
it with baked beans, thus lumbering Bill with a squawking, odiferous,
temperamental bird, noisly crapping and farting all over the office.

The dodo itself is a triumph for Visual Effects. Actually there are two
models, one a puppet operated by someone putting his arm up the neck, and
one a mechanical contrivance which can walk. In the end Bill tries to teach it to
fly, a venture which only succeeds when he teaches it to pilot a light aircraft.
The 'plane crashes, and the Goodies discover the real reason why dodos
became extinct – they're *delicious*!

Two of the shows in the seventh series fell foul of BBC censorship. The
Goodies had always received objections to some of their material, but these
editions caused an unusual amount of trouble. Jim Franklin: 'One is very close
to a programme, and what you see as being right may in someone else's eyes be
wrong. *The Goodies* occasionally offends people – I don't think that's a bad
thing – I must say, in the past I have felt annoyed about cuts that had been
forced upon us, I think in some cases for the wrong reasons. I think one should
make a statement, have faith in it, and be damned . . . probably by the public if

you're wrong. But of course, sometimes the BBC cannot take that risk.'

Bill Oddie: 'I think the BBC have monthly subjects, which are up on the wall as being worrying for them – especially ones they don't understand.' The subject of the fifth show was punk rock, which, because of the inherent and deliberate nastiness of the 1977 phenomenon given that label, caused a severe attack of fright at the BBC. Garden and Oddie had written the show with a few lines which they knew would have to be cut, just for the hell of it, but they were told that the programme could not be made at all. Garden: 'The angle was that if you push punk beyond where it's gone already, you're into a very distasteful area – and that seemed, to us, funny. The BBC couldn't understand that the whole point was that it was distasteful. What you do with these run-ins is, you say to them, "What specifically do you object to?" Nobody is ever fool enough nowadays to admit to that – people have been quoted too often on what they've objected to and what they've suggested as alternatives – so they don't fall for that any more, sadly.' After a few arguments, in which Oddie found himself, to his surprise, acting almost as mediator between the Head of Comedy and Tim Brooke-Taylor, the 'Punk' show was slightly rewritten, and went ahead.

The case of the third episode, 'Royal Command', was more complicated. First of all they wanted to include a montage of newsfilm of members of the royal family falling off horses – there is no shortage of it – as 'The Amazing Tumbling Royals'. They were stopped, on the grounds that it was forbidden to mess around with newsfilm – a ruling dating back to the Macmillan newsfilm episode in *TW3* (see page 65), but which is only invoked when it suits the BBC. Apart from this sequence, the show has a Royal Variety Performance as mounted by the Goodies, with the royal family fast asleep in their box; and then ends with the Goodies standing in for the royal family, who are all in hospital swathed in bandages.

As two members of the royal family were in fact in hospital at the time, the situation was rather touchy. Part of the BBC's sensitivity about the show apparently arose from the fact that Princess Anne was about to give birth on the day when the show was scheduled to be transmitted. Garden: 'Alasdair Milne said, "If the Princess has her baby by six o'clock on the transmission day, the show can't go out" – begging the question, what happens if she has it between six o'clock, and nine o'clock when the show's due to go out. Begging the *answer*, I presume, that by then Alasdair Milne has gone home and it's not his responsibility any more!'[36] In the event, the Princess had her baby at half past eleven in the morning, so the show was replaced by a repeat from the sixth series. There was no other choice, because all the seventh series shows were recorded only four days before scheduled for transmission. Garden: 'To show how in touch the BBC were, our administrator said, "I've got the solution – instead of putting this one out, why don't you put out the one you recorded last Friday?" We said, "This *is* the one we recorded last Friday".'

In the end, 'Royal Command' was placed where the last programme of the series would have been, and that last programme, 'Earthanasia', was shown on 22 December 1977. It has to be placed at the end of the series whatever happened, because this time the Goodies destroy the whole world. To be more accurate, it is to be destroyed by international agreement, as no-one can govern it any longer. The Goodies spend the duration of the programme examining their lives and indulging in mutual recriminations – another chance for the sort of interrelation which characterized the last show of the fifth series, quoted earlier. 'Earthanasia' does indeed end with the destruction of the world, just as several previous series had finished with the Goodies destroyed in some way. Garden: 'We were expecting something like Sherlock Holmes – that people would jam the telephone switchboards saying "Don't finish the Goodies – they must come back" . . . but nobody really tended to notice very much whether we were written out at the end of a series or not. I suppose we should take heart that nobody jammed the switchboard saying "Thank God that's over"!'

Oddie made a supreme sacrifice in the cause of humour for this show – he appears towards the end without his beard and moustache, for the first time in about eight years. The beard in the earlier scenes is genuine – he shaved it off during the recording session. Oddie: 'And of course the classic thing did indeed happen – I was half-way through, I'd got half a beard on – and they rushed in and said "Hold it!"' The producer wanted to retake the previous scene because there was a microphone boom in shot . . . Oddie just said 'Tough! – so there's a boom in shot!' After all that, his appearance without the beard fails to get a laugh. What reaction there is is more one of shock. Later in the scene he 'reveals' that he is almost bald, removing his wig – of course, he is not really bald but had been equipped with a bald-headed wig for the occasion, plus a wig to represent his normal hair.

After the seventh series the Goodies took a break before planning their next series, partly in order, as Oddie says, to go out and gain experiences in order to be able to write about them. Brooke-Taylor and Garden went on tour for six weeks in 'legitimate theatre' – a play called *The Unvarnished Truth*, which, since they had not had anything to do with the writing, gave them a rest from the total control of *The Goodies*. The play then went into the West End, which they found enjoyable but exhausting. Garden immediately laid plans to go into another play, while Brooke-Taylor concentrated on writing. He had also been involved for some time with the radio show *Hello Cheeky!*, collaborating with John Junkin and Barry Cryer; its approach depends largely on old jokes – or new jokes in the style of old jokes.

Brooke-Taylor and Garden had also been involved since 1972 with a panel game on radio called *I'm Sorry I Haven't a Clue*; Oddie also appeared in the earlier series, but by 1975 the participants were Brooke-Taylor, Garden, William Rushton and Barry Cryer, with Humphrey Lyttleton as the quizmaster.

Garden: '*I'm Sorry I Haven't a Clue* was an attempt to achieve the atmosphere and enjoyment of *I'm Sorry I'll Read That Again*, without the BBC having to pay us, and without our having to do the chore of writing a script for it. It was almost as cold-blooded as that. I put the idea to David Hatch; we put a format together, and recorded a pilot. In the first series it was all virtually ad-libbed – that was my mistake, and since then we've all learned a bit about doing panel games. We know that the audience like it a) because you appear to be witty, and b) because you appear to be put 'on the spot' and have to sweat. And those are two different things; if you've got to make up, say, a calypso, it's almost impossible to do that on the spot, and so you spend an hour or so beforehand writing it. If you have to make up a poem as it goes along, that is *just* possible, but you have to sweat.'

The early editions sound rather messy and self-indulgent, but the team's increasing experience, particularly in knowing which sections they should prepare, has led to a much improved control over the show. The team try to maintain the illusion that the entire show is ad-libbed. Garden: 'Anyone who thinks, "That wasn't done on the spot" is probably right in their assumptions; but I'd hate them to think that any of the ones we *have* done on the spot were prepared! We can write better stuff than that!'

Oddie meanwhile, having managed to get 1978 entirely clear of *The Goodies*, was working on various projects when Southern Television asked him to compère a lively Saturday morning magazine programme for children, *The Saturday Banana*, starting on 8 July 1978. Oddie: 'My reason for doing it was partly just to do something different, but rather more seriously – I do feel most "children's television" – shows done specially for children – are very bland and very safe. I do object to that – they do all have that in common; play safe, avoid controversial subjects, and don't for heaven's sake ever make adults look as though they're vulnerable.' He hoped that in *The Saturday Banana* they might be able to cover ideas and subjects not dealt with by the normal range of children's programmes. 'To a point I think we succeeded, and to a point we failed – a lot of that's to do with the technical resources available. And that's pretty chaotic – it's a live show, and obviously it goes wrong all the time, you just can't help it. What I've done when things go wrong is explain absolutely everything to the kids, and they seem to appreciate that. What bothered people was that I wasn't being funny – it didn't seem to bother the kids one little bit, and apparently they still find me quite funny, which surprised me, because I wasn't trying to be.' Certainly *The Saturday Banana* made up in verve for what it lacked in smoothness, with Oddie being prepared to try anything.

After this year away, they returned for an eighth series of *The Goodies*, running for six weeks from 14 January 1980 on BBC-2, at the earlier time of ten past eight – breaking their 'not before nine' rule but without apparent detriment. Their targets included 'Close Encounters of the Third Kind', 'Star Wars' (Graeme having built an R2D2 as a mobile dustbin, vacuum cleaner and so on), 'Evita' (Tim exhorts two girls called Marge and Tina not to cry for him), John Travolta and Margaret Thatcher; and they revealed how as two-year-olds they won World War Two.

This year away from *The Goodies* was certainly beneficial to all three of them – as with most of the 'Oxbridge Mafia' they like challenges, and to broaden their scope and experience.

The Goodies had run for ten highly inventive years on BBC Television (their transfer to London Weekend Television in 1981 falls outside the scope of this book); and although, inevitably, there were a number of less successful shows, every series produced several very funny and often spectacular programmes. To some extent the programmes have suffered by irrelevant comparisons with *Monty Python* and other manifestations of Oxbridge Mafiosity; it has sometimes been held against *The Goodies* that it is largely visual humour and makes no pretence to be 'intellectual'. This is of course its main strength – although, as we have seen, there is more in the interplay of the characters than is sometimes realized; and the programmes often take an opportunity to be socially satirical, as for example in the 'Punk show. For sheer exuberance the show is very hard to beat, and it has certainly made full use of the technical vocabulary of television. The programme could well run for a number of years yet in its new manifestation; as the team's imagination shows no signs of running out, future series of *The Goodies* should be well worth looking forward to.

10.
'Do Not Adjust Your Set'; 'The Complete and Utter History of Britain'

It is now necessary to back-track, for the tenth (and fortunately the last) time. The fourth series of *ISIRTA* ended in summer 1967. Humphrey Barclay had been producing the show up to then, but shortly after the end of the series he found himself being wooed by Associated-Rediffusion, the commercial television company which had presented *At Last the 1948 Show*. Barclay: 'I got a letter, quite out of the blue, from Jeremy Isaacs at Rediffusion asking me to come and see him . . . I thought it was something to do with the *1948 Show* – perhaps they wanted to use some material which was ours . . . I went to see him, and he said, "We like the appeal that *ISIRTA* has for children – we have decided to do a children's comedy programme, and we think you're the person to produce it." It was the shock of my life.' Barclay asked his mentor, Peter Titheradge, what he should do, and Titheradge advised him to grab the opportunity. 'It was a major decision – it's like deserting your country, to leave the BBC. I had a hysterical interview with Tom Sloan who tried to persuade me not to go, and being able to offer no good reasons, but saying so so persuasively that when I left his office I totally believed I was crazy to go and have my own series and be a producer . . . When I got outside, I thought, no, wait a minute, what was he offering instead?' The BBC offer of a possible chance to train for a possible assistant production post in their television service seemed, on cool reflection, to be insufficient; and Barclay defected to Rediffusion.

Given the brief of producing a comedy programme for children, Barclay wisely took the standpoint that it should be the funniest show they could manage, which would happen to be on at teatime. He was anxious to avoid any appearance of 'talking down' to the children; and the approach certainly produced better results than some of the previous funny programmes for children, which, even from the normally high-quality BBC stable, had tended to rely on a very basic and heavy-handed style. Barclay also decided not to use any of the *ISIRTA* team, as half of them were in the *1948 Show* and the other half in *Twice a Fortnight*. His choice fell upon Eric Idle, as the next university comic who had not been used, at any rate in a starring capacity, and Terry Jones, whom he had seen in the Oxford revue, '****', which was on in London at the same time as *Cambridge Circus*. Jones agreed to come into the show, and suggested Michael Palin; Barclay had never heard of Palin, and was a bit cautious, but in the end realized that the three would make a very good team.

Barclay felt that the intellectual side of the show ought to be balanced by one or two non-university performers, and hired David Jason as a knockabout comic (despite Terry Jones's feeling that *he* was a perfectly good knockabout comic). Barclay also needed a female member of the cast: 'I'd seen Denise Coffey at the Edinburgh Festival . . . I asked her if she minded people making jokes about her size (I thought we'd better get the air cleared over that!), and she said, no, that was the main point of being that size, to have people make jokes about it.' (Denise Coffey went on to direct for the Young Vic Theatre Company and to write plays for children.)

The shows were mainly written by Palin, Jones and Idle, although later on Coffey and Jason began to add a few ideas. The three writers agreed with Barclay's approach of not writing specifically for children. They simply wrote what seemed funny to them, and the occasional sketch which turned out to be unsuitable for children for one reason or another was simply put aside for future use.

Do Not Adjust Your Set: David Jason, Terry Jones, Eric Idle and Denise Coffey

The shows were titled *Do Not Adjust Your Set*, from the standard engineering apology caption: 'There is a fault – do not adjust your set' which could be put up to cover anything from slight interference to total loss of programme. The first series ran for thirteen weeks, starting on 4 January 1968 at 5.25, but it was due to be preceded by a Christmas special, scheduled for Boxing Day 1967. Barclay watched the transmission with mounting horror as the realization dawned that the wrong episode was being transmitted – it was the first of the series proper, and left a gap for a commercial break which the correct show did not have. Then, because it was too long for the slot allocated, it over-ran and was cut abruptly. The only saving grace was that the débâcle made headlines the following morning, which at any rate got the series off to a well-publicized start.

182

The sketches, though kept short and simple, are well written and entertaining. Having, they remember, no idea what children were supposed to like, the team instinctively developed a mildly fantastic style which was highly suitable to their audience.

> *Caption and voice-over:* 'GREAT DISCOVERIES OF OUR TIME'
> 'JAMES WATT DISCOVERS THE STEAM-ENGINE FROM THE SIMPLE KETTLE'

DENISE:	James?
JASON:	What?
DENISE:	James?
JASON:	What?
DENISE:	Do you notice anything strange about the way the kettle's boiling?
JASON:	How do you mean, Janet?
DENISE:	Well, do you not see the steam pouring out? D'you not think it could be harnessed to provide a form of transport?
JASON:	. . . You mean a travelling kettle?
DENISE:	Aye, James. A kettle that could travel from London to Glasgow in five hours flat.
JASON:	Aye, you could have express kettles, and stopping kettles, and even cattle kettles.
DENISE:	And kettle spotters.
JASON:	D'you realize, Janet, you could have kettle ways all over the world?
DENISE:	And even electric kettles . . . Aye . . . mmmmmm.
JASON:	Aye, and you know, I can see it now, on the hoardings of the land . . . 'It's quicker by kettle' . . . and – and – 'Kettle fares up'.
DENISE:	'Kettle fares down'.
JASON:	Aye, aye – and 'Kettles go slow, Prime Minister steps in'.
DENISE:	Mmmmmm – Mmmmmmm.
	(Enter Idle)
JASON:	Ah, it's you, my boy, and about time too. Look at the hour.
IDLE:	I'm sorry, father – the train was late.

The show borrowed from *ISIRTA* the idea of having a serial, with a short episode each week starring David Jason in 'The Life And Adventures of Captain Fantastic'. Dressed in a bowler hat and an old raincoat, Captain Fantastic sought to rid the world of the menace of Mrs Black and her evil Blit Men; the episodes were filmed, with a commentary, and presented a sort of dilapidated cross between Dick Barton and a non-super Superman. This serial became very popular, and went on to a series of its own after *Do Not Adjust Your Set* had finished.

Another regular item in each show was an approximately musical appearance by the Bonzo Dog Doo Dah Band, a rather wild and anarchic group consisting of 'Legs' Larry Smith, Rod Slater, Dennis Cowan, Roger Ruskin Spear, Vivian Stanshall and Neil Innes. Innes was born in December 1940, and studied art at Norwich Art School and Goldsmith's College (which is part of London University). He and the others formed the band in 1966, originally calling themselves the Bonzo Dog Dada Band (named after Dada, the anarchic art movement), but changing the name to the Bonzo Dog Doo Dah Band

Do Not Adjust Your Set: the Bonzo Dog Doo Dah Band. Rear: Neil Innes (masked), Roger Ruskin Spear, Rod Slater, Dennis Cowan and 'Legs' Larry Smith. Front: Vivian Stanshall

because they were fed up with explaining Dada. Bonzo, incidentally, was a little dog who starred in strip and animated cartoons in the 1920s. Originally the band specialized in what Innes describes as 'ricky-ticky foxtrots'; he says, 'We were offered the job of being the New Vaudeville Band when their hit record came out – because there wasn't such a thing as a New Vaudeville Band [the hit record would have been made by session musicians – this is not an uncommon practice; if the record is a hit the record company has to find a group to appear in public in a hurry] and we all said no except for the trumpeter, who went off – next week he was on *Top of the Pops*. With our act. So we changed to rock-and-roll.' The name was later shortened to the Bonzo Dog Band; but at the time of *Do Not Adjust Your Set* the 'Doo Dah' was still operative, and the band performed its own mixture of rock and plain silliness. Innes: 'Eric Idle acknowledges that the Bonzos' approach to television, which was far from professional and totally anarchic, in many ways led to the *Monty Python* sort of thinking. We would do anything which was stupid – we had a seal costume, which was the "seal of good housekeeping", and Mona Lisas with the face cut out that you could look through . . . Roger Spear had a six-foot prop arm that played a really long guitar.'

The band found the series a bit of a strain because they were on tour at the same time, and this led to a certain anarchy off the screen as well. On one occasion the television people rang up frantically asking what props they would need. Larry Smith said, 'Three cardboard boxes, a springboard, and a petrol tanker.' A plaintive phone call the next day said they were having trouble with the petrol tanker, and would an oil drum do? Innes: 'We said, "Oh – ah – that was a joke." They went mad. We nearly got out of our management contract that way – the television people were OK, they didn't mind, but our management didn't like it – they said "Clear off" – we said "Can we have it in writing" – they said "Ah, you're not getting away that easily." We wore rubber masks throughout the whole confrontation.'

One of the band's numbers in *Do Not Adjust Your Set* – 'Urban Spaceman' – became a hit record, and their songs are lively and show more intelligence in the writing than many 'straight' pop songs.

Rather to the cast's surprise, the show became something of a cult –

children liked it, but word also got around among adults, and people were rushing home from the office in order to catch the programmes. In the last show of the first series, broadcast on 28 March 1968, the team presented 'the end of *Do Not Adjust Your Set*' in the artificially hysterical style of an election broadcast – something that the children in the audience cannot have been familiar with, although that did not seem to mar their enjoyment. Indeed, the audience is highly appreciative of the whole show, and can even be heard to be cheering and groaning occasionally in the traditional *ISIRTA* manner.

One of the best items in this show presents a familiar children's situation in an adult context, with Palin and Jones as city gents, knocking at a neighbour's door.

DENISE: Yes?

JONES: Good evening, Mrs Johnson – I wonder if your husband's in?

DENISE: Yes, he is – what do you want him for?

JONES: Can he come out and play?

DENISE: No, he can't. He's just had his dinner and he's got to sit down for an hour while the food goes down.

PALIN: But we've got to go in at half-past eight.

DENISE: I can't help that – he came home late from the office so he's had his supper late.

JONES: Well, can he come and talk to us?

DENISE: No, he *can't*, he's sitting down.

PALIN: Can we come in and speak to him?

DENISE: No, you *can't* – you're always round here, you two. Why can't you play in your own garden?

PALIN: We can't.

DENISE: Why not?

PALIN: We've got visitors.

JONES: We want to play 'shipwrecks' on your old car.

DENISE: Well, Mr Johnson can't come out to play until he's had a rest, and that's that.

PALIN: Well ... can *you* come and play?

DENISE: Oh yes! Why didn't you say that before?

The fourth programme of the series was entered for the *Prix Jeunesse* International TV Festival in Munich in June 1968, where it won first prize in its category (Youth Programmes 12–15 years: Plays and Entertainment). The jury quaintly commented: 'Performers and spectators are joint in carefree *joie de vivre*.'

During this period John Cleese introduced Humphrey Barclay to Terry Gilliam, whom he had met in America and who was now staying in England. Gilliam hung around the studios and gradually got to know the participants; and later on made small contributions to *Do Not Adjust Your Set*.

Terry Gilliam was born in Minneapolis, Minnesota, on 22 November 1940. He grew up in a country area, and then moved to Los Angeles at the age of eleven, where he went to college. He says: 'I started as a physics major; I ended up as a political science major; I never majored in art because it required too many art history courses which were taught by a particularly boring professor.' He ran the college humour magazine, which provided a grounding for his first

185

job – he was hired by Harvey Kurtzman (the founder of *Mad Magazine*) as assistant editor of a magazine called *Help!*

It was at this time that *Cambridge Circus* was in New York. Gilliam: 'One of the things we did in the magazine were "fumetti" – like the Italian romance magazines which are like a comic book except that they are photographs of people, and they talk in balloons. We were getting reasonably well-known people to appear in these things, and we got John Cleese, who wasn't well-known but was funny, to appear in one.'[37]

After a period hitch-hiking through Europe, and a further year in New York working in advertising, Gilliam came to England in 1967 and worked as a freelance illustrator. After being involved in the death-throes of a magazine called *The Londoner*, he was fed up with magazine work, and phoned John Cleese to see whether he could get into television.

Cleese put Gilliam in touch with Humphrey Barclay, who remembers: 'I looked at all his drawings – they were very grotesque, but being a cartoonist myself I was intrigued by them. We all got to know him – I remember writing letters to protect him from being drafted into the American Army, because we felt that we wanted him around.'

1968 was the year of the big ITV reshuffle. From time to time the licences of the producing companies who make up the commercial television empire have to be scrutinized and renewed – or not renewed – by the Independent Television Authority. Associated-Rediffusion, as a name, disappeared from the television scene. The franchise for the London area was given to a new company (which combined the forces of Associated-Rediffusion and ABC, another producing company) called Thames Television, who took over Rediffusion's coverage of weekdays; and London Weekend Television, who took over Friday evenings, Saturdays, and Sundays from ATV.

Thames Television did not seem to be very interested in retaining Humphrey Barclay's services, but he was approached by Frank Muir – half of the one-time scriptwriting team of Muir and Norden – who was Head of Entertainment of London Weekend Television (LWT).

Do Not Adjust Your Set went on to a second series under new management; there were a further thirteen programmes starting on 19 February 1969. Once again it developed an adult cult following, which eventually led to repeats being placed later in the evening so that adults could see it. Palin and Jones brought in Ian Davidson (who had given them their chance on *The Late Show*) to act as script editor, and the series was directed, as the first had been, by Daphne Shadwell. The mixture was much as before, including a Captain Fantastic serial and some animated cartoons from Terry Gilliam.

Gilliam had been invited by Barclay to appear as a quick-sketch artist on LWT's show *We Have Ways of Making You Laugh*, which was hosted by Frank Muir. Gilliam started by doing caricature of the guests, and then drifted into animation by accident. Somebody had collected a set of disc-jockey Jimmy Young's links between the records on his radio programme, complete with awful puns. Gilliam: 'They didn't know how to present it, and I suggested I make an animated film of it. They assumed I knew how to make animated films, and I assumed that they knew I *didn't* know . . . anyway, I did one, and they really liked it, and said "Do another one". And so overnight I became an animator on national television!'

Gilliam's knowledge of animation was entirely theoretical at this stage, having been gained from textbooks. He settled for the use of paper cut-outs, which can be moved frame by frame, and are thus cheaper and quicker than the traditional Disney-type animation which involves drawing each frame out separately. Rather to his surprise, he found that he had an instinctive 'feel' for this sort of work, and produced good results right from the start. He followed the Jimmy Young film with a 'History of the Whoopee Cushion', and went on to contribute to *Do Not Adjust Your Set* and to Marty Feldman's ITV series, *The Marty Feldman Comedy Machine*.

Another Barclay production at this time was the series *Doctor In The House* (which, with slight changes of cast, went on to become *Doctor at Large* and *Doctor in Charge*) based on the best-selling books by Richard Gordon, of which Frank Muir had managed to obtain the rights. Gordon's imaginary London teaching hospital, St Swithin's, was repopulated with new characters for the series, but the basic idea, of trainee doctors and their relationship with the senior hospital staff, was retained. Muir had invited Cleese and Chapman to write the opening programme, which was transmitted on 12 July 1969, and they wrote a really excellent script. They felt unable to go on with the series at the time, and so Barclay asked Bill Oddie and Graeme Garden to continue the series (thus maintaining the obviously sensible arrangement of one of the writers also being a doctor). They expanded the number of characters in the show as time went on.

The original lead part was taken by Barry Evans, and was named Michael Upton (the name of a real-life friend of Cleese and Chapman). Other characters were also given names based on real people – for example, the anaesthetist was named Dick Stuart-Clark, after Chris Stuart-Clark of *Cambridge Circus*. After fifty-five episodes Barry Evans dropped out, and the lead was taken by Robin Nedwell in the character of Duncan Waring.

A couple of years or so later Cleese wrote a further six episodes by himself – more out of financial necessity than out of any particular desire to be reassociated with the programme. Cleese: 'I was doing a number of other things at the same time, and I tend to get fairly depressed and desperate when I'm writing a *lot* of comedy . . . particularly against the clock, it's not a very happy experience for me, I don't find it easy . . . There was a problem writing them because of the concept of what Barry Evans should be like, which meant that it was impossible to write anything funny for him. When I wrote funny lines for him, the answer was "Barry wouldn't say lines like that"; so I had to write situations so that he could stand in the middle, smiling amiably, while everyone round him did funny things.'

For one of the shows Cleese drew on his experience of staying in a hotel in Torquay run by a hen-pecked and thoroughly bad-tempered man who saw the guests as intrusions on his attempts to manage the hotel. He was so rude to everybody that Cleese was entranced, and used him as the basis for a character in a show in which the doctors stayed in such a hotel. Cleese: 'This shows what a clever man Humphrey Barclay is – at the end of the show he said, "You know – there's a series idea in that hotel"; and I remember looking at him and thinking, "Oh, you TV producer, you – that's all you ever think about".' There was indeed a series in the idea, although it was 1975 before it saw the light of day.

The various *Doctor* . . . series have been among the best comedy ever

7.35 **NEW**
DOCTOR IN THE HOUSE
BASED ON THE "DOCTOR" BOOKS BY
RICHARD GORDON
BARRY EVANS
with
Ernest Clark
Ralph Michael
Geoffrey Davies
George Layton
Robin Nedwell in
Why do you want to be a Doctor?
BY JOHN CLEESE AND GRAHAM CHAPMAN
The original *Doctor in the House*, which has been featured in books, films, plays and on radio, was written nearly 20 years ago. For television—and under the author's approving eye—it takes on a new look.

produced by ITV. They were well written by the various writing teams, and had a cast who developed their characters and timing to a high degree. Barclay is a shrewd producer of comedy, and these programmes benefited from his controlling touch.

As well as starting off the *Doctor* shows, Frank Muir was on the lookout for any other likely comedy ideas at the time when London Weekend Television began operations. He asked Palin and Jones to write and perform in their own series, and of course they jumped at the chance. They were really rather overloaded with work at this time – they were writing for Feldman, for David Frost's ITV series *Frost on Saturday*, and also wrote two pantomimes – *Aladdin* and *Beauty and the Beast* – for the Civic Theatre, Watford. Palin: 'Because of all this we really weren't able to clear the decks and concentrate as much as we needed to; they were written rather fast – the first one I was very pleased with, but the others all lacked something – I think it was preparation and care in the writing of the scripts.'

The Complete and Utter History of Britain: Terry Jones, Roddy Maude-Roxby (standing) and Michael Palin (seated)

The series was called *The Complete and Utter History Of Britain*. 'It was documentary presentation – the premise being that we would use modern television techniques to look at a historical period, but as if those techniques had been invented then; how would a television company of the Middle Ages have dealt with the Battle of Hastings, or Richard I's arrival from the Crusades?' The germ of the idea came from the 'home movie' version of the Battle of Hastings (1066) that Palin and Jones had filmed for *Twice a Fortnight*, and it was Terry Jones's brother who had suggested that there was a series in that idea.

Palin and Jones presented a pilot script to Barclay, who was very impressed by it. He hired a young Australian, Maurice Murphy, to direct, but had a little difficulty over the casting. Barclay: 'It was the kind of humour that was very difficult to cast once you went outside the actual practitioners of that humour. Mike and Terry very definitely did not want to continue with Denise Coffey and David Jason. We cast Colin Gordon to do the serious bits, Roddy Maude-Roxby to do one of the batty linking characters, and Wallas Eaton and Melinda May to play some of the other parts; they just weren't right, they weren't in tune enough with the humour.' Palin and Jones suggested that Diana Quick, whom they knew from Oxford, should also take part, and she was rather better attuned to the atmosphere they were trying to create. Jones still thinks that they might have had better results if they had performed more of the material themselves.

There were six episodes, covering history from the cavemen to Oliver Cromwell, broadcast on Sundays from 12 January to 16 February 1969. The programmes were not networked – Palin thinks that this was due to the other networks being resentful of the brash new LWT – and despite the fact that the programmes had a generous budget which allowed an unusually high proportion of film in the episodes, the overall result was not as successful as it might have been.

All the same, there are some very good ideas in the shows, particularly in the early episodes. Colin Gordon, as the narrator, introduced the items. In most cases modern stereotypes were placed in a historical setting – as for example in the case of the house-agent (Palin) trying to sell Stonehenge to a young couple (Jones and Melinda May).

PALIN: Cosy, isn't it?
JONES   (*doubtfully*): Well ...
PALIN: As I say, it's ideal for a young couple like yourselves with thirty or forty children. It's got character, charm, and a slab in the middle.
JONES: What about the gaps?
PALIN: 'Doors' ... That's another great advantage of a place like this – forty-six doors.
MELINDA: But isn't it a bit draughty in winter?
PALIN: Not if you keep running about, dear ... I mean, feel that wall – go on, feel it. That's Welsh quality for you, that is. A mountainside in your own home.
           (*Jones goes up to one of the stone uprights and taps it ... there is a creak and it falls over with a crash*)
MELINDA: Now look what you've done! I am sorry, Mr ...
PALIN: Not to worry ... you've just found the emergency exit.

The first two programmes were cannibalized into one episode on the instructions of the LWT hierarchy who felt that they were not strong enough. As a result, several good sketches disappeared when a better decision might have been to spread the cuts over all six episodes. One clever sketch which was cut – and which in fairness might have played less well than it looks on paper – demonstrates how the Britons might have had to cope with Latin after the Roman invasion. (Since the sketch was not transmitted the casting is uncertain.)

WIFE: Where been have you?
HUSBAND: Ah! Flosburga (vocative)! Well I, a cup of mead, with Egfrith, having been enjoying, I his place was about to having been making the action of being about to go, when ...

WIFE: You me that expect to believe?
HUSBAND: It the honest truth is . . . I, the hour being late and the mead having
             been much finished, not another one by with or from Egfrith would
             have been about to have had, had he, fearing lest I, thinking myself
             treated ungenerously to have been, either would feel I ought to
             have with him been staying or . . .
WIFE   (*leaping up and packing suitcase*): Of this that enough is! To my
             mother's I, this the last straw being, you too far having gone, am
             home going.
             (*She leaves*)
HUSBAND: Wait! Imperative! (*He shakes his head sadly*) This for a lark stuff.
             (*Pulls out bottle of mead from his coat*) Fear I my wife me just
             understand me not does . . .

Another deletion was a neat sketch in which St Augustine, trying to
introduce the Britons to Christianity, is taken aback to discover that they have
well-trained house gods who provide food at the murmur of a suitable prayer;
and Terry Jones still regrets losing a sketch in which a hopeful Stone Age man
attempts to patent the chair (which enables one to sit down higher up).

Sketches which were retained include Caesar's home movie version of the
invasion of Britain; a Scrapbook for 1065, a year in which nothing much
happened; and an interview with King William the Conqueror, filmed in
changing-room baths in the manner of an after-the-match interview with a
football team.

JONES (THE REPORTER): King William – congratulations on a wonderful
             victory.
PALIN (WILLIAM): Thank you, David.
JONES: You must be very pleased with the boys.
PALIN: I certainly am, David, they did a wonderful job.
JONES: Did you expect to win?
PALIN: Well, I never had any doubts, David – the boys have been fighting
             very well on the Continent, but this was the big one they were all
             looking forward to.
JONES: Were there any anxious moments?
PALIN: Well, right at the start, David, our lads weren't used to the sloping
             ground, but soon we began to open out the battle a lot more, using
             the long one down the centre, and able to split their defence right
             down the middle.
JONES: When were you sure you were going to win?
PALIN: Well, you can never be sure of a thing like that, David, but I must
             say I was pretty confident half-way through the second half when
             they were two thousand down.
JONES: Well, now, what about that 'incident'?
PALIN: Oh, you mean when Harold was knocked down . . . (*He goes all
             serious*) Well, that was a very nasty business, David, and we're all
             very sorry about it. But I think it was fair – and it certainly gave our
             lads a bit of a laugh.

The weakest point of the programme, and of all the following editions, is

Roddy Maude-Roxby as 'Professor Weaver', a dim-witted historian with a penchant for wandering off the subject. The character is uncertainly written, and Maude-Roxby was perhaps not the best person to interpret it; it would have been interesting to know what Palin or Jones themselves might have made of it.

The technique of seeing historical situations in the context of modern stereotypes is one which seems to have a particular fascination for Palin and Jones, and is one to which they subsequently returned. One of the neatest examples in *The Complete and Utter History of Britain* – and one of the few sketches to be spoken of favourably by the press when the series was reviewed – presented Palin as F. R. Launcelot, rescuing a damsel in distress, played by Diana Quick. Actually, he doesn't so much rescue her as make her fill out forms, refusing even to release her from the stake to which she has been chained.

PALIN: Now then, there's just the question of the rights . . .

DIANA: What rites *(giving him a seductive heave of her bosom)* . . . fair knight?

PALIN: Well, there's bound to be some sort of story once they hear you've been rescued, and if it gets made into a ballad, you get composition, performing and fertility rights for five years . . . Overseas distribution is covered here . . . and there's another 150 per cent if it gets into the *Anglo-Saxon Chronicle. (She signs)* Thank you.

DIANA: Now save me, gentle knight! Before the loathsome monster returneth here to claim me for his own.

PALIN: Ah! Good point! I've got to have details of your Predator or Captor . . . *(He sorts out another form)*

DIANA: A loathsome dreadful beast! Tall as the tallest mountain! Wider than a mighty oak tree!

PALIN: Hang on, hang on . . . I've got to get it down in feet and inches . . . *(writing)* Let's see . . . Tallest mountain . . . that's about 28,000 feet . . . Widest oak tree . . . well, let's say about eight foot. So he's tall and thin. Shouldn't have much trouble spotting him. *(Putting everything away and starting back to his horse)* Well, that seems to be everything. Thank you very much.

DIANA: And know I am yours, parfit, gentil knight! Loose me from these vile things . . .

PALIN: Certainly, madam. I'll get these forms in first thing tomorrow and we should have someone round by the end of the week. Friday a good day for you?

DIANA: But I may perish ere Friday!

PALIN: Well . . . a lot of the lads are on nights. We're a bit short staffed. But I'll see what I can do. Cheerio, then.
    (He clambers on his horse and sets off)

DIANA: But the loathsome beast! *(sounds of retreating hooves)* The loathsome beast! *(Hooves disappear)* The loathsome beast finishes his work to rule on Thursday!

Critical reaction to the first programme was generally unfavourable, with comments about 'undergraduate humour', and the subsequent programmes

191

were for the most part ignored altogether. The later programmes are certainly thinner, although there are some good ideas, and some of the more visual filmed material has been carefully done and builds a convincing atmosphere. The Battle of Calais (1558) is presented in a knockabout style reminiscent of *Twice A Fortnight* – the French win by means of their secret weapon (garlic); and there is a rather odd film with four simultaneous William Shakespeares. Other good studio sketches include the proud owners of a Book who go through all the standard reactions to having a new television; and Oliver Cromwell appearing on 'The Samuel Pepys Show' where Pepys has a remarkable resemblance to David Frost.

The Complete and Utter History of Britain is something of a lost opportunity. The scripts were very promising, although as Palin says they needed a little reworking in places, but the mistakes in the casting helped to make the shows less effective than they might have been. Even so, there are many lively ideas in the programmes, and Palin and Jones were able to extend their humour into more of an individual style than they had attained previously. They also gained useful experience as performers. Palin was able to demonstrate a wide range of characterizations, while Jones showed that his faith in himself as a knockabout comedian was justified. His style of physical comedy and mime is quite individual, and he was able to give it better expression in *The Complete and Utter History of Britain* than in much of his later work.

The Complete and Utter History of Britain: Michael Palin as Richard I

From the point of view of Independent Television the series had been a failure, and it seemed unlikely that Palin and Jones would be invited to contribute to ITV for some time. Meanwhile Cleese was beginning to feel that he might be prepared to work in television again on a regular basis; Chapman and Idle had been developing as writers on their own; and Terry Gilliam had established himself in a small way as an animator with an individual style. The series of accidents which had diverted all of them from their chosen careers and brought them together in various combinations had now prepared the scene for their collaboration as a team – a formidable array of talents indeed, and one which would change the face of television comedy.

The Complete and Utter History of Britain: the head of Johnny Vyvyan, Terry Jones and Wallas Eaton

Monty Python, Tunisia 1978

A typical British comedy group – Monastir, Tunisia 1978
Un groupe typique de comiques Brittaniques folkloriques 1978iques
Ein typische Tommi giggelmachengruppe volkslorische 1978

Imprimé en Ba...

John and Tony Smith
in association with
Python Productions Ltd.
and Charisma Records
present

Starring
Graham Chapman
John Cleese
John Gilliam
Eric Idle
Terry Jones
Michael Palin
and
Carol Cleveland
Neil Innes

MONTY PYTHON'S
1ST FAREWELL TOUR
OFFICIAL PROGRAMME

11.
'Monty Python's Flying Circus'

Although *Do Not Adjust Your Set* had been aimed at children, it was also watched by many adults. Among them were John Cleese and Graham Chapman, who knew Palin and Jones from the joke factory of *The Frost Report*. Cleese rang Palin and suggested that the four of them might work together. Palin and Jones, who now felt themselves to be in a weak position with Independent Television because of the relative failure of *The Complete and Utter History of Britain*, fell in with the suggestion, and suggested that Eric Idle should also be included. Idle, in a sort of chain reaction, brought Gilliam into the group; and they all approached Barry Took, who had been one of the writers on *The Frost Report*. Took was at this time a sort of 'roving producer', and he acted as a go-between and put the idea up to the BBC. They were all familiar to the BBC, except Gilliam; Cleese had a reputation as a performer, and they had all proved themselves as writers to the BBC's satisfaction by helping *The Frost Report* to win a prize at Montreux. It was obvious that they could be trusted to produce a series which would not fall flat on its face. The BBC commissioned them to do a series of thirteen, without insisting on a 'pilot' programme.

Choosing a title proved rather difficult. The team were anxious not to have a title which might give away the content of the show in any way – which would in any case have been difficult because at this stage they were themselves vague as to the content. Various deliberately silly names were tried out – *Owl Stretching Time* and *A Horse, A Spoon And A Bucket* were two early attempts, and they also toyed with the idea of using the names of a football forward line that Cleese had invented for one of his early monologues: *Bunn, Wackett, Buzzard, Stubble and Boot*. This indecision inevitably caused inter-departmental confusion at Television Centre, where make-up would have one title, props would be booked out to another, and contracts made out to a third.

Being rather chary of the whole operation, someone in the BBC's upper echelons – probably Michael Mills – had dubbed the whole exercise a 'flying circus' (a term readily applicable to any collective source of annoyance and confusion ever since Baron Von Richthofen, the World War I flying ace). Palin had seen a name which amused him in a Women's Institute magazine – Gwen Dibley – and for a short time it looked as if the unknown and innocent Ms Dibley might be held titularly responsible for this ménage; however, *Gwen Dibley's Flying Circus* was yet another name which paled in the cold light of morning, and was abandoned. In the end, the names 'Monty' and 'Python' came up in the course of discussion, and caused great amusement. The next day a few rapid phone calls established that everyone still thought that these were funny, although there may have been an element of exhaustion in this, as with the naming of *Private Eye*. So with their own 'Monty' and 'Python', and the BBC's 'Flying Circus', they were at last in business. Everyone was glad to have that sorted out, not least the variously confused BBC departments; and the title was fixed as *Monty Python's Flying Circus*.

At the start the team were not entirely sure what they wanted the show to be like – apart from funny, of course. Although their common ground was the framework of *The Frost Report*, Cleese thinks that they did not deliberately set out to break its conventions: 'If somebody had said, "Do you intend to break the conventions of *The Frost Report*?" we would have spent five seconds thinking what it meant; and *then* said "Yes". We never saw it in those journalistic terms.' Where they did hope to improve on *The Frost Report* was in the inclusion of rather more bizarre humour. Attempts to get this sort of material into *The Frost Report* tended to lead to the official reaction, 'They wouldn't understand that in Bradford' (although what was supposed to be so backward about Bradford was never explained).

One of the things which acted as an influence on the programme was a cartoon that Terry Gilliam had done for *Do Not Adjust Your Set*, called 'Elephants'. It threw away all logical thought and progression, and simply ran from one idea to the next in a stream-of-consciousness manner. A clinical description of the cartoon serves only to underline its oddity: a man who ignores a sign saying 'Beware of Elephants' is crushed by a falling elephant; his head, left sticking out of the ground, is kicked around by a football team whose heads gradually join his in bouncing around. These heads now recede until they become mere specks of dirt, part of an advertisement for soap powder presented by an animated Enoch Powell. A white sheet, held up by Powell, becomes the scene of gunfire between a fort and a man on a horse; this gunfire perforates the packet of soap powder, which falls like snow – and in fact becomes snow – a snow-covered scene complete with a stagecoach. An outlaw holds up the coach, but on his demand 'Hands Up!' he is squashed flat by a huge hand coming out of the coach.

This cartoon planted in the minds of Palin and Jones the idea that the whole show might be done in a similar manner, with ideas simply flowing on, one to the next, instead of the formalized use of sketches with a beginning, a middle and an end, which had been normal up to then. Cleese and Chapman were less interested in the overall format of the show, but fell in with the general idea because they felt that it would enable them to explore new ground in their sketches. Gilliam: 'When we began, we were always talking in terms of that film as what we wanted to do – so that anything in an idea could spring you off to the next direction. I think everyone's background was in writing ordinary sketch material, so it took longer than we thought to break away from it.' Certainly Gilliam was a major influence in breaking the others away from the more rigid format they had been used to, and encouraging them to use 'lateral thinking'. Gilliam himself was influenced by several things the others were not aware of: 'Ernie Kovacs did a television show in the States that was very visual, with very bizarre things. I know that influenced me at the time a lot, it was unlike anything else that American television ever produced. I think he was born in Czechoslovakia, and he's got that sort of weird Eastern European attitude to things.'

Gilliam was also very influenced by Buster Keaton's film *Sherlock Junior*, made in 1924, which he saw when it was shown in New York in the early 1960s, having been thought lost for many years. Keaton plays a projectionist who dreams that he takes part in the film he is showing – this is done in a superb shot which creates the exact illusion of a cinema screen with a film being projected, into which Keaton climbs. He is then further confused when the film 'cuts' around him, leaving him in the same place in the frame, but in different surroundings. In its use of the medium, *Sherlock Junior* foreshadows the way *Monty Python's Flying Circus* exploited the medium of television. A later film which made similar (though rather heavy-handed) jokes about the actual film medium was *Hellzapoppin* (1941), but in fact Gilliam never saw it.

The one step that the team were anxious to make was to escape from the tyranny of the punch line. Peter Cook had said to Cleese at the time of *Not Only But Also* that he could never see that you should lose a sketch simply because it did not have a strong punch line to round it off. Indeed several of his sketches simply wind up, tidily but without any attempt to 'cap' the sketch with a punch line. However, up to the start of *Monty Python's Flying Circus* it was generally considered necessary for any television sketch to terminate with a strong joke, and any idea which did not lead to such an ending had to be abandoned. It was this constriction which the team hoped to break away from by the use of Gilliam's stream-of-consciousness cartoons to link the sketches.

While the discussions about the series were in progress, the first of Spike Milligan's 'Q' series was broadcast – *Q5*. (This was followed in later years by *Q6, Q7, Q8* and *Q9*.) Jones: 'I remember looking at those shows and thinking, "Shit! – he's done it!" He just totally ripped up all form and shape – and there we'd been writing three-minute sketches with beginnings, middles and ends – and Milligan started a sketch, and then it turned into a different sketch, then it turned into something else.' Certainly Milligan had beaten the Python team to the abandonment of the punch line, although his shows have an improvised feel to them and he frequently terminates a sketch he has had enough of by walking off the set muttering 'Did I write this?'

The Python team's style is quite different from Milligan's, although it can fairly be said that *Monty Python's Flying Circus* occupies an equivalent place in television history to that of *The Goon Show* in radio history, as the show which above all others pushed back the boundaries of the medium and became a cult, even long after the original transmissions. The Python teaming was a very strong one – Cleese and Chapman brought to the team their hardness of approach, Palin and Jones their feeling for atmosphere, Idle his skill with words and escalating nonsense, and Gilliam his stream-of-consciousness linking which, together with the sheer savagery of his material, gives the show much of its style.

Most of the actual performing in the shows was done by Cleese, Chapman, Palin, Jones and Idle, with Gilliam making occasional small appearances, and additional support from Connie Booth; the main female performer was Carol Cleveland, whose appearances were brief but who made an ideal foil to the others.

The first series was recorded during the period August 1969 to January 1970, and transmitted on BBC-1 at various times around eleven o'clock at night, for thirteen weeks from 5 October 1969 to 11 January 1970. The shows were not transmitted in the same order as that in which they were recorded; this is a common practice, which enables the running order for the series to be

Monty Python's Flying Circus:
Terry Jones

juggled to place the best episodes near the beginning and end of the series.

In so far as the series has any particular approach, it is to mock the techniques of television. There seems to be something of an obsession with television presentation, and the programmes regularly parody the use of captions and the then current BBC-1 'trade mark' (which shows a revolving globe). The new-found freedom in the sketches led to several techniques which were new in themselves, and for which it is helpful to coin new expressions. The idea of taking a basic premise and reversing it is older than Python – *TW3* used it, as did the later satire shows – and this might be called a *reversal sketch* (for example, 'I was a Heterosexual'); but a particularly Python development of this is to take the format of something like a television quiz programme or discussion – or indeed anything with a strong and recognizable style of presentation – and then empty the content out of it, replacing it with something ludicrous. The most suitable term for this would be a *format sketch*. Another typically Python technique is to take an idea, and then allow it to get wildly out of hand, so that absurdity builds on absurdity. Idle's material often demonstrates this sort of approach, and much of this sort of writing also arose out of the discussions between the group where ideas could be expanded. The resultant effect suggests, at any rate to a technical mind, the effect obtained by overloading the input to a tape recorder, and thus producing a highly distorted recording in which the original material has become almost unrecognizable; but since the effect is normally produced by successive steps of logical escalation, the result can be labelled an *escalation sketch*. This, and the Gilliam linking technique, is often coupled with a delight in sheer silliness for its own sake. It was said of *The Goon Show* that it brought situations to their illogical conclusion; it would be more true of *Monty Python's Flying Circus* to say that it takes ideas to their *logical* conclusion, and then beyond that for a considerable way.

As Gilliam says, the team's experience in producing sketches with punch lines took some time to overcome – this could well be because sketches are

often conceived from the punch line, and then written to lead up to it. Certainly the earlier shows in the first series consist largely of sketches which have punch lines, even though they are not always intended to 'cap' the sketch but simply to bring it to a neat close – a full stop rather than an exclamation mark.

A good example of what one might label a 'soft' punch line is at the end of the very first sketch in the first programme to be recorded (although the second to be transmitted). Written by Cleese and Chapman, it has Chapman, as a farmer, and Jones, as a visitor, discussing the unsuccessful attempts of some off-screen sheep to fly.

JONES: But where do they get the idea from?
CHAPMAN: From Harold. He's that sheep over there under the elm. He's that most dangerous of animals – a clever sheep. He's the ringleader. He's realized that a sheep's life consists of standing around for a few months and then being eaten. And that's a depressing prospect for an ambitious sheep. He's patently hit on the idea of escape.
JONES: Why don't you just get rid of Harold?
CHAPMAN: Because of the enormous commercial possibilities should he succeed.

Taken by itself, this is a quite normal – and very funny – sketch. However, it is then escalated into a discussion (with diagram) of the possibilities of an airliner in the shape of a sheep, conducted by Cleese and Palin in what can only be described as 'Jabberwock-French', which is funny in a much more bizarre way (and has the audience somewhat confused).

On the other hand, many of the sketches have the traditional 'hard' punch lines, which act as the *raison d'être* of the whole sketch. This applies to Idle's sketch 'Nudge Nudge', which has put the expression 'Nudge nudge, wink wink, say no more' into the language, even though most people seem to have forgotten the punch line which turns the whole idea on its head. Idle is the blazered and beer-drinking know-it-all who is harassing the reserved city-gent-type Jones in a pub.

IDLE: Your wife interested in . . . photographs? Eh? Know what I mean –

Monty Python's Flying Circus on stage in New York – 'Nudge Nudge' with Terry Jones and Eric Idle

photographs? He asked him knowingly –

JONES: Photography?

IDLE: Yes – nudge nudge, snap snap, grin grin, wink wink, say no more.

JONES: Holiday snaps?

IDLE: Could be – could be taken on holiday, could be – yes – swimming costumes, you know what I mean? *Candid* photography, you know what I mean, nudge nudge?

JONES: No, no – we don't have a camera.

IDLE: Oh. Still – *cor!* – eh? – *cor!* – eh?

JONES: Look – are you insinuating something?

IDLE: Oh, no – no – no . . . yes.

JONES: Well?

IDLE: Well, I mean – you're a man of the world, aren't you, I mean – you've been there, haven't you, I mean you've been around, eh?

JONES: What do you mean?

IDLE: Well, I mean, like – you've done it. With a lady. You've slept with a lady.

JONES: Yes.

IDLE: What's it like?

It took until about the eighth programme of the first series for the idea of completely abandoning a sketch in mid-scene to be tried; in this show (which is number eight both as recorded and as transmitted) Chapman plays an army colonel who terminates an interview with Idle as a soldier who doesn't like the idea of being killed: 'That's a very silly line. Awfully bad.' He is then faced by Palin and Jones as a couple of mafia racketeers offering 'protection': this is a sort of 'format sketch', and was written by the unusual combination of Cleese and Palin.

PALIN: We can guarantee you that not a single armoured division will get done over for fifteen bob a week.

CHAPMAN: No – no –

PALIN: Twelve-and-six . . . eight-and-six . . . five bob?

CHAPMAN: No, this is silly.

JONES: What's silly?

CHAPMAN: No, the whole premise is silly, and it's very badly written. I'm the senior officer here, and I haven't had a funny line yet, so I'm stopping it.

JONES: You can't do that!

CHAPMAN: I've done it. The sketch is over.

IDLE: I want to leave the army, please sir, it's dangerous.

CHAPMAN: Look, I stopped your sketch five minutes ago, so get out of shot. Right – director – close-up – zoom in on me (*the camera does so*) – that's better.

PALIN: It's only because you couldn't think of a punch line.

CHAPMAN: Not true, not true. It's time for the cartoon – cue telecine . . . ten, nine, eight . . .

JONES: The general public's not going to understand this, are they.

The colonel subsequently interrupts several more sketches on account of their silliness, but he is fighting a losing battle. However, the idea of abandoning sketches without a punch line was coming to life. In a later programme, a young couple trying to have a quiet evening together are invaded by noisy and unwelcome visitors – led by the character from the 'Nudge Nudge' sketch. This sketch escalates into a 'rave-up' ending which rather gives the impression that the team couldn't think how else to get out of it, and there are several other sketches in the series which terminate without ending.

The stream-of-consciousness feeling which holds the shows together also percolates into some of the sketches. In another of Chapman and Cleese's trial scenes – this one having a witness in a coffin who raps on the lid to give his answers – Chapman, in quite a different character to his colonel, gives his evidence in a very distinctive way, which is not so much stream as torrent-of-consciousness; in effect, an 'escalation' monologue.

CLEESE: I'm sorry I'm late, m'lud, I couldn't find a kosher car park. Don't bother to recap, m'lud, I'll pick it up as we go along. Call Mrs Fiona Lewis.
(Enter Chapman, in drag)

CHAPMAN: I swear to tell the truth, the whole truth, and nothing but the truth, so anyway, I said to her, I said, they can't afford that on what he earns, I mean for a start the feathers get up your nose, I ask you, four and sixpence a pound, and him with a wooden leg, I don't know how she puts up with it after all the trouble she's had with her you-know-what, anyway, it *was* a white wedding, much to everyone's surprise, of course they bought everything on the hire purchase, I think they ought to send them back where they came from, I mean you've got to be cruel to be kind, so Mrs Harris said, so she said she said she said, a dead crab she said she said? well, her sister's gone to Rhodesia, what with her womb and all, and her youngest, as fit as a filing cabinet, and the goldfish, the goldfish, they've got whooping-cough, they keep spitting water at the Bratbys, well, they *do*, don't they, I mean, you *can't*, can you, I mean they're not even married or anything, they're not even *divorced*, and he's in the KGB if you ask me, he says he's a tree surgeon, but I don't like the sound of his liver, all that squeaking and banging every night till the small hours, well, his mother's been much better since she had her head off, don't you talk to me about bladders, I said . . .

The 'format sketches' include a *Panorama*-type exposé of men who dress up as mice, done in the manner of a drug addiction documentary (this was one of the sketches rejected from the second series of *Marty*) and a television discussion which proves rather unproductive because it is between a duck, a cat and a lizard (all stuffed). Several shows also have 'vox pops' sections, parodying the street interviews with members of the public which tend to disfigure television coverage of election or budget days. Chapman sees format sketches as their way of getting at what is going on in the mind of someone presenting a television programme: 'He's presenting what he has written down, or what's been worked out beforehand, and is very little other than a "front man". Although he appears to be quite intelligent on the subject, in actual fact he could just as well be talking to a cat, or a lizard; it wouldn't really matter.'

The pretentiousness of much television made it an ideal target, and as Cleese points out: 'We were acutely conscious that it was a television show, and were also very aware that the best parodies of television are done *on* television, and the best parodies of the theatre are done in the theatre ... One of the loveliest things that people used to say to us was that once the show came off the air and the next thing came on, which was a regional magazine programme, it was impossible to watch it without finding it terribly funny.'

Monty Python's Flying Circus (18 January 1973): Eric Idle, looking not entirely unlike Richard Attenborough, hosts the TV awards ceremony

However, television presentation is not the only target, and there is a very wide range of styles and ideas in the first series. Many of the shows have a longer item in the form of a feature at the end – the 'Mouse Problem' sketch is one such – one of the best of which is in the first programme to be transmitted. Written by Palin and Jones, it tells the story of the Funniest Joke in the World – so funny as to be lethal to anyone reading or hearing it. The British Army takes an interest in it, proving that it can kill a soldier at fifty yards, and develop it into a Secret Weapon for use in World War Two. Translated (word by word, for reasons of safety) into German, it is used to terrible effect. With sensible regard for the safety of their viewers, the Python team never let us hear the English version; but here, for the record, is the German version of the Funniest Joke in the World:

> '*Wenn is dass nöd-schtuck git un slottermeier?*'
> '*Ja, beyerhunt das oder die flipperwalt gershput.*'

There are a number of regular characters in the show – the colonel makes a few appearances, but more regular inhabitants of the Python world are the Gumbies and the Pepperpots. A Gumby is a brainless sub-human with rolled-up trousers, braces, round steel-rimmed spectacles, a small moustache, and a handkerchief with the corners knotted as a headpiece. The Pepperpots are a group of noisy women, so called because their shape is reminiscent of pepper-

Monty Python's Flying Circus on stage in New York – Michael Palin as Mr Gumby

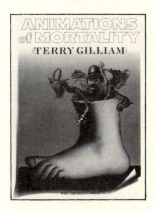

pots – although the name is not used in the programmes, only in the scripts as an identification. Another regular walk-on character in the first series is a knight in armour, carrying a plucked chicken; he has very little to do, merely hitting people over the head with the chicken occasionally. The team found that characters such as the knight and the colonel became popular in themselves, rather like a visual equivalent of the catch-phrase, which they despised as a cheap way of raising a laugh; these characters were later phased out.

Gilliam's cartoons provide most of the linking between sketches or groups of sketches. 'I was given a starting point and an ending point – from where the last sketch ended to where the next one began – and then I just let my mind wander in between. Nobody really knew what I was doing until the day of the actual recording – I'd just arrive with a can of film, and present it, and generally it seemed to work.' Gilliam deliberately does not analyse the way his mind works: 'I think naïvety is part of the creative process – the minute I become aware of what I'm doing I've killed it. I surround myself with lots of things and I absorb a lot of material, but I don't try to categorize it . . . I keep meaning to organize my books, and put them in some sort of order so that I can put my finger on what I want immediately – and I never get around to it because there's a usefulness in keeping them out of order, because as I'm looking for one thing I bump into a lot of other things.' Certainly his books are in a gorgeously abundant disarray, with serious art books rubbing shoulders with reproductions of Sears and Roebuck catalogues from the 1920s.

These Sears and Roebuck catalogues are among the sources of the cut-out items for his cartoons. He takes a great delight in 'stealing' from photographs, drawings and prints to provide the individual style of the cartoons: 'I can use Albert Dürer if I want to, I can use Doré, or anybody . . . most of these things are very common, it's just the business of taking them out of their context – it's nice to be able to take "cherished images" and fiddle about with them. What's good about using cut-outs is because they are just pieces of paper, lying around

on my desk, things accidentally fall on top of other things and create combinations.'

Apart from their distinctive visual style – which is due partly to the use of an air-brush which, by applying paint in a fine spray, can be used to give the characters a rounded appearance which belies their reality as paper cut-outs – Gilliam's cartoons are principally noted for their sheer savagery. The cartoons feed on the implicit savagery of some sketches (particularly Cleese and Chapman's) and give the show a violent aspect not normally found in television comedy. Gilliam: 'I try to say it's not me at all, it's the technique – I'm not sure if that's very convincing . . . The thing is, because they're cut-outs they're very limited – it's like a Punch and Judy show – the easiest things are violent and sudden things. I have a feeling the technique and I found each other . . . I would be working literally seven days a week, and spend at least two nights a week up all night; about two or three o'clock in the morning is when it starts happening, and I'm usually very angry at the entire world by then – a lot of pent-up rage comes out.'

In the first series Gilliam's cartoons, with their style suggestive of Salvador Dali with a migraine, are obviously a severe puzzlement to the studio audience. There are occasional reactions of disgust at the more violent happenings, but in general the audience's reaction to the cartoons and to the whole style of lateral-thinking-linking is one of amused bewilderment. They are also uncertain what to make of the signature tune: Gilliam's cartoons have ruined Sousa's march *The Liberty Bell* for ever for experienced Python fans, who can never hear it without expecting a large bare foot to come crashing down on them in bar thirty-two.

On the whole the original audiences are appreciative of individual sketches, even if they are puzzled by the overall shape of the show; most of the sketches are well received, but it is a little odd to hear the comparatively muted reaction to what later became one of the most famous of all the Python sketches – Cleese and Chapman's 'Dead Parrot' sketch. A 'format sketch' described by Cleese as illustrating 'the impossibility of getting service', it features Palin as a shifty pet-shop proprietor, and Cleese as a dissatisfied customer.

CLEESE (*entering shop with a dead parrot in a cage*): Hallo, I wish to register a complaint . . . Hallo – miss?
PALIN: What do you mean, 'miss'?
CLEESE: Oh, I'm sorry – I have a cold. I wish to make a complaint.
PALIN: Sorry, we're closing for lunch.
CLEESE: Never mind that, my lad, I wish to complain about this parrot what I purchased not half an hour ago from this very boutique.
PALIN: Oh yes, the Norwegian Blue – what's wrong with it?
CLEESE: I'll tell you what's wrong with it – it's dead, that's what's wrong with it.
PALIN: No, no – it's resting, look . . .
CLEESE: Look, my lad, I know a dead parrot when I see one, and I'm looking at one right now.
PALIN: No, no – it's not dead, it's resting.
CLEESE: *Resting?*
PALIN: Yes. Remarkable bird, the Norwegian Blue. Beautiful plumage, ain't it?

CLEESE:	The plumage don't enter into it – it's stone dead.
PALIN:	No, no – it's resting.
CLEESE:	All right then – if it's resting I'll wake it up. (*Shouts into cage*) Hallo, Polly! I got a nice cuttlefish for you when you wake up, Polly Parrot!
PALIN	(*jogging cage*): There, it moved.
CLEESE:	No it didn't! That was you pushing the cage!
PALIN:	I did not!
CLEESE:	Yes you did! (*Takes parrot out of cage*) Hallo Polly! (*Shouting in its ear*) PO-LLY! PO-LLY! (*Bangs it against counter*) Polly parrot – wake up! PO-LLY! (*Throws it in the air and lets it fall to the floor*) Now that's what I call a dead parrot.
PALIN:	No, no – it's stunned.
CLEESE:	Look, my lad – I've had just about enough of this! That parrot is definitely deceased! And when I bought it not half an hour ago, you assured me that its lack of movement was due to it being tired and shagged out after a long squawk.
PALIN:	It's probably pining for the fiords.
CLEESE:	Pining for the fiords – what kind of talk is that? Look, why did it fall flat on its back the moment I got it home?
PALIN:	The Norwegian Blue prefers kipping on its back. It's a beautiful bird – lovely plumage . . .
CLEESE:	Look, I took the liberty of examining that parrot, and I discovered that the only reason it had been sitting on its perch in the first place was that it had been nailed there.
PALIN:	'Course it was nailed there, otherwise it would have muscled up to those bars and voom!
CLEESE:	Look, matey, this parrot wouldn't 'voom' if I put four thousand volts through it. It's bleeding demised.
PALIN:	It's not – it's pining!
CLEESE:	It's *not* pining – it's passed on! This parrot is no more! It has ceased to be! It's expired and gone to meet its maker! This is a late parrot! It's a stiff! Bereft of life it rests in peace – if you hadn't nailed it to the perch it would be pushing up the daisies! It's rung down the curtain and joined the choir invisible! THIS IS AN EX-PARROT!
PALIN:	Well, I'd better replace it then.
CLEESE	(*to camera*): If you want to get anything done in this country you've got to complain until you're blue in the mouth.
PALIN:	Sorry, guv, we're right out of parrots.
CLEESE:	I see, I see – I get the picture.
PALIN:	I've got a slug.
CLEESE:	Does it talk?
PALIN:	Not really, no.
CLEESE:	Well it's scarcely a replacement, then, is it.

The reaction all this gets from the original audience is quite good, but nothing compared with later stage performances where the sketch was noisily hailed as an old friend and got hysterical reactions all through. In this original appearance, the whole idea escalates (as usual) – Cleese is directed to another pet shop in Bolton, the manager of which (Palin again) first pretends that it is

And Now for Something Completely Different: Cleese with the ex-parrot

really in Ipswich, and then that 'Ipswich' is a palindrome of 'Bolton'. ('It's not a palindrome,' protests Cleese. 'The palindrome of Bolton would be Notlob!') In any case, further discussion of whether it is a palindrome (or even a Palin-drome) is precluded by the arrival of Colonel Chapman, who proclaims the whole thing 'silly' and terminates the sketch.

The series as a whole works very well, with a 'sparkle' caused by the sheer profusion of ideas. In the early shows the direction – in particular the vision mixing – is a little slack, but in the later shows everyone seems to have got the feel of the pacing, and the overall style is lively and tightly controlled, with good timing. The director on all but the first four to be recorded was Ian MacNaughton, who directed the film inserts for the whole series, and went on to direct all the subsequent programmes. As with the first two series of *The Goodies*, the studio direction was by John Howard Davies, but this time he did only the first four programmes.

Part of the reason for the success of the series was that the BBC, having commissioned thirteen programmes, left the team alone to get on with it – in this they were perhaps the last people to benefit from Hugh Greene's influence at the BBC. Greene left the BBC on 1 April 1969, and it did not take long for the freedom he had bequeathed to evaporate. Terry Jones had been on a BBC director's course: 'I remember Huw Weldon and David Attenborough coming and talking to us, and I was so impressed by them . . . At that time a producer was responsible for whatever he put on under his name – the producer was the ultimate authority, and any head of department would back up his producer. It's terribly changed now – nobody can make a decision; the producer can't make any decision without conferring with the head of his department, and the head of his department can't make any decision without conferring with the head of BBC-1, and the head of BBC-1 can't make any decision without going to the Controller of Programmes . . .'

Certainly by the time the series was actually transmitted the reaction of those in authority was far less tolerant, and it was probably only the fact that the show got a very good critical reaction in the press that prevented it from being terminated. Chapman: 'I think if the authorities had been aware of what we wanted to do right from the beginning we would never have been allowed to do the programme . . . I don't think the BBC really wanted us around the building very much – in fact we seemed to get worse and worse offices as we went along, and for the last series we were in a shed near the gate.' This attitude of distaste for its offspring in some sections of the BBC contrasts oddly with the self-congratulatory glow indulged in by *Radio Times* ten years later in June 1979, when the tenth anniversary of the first show was marked by a full-colour cover, a long article and a special programme. But by that time, of course, the team were safely off the premises.

Whatever the reservations of the BBC hierarchy, however, a second series of *Monty Python's Flying Circus* was commissioned. It was recorded from June to October 1970, and broadcast for thirteen weeks from 15 September to 22 December 1970. Unfortunately, the BBC chose to schedule it at a time on BBC-1 when the various regions opted out for their own late-night programmes; most regions never saw it at all, one or two saw just the odd programme, and Scotland saw it on a different night. It was only when the series was repeated that the regions were able to see what they had been missing. This unfortunate scheduling did nothing to increase the team's respect for the BBC, and in a sketch in the following series the intelligence of BBC programme planners was compared unfavourably with that of penguins.

As with the preceding series, the second series shows were transmitted in a different order from that in which they were recorded (and where a show is identified by its number in this book it is the order of transmission which is being quoted). This enabled one of the best shows to be placed at the beginning of the series; it is one of the few shows to contain one of the long features which had been typical of the first series – an exposé of a hardened criminal called Dinsdale Piranha who laboured under the delusion that he was being pursued by a giant hedgehog called Spiny Norman. (In fact Spiny Norman turns out to have an existence, in the form of a Gilliam cartoon.) This first show is, however, even more memorable for perhaps the most famous Python sketch – 'The Ministry of Silly Walks', written by Palin and Jones from an idea by Cleese and Chapman. It opens with Cleese walking – or rather proceeding – down Whitehall in a quite extraordinary manner, involving complex movements of his very long legs. Many of the film inserts for *Monty Python's Flying Circus* are, unlike those for *The Goodies*, filmed in populated areas, and are notable for the presence of bemused passers-by. In the case of Cleese's Silly Walk, a line of puzzled pedestrians can be seen following him at a safe distance.

Cleese has become rather haunted by the Silly Walk. There was a period when he was likely to be hailed in the street by lorry-drivers shouting, 'Oi, Monty, do your silly walk!' – and has taken a dislike to the sketch, which is a pity, because it really is very funny. In the studio-performed section of the sketch, a young hopeful (Palin) brings his not-very-silly walk to Cleese's notice in the hope of obtaining a government grant; and the idea then escalates into the Anglo-French Silly Walk, with a demonstration – by the Jabberwock-Frenchmen from the first series – of '*La Grande Marche Futile Française*'.

As with the Dead Parrot sketch, the audience reaction to the Silly Walks is good, but not as great as might have been expected considering that the sketch is now generally considered as one of the classic Python items. It seems to be a characteristic of Python sketches that they do not make their greatest impact at first, but lie in the subconscious like a time-bomb. Jones: 'There's something about *Monty Python*, I don't know what it is – like the Spanish Inquisition sketch, it improves on the telling; when you actually see it, it's not done all that well in a way, it creaks a bit ... but you can tell people about it and it sounds very funny – it matures in the mind.' Jones is underrating the Spanish Inquisition sketch, which he and Palin wrote for the second show of the second series; it is performed well, and is received quite well by the audience; but, as he says, the idea tends to take root in the mind, and the sketch actually seems funnier on subsequent viewings than the first time, instead of diminishing in its effect with familiarity.

CHAPMAN: Trouble at mill.

CLEVELAND: Oh, no – what kind of trouble?

CHAPMAN: One on't cross beams gone owt askew on treddle.

CLEVELAND: Pardon?

CHAPMAN: One on't cross beams gone owt askew on treddle.

CLEVELAND: I don't understand what you're saying.

CHAPMAN (*slightly irritatedly and with exaggeratedly clear accent*): One of the cross beams has gone out askew on the treddle.

CLEVELAND: Well what on earth does that mean?

CHAPMAN: *I* don't know – Mr Wentworth just told me to come in here and say that there was trouble at the mill, that's all – I didn't expect a kind of Spanish Inquisition.

GRAMS: JARRING CHORD
(*The door flies open and Cardinal Ximinez of Spain* (Palin) *enters flanked by two junior cardinals. Cardinal Biggles* (Jones) *has goggles pushed over his forehead. Cardinal Fang* (Gilliam) *is just Cardinal Fang*)

PALIN: Nobody expects the Spanish Inquisition! Our chief weapon is surprise – surprise and fear ... fear and surprise ... our two weapons are fear and surprise – and ruthless efficiency ... our *three* weapons are fear and surprise and ruthless efficiency and an almost fanatical devotion to the Pope ... our *four* ... no ... *Amongst* our weapons – amongst our weaponry – are such elements as fear, surprise ... I'll come in again. (*Exit and exeunt*)

CHAPMAN: I didn't expect a kind of Spanish Inquisition.

GRAMS: JARRING CHORD
(*The cardinals burst in*)

PALIN: Nobody expects the Spanish Inquisition! Amongst our weaponry are such diverse elements as: fear, surprise, ruthless efficiency, an almost fanatical devotion to the Pope, and nice red uniform – Oh damn! (*To Cardinal Biggles*) I can't say it – you'll have to say it.

JONES: What?

PALIN: You'll have to say the bit about 'Our chief weapons are ...'

JONES (*rather horrified*): I couldn't do that ...
(*Ximinez bundles the cardinals outside again*)

CHAPMAN: I didn't expect a kind of Spanish Inquisition.

GRAMS: JARRING CHORD
(*The cardinals enter*)

JONES: Er ... Nobody ... um ...

PALIN: Expects ...

JONES: Expects ... Nobody expects the ... um ... the Spanish ... um ...

PALIN: Inquisition.

JONES: I know, I know ... Nobody expects the Spanish Inquisition. In fact, those who do expect –

PALIN: Our chief weapons are ...

JONES: Our chief weapons are ... um ... er ...

PALIN: Surprise ...

JONES: Surprise and –

PALIN: O.K., stop. Stop. Stop there – stop there. Stop. Phew! Ah! ... Our chief weapons are surprise – blah blah blah ... Cardinal – read the charges.

GILLIAM: You are hereby charged that you did on diverse dates commit heresy against the Holy Church. 'My old man said follow the –'

JONES: That's enough. *(To Cleveland)* Now, how do you plead?

CLEVELAND: We're innocent.

PALIN: Ha! Ha! Ha! Ha! Ha!
              (Superimpose caption: 'DIABOLICAL LAUGHTER')

JONES: We'll soon change your mind about that!
              (Superimpose caption: 'DIABOLICAL ACTING')

PALIN: Fear, surprise, and a most ruthless ... *(controls himself with a supreme effort)* Ooooh! Now, Cardinal – the rack!
              (Biggles produces a plastic-coated washing-up rack. Ximinez looks at it and clenches his teeth in an effort not to lose control. He hums heavily to cover his anger)

PALIN: You ... Right! Tie her down.
              (Fang and Biggles make a pathetic attempt to tie her on to the rack)

PALIN: Right! How do you plead?

CLEVELAND: Innocent.

PALIN: Ha! Right! Cardinal – give the rack – (oh dear) – give the rack a turn.
              (Cardinal Biggles stands there awkwardly and shrugs)

JONES: I ...

PALIN *(gritting his teeth)*: I *know*, I know you can't. I didn't want to say anything, I just wanted to try and ignore your crass mistake.

JONES: I ...

PALIN: It makes it all seem so stupid.

JONES: Shall I ...?

PALIN: No, just pretend for God's sake. Ha! Ha! Ha!
              (Biggles turns an imaginary handle on the side of the dish-rack)

At this point Chapman, who has been standing by through all this, detaches himself from the sketch in order to take part in the Joke Salesman sketch; and it is some time later in the programme that we meet the Spanish Inquisition again. They are now torturing a dear old lady (Marjorie Wilde):

PALIN: Now, old woman – you are accused of heresy on three counts – heresy by thought, heresy by word, heresy by deed, and heresy by action – *four* counts. Do you confess?

WILDE: I don't understand what I'm accused of.

PALIN: Ha! Then we'll make you understand! ... Biggles! Fetch – the cushions!

GRAMS: JARRING CHORD
              (Biggles holds out two ordinary modern household cushions)

JONES: Here they are, lord.

PALIN: Now, old lady – you have one last chance ... confess the heinous

209

	sin of heresy, reject the works of the ungodly – *two* last chances. And you shall be free – *three* last chances. You have three last chances, the nature of which I have divulged in my previous utterance.
WILDE:	I don't know what you're talking about.
PALIN:	Right! If that's the way you want it – Cardinal! Poke her with the soft cushions!
	(*Biggles carries out this rather pathetic torture*)
PALIN:	Confess! Confess! Confess!
JONES:	It doesn't seem to be hurting her, lord.
PALIN:	Have you got all the stuffing up one end?
JONES:	Yes, lord.
PALIN	(*angrily hurling away the cushions*): Hm! She is made of harder stuff! Cardinal Fang – fetch – the Comfy Chair!
GRAMS:	JARRING CHORD
	(*Zoom into Fang's horrified face*)
GILLIAM:	The Comfy Chair?
	(*Biggles pushes in a comfy chair – a really plush one*)
PALIN:	So you think you are strong because you can survive the soft cushions. Well, we shall see … Biggles! Put her in the Comfy Chair!
	(*They roughly push her into the Comfy Chair*)
PALIN	(*with a cruel leer*): Now – you will stay in the Comfy Chair until lunch time, with only a cup of coffee at eleven. (*To Biggles*) Is that really all it is?
JONES:	Yes, lord.
PALIN:	I see. I suppose we make it worse by shouting a lot, do we? Confess, woman. Confess! Confess! Confess! Confess!
JONES:	I confess!
PALIN:	Not you!

One of the reasons that sketches like this stand up to repetition is that, with a cast of anything up to six comedians present (instead of the one or two of more ordinary comedy programmes), there is simply a lot to watch – certainly more than can be taken in at a single viewing. Apart from this, it is not only the team's skill with words but the sheer strength of their ideas that makes these sketches take a hold on the mind. The show that contains the Spanish Inquisition sketch also has the neat idea of *Wuthering Heights* being performed in semaphore, and the execution matches the strength of the idea. This idea then escalates into *Julius Caesar* being performed in Morse on Aldis lamps and *Gentlemen Prefer Blondes* in smoke signals.

With the second series there is more linking between shows, as well as within them. Palin's Cardinal Ximinez appears again in show four, in a Vox Pops sequence, and is greeted with a big laugh; and in show three Palin appears briefly as a bishop rehearsing his lines, who claims that he is not due to appear until show eight. He appears in several other shows, still rehearsing, but not in show eight.

The team mostly wrote in the same combinations – Palin with Jones, Cleese with Chapman, and Idle by himself ('which meant' says Cleese 'that he only got one vote'). Occasionally the team regrouped – Cleese wrote the sketch about a

'Mr Hilter' taking part in the North Minehead by-election with Palin, and one about a mountaineer with double vision with Idle; he regrets that they did not split up more. To some extent it is possible to identify who wrote particular sketches by their style. Cleese: 'We used to have certain jokes – most of the sketches with *heavy* abuse in them were Graham's and mine; any sketch that started with a slow pan across countryside and impressive music was Mike and Terry's; and anything that got utterly involved with words and disappeared up any personal orifice was Eric's.' Palin: 'John and Graham had a lot more reference books than Terry and I, and they would write what we called "Thesaurus sketches" – they would find a word and then repeat it endlessly, in all the synonyms. We tried to do abuse, but no one's as good at abuse as John is – except Graham ... as a partnership they're most intimidating.'

As the second series progressed, the team were getting more adept at packaging the shows by linking ideas throughout individual shows instead of just from sketch to sketch. In the seventh show, several ideas are allowed to interact. The show opens with 'The Attila the Hun Show', which, complete with prerecorded laughter, is a savage 'format sketch' parody of American television's *The Debbie Reynolds Show;* this then links to 'Attila the Nun' – a ton-up nun on a motor-bike. Subsequently a sketch and cartoon about killer sheep is linked into an item about various animals taking on human jobs, which leads to 'The News for Parrots'. This 'format sketch' by Palin and Jones satirizes the BBC News technique – since dropped, or at any rate played down – of announcing, after news of a foreign disaster such as an air crash, that 'No Britons were involved'.

PALIN: Good evening. Here is the News for Parrots. No parrots were involved in an accident on the M1 today when a lorry carrying high octane fuel was in collision with a bollard. ... that is a *bollard* and not a *parrot*. A spokesman for parrots said he was glad that no parrots were involved. The Minister of Technology
(*photo caption of Minister with a parrot on his shoulder*)
today met the three Russian leaders
(*cut to photo of Breznhev, Podgorny and Kosygin, all in a group and each with a parrot on his shoulder*)
to discuss a £4 million airliner deal.
(*cut back to Palin*)
None of them went in the cage or swung on the little wooden trapeze, or ate any of the nice millet seed, yum yum.

The news for parrots is followed by part three of 'A Tale of Two Cities', adapted for parrots by Joey Boy. This is followed by the beginning of the News for Gibbons, which itself is faded under a Parliamentary Report for Humans – a distinctive piece of Idle 'escalation'.

IDLE: In the debate a spokesman accused the government of being silly and doing not at all good things. The Member accepted this in a spirit of healthy criticism, but denied that he had ever been naughty with a choirboy. Angry shouts of 'What about the Watermelon then?' were ordered by the speaker to be stricken from the record and put into a brown paper bag in the lavvy. Any further interruptions would be cut off and distributed amongst the poor. For the government a front bench spokesman said the agricultural tariff would have to be raised and he fancied a bit. Furthermore, he argued, this would give a large boost to farmers, and a lot of fun to him, his friend, and Miss Moist of Knightsbridge. From the back benches there were opposition shouts of 'Postcards for sale' and 'Who likes a sailor then?' from the Minister without Portfolio. Replying, the Shadow Minister said that he could no longer deny the rumours but he and the dachshund were very happy; and in any case, he argued, rhubarb was cheap and what was the harm in a sauna bath.

(cut back to Palin: superimpose caption '7 HOURS LATER')

PALIN: ... were not involved. The Minister of Technology

(cut to photo of Minister with a wombat on his shoulder)

met the three Russian leaders today

(Russian leaders again, all with wombats on their shoulders)

to discuss a £4 million airliner deal. None of them were indigenous to Australia, carried their babies in pouches, or ate any of those yummy eucalyptus leaves.

(cut back to Palin)

That's the News for Wombats, and now Attila the Bun! *(cut to animation of vicious bun doing whatever our award-winning animator normally does when he's at home)*

Monty Python's Flying Circus (10 November 1970). If this photo had been taken two seconds earlier it would have shown Attila the Bun rampaging across the table. As it is, it's just been eaten

Gilliam interprets this script instruction by showing a bun rampaging across a tea-table brandishing a sword. It is interesting to notice that the word 'Gibbons' produces a cheer from the audience, evidently from people who recognize it as one of *ISIRTA*'s running gags.

The team's refusal to regard any subject as sacrosanct caused objections, both from inside the BBC and from viewers. A Palin/Jones sketch, 'Ypres 1914', was castigated for 'sending up the First World War', when, like *Beyond the Fringe*'s 'Aftermyth of War', it was in fact more of a dig at the British 'stiff upper lip', at any rate as portrayed by the cinema.

One of Gilliam's cartoons was censored on the later repeats – it is the story of a prince who develops a spot, foolishly ignores it, and dies of cancer. (The spot, however, survives and goes on to get married and live happily ever after.) After objections that cancer was no fit subject for jokes, the word was removed and 'gangrene' substituted – a joke being made of this by the fact that it is in a quite different voice. Chapman looks at this incident from a medical viewpoint: 'Why not use a word like "cancer"? It's silly to be afraid of it and hide the thing away – a lot of people do die of cancer, and if more people spoke about it more openly then more of them would be cured. It's silly to have this fear – and that's what censorship is, really – it's fear.'

The team deny setting out to shock, although they admit that the cartoons are more disturbing than the sketches because they do not have what Palin, tongue in cheek, calls 'Our reassuring selves'. Cleese, he thinks, can get away with anything because he looks so respectable. Cleese himself thinks they overdid the use of shock, although not out of a deliberate intent to upset people: 'What you discover is that stuff with an element of shock does have the ability to make an audience laugh much more than stuff without it; and therefore when you're a little bit short of material it's awfully easy to start flailing around in all directions – rather like *Private Eye* the last ten years. If you say "you daft bugger", it gets more of a laugh than saying "you're not behaving very sensibly". At the end of a BBC party after the first series, David Attenborough said to me, "Use shock sparingly", which was the best advice we ever had. I don't think we actually stuck to it . . . but of course what happens is that the more you are in this business, the more you tend to abandon, personally, a lot of the taboos you may have held when you were fifteen, twenty, or even twenty-five; so some of the things we do, which are no longer even remotely shocking to us, may be quite shocking to a Presbyterian minister's daughter brought up in Ayr, to take an extreme example.'

The last programme of the second series has a definite end-of-term feel to it, and ends with a sketch by Cleese and Chapman which looks suspiciously like an attempt to see just what they can get away with. In fact when Cleese first read it out to the group, Terry Jones felt a bit shocked; but on reflection he thought 'why not'. Cleese plays a man who brings his dead mother – in a sack – into an undertakers. Chapman, as the undertaker, suggests burial, cremation – and then eating:

CLEESE: Are you suggesting eating my mother?
CHAPMAN: Yes – not raw – cooked. Roasted – two French fried, broccoli . . . horseradish sauce?
CLEESE: Well, I do feel a bit peckish. Can we have some parsnips?
CHAPMAN: 'Course. (*Calling off*) Fred – get some parsnips. (*To Cleese*) Right – how about stuffing?
CLEESE: No – honestly – I really don't think I should.
CHAPMAN: Look, tell you what – we'll eat her; if you feel a bit guilty about it afterwards, we can dig a grave and you can throw up in it.

As Jones says, it is the sheer awfulness of the idea that makes it funny; but it was a bit too much for the BBC. After some negotiation, it was agreed that the sketch could be performed only if the audience were heard to protest against it, and then revolt and climb on the stage to stop it. In the event, the whole exercise looks a trifle forced; for one thing, the audience start to shout too soon (and in reality, a shocked audience would react with an embarrassed silence)

and, because of the fire regulations, only about a quarter of the audience were allowed on the stage. This looks rather obvious as it is only one section of audience which gets up – the rest just sit there laughing. The sketch was shown again later the same evening, on *Late Night Line-Up*, prior to an interview with the team which was remarkable only for its lack of coherence.

The whole incident appears to have been an embarrassment to the BBC, and, even though the show has never been repeated by them, the Undertakers sketch has mysteriously disappeared from the video tape, having been replaced by something innocuous from another show.

Once they had finished recording the second series, the team worked on a film version of material from the first two series, entitled *And Now For Something Completely Different* – this being a first series catch-phrase, read by Cleese at a BBC newsreader's desk which turned up in a variety of locations. The film was made at the suggestion of Victor Lownes, who put up some of the money, and was intended to appeal to the massive student audience in America who had not seen the programmes (it was another four years before they were shown by Public Service television). The cast spent five weeks at the end of 1970 filming in a dank deserted milk depot in Totteridge, and the result is surprisingly effective. Revue format films are not normally successful – and even with this one they found that whatever order they put the items in, the audience tended to flag after fifty minutes and revive about fifteen minutes later. There seems to be a fifty-minute barrier in the use of a lot of short items, but in this case the original television material has been tightened up and in some cases improved, and the result is on the whole very enjoyable.

At this point their calculations turned out to be wildly wrong; the team had been against the film being shown in England because the material was familiar, but when the film was released in October 1971 it got its money back quickly, whereas in the United States it did not gross enough even to cover its advertising costs. Evidently America was not yet ready for the Pythons.

The Pythons gained respectability in the eyes of the BBC by winning the Silver Rose at the Montreux Festival with a special compilation edition, broadcast in Britain on 16 April 1971. Cleese's aura of respectability was further increased by his being invited to become the Rector of St Andrews University – an honorary position held for a year and elected by the students. In his speech at the installation ceremony on 21 April, he said: 'I have now to deliver a Rectoral Address, something that I am almost uniquely unqualified to do, since the one subject I might talk about with any semblance of knowledge or authority, which is Humour, is the most exquisitely dull and stupefyingly uninteresting topic known to man, the Law of Real Property not excepted . . . I cannot even hope to be diverted by an enormous *papier mâché* foot crashing down on this platform or by a colonel entering the hall and bringing the proceedings to a close by announcing that the whole thing is too silly.' He went on to give a closely reasoned – and not entirely unserious – speech in favour of Cowardice as a Way of Life.

Another outlet for the Python team's energies around this time was in the making of a few advertising films – not intended to be seen by the public, but for showing to salesmen as a way of putting over the company's policy. The most interesting one was made for Birds Eye Frozen Foods, and spends some twenty minutes emphasizing the point that Birds Eye peas are picked early so that they should be as tender as possible. The film is well made and entertaining, and includes a dig at advertising jargon, here demonstrated by Palin, with Jones as an interpreter. He has been asked how the product can be improved:

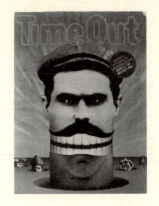

PALIN: Postulating a strategy of substantive and non-image USP reformation, assuming constant ABP, explicit to a maximization of point-of-sale realization, increased media activity or in-style promotional usage – instigate an in-depth motivational analysis on the full A-to-E spectrum with Pollinated Empiric Limited Placement Merchandising.

JONES: It says, 'Ask some housewives'.

BOTH: Boom-boom!

The film also includes a sequence with multiple Alan Whickers, each picking up the preceding one's sentence. Alan Whicker's individual style of television reporting, familiar from *Tonight* and *Whicker's World*, is the basis for a number of imitations throughout all the series; and indeed Whicker himself has lately come to sound alarmingly like Eric Idle. The multiple Whickers idea was expanded for the first programme (as transmitted) of the third series, where they are confined to a tropical island, ceaselessly searching for someone to interview.

The third series was recorded from December 1971 to May 1972, and transmitted from 19 October 1972 to 18 January 1973. Cleese was by this time starting to get tired of the whole exercise, and has said that he feels that the quality tails off during this series. In fact most of the best material in the series, as with the preceding two, is in the first few shows to be recorded. Even so the series stands up quite well, although towards the end there is a tendency for some of the material to become weird, rather than funny. Certainly Cleese is less in evidence – he takes part in every show, but there are far less of the typical Cleese/Chapman confrontation sketches than in the first and second series.

There is a generally 'harder' feeling to the entire series, and this may to some extent arise from the conflicts among the group. Apart from the linking material which had been written in committee, all the sketches had always been subjected to group scrutiny which, since everyone respected everyone else's opinion and was therefore prepared to cede points rather than hang on to material simply because it was theirs, helped to maintain a very high standard. Palin and Jones were more interested in the overall shape of the show than Cleese and Chapman; and conflicts arose because Cleese and Chapman were very insistent on maintaining the 'internal logic' of sketches, something which Palin and Jones were not so concerned about. By this time, the group had been practically living in each other's pockets for three years, and it would have been surprising if internal tensions had not sprung up. The opposing poles tended to be Cleese, who is highly articulate and logical; and Jones, who is much more an instinctive writer and performer, and who is not as immediately articulate. The dissensions led to different combinations of agreement and disagreement which Cleese later described as 'Balkanization'.

Palin says: 'In a way we were a little spoilt – it wasn't as if we were just happy with a successful television show, it had to be something more; and what it was about, and what each of us was expressing of ourselves was also important. I don't think the show would have been successful if people hadn't been pulling in various directions.' However irritating these conflicts may have been at the time, they probably helped to give the show much of its characteristic 'bite' and once the team had split up to work on their own the tensions between them subsided.

Arising from his interest in the overall 'feel' of the show, Terry Jones started to take an interest in the technical and production aspect of the programmes. The shows were habitually recorded some five minutes over length, so that they could be tightened up later in the editing sessions – the principle being, if it doesn't get a laugh, cut it. Jones became closely involved in the editing sessions, and feels that he probably made himself a nuisance to Ian MacNaughton; but, as with Jim Franklin and the Goodies, once Mac-Naughton realized that Jones was not just interfering for the sake of it, he accepted this interest in the technical side as useful.

As the third series progressed, the BBC made a number of 'requests for reconsideration' of jokes. Cleese thinks that on the whole the BBC were very good: 'I always felt that the others over-reacted to the slightest hint of censorship. I thought that once or twice the BBC were very silly, but on the whole they were very good in the freedom they gave us.' Palin: 'During the third series we had a list of thirty-two points presented to us, which they wanted changed; which we fought, and I think we got it reduced to about ten. This involved having meetings with the BBC in which we would discuss whether we should say "masturbation" or not – with six of us and one of the BBC, they were bizarre meetings.'

That particular example came from the Palin/Jones Summarize Proust Competition sketch in programme five, when Graham Chapman, as one of the contestants, listed his hobbies as 'golf, and strangling animals, and masturbation'. The BBC won that argument, and the words 'and masturbation' were cut from the sound-track – although not from the vision, which meant that anyone who could lip-read could still appreciate what the huge laugh was actually for. To confuse matters further, when the show was repeated in 1979, an uncensored version of the sketch was shown (perhaps by accident).

The Summarize Proust Competition requires its contestants to summarize Proust's series of novels *A La Recherche du Temps Perdu* in fifteen seconds. Chapman, Palin and the Fred Tomlinson singers (who madrigalize their attempt) having failed to gain any points, the prize is awarded to the girl with

Monty Python's Flying Circus (16 November 1972): Terry Jones, Graham Chapman and the Proustometer

the biggest tits. This sketch has been cited by both Alan Bennett and Jonathan Miller as an example of the intellectualism of *Monty Python's Flying Circus*; but in fact no knowledge of Proust is needed to understand the sketch. It is quite obvious that the books in question are very long and complex and could not possibly be summarized in fifteen seconds (although, for those who are listening closely, Chapman gives a brief assessment of the whole work which might be of some educational value), and any feeling of 'intellectualism' is in fact a clever optical illusion.

Like many of the third series sketches, the Summarize Proust Competition is tightly written, packing into a short time a number of barbs at the expense of various foibles of television presentation. The intensity of the writing is in many cases matched by a noticeably increased savagery which may partly have spilt over from the cartoons. By now the audiences were used to this sort of thing, and the following example is typical in being greeted purely with laughter with no hint of restraint. Cleese and Chapman are Pepperpot women in a launderette.

CHAPMAN: Hullo, Mrs Premise.
CLEESE: Hullo, Mrs Conclusion.
CHAPMAN: Busy day?
CLEESE: Busy? I just spent four hours burying the cat.
CHAPMAN: *Four hours* to bury a cat?
CLEESE: Yes – it wouldn't keep still.
CHAPMAN: Oh – it wasn't dead, then?
CLEESE: No, no – but it's not at all well, so as we were going away for a fortnight's holiday I thought I'd better bury it just to be on the safe side.
CHAPMAN: Quite right – you don't want to come back from Sorrento to a dead cat. It'd be so anticlimactic. Yes, kill it now, that's what I say. We're going to have to have our budgie put down.
CLEESE: Really – is it very old?
CHAPMAN: No, we just don't like it. We're going to take it to the vet tomorrow.
CLEESE: Tell me, how do they put budgies down, then?
CHAPMAN: Well, it's funny you should ask that, because I've just been reading a great big book about how to put your budgie down, and apparently, you can either hit them with the book, or you can shoot them just there, just above the beak.
CLEESE: Just there? Well, well, well. 'Course, Mrs Essence flushed hers down the loo.
CHAPMAN: No, you shouldn't do that – no, that's dangerous. They *breed* in the *sewers*!

Even Cleese and Chapman's unappetizing menu doesn't seem to worry the audience of show number three:

JONES: What do you want with your jugged fish?
IDLE: Halibut.
JONES: The jugged fish *is* halibut.
IDLE: What fish have you got that isn't jugged, then?
JONES: Rabbit.

IDLE:	Rabbit fish?
JONES:	Yes – it's got fins.
IDLE:	Is it dead?
JONES:	Well, it was coughing up blood last night.

But probably the nastiest sketch – and one which does worry some sections of the studio audience slightly – is 'Sam Peckinpah's Salad Days' in programme seven; it starts innocently enough, with a picnicking group round a piano, but gradually the scene becomes a bloody collection of severed limbs, with blood spouting everywhere in a manner inspired by Peckinpah's final shoot-out in *The Wild Bunch*.

By this time the team had not only abandoned punch lines, but had also stopped bothering to make comments about the fact that they had abandoned them. The linking devices in the third series are less obvious than in the first, and the team also play tricks with the overall shape of the shows – putting the closing titles near the beginning, indulging in false endings, and on one occasion starting with the trademark of a rival television station (and one of its announcers). None of this seems to confuse the audience, who have obviously got used to the style. It is tempting to see the early comments by the cast on, for example, the lack of punch lines as an attempt to educate the audience; but Cleese says that they had no such idea in mind: 'It wasn't that we were signalling it to the audience, it was that the whole concept was new to us; the whole idea of doing something without a punch line struck us as being funny. The whole idea of breaking a convention was right in the front of our minds; but very rapidly, once you've destroyed a convention then the fact that the convention no longer exists itself becomes a convention, so then of course there wouldn't be any point in commenting on it.'

The last major comment about not using punch lines comes at the end of show three (the first to be recorded):

IDLE:	Right – I'm arresting this entire show on three counts; one – acts of self-conscious behaviour contrary to the 'Not In Front Of The Children' Act; two – always saying 'It's so-and-so of the Yard' every time the fuzz arrives; and three – and this is the cruncher – offences against the 'Getting Out Of Sketches Without Using A Proper Punch Line' Act, namely, simply ending every bleeding sketch by just having a policeman come in and . . . wait a minute . . .
CLEESE	(*entering and placing a hand on Idle's shoulder*): Hold it.
IDLE:	It's a fair cop!
	(*A large hand appears through the door and places itself on Cleese's shoulder . . . Blackout*)

There are a number of running jokes throughout the series – partly because the filming was evidently completed before the studio recordings started, and many of the locations and characters turn up in more than one show; and some of the prerecorded studio material is also split up and distributed round the shows. All this helps to give the whole series an identity, rather than its being a collection of unrelated programmes.

All five of the main members of the team play a wide variety of characters in all the series, but certain impersonations seem to aggregate to make a 'persona' with which each performer becomes associated. Cleese and Chapman tend to specialize in assertive authority figures – partly, Chapman says, on account of their height: 'The others are awfully short, really ... My father was a police inspector, I suppose that's where that background comes from, that and the medical side of ordering people around.' This family connection may explain Chapman's superb glassy stare when he is being the colonel or a similar authority figure. It is interesting to note that, where Chapman plays senior authority types, Cleese tends to be a constable, or a traffic warden. He is also very good at infuriated upper-middle-class types.

Idle, whom Chapman describes as 'a word freak', creates a range of characters who have a sort of withdrawn aggressiveness; many of them have verbal peculiarities, such as the Man Whose First Answer is Always a Rude One, the Man Who Has Problems with Wrong Word Order, and, in this example, the Man Who Speaks in Anagrams.

PALIN: Hello, good evening and welcome to another edition of Blood Devastation Death War and Horror, and later on we'll be meeting a man who *does* gardening. But first on the show we've got a man who speaks entirely in anagrams.

IDLE: Taht si crreoct.

PALIN: Do you enjoy it?

IDLE: I stom certainly od. Revy chum so.

PALIN: And what's your name?

IDLE: Hamrag – Hamrag Yatlerot.

PALIN: Well, Graham, nice to have you on the show. Now, where do you come from?

IDLE: Bumcreland.

PALIN: Cumberland?

IDLE: Staht sit sepricly.

PALIN: And I believe you're working on an anagram version of Shakespeare?

IDLE: Sey, sey – taht si crreoct, er – ta the mnemot I'm wroking on *The Mating of the Wersh*.

PALIN: *The Mating of the Wersh*? By William Shakespeare?

IDLE: Nay, by Malliwi Rapesheake.

PALIN: And what else?

IDLE: *Two Netlemeg of Verona, Twelfth Thing, The Chamrent of Venice* ...

PALIN: Have you done Hamlet?

IDLE: *Thamle*. 'Be ot or bot ne ot, tath is the nestqui.'

PALIN: And what is your next project?

IDLE: *Ring Kichard the Thrid*.

PALIN: I'm sorry?

IDLE: 'A shroe! A shroe! My dingkome for a shroe!'

PALIN: Ah, Ring Kichard, yes ... but surely that's not an anagram, that's a spoonerism.

IDLE: If you're going to split hairs I'm going to piss off. (*Exit*)

Palin plays perhaps the widest range of characters, from flashy quizmasters and television interviewers to dim-witted ordinary little men or naïve overgrown schoolboys. One of his classic creations is Mr Pither, the hero of the

Monty Python's Flying Circus: 'The Cycling Tour' (7 December 1972). Communist police (Chapman, Idle, Cleese) confront Mr Pither (Palin); hotel clerk Terry Gilliam looks on

only edition of *Monty Python's Flying Circus* to have a single straight-through plot. This is the eighth show of the third series, subtitled 'The Cycling Tour', and was one of several Palin/Jones half-hour scripts which had been rejected by the BBC. After going through the usual group criticism process, it became a Python show, with Palin as the central character. Mr Pither is a close relation of an earlier Palin characterization, Arthur Putey, who is an ineffectual man with marital problems in a first series sketch, and who is also the applicant to the Ministry of Silly Walks in the second series. Pither is very like this character – he is a sort of super-intelligent Gumby (which makes him a very dim human being). Palin: 'I do like playing rather gullible characters like that, but I like giving them that extra dimension – Pither is a simple-minded chap, really, and yet awfully aggressive in a way – he won't let you go. I don't actually like bright, sharp, clever, pushy people – so I tend to go for the sort of characters that would infuriate them; those are the sort of characters I like to play.' Pither's aggressiveness consists of reciting to anyone who will listen (and several who don't want to) the details of his latest cycling accident, and the damage thereby sustained to his packed lunch. The only person who will listen to him is Terry Jones, as a character who has invented food which will self-eject just *before* an accident.

Jones is quite capable of playing a flashy character – the compère of the 'Summarize Proust Competition', for example – and he also does a nice line in cut-price crooks. Many of his characterizations, however, are of an ordinary man caught in the middle of a lunatic situation – the Englishman surrounded by Australians who are all called 'Bruce', or the City gent who is trapped by Idle in 'Nudge Nudge'; and he is the judge in most of the court sketches. He says that he does not basically think of himself as a funny person: 'It's all a bit defensive, I think, doing things to make people laugh ... As a child I had difficulty in pronouncing my "r"s, and saying my name – "Tewwy Jones" – this gets a sort of ribald reaction and you can't understand why.' This difficulty with 'r's still emerges, rather endearingly, when he plays his more pompous characters. Their bewilderment perhaps reflects his own uncertainties: 'I suppose I've spent a lot of time trying to find out what other people laugh at – I mean, not what *I* laugh at – I laugh at poetry; I laugh at things that look beautiful; if I see anything that looks really nice, that makes me smile with happiness. Learning what makes people laugh ... I still don't know!' Not knowing does not seem to prevent him from being able to make people laugh; but it prevents him from being able to analyse how he does it.

By the end of the third series the team had demonstrated their abilities to make not only English viewers laugh – and even English television critics – but also German viewers. A special programme, entitled *Monty Python's Fliegende Zirkus*, was made in Germany, *in German*, but never shown in Britain; and a second German production was made in English and, to the cast's relief, dubbed into German. This edition was shown on BBC-2 (in English, of course) on 6 October 1973. There are some excellent sketches, including one which originated in the *1948 Show*, detailing total confusion in a contact lens and hearing aid shop – and a long fairy story written by Cleese with Connie Booth: 'Happy Valley, or, The Princess with Wooden Teeth'. Connie Booth is the princess in question, with Terry Jones as the king, her father, who spends his time singing very odd songs at an electric organ and setting impossible tasks for her suitors.

This was Cleese's last television appearance as part of the Python team. He had been getting progressively less interested during the third series, and finally announced his decision to leave. The press immediately speculated that this would be the end of *Monty Python's Flying Circus* – and indeed the BBC seriously considered cancelling the planned fourth series. Meanwhile, however, he went on tour in 1973 with the team in a stage version of the show, using many of the most popular sketches. They had done a stage show in 1970 at the Belgrade Theatre, Coventry, which had gone down very well, and they felt that it would be an interesting new departure to do a stage tour.

They were joined by Neil Innes, who had been doing studio warm-ups for the television recordings since the Bonzo Dog Band had broken up. He provided musical interludes with such songs as 'How Sweet to be an Idiot', a semi-straight, semi-humorous song he had written while working with Vivian Stanshall and the group called 'Scaffold' after leaving the Bonzo Dog Band.

The tour consisted of a series of one-night stands in places including Sunderland and Glasgow, and the team found it a rather exhausting experience, rushing from theatre to hotel, and from hotel to another theatre for a technical run-through, and so on. Palin had always enjoyed being a Gumby on television: 'It was very therapeutic to do – lovely to be able to stand there and just yell. Until I had to do it in the stage show and then I realized the disadvantage – six weeks with laryngitis.' The cast started to use radio-microphones fairly early on because of the difficulties of projecting to a large auditorium. Cleese remembers: 'By the time we got to Leeds four out of the six radio mics were not functioning, and every time people came off-stage there was a scrimmage while the next people on grabbed the nearest mics; we would gather into two knots on the stage – you got near to whoever had the mic and said the lines to his tie!'

As if this was not enough, the team then went on tour across Canada. They began in a small theatre in Toronto, which Cleese thoroughly enjoyed because, as with *Cambridge Circus* in Greenwich Village, he could act rather than having to project; but as they made their way through Montreal, Ottawa, Winnipeg, Edmonton, Calgary and Vancouver, they found themselves playing to audiences of about three thousand people in huge halls, which required what Cleese

Monty Python Live at Drury Lane

describes as 'opera acting'. As these were mostly one-night stands, everyone was soon totally exhausted.

The following February, having recovered somewhat, they opened for a season at the Theatre Royal, Drury Lane, London, where they played to packed houses of Python fans. Cleese was puzzled by the reactions of the audience – they would applaud a sketch upon recognizing it, laugh a moderate amount through it, and then clap and cheer enthusiastically at the end. It began to make sense when he realized that the show was really the equivalent of a pop concert, and that the audience were celebrating the performance of old favourites. Theatre critic Harold Hobson, writing in the *Sunday Times* on 3 March 1974, also commented on this behaviour of the audience, and concluded that the team had achieved theatrical 'relevance' – not in the usual sense of relevance to the current social or political scene, but relevance of mood.

Cleese found this sort of audience reaction disconcerting: 'The best audiences are not the ones who laugh the most, but the ones who laugh quickly and loudly, and then shut up. I remember the joy of performing the revue at Oxford – the audiences were fabulous, and the pace kept going; a Saturday night audience can laugh so much that you lose pace, and the show tends to die a bit.'

After the stage tour ended, preparations were made for the fourth television series, which the BBC had now decided to commission after all. Retitled simply *Monty Python*, the series consisted of only six programmes, each recorded very close to its transmission date and thus broadcast in the same order as recording. The transmissions began on 31 October 1974. As the order could not be reshuffled, and also since they had been unable to follow their earlier practice of recording about five minutes over length and then editing down, the shows were placed at a disadvantage even without the absence of Cleese. Palin: 'There was an ingredient missing – the sort of middle-class ferocity that John could express so well wasn't quite there; also Terry Gilliam wasn't able to do much animation, and Eric wrote very little.'

The fourth series contains one really superb show (the third); one good show (the last); and the remainder don't quite come off. However, the series does not really justify the very bad press reaction, and is worth it if only for that third show, which carries the linked surrealism which is the Python trademark to new heights. Various sketch ideas recur – the Pepperpots watch themselves on television watching an earlier sketch ('bloody repeats!'); and the show is given a sort of subconscious thematic unity by the fact that all the music – for example the skit on the 'Steptoe Theme' – is based on the melody of Neil Innes's song 'When Does A Dream Begin' which he sings to Gilliam's wife and a Spitfire aeroplane (all three being in RAF uniform).

This song, which ends the show and takes place on an RAF airfield, filmed in scratchy black-and-white, is one of several items with a wartime RAF slant. Earlier in the show a long and complex introduction leads to a sketch set in a wartime RAF station:

JONES: Morning, Squadron Leader.
IDLE: What-ho, Squiffy.
JONES: How was it?
IDLE: Top-hole. Bally Jerry, pranged his kite right in the how's-your-father; hairy blighter, dicky-birded, feathered back on his sammy,

took a waspy, flipped over on his Betty Harpers and caught his can in the Bertie.

JONES: Er, I'm afraid I don't quite follow you, Squadron Leader.

IDLE: It's perfectly ordinary banter, Squiffy. Bally Jerry, pranged his kite, right in the how's-your-father; hairy blighter, dicky-birded, feathered back on his sammy, took a waspy, flipped over on his Betty Harpers and caught his can in the Bertie.

JONES: No, I'm just not understanding banter at all well today. Give us it slower.

IDLE: Banter's not the same if you say it slower, Squiffy.

JONES: Hold on then – Wingco! – just bend an ear to the Squadron Leader's banter for a sec, would you?

CHAPMAN: Can do.

JONES: Jolly good. Fire away.

IDLE: Bally Jerry ... (*he goes through it all again*)

CHAPMAN: No, I don't understand that banter at all.

IDLE: Something up with my banter, chaps?

GRAMS: AIR RAID SIRENS
(*Enter Palin, out of breath*)

PALIN: Bunch of monkeys on the ceiling, sir! Grab your egg-and-fours and let's get the bacon delivered!

CHAPMAN: (*to Idle*): Do *you* understand that?

IDLE: No – I didn't get a word of it.

CHAPMAN: Sorry, old man, we don't understand your banter.

PALIN: You know – bally tenpenny ones dropping in the custard!
(*no reaction*)

PALIN: Um – Charlie choppers chucking a handful!

CHAPMAN: No no – sorry.

JONES: Say it a bit slower, old chap.

PALIN: Slower *banter*, sir?

CHAPMAN: Ra-ther.

PALIN: Um – sausage squad up the blue end?

IDLE: No, still don't get it.

PALIN: Um – cabbage crates coming over the briny?

THE OTHERS: No, no.
(*Film of air-raid*)

IDLE (*voice-over*): But by then it was too late. The first cabbage crates hit London on July the 7th. That was just the beginning.
(*Chapman seen sitting at desk, on telephone*)

CHAPMAN: Five shillings a dozen? That's ordinary cabbages, is it? And what about the bombs? ... Good Lord, they *are* expensive.

All this leads to accusations of trivializing the war, which develop into a trial scene in which Idle is accused of flicking at the enemy with wet towels, among other crimes. This is the only Python trial scene not written by Cleese – to be accurate, it is really a court martial, and a rather peculiar one at that. The 'rave-up' ending of this sketch is seen again when the characters in a later sketch switch on their television, and that leads on to one of Gilliam's sourer cartoons.

There is then a shift of mood into a 1920s-style drawing room, whose occupants seem to be obsessively philological:

CHAPMAN: I say!

CLEVELAND: Yes, Daddy?

CHAPMAN: Croquet hoops look dam' pretty this afternoon.

CLEVELAND: Frightfully damn pretty.

IDLE   (*as her mother*): They're coming along *awfully* well this year.

CHAPMAN: Yes, better than your Aunt Lavinia's croquet hoops.

CLEVELAND: Ugh! Dreadful tin things.

IDLE: I did tell her to stick to wood.

CHAPMAN: Yes, you can't beat wood. Gorn.

IDLE: What's gone, dear?

CHAPMAN: Nothing, nothing – just like the word, it gives me confidence. Gorn. Gorn – it's got a sort of *woody* quality about it. Gorn. Go-o-orn. Much better than 'newspaper' or 'litter bin'.

CLEVELAND: Ugh! Frightful words!

IDLE: Perfectly dreadful!

CHAPMAN: 'Newspaper' – 'litter bin' – 'litter bin' – dreadful *tinny* sort of word.

CLEVELAND (*screams*)

CHAPMAN: Tin, tin, tin.

IDLE: Oh, don't say 'tin' to Rebecca, you know how it upsets her.

CHAPMAN: Sorry, old horse.

IDLE: 'Sausage.'

CHAPMAN: 'Sausage'! There's a good woody sort of word, 'sausage'. 'Gorn.'

CLEVELAND: 'Antelope!'

CHAPMAN: Where? On the lawn?

CLEVELAND: No, no, Daddy – just the word.

CHAPMAN: Don't want antelope nibbling the hoops.

CLEVELAND: No, no – 'ant-e-lope'. Sort of nice and woody type of thing.

IDLE: Don't think so, Becky old chap.

CHAPMAN: No, no – 'antelope' – 'antelope', *tinny* sort of word.

CLEVELAND (*screams*)

CHAPMAN: Oh, sorry old man.

IDLE: Really, Mansfield.

CHAPMAN: Well, she's got to come to terms with these things. 'Seemly.' 'Prodding.' 'Vac-u-um.' 'Leap.'

CLEVELAND: Oh – hate 'leap'.

IDLE: Perfectly dreadful.

CLEVELAND: Sort of PVC sort of word, don't you know.

IDLE: Lower-middle.

CHAPMAN: 'Bound!'

IDLE: Now you're talking!

CHAPMAN: 'Bound.' 'Vole!' 'Recidivist!'

IDLE: Bit *tinny* . . .

CLEVELAND (*screams and rushes out sobbing*)

IDLE: Oh, sorry, Becky old beast.

CHAPMAN: Oh dear, I suppose she'll be gorn for a few days now.

IDLE: Caribou.

CHAPMAN: Splendid word!

IDLE: No, dear, nibbling the hoops.
        (*Chapman fires a shotgun*)

CHAPMAN   (*with satisfaction*): Caribou – gorn. . . . 'Intercourse.'

IDLE: Later, dear.

CHAPMAN: No, no – the word, 'intercourse'. Good and woody. 'Inter-course.'
        'Pert,' 'pert,' 'thighs,' 'botty,' 'botty,' 'botty' (*getting excited*),
        'erogenous zo-o-one'. Ha ha ha ha – oh, 'concubine', 'erogenous
        zo-o-one', 'loose woman', 'erogenous zone' . . .
        (*Idle calmly empties a bucket of water over Chapman*)

CHAPMAN: Oh, thank you, dear. There's a funny thing, dear – all the naughty
        words sound woody.

IDLE: Really, dear – how about 'tit'?

CHAPMAN: Oh, dear – I hadn't thought about that. 'Tit.' 'Tit.' Oh, that's very
        tinny, isn't it? 'Tit.' 'Tit.' Tinny, tinny.
        (*Cleveland, who has just come in, screams and rushes out again*)

CHAPMAN: Oh dear. 'Ocelot.' 'Was-p.' 'Yowling.' Oh dear, I'm bored. Better
        go and have a bath, I suppose.

IDLE: Oh really, must you, dear – you've had nine today.

CHAPMAN: All right – I'll sack one of the servants. Simpkins! Nasty tinny sort
        of name. SIMPKINS!
        (*Enter Palin, in RAF uniform*)

PALIN: I say, mater, cabbage crates coming over the briny.

IDLE: Sorry dear, don't understand.

PALIN: Er – cow-catchers creeping up on the conning towers?

IDLE: No, sorry old sport.

PALIN: Um – caribou nibbling at the croquet hoops.

IDLE: Yes, Mansfield shot one in the antlers.

The show ranks among the best of the Python output, partly because of the linked and surrealistic feeling which permeates it. The other show of the series which is reasonably successful, the last one, has several good ideas; including 'The Most Awful Family in Britain' which is remarkable for Terry Jones, as the father, maundering on about his bowel movements, and Terry Gilliam lying on the floor liberally covered in baked beans.

With Cleese absent, Idle becoming more interested in doing his own series, and a general feeling that the team was breaking up, it was decided that it was time to stop the television *Monty Pythons*. However, a treat was in store for Python fans with the release in April 1975 of the team's second film – *Monty Python and the Holy Grail*. Cleese was involved in this and in fact some material he wrote for it which was not used in the final version found its way into the second programme of the fourth series. The finance for the film was set up by Michael White – who had brought *Cambridge Circus* and '****' to London in 1963. He persuaded a variety of people to put money into it, including the pop groups Pink Floyd and Led Zeppelin.

Despite being made on a low budget, the film works very well and looks much more expensive than it was. Feeling that modern middle-class England had suffered enough from their attentions, they set the film in the legendary period of King Arthur. However, they then peopled it with modern stereotypes, many of them readily recognizable from the television shows. Palin: 'We were able to use the considerable talents of people in Python, like

Monty Python and the Holy Grail: King Arthur and his Knights ride to Camelot

Terry Gilliam with his design, and Terry Jones's direction, and all of our feelings for historical period. We felt we were using an area of ourselves which we hadn't really explored in the television series.'

The two Terrys – Jones and Gilliam – co-directed, and the script was a team effort. Being still firmly rooted in the sketch format, the team produced a result in which the story line tends to divide into a series of sketches; but the film hangs together well on the whole. The fascinating thing about it is that it often looks better than genuine Hollywood period epics; the team deliberately attempted to express their dislike for brash Hollywood versions of English history.

Neil Innes, who also appears – appropriately enough as a minstrel – wrote the songs and some background music, but since the low budget precluded the use of a full-sized orchestra, the background music was in the end mostly drawn from commercial mood-music records. The complete script of the film, together with many photographs, was subsequently published by Eyre Methuen.

The film makes a certain amount of play with cinematic conventions; the opening titles are hilariously confused by some very insistent subtitles in almost-Swedish, and the plot gets a trifle mixed-up with a modern historian who is killed by one of the knights, as a result of which the film ends with the main characters being arrested by the police.

The first part of the film shows King Arthur (Chapman) assembling his knights and being instructed by God (a Gilliam animation) to go on a quest for the Holy Grail. Chapman's portrayal of Arthur is very effective, with an easy and quite believable authority; Cleese plays a remarkably destructive Sir Launcelot, Idle the cowardly Sir Robin, Jones the learned Sir Bedevere, while the pure-hearted Sir Galahad is played with convincing innocence by Palin. In the central section of the film there are four individual adventures, which rather reinforces the sketch feeling. The adventure of the Three-Headed Knight and Arthur's encounter with the Knights who say 'Ni' are not as effective as the rest of the film, but the other two adventures stand up well. Sir Galahad (Palin) finds himself in a castle full of beautiful maidens, all between the ages of sixteen and nineteen-and-a-half, and all with a burning desire to be spanked and treated to oral sex. To his disgust he is rescued by Launcelot.

Sir Launcelot (Cleese) has his own adventure in which he kills or maims most of the inhabitants of a castle where he imagines a princess is being married against her will. To his chagrin ('Sor-ry!') the princess turns out to be a quite remarkably unattractive prince – a fascinating performance from an almost unrecognizable Terry Jones. Jones's individual style of mime can be seen in the scene where he shoots an arrow bearing the message which will bring Launcelot, while trying to pretend to his guards that he is not actually doing so.

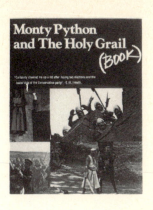

With the main characters reunited, the film moves into its final section, as they come near the end of their quest. Idle, who generally seems less able to sink himself into his parts than the others, produces a convincing monk in Brother Maynard, the senior monk in charge of the Holy Hand-grenade of Antioch; and Cleese appears as a wizard much given to explosions, and having a rather peculiar Scots accent. The film ends with the arrest of the knights, and the breaking of the camera filming the incident.

The overall 'look' of the film is extremely good, with some excellent photography; and there are a number of hilarious cameos from the team (who play many small parts in addition to the major characters). Particularly effective are some peasants with a remarkable grasp of political sociology, and Cleese's French knight who has a very bizarre line of abuse ('I wave my private parts at your aunties, you cheesy lot of second-hand electric donkey-bottom biters').

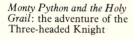
Monty Python and the Holy Grail: the adventure of the Three-headed Knight

Monty Python and the Holy Grail was far more successful in America than its predecessor, and apparently also went down very well in Russia! Perhaps the Russians liked its ostensibly anti-religious element. However, it was the last major teaming of the Pythons for four years. As Chapman says: 'Working in a group is great fun, but you need your own individual identity as well . . . if you're stuck together for almost a year doing a television series, it becomes very difficult to have a separate existence other than within the group. You virtually have to ring up to ask if it's all right to have a bath. We must develop separately as individuals for the group to survive.'

Monty Python continued to be available to its fans in the form of records and books. As with – and several years earlier than – the Goodies' books, a great deal of effort has gone into making the books work in their own terms, in particular from Eric Idle as editor. Similarly with the records – although the earlier issues are just reworkings of the television material, the later ones are conceived more as artifacts in their own right. One of them, *Monty Python's Matching Tie And Handkerchief*, revives the old idea of interlaced grooves – there are two grooves on side two, and it is a matter of luck which one is played

when the pickup is put down onto the record. This idea had been done on 78s at least as early as 1911, but the Pythons were the first to do it on a long-playing record.

The television shows, meanwhile, were gaining new fans abroad. In America, Public Service television stations took the entire first three series, starting in 1974. 'Mad Monty's Flying Circus' headlined the *Chicago Tribune*, 'you gotta see it to believe it'; many young Americans saw it and believed in it, to the extent of its becoming a campus cult.

More surprisingly, the shows achieved great popularity in Japan when they were shown, in dubbed versions, in 1976.[38] Prefaced by explanatory material of doubtful helpfulness, the shows produced a mixture of puzzlement and enthusiasm in the viewers. Some of the sketches had to be cut lest they offend some sections of the population – the 'Ministry of Silly Walks' sketch was one to disappear – but the programmes received the supreme accolade of over-taking golf in the television ratings. The success of *Monty Python's Flying Circus* is not really as surprising as it seems; the Japanese have a stronger sense of humour than many westerners imagine. Japanese films, for example, are not all in the *Seven Samurai* mould; there are many entertaining comedies, and, since the Japanese sense of humour tends to be fairly earthy and occasionally savage, it is easy to see why at least some aspects of *Monty Python* went down well with them.

The television show having become familiar in America, the team received a tremendous response when they took the stage show to New York, playing at City Center from 14 April to 2 May 1976. Here the 'pop concert' effect was even more marked than it had been at Drury Lane. Cleese: 'Almost every performance you got applause at the start of the sketch, when they recognized it; during the sketch you got very few laughs because people knew it so well; and then at the end you'd get an enormous amount of applause just after you'd decided that the sketch had more-or-less "died". It was much more a pop concert than a theatrical show.'

Meanwhile, *Monty Python* had become involved in perhaps the strangest facet of the show's history – a full-blooded lawsuit in the American Federal Court. The success of the first three series had prompted interest from the major television networks and, despite the fact that the team had said that they

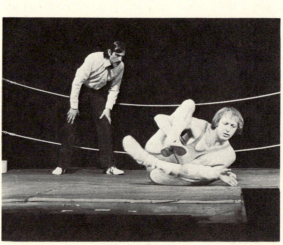

Monty Python's Flying Circus on stage in New York: self-wrestling – Graham Chapman v. Graham Chapman. Terry Jones referees

did not want the programmes sold to commercial television, the BBC's American distributors, Time-Life, sold the fourth series to ABC. The Pythons were too busy with other things to be unduly concerned about this, until Palin saw the first result – a compilation of three of the programmes into what was nominally a ninety-minute slot, but which, allowing for commercials, ran about seventy minutes. He was horrified: 'They had made numerous cuts in accordance with some federal – official but arbitrary – code of censorship; we felt what they'd done was de-gut the programmes totally to such an extent that they just were not Python.' It was not just a matter of a few cuts – the whole structure of the programmes had been irretrievably damaged, and so many sequences and even odd words had been cut that the result looked as if the Python team had produced seventy minutes of boring, pointless material.

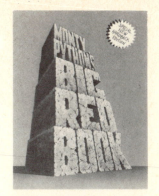

Incensed by this, the team took ABC to court in an attempt to obtain an injunction against the planned second programme – the other three episodes – being shown. Palin and Gilliam represented the Python team in court; Gilliam found the whole idea highly amusing, standing in a federal court solemnly discussing typical Python expressions such as 'naughty bits' (a euphemism dating from a second series 'lecture' on 'parts of the body'). After the court had viewed both the complete and the mangled versions of the programmes, and heard representations from both sides, Judge Lasker summed up: 'The law favours the proposition that a plaintiff has the right under ordinary circumstances to protection of the artistic integrity of his creation. In this case I find that the plaintiffs have established an impairment of the integrity of their work.' However, he felt unable to grant an injunction against the second compilation being broadcast because of the heavy financial loss which ABC would suffer; but he ruled that a disclaimer could be broadcast before the show. After Palin and Gilliam had written a disclaimer (and the judge had apparently toned it down) ABC were instructed that the broadcast might only proceed if it were preceded by the announcement: 'The members of Monty Python wish to dissociate themselves from this programme, which is a compilation of their shows edited by ABC without their approval.'

ABC's lawyers promptly rushed to the appeals court to file a motion of 'stay pending appeal' which, for procedural reasons, was heard without benefit of witnesses or viewings of the tapes. The motion was granted and the broadcast went ahead without the disclaimer, apart from a brief caption – inserted voluntarily by ABC – simply stating that the programme was 'Edited for television by ABC'.

The case continued. After much wrangling, a final final judgement was reached which was more to the Pythons' satisfaction: ABC were prevented from ever showing the programmes again, the Pythons were awarded both damages and the rights to the video tapes of all their programmes (outside Britain), and the point was established in American law that an artist had a right to exert control over his work. With this last section of the judgement *Monty Python* has earned a place in American legal history by establishing an important point of law that may, hopefully, be an embarrassment to the American television networks and their appallingly insensitive attitude to their material.

More important to Python fans is the granting of the rights in the tapes to the team. Pre-recorded video cassettes are gaining ground as a medium for home entertainment, and it seems likely that pre-recorded video discs (which have many technical advantages over tape) may become available within the next few years. The home market that these formats provide could be ideal for the *Monty Python* programmes. The continuing popularity of the shows, and the fact that they stand up well to repetition, makes them highly suitable to this new form of marketing.

Monty Python's Flying Circus on stage in New York: John Cleese and albatross

This is the best compliment one can pay to the shows. As with *The Goon Show*, they are likely to maintain their appeal as new audiences grow up, and they remain landmarks of television comedy. No other television show has ever broken so much new ground; in the same way that *Beyond The Fringe* destroyed 'old-fashioned revue', *Monty Python's Flying Circus* has virtually killed off the old-fashioned sketch show (although *The Two Ronnies* continues to inhabit the corpse). It is to the credit of the team that they were prepared to make risky experiments – and also to the BBC that it ever allowed them to – because what is perhaps most important about the show is that it was prepared to risk failure. It is comparatively easy for a television show to achieve a modest success by not taking any risks – and inevitably the pressures to succeed are so great (particularly on commercial television) that all too much television comedy settles for a safe mediocrity. *Monty Python's Flying Circus* established the right to fail; there are certainly many ideas throughout the show which do not come off – but because of the willingness to take risks, the ideas which *do* work often climb to unprecedented and dizzying heights of comedy. The sheer range of invention is unparalleled – and indeed it is a source of frustration that this chapter has been able to mention only a handful of the sketches, perforce ignoring many more which are classics.

Monty Python's Flying Circus resulted from the unique blending of six disparate talents. The collective entity known as Monty Python continues, having transferred to the medium of the cinema, which they now see as offering greater possibilities; but the group went their separate ways for a time, and their individual activities – as well as the result of their next collaboration – form the subject of the next chapter. For the television programmes which brought them together, it remains only to say that it is doubtful whether they can ever be surpassed for sheer inventive use of the medium; and that they are, and will remain, among the great classics of television comedy.

Monty Python's Flying Circus:
Alan Whicker Island

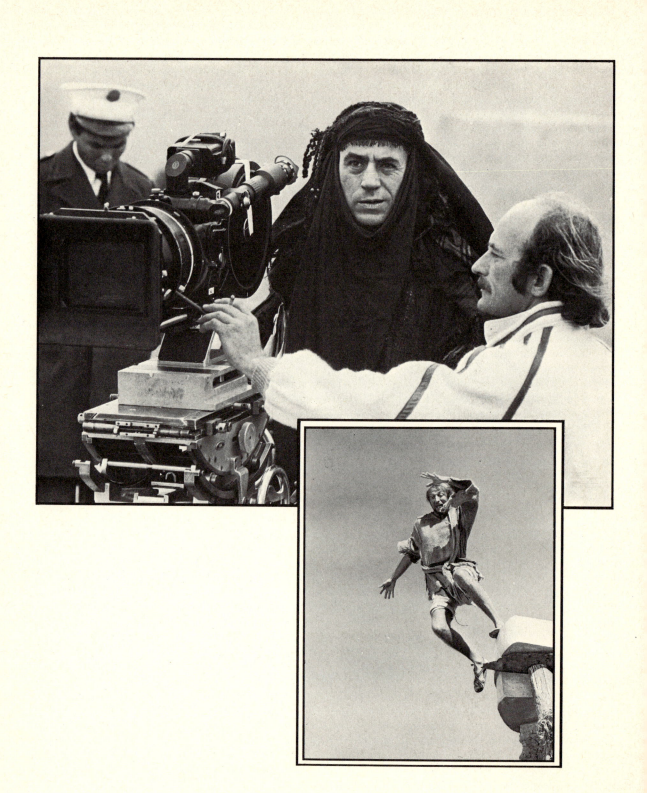

12.
'Jabberwocky'; 'Rutland Weekend Television'; 'Ripping Yarns'; 'Fawlty Towers'; 'Monty Python's Life of Brian'

'We all need to reassure ourselves that we have a separate identity.' Graham Chapman speaks for himself in saying that, but all the members of the Monty Python team have spent part of the period since *Monty Python and the Holy Grail* and the American stage tour in establishing their own identities. For Chapman this has taken the form of writing and going into film production. He has written an autobiography – in fact *A Liar's Autobiography* – published in autumn 1980, which colours the story of his life with a certain amount of imaginative embroidery.

He has also been collaborating with Bernard McKenna on a screenplay for a parody of *Treasure Island*; and prior to this had worked with McKenna on another film, *The Odd Job*. This film was Chapman's first experience of cinema production – he co-produced with Mark Forstater. The story was originally a television play by McKenna, with David Jason and Ronnie Barker. Chapman worked with McKenna on the screenplay; he had not originally intended to act in the film, but took the lead rôle because he could hire himself cheaply and thus keep the budget low. He had hoped to get Keith Moon to play the Odd Job Man himself, but Moon's commitments with The Who did not allow him to take part.

Chapman plays Arthur Harris, who in a moment of despair hires an Odd Job Man to kill him because he is a failure as a suicide. When he subsequently changes his mind – his wife Fiona, whose leaving him was the original cause of his misery, returns – he realizes that he cannot call off the assassin because he does not know his identity. Several attempts by the Odd Job Man to kill Arthur misfire, involving innocent bystanders. In the end, Arthur and Fiona find the Odd Job Man and persuade him to call off the assignment. He leaves their flat without his equipment; they call him back from their balcony, not realizing that he has booby-trapped it . . .

The film was released in October 1978, and received little critical approval. Chapman's characterization is interesting, because he abandons the authority figures of his *Python* and *Holy Grail* appearances for a more ordinary man, who is unable to cope with the situations he gets himself into; the ineffectualness of Arthur Harris is quite as convincing as the easy authority of King Arthur in *Holy Grail*.

Terry Gilliam also moved into cinema films, abandoning his animation: 'I was finding I was very restricted, and I was forced to keep doing certain things . . . it was getting tiresome, because it wasn't fresh for me any more. The limitations of the technique were getting boring, and I just wasn't willing to do proper animation – I just don't have the patience for it.'

Looking for a suitable subject for a live-action film, he teamed up with novelist Charles Alverson (an old friend, who had also preceded Gilliam as assistant editor of the magazine *Help!* in New York). They chose as their starting point the poem which Alice finds in the looking-glass house in *Through The Looking-Glass* – 'Jabberwocky':

> *'Twas brillig, and the slithy toves*
> *Did gyre and gimble in the wabe;*
> *All mimsy were the borogroves,*
> *And the mome raths outgrabe.*

> *'Beware the Jabberwock, my son!*
> *The jaws that bite, the claws that catch!*
> *Beware the Jubjub bird, and shun*
> *The frumious Bandersnatch!'*

The poem relates, in a further four stanzas, the simple story of the slaying of the Jabberwock. Gilliam and Alverson built a sardonic mediaeval legend onto Lewis Carroll's original, telling how a slow-witted cooper's apprentice kills the monster which is terrorizing the land, and thus wins the hand of a princess. Gilliam is fascinated by the mediaeval period and its legends – there is almost something mediaeval about him; he looks entirely at home as Cardinal Fang in the 'Spanish Inquisition' sketch, or the parts he plays in *Monty Python and the Holy Grail* – and compares the genre with the Hollywood Western: 'It's archetypal situations – everything is clear, the order of society is clear. I just like the visual aspect of the Middle Ages – I like castles, I like heraldry, armour – they all fascinate me.' He lists Breugel and Bosch as his two favourite painters: 'There's great humanity in the paintings – life is just teeming, it's all being lived at an extremely vital level.'

Surviving mediaeval carvings and paintings have a surprising freshness. Recently the front of the Cathedral of Nôtre Dame in Paris was cleaned for the first time since the invention of photography, and close-up photographs were taken of the carvings and friezes which are too high to be seen normally. They represent mediaeval life with an attractive directness – peasants and kings, merchants and beggars in a riotous procession. Other cathedrals have wood carvings of hunters and animals which have an amazing feeling of life to them; but all this was stifled by the Renaissance, with its fussy over-detailed art and architecture. Whatever benefits it brought to music and literature, the Renaissance has a lot to answer for where art is concerned. Gilliam's fascination for the period perhaps makes his own cartoons easier to comprehend, if they can be seen as descendants of the mediaeval tendency to blend fantasy with reality with exaggeration – animated gargoyles and anthropophagi.

Despite his affection for the period, Gilliam does not succumb to the temptation to see it through the romanticized (and sanitized) eyes of most Hollywood epics. 'It was like the potty-training period of history; with *Jabberwocky* people got very offended by the scatology – the constant defecation and people peeing off towers, and just the filth. And yet it *was* like that – I wasn't making anything up. I've got a book called *Illustrations from the Margins of Illuminated Mediaeval Manuscripts* – and here are all these little monks who have been drawing the Bible, and they put amazing things in the margins.

Extraordinary figures – strange mediaeval beasties – but the main thing is that the great majority of the figures seem to be taking a crap! They're just generally showing their bums and sticking their genitalia all over the place – it's very crude and very funny, and I like it. It's always struck me – monks sitting there in these abbeys, doing these holy books, drawing all these dirty drawings! But they *weren't* dirty drawings – it was just wallowing in the joys of physicalness, and all the things the body can do.'

Inevitably, Gilliam found the film being classed as a Python film – it was actually advertised as such in America, until he stopped it – with the result that audiences became rather confused about it. After initial showings, he altered the film considerably, because he found that audiences were laughing in the early scenes at things which were not really meant to be funny, and then gradually realizing that it wasn't basically a funny film, and losing interest. In the revised version, the film deliberately starts more slowly, so that it is more obvious to the audience that it is not a straightforward comedy.

The film was released in March 1977. Gilliam directed as well as wrote, the production designer was Roy Smith (who had also been production designer on *Monty Python and the Holy Grail*), and the lead part was played by Michael Palin. The supporting cast list is impressive – it includes John Le Mesurier, Warren Mitchell, Harry H. Corbett, Bernard Bresslaw, and John Bird, as well as Neil Innes and Terry Jones in small parts. The film looks superb – beautifully photographed, and with a better mediaeval 'look' than almost any other film ever set in the period. One or two of the sequences do not really come off – one such is a hide-and-seek competition which takes over from the extremely violent jousting tournament when it begins to run short of knights, which is just a bit too much like something out of *Monty Python*. Palin plays his part fairly 'straight', which is the best approach; and the comic acting honours go to veteran Max Wall (minus false teeth), for his magnificently decayed performance as King Bruno the Questionable.

In Lewis Carroll's original book, Alice's reaction to the poem 'Jabberwocky' was: 'It seems very pretty, but it's *rather* hard to understand'; and this summarizes the attitude of many reviewers very accurately. Everyone agreed that it looked excellent; but many reviewers seemed bemused by the fact that the vast comic experience of the cast was not allowed to produce a belly-laugh every few seconds. The comic effect of the film is cumulative, depending upon the carefully constructed atmosphere; the best jokes grow out of the situations, as when Palin attempts to improve the routine of an armourer's factory by moving a tin of nails closer to the person using them – by upsetting the routine he causes a domino-like chain of disasters which end in the total collapse of the factory. There are a number of jokes which seem to be imposed on the subject rather than arising from it, which is largely due to the influence of Pythonism on Gilliam: 'I don't think we were bold enough when we wrote the thing; there are certain areas which are very Pythonesque in it, and we didn't completely make the break from Python. It was like a transitional film – it went about half-way to where I wanted to go. It got much clearer reactions when it went to countries that don't know Python; anywhere that had seen Python the reviews either say "it's great" or "it's the worst piece of shit that's ever been made" – there's nothing in between! It's invariably compared to *Holy Grail* – I suppose I asked for trouble by doing a mediaeval film immediately after Python.'

Part of the reviewers' difficulties arise because the film refuses to be

Terry Gilliam's sketches of
the Jabberwock

pigeon-holed as just a comedy or just a horror film; but for people prepared to approach it with an open mind – and forget about Monty Python – there is much to enjoy. Almost incidentally, the film creates a monster which is possibly the most effective monster in the history of the cinema – a truly terrifying creation. The official special effects man had failed to produce a monster by the time all the other filming had been completed, and in the end Gilliam and a handful of other people created the monster themselves. Gilliam was deliberately trying to avoid copying Tenniel's original illustration in *Through the Looking-Glass*: 'In the end, it is and it isn't the Tenniel one – there's certainly a connection between the two. Most people couldn't work out how it actually worked – there's a man in it backwards, so that his legs bend like a bird's legs, with the joints the other way round; and his arms do the wings.' The monster was made to look huge by confronting it with a miniaturized suit of armour four and a half feet high, containing a child.

The best compliment to the film came from Stanley Kubrick, who rang up Gilliam to say that *Jabberwocky* was more successful at creating its period than Kubrick's own *Barry Lyndon* – even more of a compliment in view of *Jabberwocky*'s low budget of £500,000. However, in future Gilliam intends to pick a period which can be created without pumping the studio full of smoke and fuller's earth. 'Every day, there wasn't a pore in your body that wasn't clogged . . . foul! It was just so awful!'

While Gilliam was clogging his pores with fuller's earth, the remaining members of the Python team were making their own separate marks in television. Eric Idle made two series for BBC-2 under the title *Rutland Weekend Television*. The basic premise of the series was that the show was being presented by a hard-up small local television company – in Rutland – and the whole atmosphere of the shows is a sort of inspired tattiness. It was not so far from the truth, either – the first series was recorded in studio 'Presentation B' at Television Centre – which is about the same size as the studio used for the

Rutland Weekend Television:
David Battley and Eric Idle

236

weather forecasts – and the second series in Bristol, in the BBC's larger, but not exactly oversized, Studio A. There was of course no audience. The cast included David Batley and Henry Woolf and Idle invited Neil Innes to take part and write a few songs. Innes remembers BBC spokesmen saying at a press showing of the first series, 'This whole series has cost only slightly more than one "Lulu" show', and then being unable to find the key to the drinks cabinet.

Writing within this framework, Idle produced a number of lively sketches, many of which poked fun at various aspects of television presentation – there was much play with different methods of announcing the items, all of them deliberate failures. The first series of six was broadcast starting on 12 May 1975, and the second series consisted of seven shows broadcast from 12 November 1976; there was also a Christmas edition on Boxing Day 1975.

One of the sketches takes to its limit the Python technique of the format sketch. Here, instead of emptying the content from a familiar format and pouring something silly into its place, Idle empties the content from a typical television interview and replaces it with meaningless gibberish. Idle is the interviewer, and the interviewee is played by Henry Woolf.

IDLE: Foreskin, mousetrap view Mount Everest tin tray lobotomy in England?

WOOLF: Saddleback, saddleback. Lechery billboard kettle bum simpering, snuff masticated boss-eyed hand-set, lemonade enterprisingly apartheid rubberized plum joint curvaciously mucking squirrels.

IDLE: I see. Rapidly piddle pot strumming Hanover peace pudding mouse rumpling cuddly corridor cabinets.

WOOLF: Sick in a cup. Door jamb whisper tap Sunderland shower curtain iced wallpaper cups graunchingly rubbed king-rap buttock kissing feathers, definitely pheasantry daughter successfully douche dinner bottom.

IDLE: Machine rapped with butter?

WOOLF   (*nodding*): Machine rapped with butter.

Other sketches include a Stanley-Holloway-type monologue about a wife-swopping party; a feature on prisons run by suburban housewives in suburban houses; and the story of an insurance salesman who makes a pact with a man who claims to be the Devil, but in reality works in an electrical shop.

The most interesting sketch, however, in terms of future development is one about a pop group called the 'Rutland Stones', complete with a very Beatle-ish song by Innes. This was presented in the same sort of visual style that Richard Lester used in the Beatles' film *A Hard Day's Night*. During 1977, Idle was hosting the American television programme *Saturday Night Live* – a sort of vaguely satirical comedy show – which had a running gag about the possibility of the Beatles coming together. Idle capped this by showing the film of Innes's Beatles-style song, billed as 'The Rutles'. It got a tremendous response – viewers kept sending in Beatles record covers, amended to read 'The Rutles', for signatures; and NBC suggested that Idle should present the entire story of the Rutles. He agreed, and Innes found himself frantically writing more Beatle-ish songs.

Idle co-produced *The Rutles* with Lorne Michaels (the producer of *Saturday Night Live*); it was largely made in Britain, although to American technical

Sleeve of *The Rutles* record

standards. It was originally scheduled to be shown out of peak hours, but in view of the enthusiasm with which NBC reacted to it, it was shown in 'prime time', on 22 March 1978; it was seen in Britain on 27 March, on BBC-2. The programme is very ambitious, running sixty-five minutes and being presented in the style of a documentary film, complete with 'archive film' and interviews. An immense amount of care has been taken to make the programme look right – actual film of rioting Beatles fans is matched perfectly with footage of the four Rutles, and the period atmosphere of the early 1960s is accurately maintained. There is also a short cartoon sequence which copies exactly the style of animation created by Heinz Edelmann and George Dunning for *Yellow Submarine*.

Innes's songs are also perfectly in the Beatles' style – perhaps too perfectly, for they come out as pastiches rather than parodies. The cast list contains some very impressive names. Mick Jagger (commenting on how awful the Rutles were) and Paul Simon appear as themselves in interviews. Bianca Jagger decorates one scene as the girlfriend of a Rutle; and the joke becomes ingrowing as George Harrison, heavily disguised as a journalist, interviews a fictitious character played by Michael Palin while in the background a succession of people steal things from the Rutles' equivalent of the 'Apple' offices.

On the minus side, there is a tendency for one-line gags to be imposed on the material; this has presumably been done in the interests of giving it some 'lift', but in fact they are merely intrusive and the whole thing would have been funnier if it had been allowed to rest on its atmosphere alone. The story parallels that of the Beatles very closely, but it is fair to comment that as a parody the whole programme lacks depth – perhaps in paying such attention to fine detail Idle has lost the chance to have a really close satirical look at the Beatles phenomenon. However, as Innes points out, the programme is really more of a dig at the way the media handled the Beatles – and indeed there are several cracks at the expense of the sort of glossy documentary that *enfant terrible* Tony Palmer was making for ITV on the subject of pop music around this time.

Idle had also been closely involved with the production of the Monty Python books and his own *Rutland Dirty Weekend Book*, which are cleverly laid out and exploit the possibilities of book and magazine styles in a variety of ways; and in 1975 he wrote a novel, *Hello Sailor*, published by Weidenfeld and Nicholson. It is a riotously exaggerated tale of corruption and sexual excesses in the corridors of power, and certainly makes up in sheer hilarity for whatever it may lack in the way of depth or discipline.

Rutland Weekend Television, as well as leading on to *The Rutles*, also led to a very interesting series from Neil Innes. The producer of *Rutland Weekend Television*, Ian Keill, suggested doing a special hour-long programme of songs, to be called *The Rutland Weekend Song Book* and consisting of the musical items from the series. Innes: 'Then Aubrey Singer said, "Why don't you do thirteen?", and I fell about with laughter – *thirteen! . . .* that ended up being a concrete offer of six. Originally I thought I'd call it *Parodies Lost*, because I liked the title; I looked at *Paradise Lost* to see if there was anything there I could parody – I thought, Oh God, it's only Good and Evil and Love Interest . . . it's *Crossroads*!' In the end the series (which started on 17 January 1979 on BBC-2) was titled *The Innes Book of Records*. Despite being made on a tiny budget, and very rapidly, the programmes are fascinating; they consist of a number of songs, with minimal linking, performed by Innes in a variety of costumes and surroundings. There are appearances by various guest artists, including John Betjeman and Jake Thackray, but it is Innes's songs which hold the attention. Some of them are reworkings of existing items, including several from *Rutland Weekend Television* and 'When Does a Dream Begin' from *Monty Python*; a few of them enlist the help of members of the public, notably a song about everything being all right in Shangri-La which is sung by Innes in Superman costume, with help from the inmates of a holiday camp.

There is a general atmosphere of slight sadness – Innes always seems to look a little sad, even off-screen – and in so far as there is any theme to the songs, Innes says: 'I tend to be rather anti-consumer society – I don't know why, because I'm just as much a supporter of it, I've got a video recorder and a car – but I slightly feel that the quality of life is not the same as it was.'

The Innes Book of Records is an intriguing series, and indeed Innes may be the first in a field which could well develop as a result of the availability of prepackaged video recordings – a sound-and-vision equivalent of the 'concept album'. Certainly many of the items would stand up to more than one viewing.

In his use of atmosphere rather than actual gags for his series, Innes is in a way more comparable to Michael Palin and Terry Jones than to Eric Idle, from whose series *The Innes Book of Records* originally grew. Palin and Jones's major post-Python work was also in this use of atmospheric comedy; but prior to this they had branched out into the field of television drama, with their play, *Secrets*, written between the third and fourth series of *Monty Python*. Theirs was the first of six plays broadcast by BBC-2 under the overall title *Black and Blue* – the premise being that the humour would be either black or blue – or both.

Secrets was transmitted on 14 August 1973, with Warren Mitchell in the leading rôle (Palin and Jones did not appear). The play tells the story of some men who fall into the mixing vat at a chocolate factory. Before anyone can stop the mechanism, they have made their exit from the factory in the form of filling for chocolates. Horror and confusion reign in the works, until reports from the unsuspecting area to which the chocolates had been sent indicate that they are selling very well. Attempts to duplicate the results by incorporating beef and other animal meat into the sweets produces only complaints, so in the end the factory advertises for people willing to be cannibalized for a high price, and finds no shortage of volunteers. The chocolates, tactfully promoted under the name 'Secrets' as containing 'non-animal meat', prove best-sellers; and the play ends with an advertisement which states, 'We let people into our Secrets'.

Terry Jones: 'We were told the brief was a series of farces – either black or blue – but actually, we didn't really write a farce; we wrote almost a documentary about what would happen if somebody fell in some chocolates. But they did it as a farce; that was the bit I didn't like, when I saw it – I thought it was done very well, but there were certain scenes that they played up as if they were farce. We researched it thoroughly – we bought a book called *Marketing Strategy* by the Professor of Marketing Strategy at Stirling University. It was a very good book, except that one thing it didn't ever question was the morals of actually persuading somebody to buy something. *Secrets* was just this book applied to this situation – somebody's fallen into the chocolate vat, what do you do? You work out whether it's going to pay!' The play was highly entertaining, despite the alterations made to it so that it would fit the specification for the series more closely; it was well received by the critics, but the BBC received a number of complaining telephone calls that evening ('This is the sickest show I have ever seen . . . I was watching it with my uncle – I was shocked').

Palin then took on a couple of straight acting rôles; one was in a television version of *Three Men in a Boat*, the other the lead part in Gilliam's *Jabberwocky*. He was then approached by BBC producer Terry Hughes with the idea of doing some sort of a series; he and Terry Jones went away and racked their brains for an idea. Palin had given Jones an old book, called *Ripping Tales*, which was full of rousing schoolboy stories of the sort which nowadays sound hilarious. It was Terry Jones's brother, who had suggested *The Complete and Utter History of Britain*, who pointed out that there was a series lurking in this book. (Jones's brother seems to have missed his vocation – he should have been a television producer.)

Palin and Jones wrote a 'pilot', called *Ripping Yarns* and subtitled *Tomkinson's Schooldays*. The programme was entirely made on film, rather than in the studio, and very careful attention was paid to period detail and atmosphere. Basically, the programme is an extended reversal sketch. For example, the

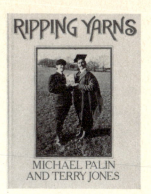

School Bully is salaried by the school because parents send their boys there to be properly bullied. There is also a certain amount of escalation of ideas, so that the programme has a slight touch of Monty Python about it, which is absent from its successors. *Tomkinson's Schooldays* was transmitted on 7 January 1976, and repeated on 20 September 1977 in order to 'lead off' a series of five more Ripping Yarns which ran in the following weeks.

Like *Tomkinson's Schooldays* the remaining shows were entirely made on film. This enabled the period 'feel' to be obtained more satisfactorily than if they had been done in a studio in the normal way, with an audience. They are all beautifully photographed; and were sensitively directed by Terry Hughes, who did two of the five, and Jim Franklin (taking a rest from *The Goodies*).

The fact that the programmes, when assembled, had no audience meant that a decision had to be taken as to whether to add laughter. This is normal practice for a comedy show which has been made away from the studio (although it happens rarely); the film is shown to an audience, and their reactions added to the soundtrack. Two of the shows (*Escape From Stalag Luft 112B* and *Across the Andes by Frog*) were transmitted without an audience, and predictably came across in a rather muted way; and there were technical problems about the recording of the audience on the other shows which led to the laughter track having to be rather quieter than it should have been, thus giving the impression that the audience were unenthusiastic. When the series was later repeated, all six shows were shown to audiences under more satisfactory recording conditions; so that all the shows had an audience, and those that had had one before now had a new one. The general effect was more satisfactory.

The original audience had almost killed one of the best shows, *The Testing of Eric Olthwaite*, by tittering in a tense dramatic scene because they were not too sure what to make of it; they were 'mixed off' the soundtrack in that sequence. The film tells the story of Eric (played by Palin), a Yorkshire boy

Ripping Yarns: Michael Palin as Eric Olthwaite

who is accurately described by his sister as 'a boring little tit'. His conversation is limited to the subjects of shovels ('Howard Molson's got a new shovel . . . he's hung it next to his other one') and rainfall figures. He is so boring that his father pretends to be French in order to avoid having to talk to him; and one day he wakes up to find that his family have abandoned him . . . they have even taken the outside toilet. Rejected by all the people in his town because he is so boring, he is captured as a hostage by a bank robber. The robber is about to shoot him in order to get away unidentified – this is the scene which bewildered the original audience – when they discover a common interest in shovels and rainfall. Eric is reprieved, and together they form a gang. Several bank robberies later he is so famous that he is accepted by his old town – and made mayor. The story is told with a loving attention to detail and the look of 1930s Yorkshire. Palin, interviewed on television, gave away a secret: 'Actually, we filmed in Durham, because Yorkshire wasn't grotty enough . . . Oh! Sorry, Durham! . . . (Oh God . . .).'[40] Eric Olthwaite himself is a classic Palin creation – Mr Pither (of the *Monty Python* 'cycling tour') as he might have been written by J. B. Priestley.

Being of a rather gentle nature, and broadcast on BBC-2, *Ripping Yarns* did not gain a particularly large audience on its first showing; however, a further series was thought worth while. Because of the high cost of making these programmes entirely on film, the BBC's budget would run to only three more programmes; Palin is quite happy to leave the total number of *Yarns* at nine, as he feels that it is not an unlimited medium.

The second series began transmissions on 10 October 1979. Again, the films were painstakingly made, with close attention to detail. In the last of them, *Roger of the Raj*, Palin plays Roger, the son of Lord Bartlesham – an elderly gentleman labouring under the delusion that his servants are all slaves (he keeps freeing them). Roger's life's ambition is to open a small chemist's shop. It is only after he has found himself the unwilling leader of a mutiny of the troops in India during World War I (largely the work of his communist Latin tutor) that he achieves his ambition, albeit by the process of adding it to the front of his stately home.

In the second film, the story of a dedicated football fan in a North-of-England town during the 1930s, there is a brief (and unbilled) walk-on appearance by John Cleese (who also made a brief unbilled appearance, with Eleanor Bron, three days later in *Doctor Who*, of all things). The three shows are well up to the standard of the first series, with the problems of recording the audience reactions under somewhat better control. Apart from their television activities, Palin and Jones earlier collaborated on *Bert Fegg's Nasty Book for Boys and Girls* (Eyre Methuen, 1974). The format of the book – for once not related to previous television material – is basically mock-educational, with many interruptions by the ghastly Bert Fegg. Items include a pre-*Ripping Yarns* version of *Across the Andes by Frog* and some fascinating wild animals such as the Turkish Wall Goat. ('Unfortunately incontinent, the Turkish Wall Goat is a constant hazard on the streets of Ankara. Its ability to climb any vertical surface and remain there for many weeks on end, have rendered some side-streets virtually impassable. Perhaps the worst feature of this anti-social animal is its habit of shouting at young women and making misleading statements to the press about the present Turkish Government.')

Terry Jones has been able to put some of the money he earned from *Monty Python* to good use; he has a deep-rooted concern for the few remaining Real Things in an increasingly synthetic age – real ale, unprocessed food and so on. He financed the experimental first edition (the 'dummy') of *Vole*, an ecologically-conscious magazine edited by Richard Boston, and has continued to back it in partnership with the Dartington Trust. Jones also financed the reopening of the Penrhos Brewery in Herefordshire, which now makes real beer as opposed to the gassed-up rubbish sold by many of the big brewing combines.

In the midst of all this activity, Jones has managed to find time to write a book which in a way is a return to the career he might have taken up originally (writing 'words about words'). Called *Chaucer's Knight*, it is a serious and close study of part of the *Canterbury Tales*.

John Cleese has also been keeping fairly busy since leaving *Monty Python's Flying Circus* – although not quite as busy as is suggested by his entry in *The International Film and TV Year Book*, which lists him as appearing in four totally fictitious films – *The Bonar Law Story*, *Abbott and Costello meet Sir Michael Swann*, *The Young Anthony Barber* and *Confessions of a Programme Planner*. Cleese added these to the list of his real activities, one every year, out of sheer mischievousness. However, nobody noticed, so he stopped bothering after four years.

In the real world, Cleese has made two forays into new areas – training films and situation comedy. The first dates from the period when he was still appearing in *Monty Python's Flying Circus*. At the suggestion of Antony Jay, whom he had met when Jay was writing the 'theme scripts' for *The Frost Report*, they teamed up with Peter Robinson, a TV and film director, and Michael Peacock, who at one time ran BBC-2. The object of the exercise was to produce training films for industry and the retail trades which would be rather better produced than had been usual in the past, and could combine instruction with entertainment. Under the company name Video Arts, they produced a series of films called *The Selling Line*, which have also been shown on television. In the first of them Cleese appears as a maintenance engineer given to using such confidence-inspiring phrases as 'Who sold you this, then?' and 'Here, you've been *using* this, haven't you?' Since 1972 the company has produced a number of training films, starring not only Cleese but such names as Ronnie Barker and Angharad Rees. Cleese scripted many of the earlier films, but more recently has confined himself to appearing in them, and helping to run the company.

The financial return from what has proved to be a wise investment of both money and skill has enabled him to free himself from the treadmill of television appearances. He feels that the performers who last longest on television are those who ration their appearances, and the existence of Video Arts helps him to do just that. In fact the rationing has been fairly severe; in the period since leaving *Monty Python's Flying Circus* he has made a very few appearances in other people's shows, of which the most notable was in *The Muppet Show*, broadcast on ITV on 21 October 1977. The Muppets' scriptwriting team caught something of the essentially acerbic John Cleese, as he insisted to Kermit the Frog that his contract excluded him from appearing with pigs, and then co-starred with a poofy parrot in a sketch set in a spaceship; reasonably enough, he appeared as Long John Silver.

Under his own flag, however, he has treated us to two short series in what is for him a new field – situation comedy. He was approached by the BBC, in the person of Jimmy Gilbert, and asked whether he would like to write a series. He was keen to write something in collaboration with his wife, Connie Booth – they had already written 'The Princess with Wooden Teeth' for *Monty Python's Fliegende Zirkus* – and so they put their heads together for a suitable subject. Cleese: 'We soon decided that it was pointless doing sort of Mike Nichols and Elaine May stuff, because Bron and Fortune had already done it better. There was no point in trying to do revue stuff because Python was obviously superior.' Then he remembered the rude hotel owner in Torquay who had already been the basis for one of the *Doctor* shows, and realized that Humphrey Barclay's prediction had been right – there was indeed a series in it.

Both the series and the hotel it celebrates are called *Fawlty Towers*, and Cleese plays the lead rôle of Basil Fawlty, the proprietor. Basically, the characterization is an exercise in bad temper and sarcasm, but there is more to it than that; Basil is a man to whom even the simplest problem is a major crisis, and he sees the guests as being in the way of the smooth running of the hotel. He is married to Sybil – like him, about forty; an over-dressed and over-coiffured harridan played, in a performance of truly magnificent awfulness, by Prunella Scales. Connie Booth plays Polly, an art student earning a living as

Fawlty Towers (1975): Connie Booth and John Cleese discuss a fine point of hotel management

best she can. The remaining major character is Manuel (Andrew Sachs), a Spanish waiter with minimal command of English, hired by Basil in a moment of gross over-confidence in his own ability to speak Spanish.

The first series of six episodes ran on BBC-2 from 19 September 1975. As with its true-life original, the hotel is situated in Torquay, a genteel seaside resort on the south coast of England. *Fawlty Towers* has its own pretensions to gentility – not to put too fine a point on it, Basil is a first class snob. He is therefore delighted when, in the first programme, the hotel is honoured by the presence of a certain Lord Melbury.[41] Basil fawns on him like a piece of damp blotting-paper; but Basic is no judge of men – 'Lord Melbury' is a confidence trickster and a practised liar.

Basil, on the other hand, is a very unpractised liar. He frequently tries to go behind Sybil's back in misguided attempts to save money – in the second programme he hires a useless Irish builder who makes a mess of the whole job, to Sybil's fury. ('I have seen more intelligent creatures than you lying on their backs at the bottoms of ponds. I have seen better organized creatures than you running round farmyards with their heads cut off.')

As the series progresses Basil becomes hopelessly embroiled in his attempts to deal with hotel inspectors, a wedding party, and a gourmet dinner; it is obvious that Sybil's lack of confidence in his abilities is entirely justified. Polly generally remains a neutral observer in this battleground, although she does occasionally side with Basil in ill-advised attempts to protect him from Sybil's fury. Unable to cope with Sybil, Basil generally works out his temper on the unfortunate Manuel, whose vocabulary seems largely limited to '¿Que?'.

The six shows were recorded sufficiently ahead of transmission to enable their order to be arranged for the best effect, and placing the best show last. With Sybil in hospital, Basil has a chance to exercise his sarcasm on the Sister instead of the hotel guests.[42] He has been asked to leave Sybil's room.

SISTER:	You still here?
BASIL:	Apparently.
SISTER:	A doctor's coming.
BASIL:	My God! – a *doctor*? I mean, here in the hospital – whatever do we do?
SISTER:	You can leave.
BASIL:	Why *do* they call you Sister – is it a term of endearment?
SISTER:	Now look, Mr Fawlty, I'm not going to ask you again.
BASIL:	Presumably you wouldn't mind if I said goodbye to my wife? She is under the knife tomorrow.
SISTER:	It's an ingrowing toenail!
BASIL:	Oh, you know, do you? Well, that'll help. (*To Sybil*) Take care, now, and if you can think of any more things for me to do, don't hesitate to call.
SISTER:	Finished?
BASIL:	Just. Thank you so much.
SISTER:	Not at all.
BASIL:	Charmed, I'm sure. Ingrowing toenail, right foot. You'll find it on the end of the leg.

There is a certain amount of wish-fulfilment in that scene – many people have wanted to be rude to bossy Sisters in hospital, but never quite dared. Left in sole charge of the hotel, Basil runs into complications with a test of the fire alarm, during which Manuel contrives to start a fire in the kitchen. In trying to deal with it, Basil is knocked out.

He awakes in hospital, concussed and with his head bandaged. While the doctor's back is turned, he sneaks out and back to the hotel, where his concussion causes his behaviour to be very odd. Apart from anything else it intensifies his inherent xenophobia: some German guests are very puzzled by his constant references to the war – he is in fact desperately trying *not* to talk about the war – and by his efforts to cheer up one of the German girls who he has reduced to tears.[43] Many years earlier a reviewer suggested that Cleese's stock-in-trade was 'a look of incipient madness'. In this episode the incipience finally becomes actual, leading to the wonderfully delirious moment when he offers to 'do the funny walk' and launches into an incredible goose-step.

The first series of *Fawlty Towers* was a resounding success, rather to Cleese's surprise. He and Connie Booth had simply written to please themselves, and bred a success almost by accident. The immediate question in the public mind was, 'Will there be another series?' There was, but not until 1979. Six were written, and the first five transmitted starting on 19 February; the recording of the last episode was affected by an industrial dispute, and it was eventually transmitted on 25 October 1979.

With a series forthcoming, the other obvious question was, would he be able to match the first series? He did, without any doubt. All the shows are good; two of them rank as the very highest order of comedy. In one, Basil's prurience over a male guest with an illicit girlfriend provokes a chain of complications worthy of a Whitehall farce; in the other, Basil has extreme difficulty in coping with the body of a guest who has been so inconsiderate as to die on the premises. This latter programme is a masterly demonstration of tightrope-walking. Many a lesser artist would have turned the audience against him in dealing with such a potentially touchy subject; but Cleese never loses them, even in a very uncomfortable scene in which the dead man's friends, who do not know that he is dead, are confronted by Basil, who thinks they have come from the undertaker.

Cleese says of *Fawlty Towers*: 'What we said at the start was, that they're nothing more than little half-hour farces; what actually happened was that in two or three of the shows we did take them into slightly more uncomfortable areas.' Certainly there is a lot more than farce to it; the characters obey the rule which marks out the top-class situation comedy – that they have a believable existence away from the programmes. All the major characters have a depth which prevents them from disappearing from the mind at the end of the half-hour. Basil, for example, has a definite existence in the past; we gather from a few hints that he has a certain amount of education and appreciation of the arts. The Cleese character in the sketch on page 140, faced with a domineering mother, might almost be Basil – except that it is highly unlikely that Basil ever went to university. He is quite unable to cope with people and the demands they place on him; it is also quite obvious from his tone of voice on occasions that he is a depressive.

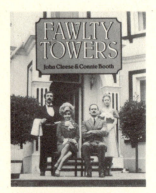

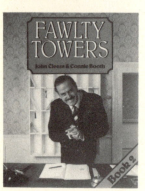

Understandably, Cleese is irritated by people who say to him, 'There must be a lot of Basil in you.' It is rather the reverse which is true – there is a lot of Cleese in Basil. Cleese: 'Connie and I have always had a thing about suppressed rage – people who can't express their rage properly, which neither of us can – we always find it very funny to see people getting really steamed up and not being able to "blast". That was part of it; and the other part was, there was a certain amount of me in him, and a certain amount of my father. And I suppose, with the suppressed anger, a certain amount of Connie, too. So it was a private thing – I never expected it to catch on anything like the way it did.'[44] It is this approach of writing to please themselves which is the secret of the programme's success; that, and the depth and development of the characters. In the very first programme, Cleese plays Basil with the sort of frustrated anger that is very close to tears, but in all the subsequent programmes Basil has at least a partial acceptance of the fact that he is surrounded by idiots – he has a sort of bad-tempered resignation to it all. We know that he and Sybil were married fifteen years earlier – a disaster in both their lives. He hates her acid tongue (which is probably partly bred out of years of coping with him); her lack of sensitivity; and her laugh, which is reminiscent of a drain-clearing device. She is of course perpetually infuriated by his incompetence, his snobbishness, his lack of tolerance – and his lack of any real sense of humour. And yet . . . on several occasions she calls for him to deal with a situation which has got out of her control; and she is genuinely upset when she thinks he has forgotten their wedding anniversary.

Polly is a less forceful character, although none the less real; she has to bear the brunt of much of Basil's behaviour, but in the later shows she has started to fight back. Manuel has also developed a little in the second series – he has gained a very small English vocabulary, but he and Basil are still permanently at cross-purposes. Cleese says he created Manuel because he is fascinated by non-communication. One of his colleagues has suggested that Manuel is 'really' Terry Jones – or at least based in part on Cleese and Jones's mutual communication difficulties during *Monty Python's Flying Circus*. However, when this theory was put to Cleese, he firmly denied it . . . when he had stopped laughing.

Manuel has become one of the most popular features of the show – at any rate in Britain; but when the 'dead body' edition of *Fawlty Towers* was entered by the BBC for the 1979 Montreux Light Entertainment Festival, the jury were not amused. A Swiss TV executive said: 'Funny foreigners may be a joke to the English. But not to us. We are your funny foreigners. Manuel is a character in dubious taste.' However, the disapproval of the Montreux jury seems rather pointless in view of the fact that *Fawlty Towers* was the BBC's best-selling programme of its overseas sales for 1977–8, going to forty-five stations in seventeen countries.

In the end Cleese did win an award at Montreux – but for a quite un-Basil-like programme he had made for Norwegian Television.

There are unlikely to be any further editions of *Fawlty Towers*. Cleese has become fed up with it after two series, which is par for the course with him; and the hotel format is essentially self-limiting. The great strength of programmes such as *Till Death Us Do Part* and *Hancock's Half-Hour* was that the central character had no positively defined job, and although the hotel situation allows for a number of plots easily from the start, it also imposes limitations. In any event, *Fawlty Towers* made more impression on a first series than any comedy series in the history of television – it normally takes several series to get a programme off the ground – and Cleese has produced twelve classics of television comedy.

Cleese made a new departure in June 1979 by directing his first stage show – the Amnesty special, *The Secret Policeman's Ball*, a successor to the 1976 show, and including Peter Cook, Michael Palin and Terry Jones in the cast. This gave him a taste for direction and, in a radio interview, he threatened to take it up to the exclusion of all else: 'I certainly don't want to go on doing the acting, because if you act on the stage there's too much repetition; if you act in the cinema then you have to get up for these appalling early mornings, and I just feel ill after three weeks; and if you act on television you never get enough rehearsal time – the whole thing is a wild, mad, last-minute improvisation. So obviously, the answer is, there are a lot of people around who are prepared to act, so the wonderful thing would be to direct them. It seems to me an ideal job, and the hours are very reasonable.'[45] Let us hope he does not carry out this threat – he would be a serious loss to television comedy.

So, each in his own way, the various members of the *Monty Python* team have flown solo for a time; their long-awaited reteaming came in autumn 1979 with the release of their third film: *Monty Python's Life of Brian*.

The ideas for the film germinated while the team were attending various premieres of *Monty Python and the Holy Grail*, and consequently spending rather a lot of time sitting round together in airport lounges. The original suggestion, made by Idle, was for a story to be called *Jesus Christ – Lust for*

Glory; but after the team had done some research into the life of Jesus and found that they did not really want to ridicule Him, they moved on to the idea of the thirteenth disciple – St Brian, who was always just that bit too late. Gradually they moved away from the life of Christ altogether, and the film emerged as the story of Brian Cohen, who is mistaken for a prophet by a crowd and finds himself hailed as the Messiah, to his horror.

Monty Python's Life of Brian: Palin as cured leper, Chapman as Brian

The film was shot on location at Monastir, Tunisia, during the autumn of 1978, with Terry Jones directing as well as taking part, and Terry Gilliam resigning his directorial responsibilities to concentrate on the art direction and making a few small appearances. The rough-cut of the film – the first time it had been assembled – was shown to an invited audience in London in January 1979, at which point it ran over two hours. Over the following months various sections were cut – some only to be reinstated – and the film screened again to different audiences, to enable the team to judge reaction to the film. In the original version the film began with three shepherds – not the ones to whom the angel brought the message of the birth of Christ, but the ones in the next field. The scene was beautifully written – it is presented in comic-strip form in the book-of-the-film – but for reasons which nobody was able to explain the first half of the film came over as much funnier when it had been removed. Various other sequences were either removed or trimmed, including Eric Idle's strange Jewish Nazi, Otto – one of the few characters who seemed to be imposed on the film rather than growing out of it. His scene is included in the published script, but in the released version of the film he appears only for a moment at the end, with his crack suicide squad.

Terry Gilliam, speaking at the time the editing was taking place, was somewhat uncertain about the technique of trying out various versions on different audiences: 'This isn't the way we used to do the television shows – and it's very confusing, because you keep thinking you've got the answer; then you show it to another audience and they react differently. Now we seem to have got it just about right – but maybe it's more of an ordinary comedy now. It's almost like letting the audience determine what they want to watch, rather than saying, "This is what you're going to watch" and taking our chances.' Terry Jones says that this is only the equivalent of their editing techniques on the television shows where, basically, they cut anything which did not get a laugh.

The film is, however, hardly an 'ordinary comedy'. Its subject matter caused the original backers, EMI, to get cold feet and withdraw; in the end the money was put up by George Harrison, apparently merely on the grounds it was the only way he could see the film. Adverse reactions were not long in coming from the outside world. As early as April 1979 the 'Festival of Light' told readers of their bulletin: 'It's a parody of the life of Our Lord Jesus Christ, showing him as an ignorant zealot in the confused political scene of First-Century Palestine. Obscene language is put into the mouth of Brian = Jesus, and his Mother is made into a comic character.'

This was fair warning of what was to come. Upon its opening in the United States in autumn 1979 the film succeeded in upsetting both Christian and Jewish organizations and getting itself banned in two states. Accusations of blasphemy were frequently made. In England, where the film opened in November, reaction was less hysterical. The film censor passed it uncut, and critical reaction was generally that the film was in bad taste but not actually blasphemous. The day after the première, 9 November, Cleese and Palin appeared on a late-night television programme with the Bishop of Southwark and Malcolm Muggeridge. It rapidly became apparent that there was no common ground, as the Bishop and Muggeridge both thought the film not only blasphemous but 'tenth-rate'. Insisting that the film was 'really' a parody of the life of Christ – despite Cleese and Palin's frequent denials – Muggeridge suggested that if the film had parodied Islam instead of Christianity there would have been an outcry from the same people who were currently praising it. Cleese retorted: 'You're right – four hundred years ago we would have been burnt for this film. Now, I'm suggesting that we've made an advance.' Muggeridge seemed not to think so.

At the root of all the objections to the film is the insistence that Brian is a lampoon of Christ; something which is clearly not so to anyone who cares to watch the film dispassionately. Christ Himself appears briefly, delivering the Sermon on the Mount (played absolutely straight by Ken Colley); the fact that the film goes on to suggest that people on the edge of the crowd might have been unable to hear clearly is hardly blasphemous, and more of a dig at similar scenes in *Ben-Hur* and *King of Kings*. Apart from this appearance, and the comic portrayal of Pilate and a cured leper (both played by Palin) all the other

Monty Python's Life of Brian: Cleese as Reg

characters are plainly fictitious, and any resemblance to persons living, dead, or resurrected is in the desire of the beholder to find blasphemy where none exists.

What the film does do is place modern stereotypes in a historical setting – very much a Palin and Jones obsession, explained by them as a desire to dress up – which enables it to indulge in a number of sharp digs, particularly at trade unionists and guerrilla organizations. The two seem to have become mingled in the form of the People's Front of Judea and their plan to kidnap Pilate's wife ('We point out that they bear full responsibility when we chop her up, and that we shall not submit to blackmail').

The main attack of the film, far from being directed at Christ, is aimed at the overreadiness of the mob to accept false prophets. Forced to pose as a prophet for a few minutes because he is being pursued by the Romans, Brian collects a crowd who insist on hailing him as the Messiah. The more he protests the more they acclaim him. In the television discussion mentioned above, Cleese said, 'The film is about closed systems of thought, whether they're political, theological, religious, or whatever ... systems by which whatever evidence is given to a person, he merely adapts it, fits it into his ideology. Once you've actually got an idea which is whirring round so fast that no other contrary evidence can come in, then I think it's very dangerous.' Unusually for the Pythons, there is a positive 'message' in the film – it might almost have a caption identifying it – when the exasperated Brian tells his followers: 'You don't need to follow me. You don't need to follow anybody. You've got to think for yourselves. You're all individuals.'

What should not be obscured by the wrangling is that *Brian* is a very funny film. The characterizations are beautifully done – particularly Cleese's leader of the People's Front of Judea, Reg; Palin's speech-impedimented Pilate; and Terry Jones's saintly passer-by, who discovers the disadvantage of emulating Simon of Cyrenia. The supporting actors are excellent, and there is a brief appearance by Spike Milligan (who just happened to be in the area) who demonstrates the difficult art of up-staging Cleese and Palin.

Unusually for a Python artefact, the film employs a conventional narrative structure, with only a handful of joke captions; and the editing has tightened up the original rather sprawling version very neatly, while managing to retain all the best material. Only the appearance of Otto in the last sequence is somewhat confusing because the scene which established him has been cut – he and his soldiers are passed off as the rival Judean People's Front.

It is this final sequence which has caused most of the complaints; Brian, together with a large number of others, is crucified on Pilate's orders. Once again, accusations that this scene lampoons *the* crucifixion are misguided – as Palin points out, crucifixion was a perfectly normal form of capital punishment in the Roman civilization. In *Brian*, the Pythons have simply extended the range of humour, adding to it the 'hard edge' which has characterized so much of their work. There is no doubt that many people will find this final scene upsetting – it is indeed a very uncomfortable sort of humour; but the fact that it rams home the point that Jesus suffered the same method of execution as many others may well add to rather than detract from the story of His life for those who see the film.

Monty Python's Life of Brian demonstrates convincingly that the Pythons can sustain a coherent full-length narrative, and indeed it is the most successful of the three Python films to date. Since they are unlikely to work together again in television, the cinema provides them with their most suitable meeting-ground and they are in fact working on a new film.

Monty Python's Life of Brian: Palin (in foreground), Cleese and Idle as worshippers; Spike Milligan is peering over Cleese's right shoulder

Monty Python's Life of Brian: Milligan

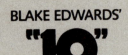

Half Term Report

The last chapter of a book of this type, which is in effect a 'history and critique', usually follows a set formula: summarize what the book has spent its length saying, wrap it all up neatly and tie a bow on it. That is all very well when the subject or subjects of the book are so considerate as to be either retired or dead, but it seems rather pointless when dealing with a group of people who are in their prime and obviously have many active years ahead of them.

For this reason it seems a more interesting approach to attempt to identify the challenges which await the Oxbridge Mafia in the future – these are, after all, people who like a challenge and will invent one if one does not exist. However, lest this chapter should sound like a severe attack of writer's arrogance, it should be emphasized that this is a purely personal assessment (guesswork, if you prefer); and that in any case these are all lively and intelligent people, who are quite capable of confounding augury by meeting some quite different challenge altogether.

Peter Cook is the natural comic genius of the group, and in many ways the most brilliantly inventive. He is an instinctive performer, who for the most part seems unable to analyse his abilities but simply follows where they lead. One of the weaknesses of the *Derek and Clive* records is that they are largely improvised, and possibly if Cook could prepare the dialogues more closely he would be able to overcome the inherent difficulties of working with such dubious material. Cook has also announced that he will be taking a closer interest in the running of *Private Eye* in future, which should produce some interesting results; he is not as keen as Ingrams on parodying the tabloid newspapers, and wants to attack the more respectable organs of the press.

There is a challenge for the BBC too, even though it never went to university. Time and again the BBC merits praise for making a programme such as *TW3* or *Monty Python* possible in the first place, and then criticism for making it difficult. From John Bird's and the Python team's experiences it would seem that the BBC likes to *have been* responsible for some programme which (though controversial) is safely past, rather than having to undergo the problems of being responsible for some such programme in the present. If there is to be a 1980s successor to *Monty Python* from any quarter the BBC will have to be a little less cautious.

For John Bird, Eleanor Bron and John Fortune, the challenge will arise only when someone at the BBC has faith enough in their very considerable abilities to give them their heads (although Bron has found a challenge in a different area with her one-woman stage show). Their comedy style is not as widely appreciated as it might be – such subtlety is not to everyone's taste – but to anyone who can understand the wish for comedy not to be constrained by rigid compartmentalization, there is still a good deal for them to say in their own oblique manner.

Obliqueness is one of Alan Bennett's trademarks as well, although his observation is sharper and has a wider range. His writing still shows occasional signs of strain at maintaining a long continuous play, although several of the plays in his ITV series were of a very high standard. For Bennett the challenge is what it has always been – to be more perfect.

Jonathan Miller finds and demolishes challenges faster than anyone could hope to devise them for him. In his time he has been a doctor, a comedian, a theatrical director, the presenter of an arts programme on television, an opera director, a sort of television doctor (with *The Body in Question*) and has most recently taken over the helm of the BBC's massive commitment to produce all the plays of Shakespeare; he seems to be a sort of latter-day Renaissance Man, barring only his self-confessed lack of any musical abilities. At the time of writing his challenge is to make the BBC's Shakespeare series both a standard work of reference and a new illumination of the plays; but he will find himself another challenge when he has done that. Perhaps the real challenge for Miller is to keep finding challenges.

Dudley Moore – in a way the baby of the *Beyond the Fringe* team – has blossomed spectacularly in the last few years, making a career for himself in comic acting, mostly in America. He does not yet have the comic stature of, say, Peter Cook, but even so is emerging as a film star in his own right.

For the Goodies, regarded collectively, the obvious challenge would be a transfer to cinema. In fact a script has been written, showing them meeting for the first time. However, the film would be extremely expensive to mount properly, because of the high cost of visual effects. *The Goodies* has already had a long life for a television comedy; the challenge of keeping it as fresh and inventive as it has been at its best will be considerable.

Eric Idle's whole comic style depends on ideas which burgeon rapidly – in a way like Peter Cook's, but where Cook builds a tottering edifice of strange thoughts, Idle's ideas tend to expand laterally, each one thrusting away from the others rather than building on them. He can pay brilliant attention to detail – *The Rutles* demonstrates that clearly – and his inventiveness is of a very high order. If he needs a challenge, it is to control this inventiveness, to direct it more purposefully – but not at the expense of his present sparkle. At the present he is a little like a scatter-gun: with a narrowed aim and the same fire-power he could be formidable indeed.

Graham Chapman, the master of the glassy-eyed authority figure, has demonstrated with *The Life of Brian* that he can sustain a full-length rôle which is not a grotesque. As his authority figures were always out of contact with reality, so his recent characterizations have little control over their surroundings, and their comic plight is well delineated in his performances. *Brian* and *The Odd Job* show that he can build a very funny sustained comic persona out of his various characterizations, given the right opportunity.

Terry Gilliam – an honorary member of the Oxbridge Mafia by virtue of his rôle in the shaping of *Monty Python's Flying Circus* – has an extremely inventive mind, teeming with a profusion of images (like his study, which contains an incredible collection of *objets d'art*, *objets trouvés*, and junk). *Jabberwocky*, and his art direction on *Brian*, demonstrate his ability to create comic atmosphere and, like Bird and Bron, he likes to overflow the narrow category of plain comedy. The challenge for Gilliam is to make a film (or films) which give his skill in the creation and juxtaposition of images free reign, while avoiding the temptation to use Python mockery. In *Jabberwocky*, the best bits are those where the film believes in itself. If Gilliam can sustain an 'inner belief' throughout a film, he can create his own world, be it mediaeval legend or science fiction.

The ability to create images, and to build the comedy on atmosphere rather than on obvious gags, is very much a factor in Palin and Jones's work. Michael Palin is far and away the best actor in the Python group, in the sense of being able to take on a wide variety of rôles and immerse himself in them; whereas the others are usually unmistakable, Palin can become unrecognizable when playing a character. It would be interesting to see him create a complex and deep characterization for the length of a feature film – there is no doubt that he has the ability. The characters in *Ripping Yarns* – except perhaps for Eric Olthwaite – operate in pastiches of a past generation's fantasy worlds. The challenge for Palin would be to create characters which have their own existence outside the story, and inhabit a world with its own reality (even if it is not the real world).

Terry Jones has a considerable ability as a mime which has not yet been taken to anything like its limit; it can be seen in some of the scenes from *The Complete and Utter History of Britain*, and also in his prince in *Grail* and his hermit in *Brian*. The existing evidence suggests that his style of movement, if developed, might lie in an area between Jacques Tati and Harry Langdon. Mime is, of course, somewhat out of fashion currently, and it would require a certain amount of ingenuity to find a vehicle which would allow him to indulge in mime without seeming contrived. Perhaps it is too impracticable a challenge – but it could be very interesting.

Unlike Palin, John Cleese can never submerge his personality into a rôle, but he has managed to create a range of parts that grow out of his character by exaggeration or inversion. The most obvious of these, of course, is Basil Fawlty; with this part Cleese has created a character whose reality is positively uncomfortable. Despite Cleese's idea of *Fawlty Towers* as being simply farce, he has hit on a very strong comic persona. The master of this technique of comedy – building the rôle almost unconsciously on to the reality, and drawing the humour out of the character's reactions to situations that could well be real – was of course Tony Hancock. It took several series of *Hancock's Half-Hour* to build the complex character which is so well remembered. Cleese, however, is most unlikely to do any more *Fawlty Towers*; he has no intention of getting trapped on the television treadmill. A challenge for Cleese, then, could be to improve on Basil Fawlty – to create a new character which allows his considerable abilities full scope, which can take on the reality and warmth of the Hancock character – without placing him in a self-limiting format, and without requiring a commitment to numerous long series. To improve on *Fawlty Towers* would be the most difficult thing Cleese has ever done. If he should accept this challenge, even failure would be interesting; success would take him into the comic stratosphere.

The Pythons, as a group, have decided not to do any more television series – they have driven that donkey about as far as it will go – but to do a cinema film every few years. *And Now For Something Completely Different* hardly constitutes a film in its own right, being a reworking of the television material; but *Grail* and *Brian* show a firm basic grasp of the cinema as a medium. The interesting thing about *Brian* is that, where *Grail* had cocked a few snooks at cinema techniques, *Brian* is told entirely conventionally. The challenge for the Pythons might be to do for the cinema what they did for (or rather to) television – to trample conventions underfoot, and to take the medium apart piece by piece and give it a thorough and beneficial shaking-up.

It is now more than twenty years since *Beyond the Fringe* opened at the Edinburgh Festival and unwittingly blazed the trail for the Oxbridge Mafia; twenty years which have been covered in this book, and are only the first half of the story. In another twenty years the participants will be around sixty, and perhaps it will be possible to write another book detailing their activities between now and then. Whatever they get up to, however they pursue their careers, and whether or not they pick up the challenges suggested in this chapter, one thing is certain – it won't be boring.

Notes

All the interview quotes are taken from the interviews I did with the people involved during the research for this book, except where indicated in the text or listed below.

1. A gramophone record of the 1976 Amnesty Show was issued under the title *A Poke in the Eye with a Sharp Stick*; and Roger Graef directed a documentary film record of the occasion, titled *Pleasure at Her Majesty's*.
2. Information on the history of the Cambridge Footlights Club from the programmes for *Out of the Blue* and *A Clump of Plinths*.
3. This and the other Bennett quotes (except as below) from a letter to the author.
4. Dudley Moore quotes from *The Observer* colour supplement, 9 December 1979.
5. Dudley Moore quote from *Parkinson*, BBC-1, 18 November 1972.
6. Michael Frayn quote from *Beyond the Fringe* – introduction to the text – published by the Souvenir Press.
7. The comment about the lack of experience in stage projection on the part of some of the Footlights people is based on the performances on the gramophone record of *Cambridge Circus*, recorded 'live' in the Arts Theatre; several of them are using a sort of 'singer's voice' in order to get the necessary power, and sound less relaxed than in their later appearances.
8. Michael Frayn quote as above.
9. Jonathan Miller quote from *Parkinson*, date as above.
10. First Jonathan Miller quote from *Parkinson*.
11. Interview with Mrs Cleese from the *Sunday Times*, 6 March 1977.
12. Humphrey Barclay's scrapbooks include programmes for the various manifestations of *Cambridge Circus*, as well as press reviews, photos and drawings; they were a very useful research source.
13. The first edition of *I'm Sorry I'll Read That Again* still exists in BBC Sound Archives.
14. My comments on *TW3* arise from having seen a large number of them during the research; most of them still exist on 16 mm telerecordings.
15. Hugh Greene's comment is supported by reports of parliamentary proceedings in the newspapers.
16. The edition of *TW3* including the Macmillan newsfilm has gone missing, but the incident was reported in several papers.
17. BBC Central Registry has a large file of letters about *TW3*; the earliest letters on the subject would not have been included, but once it became obvious that *TW3* was a sufficiently important subject, a file was opened on it and all subsequent letters included. I read them all.
18. This extract is transcribed from the gramophone record made in America; the sketch was probably semi-improvised.
19. Barry Humphries quotes from an interview in *The Listener*, 31 May 1979.
20. Many of Bron's 'Lady Pamela' sketches were co-written with Christopher Booker; however, this one, according to the BBC's paperwork, is hers alone.
21. Tynan and That Word – no telerecording now exists of this programme; information on what Tynan said from Christopher Booker.
22. This monologue reappeared in *Forty Years On*, but in a considerably modified form. The quote here is a transcript from the original broadcast.
23. Alan Bennett quote from *Parkinson*, as above.
24. Bennett's poem 'On Going To The Excuse-Me' has been published in *The New Oxford Book of Light Verse* (Oxford University Press, 1978; edited by Kingsley Amis) under the title 'Place-Names of China'.
25. *Forty Years On* is published by Faber & Faber.
26. The E. L. Wisty monologue extract is transcribed from the gramophone record, which is taken from the soundtrack of the TV show.

27. My comments on *Where Do I Sit?* made after listening to a private recording of the soundtrack.

28. Minicab sketch transcribed from the television presentation of extracts from *Behind the Fridge*.

29. ISIRTA dates: Preparatory series – three from 3 April 1964. First series – nine from 4 October 1965. Second series – thirteen from 14 March 1966. Third series – fourteen from 3 October 1966. Fourth series – fourteen from 23 March 1967. Fifth series – thirteen from 14 April 1968. Special 26 December 1968. Sixth series – thirteen from 12 January 1969. Special 25 December 1969. Seventh series – thirteen from 15 February 1970. Special 31 December 1970. Eighth series – eight from 4 November 1973.

30. For those who may be unfamiliar with them: Walter Gabriel is an elderly rustic comic-relief character in *The Archers*, a rural radio soap-opera; Eddie Waring is a sports commentator who eschews the use of consonants.

31. Hendon is a not particularly interesting area of North London.

32. The Inland Revenue tend to assess a writer or actor's tax by assuming that he earned more in the current year than he did in the previous year, and then demanding the tax derived from this guess early in the tax year, before anything like the amount guessed at has been earned.

33. The ITV companies cover different areas of the country, and assemble their own programming, taking some shows from London or elsewhere as they happen, taking others at a different time, and sometimes ignoring shows altogether. This leads to confusion and is known as 'regional broadcasting'.

34. This is not the Douglas Sirk film of the same title, which was made some ten years earlier. Despite similarities in the plot, the producer of the later film insisted that it was not a remake of the earlier one (letter to *Radio Times* published 28 June 1979).

35. The five-mile limit – this is what they actually say in the programme, but in fact the operative distance was three miles.

36. The probable reason why Alasdair Milne set six o'clock as a deadline was that if the baby had been born after that the news would have missed the six o'clock bulletins and would not be widely known until nine o'clock, by which time *The Goodies* were on the air anyway.

37. The fumetti feature in which Cleese appeared was called 'Christopher's Punctured Romance', and published in the May 1965 edition of *Help!*

38. Several newspapers alleged that the Japanese translation of the show's title came out as *The Gay Boy's Dragon Show*; but the Japanese characters printed by one of them simply read 'Monty Python' phonetically, and 'Flying Circus' literally.

39. I stand by this assessment of Gilliam's monster, at any rate in terms of any *original* monster – King Kong is, after all, only an oversized ape, and the Frankenstein monster is perverted humanity; excepting these, which are effective in rather different terms (and both somewhat sympathetic) the Jabberwock stands comparison with any monster in the long history of horror films.

40. Michael Palin quote from *The Pythons*, BBC2, 20 June 1979.

41. 'Lord Melbury' was played by Michael Gwynn.

42. 'Sister' played by Brenda Collins.

43. 'German guests' played by Nick Lane, Lisa Bergmayr, Willy Bowman and Dan Gillian.

44. Second John Cleese quote from *The Pythons*, as above.

45. John Cleese quote from *Kaleidoscope*, BBC Radio 4, 27 June 1979.
   pp.268–9: the cast of the 1976 Amnesty show – (front) Carol Cleveland, Terry Jones, Neil Innes, Peter Cook, Eleanor Bron, John Bird, (back) Alan Bennett, John Cleese, Jonathan Lynn, Michael Palin (obscured), Bill Oddie, Graham Chapman, John Fortune, Jonathan Miller, Desmond Jones, Graeme Garden. Insets: Dame Edna Everage, Tim Brooke-Taylor, Eric Idle, Michael Palin, Dudley Moore, Terry Gilliam.

Index

The Family

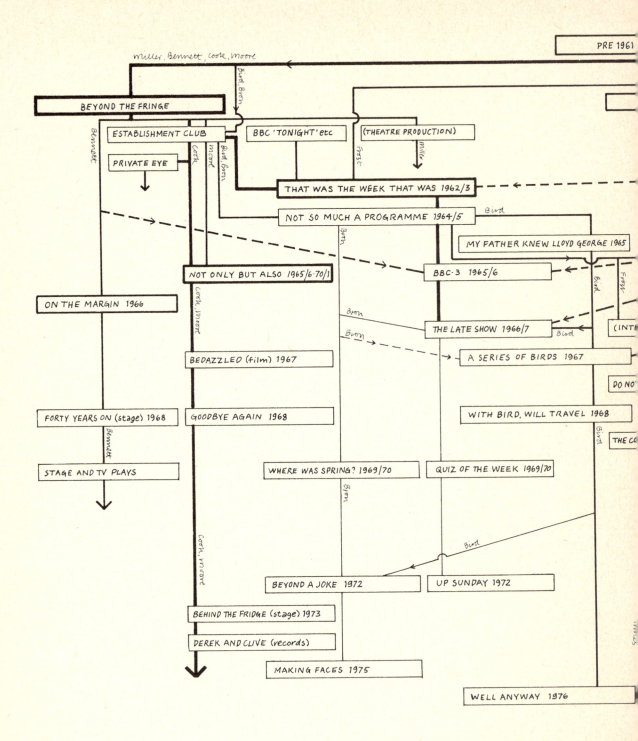

PRE 1961

Miller, Bennett, Cook, Moore

BEYOND THE FRINGE

ESTABLISHMENT CLUB   BBC 'TONIGHT' etc   (THEATRE PRODUCTION)

PRIVATE EYE

THAT WAS THE WEEK THAT WAS 1962/3

NOT SO MUCH A PROGRAMME 1964/5

Bird

MY FATHER KNEW LLOYD GEORGE 1965

NOT ONLY BUT ALSO 1965/6·70/1   BBC·3 1965/6

ON THE MARGIN 1966

THE LATE SHOW 1966/7

(INT

BEDAZZLED (film) 1967   A SERIES OF BIRDS 1967

DO NO

FORTY YEARS ON (stage) 1968   GOODBYE AGAIN 1968   WITH BIRD, WILL TRAVEL 1968

THE C

STAGE AND TV PLAYS   WHERE WAS SPRING? 1969/70   QUIZ OF THE WEEK 1969/70

Bird

BEYOND A JOKE 1972   UP SUNDAY 1972

BEHIND THE FRIDGE (stage) 1973

DEREK AND CLIVE (records)

MAKING FACES 1975

WELL ANYWAY 1976

THE INNES BOOK OF RECORDS 1979

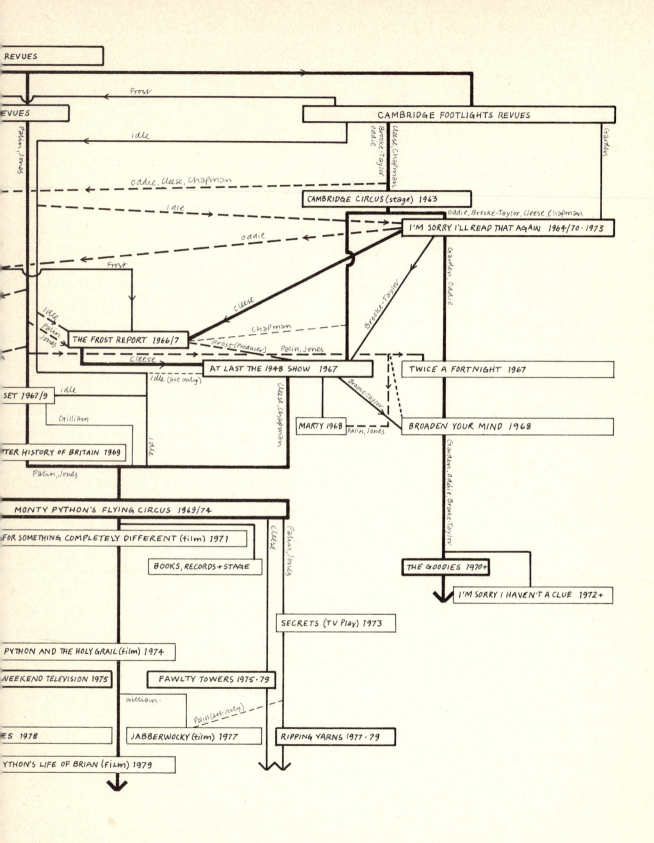

REVUES

EVUES

CAMBRIDGE FOOTLIGHTS REVUES

Frost

Idle

Garden

oddie, Cleese, Chapman

CAMBRIDGE CIRCUS (stage) 1963

Idle

oddie, Brooke-Taylor, Cleese, Chapman

oddie

I'M SORRY I'LL READ THAT AGAIN   1964/70·1973

Frost

Garden, Oddie

Idle

Cleese

Brooke-Taylor

Palin, Jones

Chapman

THE FROST REPORT 1966/7

Frost (Producer)

Palin, Jones

Cleese

TWICE A FORTNIGHT 1967

Idle (act only)

AT LAST THE 1948 SHOW   1967

Brooke-Taylor

SET 1967/9

Idle

Gilliam

MARTY 1968

Palin, Jones

BROADEN YOUR MIND 1968

TER HISTORY OF BRITAIN 1969

Cleese, Chapman

Palin, Jones

Garden, Oddie, Brooke-Taylor

MONTY PYTHON'S FLYING CIRCUS 1969/74

Cleese

FOR SOMETHING COMPLETELY DIFFERENT (film) 1971

BOOKS, RECORDS + STAGE

Palin, Jones

THE GOODIES 1970+

I'M SORRY I HAVEN'T A CLUE 1972+

SECRETS (TV Play) 1973

PYTHON AND THE HOLY GRAIL (film) 1974

NEEKEND TELEVISION 1975

FAWLTY TOWERS 1975·79

Gilliam

Palin (act only)

ES 1978

JABBERWOCKY (film) 1977

RIPPING YARNS 1977·79

YTHON'S LIFE OF BRIAN (film) 1979